Raphael Zähringer
Hidden Topographies

Buchreihe der ANGLIA/ ANGLIA Book Series

Edited by
Lucia Kornexl, Ursula Lenker, Martin Middeke,
Gabriele Rippl, Hubert Zapf

Advisory Board
Laurel Brinton, Philip Durkin, Olga Fischer, Susan Irvine,
Andrew James Johnston, Christopher A. Jones, Terttu Nevalainen,
Derek Attridge, Elisabeth Bronfen, Ursula K. Heise, Verena Lobsien,
Laura Marcus, J. Hillis Miller, Martin Puchner

Volume 57

Raphael Zähringer

Hidden Topographies

Traces of Urban Reality in Dystopian Fiction

DE GRUYTER

For an overview of all books published in this series, please see
http://www.degruyter.com/view/serial/36292

ISBN 978-3-11-063528-7
e-ISBN (PDF) 978-3-11-053585-3
e-ISBN (EPUB) 978-3-11-053396-5
ISSN 0340-5435

Library of Congress Cataloging-in-Publication Data
A CIP catalog record for this book has been applied for at the Library of Congress.

Bibliografische Information der Deutschen Nationalbibliothek
Die Deutsche Nationalbibliothek verzeichnet diese Publikation in der Deutschen Nationalbibliografie; detaillierte bibliografische Daten sind im Internet über http://dnb.dnb.de abrufbar.

© 2018 Walter de Gruyter GmbH, Berlin/Boston
This volume is text- and page-identical with the hardback published in 2017.
Druck und Bindung: CPI books GmbH, Leck

♾ Printed on acid-free paper
Printed in Germany

www.degruyter.com

Dedicated to my father, a lion

Acknowledgments

This book was accepted as a dissertation at the Faculty of Humanities of the Eberhard Karls Universität Tübingen in the winter term 2015/2016. More than four years have passed since I started this book, this project – and I would have been unable to complete it without the support of numerous persons and institutions. My sincere thanks go to all the people who gave me feedback on my chapters: Rebecca Hahn, Eike Hinner, Jutta Kling, Prachi More, Amrei Nensel, Amir Taha, and more unsung heroines and heroes of my doctoral colloquium. I would also like to thank Caroline Edwards and Tony Venezia, who hosted the first international conference on China Miéville's work (and who gave me the opportunity to present a few of my ideas there). Gratitude also to all the people at Gylphi (especially Anthony Levings) for publishing a condensed version of what later became chapters III.1 and III.2.1 of this study. I am also seriously indebted to the Professor Dr. Friedrich Schubel-Stiftung (in particular to Gerhard Stilz and Christoph Reinfandt for valuable advice on the initial draft), and the Landesgraduiertenförderung Baden-Württemberg – both thought my project absolutely worth their money and helped me to get it going. I would also like to thank Brigitte Breitel, Heike Winhart, and Stefan Zauner, on whom I could always rely with regard to administrative questions. My deepest gratitude goes to Ingrid Hotz-Davies and Russell West-Pavlov for their thorough and enthusiastic assessment of my work and, of course, to Christoph Reinfandt: since I do not even know where to begin (maybe in the summer term 2007 when I attended my first course taught by him?), I will simply state that I would not have even considered doing my PhD and going through with this project without him (not to mention its funding, fine-tuning, and the overall direction it took). I am also deeply indebted to all the people who helped to turn the manuscript into this book: Martin Middeke along with the other editors of the Anglia series, and Katja Lehming at De Gruyter, for answering an almost neverending flood of questions on my part. Last but not least, I would like to thank my family: my wife Janina and little Ben, who make my days brighter than anyone else; my mother Angela and my sister Judith for their general support and continuous inquiries ("When do you think you will hand in this thing?") – and my father, Berthold Zähringer, who died two days after the defence of my doctor's thesis, and who was proud of what I was doing.

Thank you.

Contents

List of Figures —— XI

List of Tables —— XI

List of Abbreviations —— XI

I **Introduction** —— 1
 Project Outline —— 3
 Strategy of Inquiry —— 4
 The Novels —— 5

II **From More to Miéville: the Dystopian Tradition** —— 7
II.1 The Literary History of Utopia, Anti-Utopia, and Dystopia —— 7
II.2 Brave New Worlds: Key Coordinates of Five Dystopian Novels —— 14
II.2.1 *Perdido Street Station* (2000) —— 15
II.2.2 *The City & The City* (2009) —— 19
II.2.3 *City of Bohane* (2011) —— 22
II.2.4 *Lilac and Flag: An Old Wives' Tale of a City* (1990) —— 26
II.2.5 *Divided Kingdom* (2005) —— 29

III **Literature and Maps, Maps and Literature** —— 35
III.1 Maps and Literature: Cartography and Literary Studies —— 35
III.2 Places to Get Lost: Literature and Maps —— 49
II.2.1 "Strange Tricks of Cartography": The Map(s) of *Perdido Street Station* —— 49
III.2.2 X Marks the Spot – Not: *Divided Kingdom* —— 65
III.2.3 The Metafictional Square: *City of Bohane* —— 71

IV **Urban Spaces: Taking a Stroll** —— 79
IV.1 From Lefebvre to the City as a Body: A Model for Topographic Analysis —— 79
IV.2 Walking the Urban Dystopias —— 86
IV.2.1 *Perdido Street Station*: The City as a Body, the Body as a City —— 86
IV.2.2 *The City & The City:* Perceived Space and the Force of Unseeing —— 109
IV.2.3 *City of Bohane:* The Back Trace of Memory —— 116
IV.2.4 *Lilac and Flag:* Opening Urban Oysters —— 132
IV.2.5 *Divided Kingdom:* Conceived Space, Ideology, and Identity —— 151

V Against the Grain: Borders and Transgressions —— 169
V.1 Interdisciplinary Approaches towards Transgression —— 169
V.2 Transgressive Performances —— 176
V.2.1 *Perdido Street Station* and the Hybrid Zone —— 177
V.2.2 *The City & The City:* Once More onto the Breach —— 194
V.2.3 *Divided Kingdom:* Withour Colour, without Place —— 209

VI Systems Theory and the Fiction of Probable Reality —— 222
VI.1 Systems Theory, Dystopian Literature, and Complexity —— 222
VI.2 Final Readings —— 235
VI.2.1 *Perdido Street Station:* The Dynamics of Transition and Hybridity —— 235
VI.2.2 *The City & The City:* Caught in Borderlessness —— 244
VI.2.3 *City of Bohane:* Bittersweet Memories —— 249
VI.2.4 *Lilac and Flag:* The Only Way Out —— 253
VI.2.5 *Divided Kingdom: Eukrasis* Is White —— 255

VII Conclusion —— 261

Works Cited —— 267
Primary Sources —— 267
Secondary Sources —— 267
Dictionaries —— 272

Name Index —— 273

Subject Index —— 275

List of Figures

Fig. i: Ebstorfer Map of the World (1284); copyright bpk / Staatsbibliothek zu Berlin / Ruth Schacht —— 36
Fig. ii: Hartmann Schedel's Map of the World (1492); copyright bpk / Dietmar Katz —— 37
Fig. iii: Model of Map, Territory, and User/Producer —— 47
Fig. iv: Map of the Divided Kingdom (© Rupert Thomson, 2005, *Divided Kingdom*, Bloomsbury Publishing Plc.; reproduced by permission of the author c/o Rogers, Coleridge & White Ltd., 20 Powis Mews, London W11 1JN) —— 66
Fig. v: City Space Model —— 86

List of Tables

Table i: Border Types Model 1 —— 173
Table ii: Border Types Model 2 —— 175
Table iii: The Dystopian Scale —— 264

List of Abbreviations

Titles of primary texts quoted in the running text will usually be shortened as follows:

City of Bohane	CoB
Divided Kingdom	DK
Lilac and Flag	L&F
Perdido Street Station	PSS
The City & The City	TC&TC

I Introduction

I do not remember the exact year, but I assume I was about twelve years old when I read a story in my Donald Duck pocket book #181 (*Lustiges Taschenbuch* in German); it was called "Der Traum vom großen Onkel" ("The dream of the Big Uncle"). The story took place in 2084 in a world quite unlike the Duckburg I had known from other Donald Duck stories. In "Der Traum vom großen Onkel", Uncle Scrooge figured as a despotic tycoon who ruled with an iron fist. Donald (called Donaldon or employee 00001 in this particular story), along with the rest of the population, suffered from Scrooge's rule: hard work, repression, TV sets with in-built surveillance cameras, and omnipresent floating camera drones took their toll on Duckburg in 2084. At the end, however, Uncle Scrooge went one step too far: taking away people's last resort (the daily ration of sweets) resulted in a riot as the workers, along with part of the police force (Daisy being one of them – as so often, Donald was hopelessly in love with her) tore apart all means of oppression and surveillance. The rule of the big uncle was over, the forces of good triumphed. Not much later, I also read the novel "Der Traum vom großen Onkel" was actually based on – George Orwell's *Nineteen Eighty-Four*, of course. Right from the beginning, I was taken aback by this fictional world that was so much like Duckburg. Winston was Donaldon, Julia was Daisy, Big Brother was Uncle Scrooge, the telescreens were there again – it was stunning. At the same time, it was much more real because the story did not take place in happy, four-coloured Duckburg, but in 'my' world – or in a world that was very similar to mine, and I could well imagine how our world might turn into Winston's one day. What "Der Traum vom großen Onkel" had not prepared me for, though, was the quite different reading experience of *Nineteen Eighty-Four*. In contrast to the Duckburg version, good did not triumph over evil. As I arrived at the final, devastating sentence, Winston did not pull through. "He loved Big Brother". I do not remember how long I sat there with the open book in my lap, but I remember perfectly that I cried. I had read rather pessimistic pieces of fiction before, but none of them had been able to show me in such a merciless way that something was wrong with this world.

It was at this point that I became fascinated with what I would later learn was utopian, anti-utopian, and dystopian fiction. It still strikes me that my very first encounters (I think) with this literary tradition already showed me both ends of the scale: "Der Traum vom großen Onkel" may not start as a utopia (the 'good place'), but at the end, the way is paved for it. The system is taken down, and something new, something full of hope, can be built on its ruins. Conversely, *Nineteen Eighty-Four* thwarts all hope, only offering despair. Utopia and

DOI 10.1515/9783110535853-001

anti-utopia, in the form of two narratives about places quite different and not so different from our actual world, have been with me for quite a while, and they already showcased the two most extreme forms alternative world designs can assume. However, there lingers third a category between the two: dystopia. It is a term that is sometimes used synonymously with anti-utopia, but other contemporary scholars such as Tom Moylan claim it as a category of its own (a claim which I am going to follow for the purposes of this study). The main argument for treating dystopia as a third, in-between mode is that utopia and anti-utopia as two extreme and strictly separated forms often do not do justice to the text at hand. Whether a fictional world is rather good/utopian or bad/anti-utopian is a question of perspective, and quite often, a text will show attributes which qualify it for either side. The dystopian category, then, provides a productive middle ground for negotiating between utopia and anti-utopia, a vast in-between space which is able to take into account both hopes and fears articulated in a particular text.[1]

The dystopian tradition as a mode of writing is, of course, much older than Orwell (or Duckburg). After early harbingers such as Plato's *The Republic* (ca. 380 BC) and Thomas More's *Utopia* (1516), the first crucial period for dystopia is the Romantic period because it is the first period in which the relationship between the individual and the world was increasingly perceived to be problematic against the backdrop of modernisation. As O'Flinn states: "I should like to underline this idea of tensions, hopes and fears, because it is out of that complex of emotions that most of the best Romantic poetry gets written" (O'Flinn 2001: 2). Romantic poetry's negotiation between hopes and fears is due to crucial and wrenching social, political, and epistemological changes in the late 18th and early 19th century usually attributed to three major revolutions (Industrial, American, and French Revolution), all of which contribute to a persistent unease, a rift between the individual and the world. This unease was carried forth to the Victorian Age due to the period's full onslaught of industrialisation and the continuing social and political changes. Questions about the relation between the 'I' and the world become even more pressing: "[d]espite the progress in technology, social reform, individual freedom, and independence in the Victorian era, by the end of the nineteenth century, the formation of an individual self was accompanied by all the psychological drawbacks of modern humanity: estrangement from the world, alienation, disorientation, loss of meaning" (Middeke 2012: 56). The early 20th century, marked by the First World War, condensed these

---

[1] See chapter II.1, which elaborates on the literary history of the three terms as well as Moylan's insistence on dystopia as a third category. See also Moylan (2000: 181).

wrenching changes and all the questions they raised into the watershed texts (and worlds) of Wells, Zamyatin, Huxley, and Orwell, with varying focus on fascism, totalitarianism, and collectivism. The individual was still struggling, primarily with the world as a nation state. One could say that the modern era abandoned the idea of a clear-cut separation between good and evil of earlier periods, which was replaced by a world that is ambiguous and equivocal. The modern world, it seems, had become fairly dystopian itself, a notion supported later by the Second World War, Watergate, the Vietnam War, and other epistemological crises. The most recent development since the 1980s is the shift away from totalitarian nation states and dictatorships towards epistemological, ecological, social, and numerous other crises right at people's doorsteps, and the dystopian tradition has picked up on this shift. There is a considerable amount of recent dystopian fiction which, while still indebted to the rich tradition, is rather concerned with the typical way of life of the late 20th and early 21st century and its new pressing problems: these texts are concerned with urban life and the city at large. This new focus provides a huge field for investigating the tensions between hopes and fears in urban spaces while still asking the same fundamental question the tradition has been concerned with since its roots in the Romantic period: the question about the relation between the individual and the world.

Project Outline

Against this backdrop, this study strives to explore the urban topographies of recent dystopian fiction. Its basic assumption is that fictional worlds in general, and dystopian ones in particular, are approximations of the actual world. Dystopian texts force their readers to pit these two worlds against each other; in this arrangement, it is precisely the difference between the two that will prove to be productive. As fictional worlds, recent dystopias employ or call upon real scenarios with particular emphasis on urban spaces and topographies (as representations of areas) in a narrated space that appears to be mappable. This study's aim is to outline how these dystopian texts can be connected to notions of reality and fictionality as well as dimensions of meaning. Based on systems-theoretical, narratological, and spatio-philosophical concepts, it comes to terms with these texts' specific operations of spatial construction and presentation as hidden topographies in which the links between fictional world and actual world often are elusive, covert, and indirect. This 'indirectness' of hidden topographies is crucial for understanding the critical potential of dystopian fiction. The fictional worlds described in these texts are very different from the actual world and, by nevertheless insisting on realistic strategies of representation, it is exactly the exploitation of this difference that enables the dystopian mode of writing to effectively comment on actual-world problems: fictional worlds in general hinge on their capability to provide their recipients with a crisper version of reality by highlighting certain elements (and ignoring others), and critical dystopias take this necessary difference to extremes in order to maximise literature's critical potential.

Three areas of research are crucial for this task and provide an interdisciplinary working environment. Firstly, this study draws upon concepts from the so-called *spatial turn*, a paradigm shift in cultural studies which, roughly since the 1980s, emphasises the formerly underestimated role of space across the disciplines (see Bachmann-Medick 2006/2014: 285–329). Secondly, it takes into account established research on the dystopian tradition and its umbrella category of Science Fiction by relying on the tradition's negotiation of utopian hope and anti-utopian despair as well as notions of fictionality in the context of critical irrealism (i.e. a mode of writing which presents a place quite unlike the actual world, but in a very realistic fashion). The latter directly connects to the third discipline: systems-theoretical literary studies. This line of thought is added in order to show that critical irrealism (and dystopian fiction as a crucial mode of critical irrealism) can be taken as a follow-up to the differentiation and rise of the modern realist novel. Furthermore systems theory, due to its concern about the relations between literature and other systems (and society at large), provides an opportunity to elaborate on literature's oscillation between fiction and reality as well as literature's attempts at describing something as complex and undescribable as modern society.

Strategy of Inquiry

This study starts with an overview of the dystopian tradition by problematizing the history of the terms utopia, anti-utopia, and dystopia, and by identifying key characteristics of works of fiction indebted to this literary tradition. It then highlights the preference for dystopia over the other two terms by claiming that the (urban) dystopia is not only closer to our actual world than the simplifying extremes of utopia and anti-utopia, but also more productively embedded in the literary tradition of Science Fiction at large. This outline is followed by an overview of the five dystopian novels this study will work with; the overview introduces the novels' settings, story lines and plots, major characters, and the narrative techniques employed (chapter II). In the next step, this study explores the interrelations between maps and literature; both share a long history, and both offer rich interrelations with regard to representation as well as to questions of reality and fictionality. These interrelations are then elaborated on by three close readings of dystopian novels which not only feature a printed map of the fictional territory, but are also generally concerned with cartographic means of reference and representation (chapter III). Thus, a way is paved for the core of this study, the spatial analyses of urban dystopias. By drawing upon several scholarly paradigms of spatial research, most importantly Henri Lefebvre's *The Production of Space* (1974/1991), I develop a model for topographic analysis which I then use to shed light on spatial strategies in urban dystopias, mostly by focussing on the interplay between the individual and the city in the force field of materiality (i.e. what spaces are 'there') and discursivity (i.e. what one can 'do' with these spaces discursively) (chapter IV). Afterwards, the focus is sharpened and redirected from urban spaces in general towards borders and individual performances of transgression by dystopian outsider characters (who seem to embody the very basic idea of transgression in a spatial, mental, and bodily sense). The result is an analytical toolkit based on Lotman's concept of the semiosphere as well as Monika Fludernik's systematic model of border types, which is then put to the test by three close readings (chapter V). Lastly, a larger frame of reference is provided by building a bridge between the modern realist novel and postmodern irrealist dystopian fiction, both of which attempt to critically come to terms with describing the world. Systems-theoretical lines of thought are added in order to embed dystopian fiction into the larger context of how literature as a system relates to the world and vice versa (chapter VI). This also provides a link back to the literary history of dystopian fiction outlined in the beginning.

The Novels

A total of five dystopian novels will be examined in detail for the purposes of this study. All of them can be called dystopian, and all of them offer excellent opportunities to explore the notions outlined above. *Perdido Street Station* (2000) by China Miéville is an urban fantasy novel, set in a very grim city which features numerous highly relevant characteristics of urban space and topographies in a dystopian context. The novel is outstanding in the way it shows the transposition from totalitarian states to urban dystopias in a city space with many smaller systems and subsystems in a confusing clutter of reciprocal performances attributed to the novel's characters and its readers on various levels (e.g. the city map printed in the book, characters' ways of integrating themselves into the city, and the physicality of transgression). In a way, *Perdido Street Station* is the culmination of what this study is concerned with, and was the first text to find its way into the project.The second novel, also by China Miéville, is *The City & The City* (2009). It is relevant for this study primarily because of a specific, indoctrinated performance called 'unseeing,' which results in treating one city space as two separate cities. Due to this arrangement, the text is also crucial with regard to notions of compliance and transgression. Similarly, Irish writer Kevin Barry's *City of Bohane* (2011) made it into this study because of its double topography: first, Bohane is a city dominated by gang politics, which severely influences the city's mood, structure, and story. A second topographical layer is added to this gangland topography by the novel's emphasis on the nostalgic remembrance of the past, which infuses the city with history and personal memory. Novel number four is John Berger's *Lilac and Flag: An Old Wives' Tale of A City* (1990), the last volume of Berger's *Into Their Labours* trilogy. As in *City of* Bohane, the novel confronts an anti-utopian city present with a utopian rural past, but with an additional emphasis on the gap between the mythic, elusive elements of ancient Greek Troy on the one hand and the modern, capitalist paradigm of the cosmopolis on the other. *Divided Kingdom* (2005) by Rupert Thomson completes the array of this study's chosen dystopian novels. It was included primarily because of its strategies of cartographic selection and omission and its focus on the psychological as well as material effects of borders on national and personal identity. Together, these five novels shed light on a vast array of issues recent urban dystopian fiction is concerned with as they tackle questions of the individual finding (or not finding) its place in a dystopian, urbanised world from different angles: for instance, the texts explore the relations between immediacy of urban experience and distanced observation, between past, present, and future, between isolation/individuality and interaction/community, between conformity and transgression, between spatial concepts and spatial practices. Finally, all five texts are concerned with the dystopian key concept of being torn between hope and despair as they play out in the city.

II From More to Miéville: the Dystopian Tradition

The following chapter is concerned with dystopia as a literary tradition. Part one provides an overview of the development of the dystopian tradition and starts out with an outline of typical dystopian elements in fiction as well as a quick glance at the sometimes problematic excessive supply of terms (utopia, anti-utopia, dystopia, to name only the most prominent ones). After that I will, by and large following Tom Moylan, object to the assertion that the utopian/anti-utopian tradition, in the 21st century, is dead and without purpose by showing how this literary tradition productively repositions itself with regard to an urbanised world, to the genre of Science Fiction, and the tradition's capability of "daring to dream" (Moylan 2000: 67), all under the subheading of dystopia. Part one then ends with a brief follow-up on the dystopian tradition's peculiar stance between reality and fictionality which is closely linked to this repositioning. Section II.2 introduces the five novels chosen for this study by presenting their general outlines (spaces, narration, story and plot, and dystopian elements).

II.1 The Literary History of Utopia, Anti-Utopia, and Dystopia

The Dystopian Tradition: Terminology and Typical Elements

What is striking from the very beginning in the context of utopian/dystopian literature is the overabundance of terms used in literary studies in order to systematise all the texts and categories orbiting around Thomas More's *Utopia* (1516), which gave the tradition its name. Three key terms have dominated the debates since their establishment by Lyman Tower Sargent in 1967 (see Moylan 2000: 70–71): utopia, anti-utopia, and dystopia.[1] However, their exact meanings as well as the relations between them are far from being clear and vary from scholar to scholar.

I start with the term utopia itself, as coined by More, which is more than simply the 'good place' because it carries a pun. While the 'topia' in 'utopia' refers to the Greek expression for place, spelling and pronunciation of the word leave it open whether the etymological root refers to the Greek 'eu' (good/beautiful) or to 'ou' (non/not). Therefore, utopia has a double meaning which will become highly important for this study, particularly for chapter IV: it is the good place, but at the same time it is also the non-place, i.e. the place that does not exist because it cannot exist. This double meaning is at the heart of utopia's function:

---

[1] For a thorough overview of more terms, see Meyer (2001: 17–33).

it provides a desirable, but unreachable vision of a perfect world (see Meyer 2001: 17). Anti-utopia, then, poses as the alternative draft of utopia: another non-place, but the 'eu' meaning is countered – it is a non-good non-place. The third term, dystopia, is free of the pun, and can more directly be called a 'bad place'.[2]

How are these three terms related? Sometimes, utopia is established as an umbrella term with dystopia and/or anti-utopia as negative variations, usually based on a historical argument (i.e. these approaches take into account that the utopian category came first, as in More's *Utopia* or in Plato's *The Republic*, while dystopia and anti-utopia are treated as responses which followed later). In other cases, utopia and anti-utopia are considered to be on equal footing and therefore rather two sides of the same coin which cannot exist without each other. What is more problematic is the differentiation between anti-utopia and dystopia because both, in a way, function as negative counterparts to utopia. Some scholars simply use one of them while dismissing the other;[3] other scholars, such as Chad Walsh, use them synonymously (see Walsh 1962: 14); and a third group uses both of them, treating anti-utopia and dystopia as separate (which I will be doing as well in this study). A good reason for using the latter approach has been provided by Tom Moylan in his book *Scraps of the Untainted Sky. Science Fiction, Utopia, Dystopia* (2000), which has also been used as a starting point for Graham J. Murphy's chapter on dystopia in *The Routledge Companion to Science Fiction* (see Murphy 2009: 473). According to Moylan, it is important to distinguish between anti-utopia and dystopia because the reduction of the two "to a single 'anti-utopian' category" and the resulting "development of a simple binary opposition between Utopia and Anti-Utopia efface[s] the continuum that stretches between these powerful forces"(Moylan 2000: 122). Therefore, Moylan still treats utopia as the good place and anti-utopia as the bad counterpart – but between these two extremes, there is the dystopia as a vast in-between category "[f]or those who are unwilling to capitulate to an unqualified triumphalism or a static cynicism" by "open[ing] onto the continuum of utopian and anti-utopian contestation without necessarily falling into either camp" (Moylan 2000: 105). Dystopia opens up a "contested or undecided space between militancy and resignation" (Moylan 2000: 181).

This definition of dystopia thus refers to a negotiation between two extremes, and it makes much sense for two important reasons. Firstly, the bounda-

---

[2] For an extremely thorough history of the shifting terminology, see Moylan (2000: 29–145).
[3] Meyer uses anti-utopia, thus dropping dystopia, because he considers the former the more established term (see Meyer 2001: 17).

ries between utopia and anti-utopia are not as clear-cut as one might think at first glance. Almost all characters inhabiting Huxley's *Brave New World*, for instance, are absolutely happy with their lives – and still, few readers would call it a good place. Conversely, these characters live in a world where many dreams of mankind have been fulfilled, and where one can live in happiness – but still, there are characters who would not call it a perfect world. Often, only a slight modification or change of perspective may cause utopia to tip over into its negative counterpart or the other way round (see Meyer 2001: 91). Especially if one looks at the proclaimed models of state and society which can be found in (anti-)utopian world designs, it is striking how similar utopia and anti-utopia can be. The second reason is directly connected to this point: what is considered to be good or bad is very much in the eye of the beholder. Thus, a reader-based argument finds its way into the debate, and it persists since Darko Suvin, in his classic definition, has hinted at the power of the reader in deciding how to take the presented world. "Thus, some texts intended (and internally marked) as utopian or dystopian (or perhaps not written within a utopian/dystopian strategy at all) can be received by readers as utopian or dystopian according to their own aesthetic or political judgments" (Moylan 2000: 155; see also 138). The interstitial stance of dystopia therefore enables much more productive readings.

The basis of dystopian and anti-utopian thought is, generally speaking, discomfort concerning utopian thought. Thus, the forms are closely linked from the very beginning. Reactions may include many different responses that attempt to falsify the utopian state and society, reaching from a critical attitude towards utopia to counter-utopian and utopia-negating ideas. The first watershed in the development of this literary tradition can be identified in early Romanticism where its satirical attitude in general gave way to specific concerns about society and to critical statements on events of the day (see Meyer 2001: 14). Criticism in the (anti-)utopian context aims at a variety of utopian elements. Firstly, it aims at basic ideas of how to define humankind and thus at the foundations of utopian society, the main point being that the utopian world denies the possibility of evil as such. Closely related to this point is the so-called 'realism argument': instead of strolling through ideal (and thus unreal, illusory) worlds, one should be working on real, everyday grievances (see Meyer 2001: 13). Thus, the realism argument is directly tied to the functionality of utopia: the world presented is too perfect and its highly positive status will never be achieved in the actual world, where good cannot exist in a totality without evil. Of equal importance is dystopia's/anti-utopia's critique of technological progress and reason, the former gaining particular importance in the late 19th century in the course of industrialisation. Dystopianists/anti-utopianists are worried about utopia's repression of individualism which goes hand in hand with an increase in isolation and alienation due to technological innovations. In short, the concern is that the development of ethics and morality might not keep up with developments in technology and thus be left behind without being able to respond properly to the questions and challenges raised by technological progress. Hence, in combination with a loss of traditional values and virtues, hummankind may not only be alienated from, but also threatened by and afraid of its very own products, the atomic bomb being the primary example (see Meyer 2001: 14). Twentieth-century texts mostly feature criticism on totalitarianism as a specific form of anti-individualism. Utopia as a closed, static society usually aims at a homogeneity and/or collectivism that sacrifices individuality for the well-being of the state – which is one of the reasons why dystopian and anti-utopian narratives tend to tell the story of an outsider as a counter-figure (see Meyer 2001: 14–15).

As a result, the societies these characters live in typically feature several recurring elements. With regard to politics, dystopias/anti-utopias tend to have a one-party system and/or a single dictator-like leader figure at the top. As pointed out, the government's basic idea is to keep society closed and static, thus maintaining a status quo which benefits the few at the expense of the many. Totalitarianism plays an important role in keeping people in check. Obedience is often assured by military force or a militarised police force, severe punishment, torture, and spies who keep an eye on those who question the authorities. As far as the economy is concerned, dystopias tend to be societies of lack (*Brave New World* being the most famous exception, *Nineteen Eighty-Four* being the most famous example). Again, a few people benefit from the poverty of many, which sometimes goes hand in hand with rich and powerful corporations exploiting a vast working class. A look at the design of these societies' communities very often reveals weakened, estranged, or even disbanded families, the reason being deeply rooted in the fundamental concept of any totalitarian system: in order to make people devote themselves to the state entirely, one needs to take away other relations which establish strong bonds, namely families, unions, and other social groups. Therefore, citizens of dystopias/anti-utopias also tend to have hardly any private life (which would give them the opportunity to spend time on things not related to the state). For the same reason, people's lives often also are loveless and sexless. Furthermore, these societies often have a technocratic touch. Technology functions as another means to keep people in check, either by surveillance (cameras, bugs, drones) or control (genetics, brainwashing, drugs). Lastly, media, culture, religion, and art as a counterbalance to the government are typically weakened by censorship and control, and may also be corrupted by propaganda (see Meyer 2001: 35–90).[4]

Repositionings: Dystopian Literature and Science Fiction
So far, this chapter has mostly been concerned with the broad categories of utopian, anti-utopian, and dystopian fiction and with what scholars have treated as the history of this literary tradition and its basic purpose as criticism. In the following, the focus will shift towards the striking development of this literary tradition from – roughly – the 1950s until today, which is characterized by a peculiar opposition between the proclaimed end(s) of utopian/anti-utopian writing on the one hand and productive repositionings and blurrings of genre on the other. An overwhelming number of voices who dismiss utopia (and anti-utopia) as a literary genre have been collected by Meyer (see 2001: 471–489). Most of these dismissals are politically or socially charged, but the arguments offer a vast panorama of reasons and lines of thought nevertheless, a few of which I will discuss in this section.

What stands out is how almost all critical voices hinge on the clash between the actual world and the representation of the utopian world in question. Jürgen Habermas, for example, states that utopia's promises were shattered because of how the actual world turned out so far, thus dismissing the utopian idea altogether (see Meyer 2001: 473).[5] Walsh, although he agrees that utopia has to be considered a failure when the actual world's development in the 20th century is compared to people's expectations in the 19th century, insists that utopia actually has been successful, most importantly in the realm of technology. Many things which people before 1900 could only dream of have actually become true; however, even if one admits that technology made men land on the moon, stay in touch with each other over vast distances, and defeat all kinds of illnesses, these technologies have often also been put to negative use (the paramount example being nuclear energy as a power beyond imagining which was not only turned into electricity, but also into a weapon). Actual world and utopia, then, differ so much because of utopia's totalised design – it presents a world which is simply too perfect, according to, for example, Karl Popper (see Meyer 2001: 481). Theodicy finds a way into the requiem for utopia with Gottfried Wilhelm Leibniz: there is no point in confronting humankind with ideal worlds be-

---

[4] For another collection of similar points, see Moylan (2000: 148–150).
[5] The underlying assumption that the actual world is a rather bad (and therefore dystopian) place will become very important later on.

cause we already live in the best of all possible worlds (see Meyer 2001: 481). Others still state that there is a better alternative to the status quo indeed, but with another challenge: humankind does not have a problem with regard to imagining desirable goals, but how to get there (see Meyer 2001: 483) – and how to deal with negative side effects (of, for example, technological progress). There seems to be no ultimate method of thought or action which could lead humankind to a happy future (see Meyer 2001: 481). Other voices highlight the dismissal of socialism and the rise of capitalism as key factors for the end of utopia. Utopia, it seems, used to be about an incalculable fantastic, while the actual world is more and more concerned with calculating the future, thus having no need for utopian imagination anymore (see Meyer 2001: 473). The rise of capitalism and the civil society, according to Fukuyama, put an end to socialism, and therefore to history and utopia as well (see Meyer 2001: 483). What is the result? While Joachim Fest, in a quite fatalistic manner, states that a life without utopia is simply the price to be paid for modernity (see Meyer 2001: 486), the more general claim across the disciplines and schools of thought is that people have to reduce their expectations as in the 'realism argument' mentioned earlier on. Instead of longing for a perfect but unreachable utopia, humankind needs to focus on what is 'realistically' possible (see Meyer 2001: 473). Utopia, it seems, is dead. From the beginning of its critical requiem in the 1950s and 1960s (marked mainly by nuclear warfare, two world wars, and the Cold War) to more recent renditions from the 1990s until today (marked by an ever-growing capitalism which may devour itself in the end, and by anxieties concerning the edge of technological progress over morality and social values), utopia is reduced to a disenchanted anachronism which has failed. Anti-utopia, be it as utopia's counterpart or as its follow-up, is not granted a place anymore either. Again, the fictional design is considered too unrealistic and thus, according to Eckhard Jesse, humankind is said to be unable to benefit from either images of a pessimistic (anti-utopian) apocalypse or (utopian) promises of bliss (see Meyer 2001: 489).

What is the point of dystopian literature, then? Maybe one has to accept utopia as what it is – a good place, but a non-place also. However, at the same time, the actual world itself seems to become more and more of a bad place despite or precisely because of technological progress. Thus, while the good place is dismissed conceptually, the bad place is right at our doorstep. So, maybe utopia as a totality has come to an end indeed (why dream of something you can never achieve when you might be able to achieve something along rather down-to-earth lines of thought?), and maybe anti-utopia has come to an end, too (why fear fictional or future grievances if they have already crept up on the actual world?). It is precisely this development which enables the rise of dystopia as a highly productive literary tradition. In contrast to Jesse's claim that neither utopian nor fully fledged anti-utopian visions can help us, there *is something between pessimistic apocalypse and inflated promises of bliss*, and this inbetween is incorporated by dystopia as a negotiation between utter despair and glimmers of hope. Humankind today, it seems, needs both extremes to a certain extent: it is hard to deny the bad place and, if it shapes the world, it certainly also shapes people's ways of coming to terms with this world; but people also need something good to cling to and dream of. All this is concentrated in dystopia.

One of the main reasons for its productivity and persistence, I suggest, is its transposition into urbanity. Dystopian literature's focus of the post-war era seems to have shifted from Orwell's Oceania to particular cities still influenced by the totalitarian socio-political system framing it. Out there, in the city as the emergent form of life of modern and postmodern society, dystopia finds enough elements of the bad place (crime, aggressive capitalism, anti-individualism, surveillance, downsides of technological progress) as well as glimmers of hope (free public transport, renewable energy, give-away shops, labour unions) to work with; it is thus able to narrow down the scope from state to city, from the abstract to everyday life, "seek[ing] a formal strategy that speaks to the moment without abandoning utopian contestation" (Moylan 2000: 105). It becomes clear why the repositioning into urbanity as a reaction to an urbanized world is crucial: under the precondition that the city embodies modernity with all its ambivalent implications (see Sarkowsky 2014: 14), utopia's promises and problems move closer to pressing concerns of the day and their solutions. In Moylan's words, "the conditions for moving forward are not to be found in some idealized future but are with us in the very societies in which we live" (Moylan 2000: 107) – just like the anti-utopian elements.

Second, dystopia's rise and productivity as a negotiation between utopia and anti-utopia is also due to its blending with another highly productive genre: Science Fiction.[6] Moylan points out that this blending process started in the 1970s and 1980s, boosted by cross-disciplinary scholarship and the launch of several influential journals (e.g. *Science Fiction Studies* and *Alternative Futures*, or the Newsletter *Utopus Discovered*), the 1967 article "The Three Faces of Utopianism" by Sargent figuring as the emerging scholarship's harbinger (see Moylan 2000: 69–70). The resulting dystopian texts "work within the shell of the old utopian aesthetic as it plays out in the familiar discursive universe of sf" (Moylan 2000: 105). Questions such as the following provide potential interrelations between these two traditions of writing: (how) can morality and ethics keep up with tech-

---

6 See Moylan (2000: 77) for utopian literature as a subgenre of Science Fiction.

nological progress? (When) does the greater good prevail over individual happiness? (When) do the ends satisfy the means? And, most importantly and more generally, "[w]here in the world am I? What in the world is going on? What am I going to do?" (Moylan 2000: 3).[7] All these questions, tensions, hopes, and fears can then be negotiated in the form of the critical dystopia on the grounds of urbanity.

II.2 Brave New Worlds: Key Coordinates of Five Dystopian Novels

The following subchapters introduce the five novels that are at the heart of this study.[8] Every subchapter is concerned with four core areas. Firstly, the sections named "Spaces" briefly describe the setting of the novel in question by explaining its typical (mostly urban) spaces. "Story and Plot" sections then provide an overview of the story in a nutshell as well as the novels' main characters. Thirdly, "Narration and Perception" passages describe how the story in question is conveyed to the reader by briefly outlining the narrative perspective and how it affects the mediation of events. Lastly, the sections named "Dystopian Turn and Development" highlight the story worlds' dystopian elements and how what I call the "dystopian turn" came about in the fictional world. I use this term in order to highlight how many dystopian novels use the actual world as a blueprint before, at a certain point of time, the story world takes a wrong turn and develops differently from the actual world, thus creating an alternate history which then finally arrives at the status quo described as the present of the story world (see Moylan 2000: 106–107, who uses the term differently, namely as a scholarly paradigm shift as in, for instance, *linguistic turn* or *spatial turn*).

---

[7] See also Luckhurst (1994: n.pag.), who identifies Science Fiction's desire for a (re)entry into the 'mainstream' of fiction, i.e. for getting rid of the degrading label of popular genre fiction, as the most pressing motivation for asking such questions.
[8] While I am absolutely aware that literary scholars usually do not start with some kind of summary of primary texts, I deem this subchapter necessary because it (instead of merely retelling the novels) already provides problem-oriented perspectives on the fairly dense novels at hand. Additionally, a section which presents the texts' key aspects is helpful because this study, as indicated in the table of contents, works with each text in several steps for the sake of an increasing complexity of analysis and interpretation.

II.2.1 *Perdido Street Station* (2000)

Spaces

China Miéville's *Perdido Street Station* (*PSS*) is one of the most striking examples of urban topographies in recent dystopian novels. The title points to the importance of urban space and infrastructure before the reader starts on the first page, with Perdido Street Station being the largest traffic junction of New Crobuzon, a dark, sprawling metropolis, located in the fictional world of Bas-Lag.[9] The city is dominated by steampunk technology, mostly in the form of gaslights, airships, railways, skyrails, constructs (i.e. small robots or machines, equipped with poor artificial intelligence) and heliotypes (the Bas-Lag equivalents of photographs).

The city is inhabited by a vast variety of humanoids; besides humans, numerous hybrid races can be found: the frog-like vodyanoi, the massive cactacae (a folk of warriors with cactus-like bodies), and the fragile khepri with human bodies and whole scarab beetles instead of human heads, to name but the largest groups. All these different groups display very different ways of perceiving, interpreting, and constructing urban space and society, which go together with different designs of the communal space. Every quarter in New Crobuzon has its own characteristics and works according to its own rules. While some of them are almost completely separated from the rest of the city (e.g. the cactacae's heavily-guarded dome, which is simply called the Glasshouse), others overlap and interchange in a dynamics of living together, against and along with each other. Characters in the book are often torn between cultures or social groups, sometimes in a very physical sense; terms such as "transition" and "hybrid zone" figure as the key words for the entire city's lifestyle and flair.[10]

New Crobuzon is, unquestionably, a grim place, a "nightland" (*PSS*: 2). It is huge, crowded, polluted, and intriguingly torn: industrial decay is pitted against sprawling, rotting, and organic elements. Disease and crime are commonplace in "this great wen, this dusty city dreamed up in bone and brick, a conspiracy of industry and violence, steeped in history and battened-down power, this badland" (*PSS*: 4). Gangs, mutants and unspeakable creatures roam the narrow streets at night. Some of these horrors are spelled out explicitly, others are touched upon only briefly, and others may only be urban legends. Since they

---

9 *Perdido Street Station* was followed by two further Bas-Lag novels: *The Scar* (2002) and *Iron Council* (2004).
10 This will be discussed further in chapter V.2.1.

are described by various characters and from different narrative perspectives, they seem to be everywhere. The result is a scenario of constant insecurity.

The city's government, a parliament under the reign of mayor Bentham Rudgutter (a twisted allusion to Jeremy Bentham, 1748–1832, the figurehead of modern utilitarianism), appears like the last poor remains of the classic dystopian surveillance state. Wealthy humans have the best life in terms of economy, rights, and housing; poor non-humans (which are subsumed under the term 'xenians') the worst. There is no equality; xenians, especially the khepri, face severe segregation and racism. Several parties that struggle for power at all cost are mentioned, some of which are obscure cults rather than political parties. Furthermore, New Crobuzon's inhabitants right to vote is limited to a corrupt lottery of votes, and one is not allowed to state their opinion openly. Instead, the militia and its looming towers control the people and try to take out enemies of the system as quickly and silently as possible. Corruption, involvement in drugs, prostitution, and mob crime are said to be commonplace among politicians, or as Benjamin Flex, the editor of the underground newspaper *Runagate Rampant* puts it: "Shit, sure as eggs Rudgutter's got fingers in every fucking pie you can think of. They all have. Churn out the commodity, grab the profit, get the militia to tidy up your customers afterwards, get a new crop of Remade or slave-miners for the Arrowhead pits, keep the jails full... nice as you like" (*PSS:* 119–120.).[11] New Crobuzon's government does not live up to its classical dystopian predecessors when it comes to totalitarianism because of its lack of control of space, but still it is a rough place. Punishment is extremely cruel and ranges from prison, slavery, torture and execution to Remaking (the magical – and violent – merging of two bodies; see, for example, *PSS:* 82). Power is a very fuzzy issue in *Perdido Street Station*. While the government is eager to rule with an iron fist while posing as something like a city-state republic, it is at the same time unable to control the city with all its milieus, subsystems, and forms of more or less organised resistance. In addition, it seems powerless against legendary individuals (such as Jack Half-a-Prayer, New Crobuzon's figuration of Robin Hood) and supernatural entities (such as the slake-moths, nocturnal predators which feed on people's dreams; see below). Since pollution, crime, and disease are the status quo, one might even say that the government is powerless against the city as such, which sprawls and grows, against "this behemoth that eats its citizens" (*PSS:* 2). With regard to the spaces of *Perdido Street Station*, it is also worth mentioning that the novel comes with an intriguing map of New Crobuzon (a detailed analysis is provided in chapter III.2.1).

---

11 See also the government's involvement in illegal gladiator arenas (*PSS:* 178–179).

Story and Plot

The novel's main character is the human Isaac Dan der Grimnebulin, an eccentric scientist, who tries to hide his relationship to Lin, a khepri artist. One day, a stranger comes to his lab: Yagharek, a garuda (a half-human, half-bird race of nomadic hunters from the faraway Cymek desert). Yagharek committed a serious crime when he was still with his tribe, and his wings were sawed off his back as punishment. As an outcast deprived of his ability to fly, Yagharek asks Isaac to make him fly again. A series of experiments and research commences, unfortunately triggering a dark force that threatens the entire city: Isaac obtains a rare grub that turns into a large and powerful slake-moth which escapes and frees four other moths from a governmental research lab. The moths feed on people's dreams, thus haunting the entire city, leaving their victims mentally devastated. At the same time, Lin is approached by Motley, an underworld boss, who wants her to create an intriguing and horrifying piece of art. Motley is a hybrid creature in the truest sense of the word, a so-called Remade, his body being a wild nightmare of both human and animal body parts. He wants Lin to make a statue of khepri-spit (a viscous liquid that Lin produces in her beetle head and which she uses for her art) depicting himself. While Lin, obsessed with her artistic project, becomes a prisoner of Motley, Isaac and Yagharek are the main protagonists of a wild hunt. The government is after them and some of their friends (most importantly the left-wing activist Derkhan Blueday), while Isaac's group is after the moths.

Narration and Perception

The novel provides two different modes of narration. Beginning and ending, as well as occasional passages in between, are dominated by homodiegetic passages from Yagharek's perspective with fixed internal focalisation. This personalised approach offers a clever way of introducing the reader to the unfamiliar story world which draws upon classic beginnings of works of Science Fiction: since the story world is strange, unfamiliar, and different from what the reader knows to be his/her actual world, one cannot take in the new world in its entirety right from the start. Instead of overwhelming the reader with innumerable details, Science Fiction novels tend to take their readers by the hand and show them a way in (see Moylan 2000: 6). The beginning of *Perdido Street Station*, by presenting the world through Yagharek's eyes, does exactly that: Yagharek is a newly arrived stranger in New Crobuzon just as the reader is a newly arrived stranger in Bas-Lag in general and in New Crobuzon in particular, and both crave for orientation. Providing more homodiegetic passages over the course of the novel ensures that readers can see Yagharek's progress as well as their own, in order to end up, at the close of the novel, as fully fledged citizens of the nightmarish city.

The main part of the novel is, however, narrated by a heterodiegetic narrator with flexible focalisation. Most of the time, Isaac as the main protagonist functions as the focaliser, but shorter passages also reveal the perspectives of his associates (e. g. of his girlfriend Lin or their friend Derkhan Blueday) and mayor Rudgutter. What these characters have in common is that they are locals who know their way around, thus rather providing an informed overview for the reader which functions as a counterpoint to Yagharek's passages.

These two different, oscillating levels thus play around with the entire process of coming to terms with the strange and unfamiliar story world. Yagharek's perspective lets the reader enter the city as a walker on street level, while the heterodiegetic passages provide a glance at New Crobuzon 'from above.' This interplay of proximity and distance, of particularisation and totalisation, will be elaborated on in the context of Michel de Certeau's book on *The Practice of Everyday Life* (1984) in chapter IV.

Dystopian Turn and Development

In contrast to other dystopian novels, *Perdido Street Station* does not give much information on how the dystopian status quo came about. The only significant event that is mentioned is the arrival of the first khepri about 700 years ago (see *PSS:* 184–185). An unspecified apocalypse (called The Ravening) on the eastern continent forced the khepri to migrate. 10,000 years of khepri history and memory were lost due to the unspeakable terror of The Ravening, and a new historical period was announced by the survivors and their descendants: the City Cycle. Another passage deals with what passes as Bas-Lag's equivalent of nuclear power: the Torque.[12] Due to unspeakable experiments, some kind of rift called the Cacotopic Stain opened.[13] Secret research and experiments were conducted in order to develop weapons to be used in a war against the city Suroch, which was then completely melted, transformed, and devastated, the only remains being "a drab panorama of what looked like crushed glass and char-

---

[12] A reminiscence of other dystopian histories since the 1980s, where the dystopia is often preceded by or at the brink of a nuclear war or catastrophe. See, for example, Alan Moore's *V for Vendetta* (1988–1989) and *Watchmen* (1986), or Russell Hoban's *Riddley Walker* (1980).
[13] Isaac also gives the translation of Cacotopos: "Bad Place" (*PSS:* 200). Interestingly enough, cacotopia is the term Anthony Burgess, according to Meyer, had been using for his novel *1985* (see Meyer 2001: 22).

coal" and horribly mutated life forms (*PSS:* 198). The Torque is a random force beyond human ken, not to mention control.

All in all, the dystopian elements in *Perdido Street Station* fray into conflicts between individuals, remains of classic dystopian institutions, social groups, supernatural entities, and the city itself. The result is a dark, muddled web of structures and relations where nobody is safe and in which everything seems to be possible. Constant insecurity, due to constant change and fuzzy edges – that is New Crobuzon as an urban dystopia.

II.2.2 *The City & The City* (2009)

Spaces

The City & The City (2010), one of Miéville's more recent novels, depicts a quite different city – or two (or even three) cities. One metropolitan area somewhere in Europe is divided into the dull, rainy, film noir-like cities (or city states) of Besźel and Ul Qoma. Judging from the names of inhabitants and streets, from clothing styles and architecture, Besźel has a rather Eastern European touch, whereas Ul Qoma appears to be rather Arabic. What is striking is the way these two are divided because in contrast to Berlin before the Fall of the Wall or other split cities in the real world, there is no material border that runs between Besźel and Ul Qoma. No walls, no fences, no barbed wire can be found. There is an official border crossing called Copula Hall, but that is it. In fact, the cities even overlap, and are "grosstopically" close to each other (see *TC&TC:* 160 – 161).[14] The two cities are not divided physically, but mentally: citizens are used to only perceiving what is happening in their city while shielding themselves from impressions of the other city (a subconscious performance called unseeing). Streets and buildings are either classified as total, as alter, or as cross-hatched. Total areas belong to one city only, namely the one the speaker is actually in. Alter spaces always refer to the other city and have to be ignored completely. The only way to legally look at alter spaces is to get a visa and then walk (or drive) through Copula Hall as the connecting (and separating) building: "If someone needed to go to a house physically next door to their own but in the neighbouring city, it was in a different road in an unfriendly power. […] A Besź dweller cannot walk a few

---

14 Basically, grosstopically means something like "bluntly geographically speaking without the practice of unseeing". Two houses in a crosshatch zone can be grosstopically right next other, but be located in different cities – as explained in the quote above, in order to get from one house to the other, one would have to go to Copula Hall first, cross the border, and walk to the other house in the other city.

paces next door into an alter house without breach" (*TC&TC:* 86). Crosshatch areas, however, are usable by both cities. Thus, it is common that citizens of Besźel and Ul Qoma walk the same stretch of land just a few inches away from each other trying not to notice each other. Crosshatch areas usually have different names in the two cities and are strictly treated as being separate. Illegal crossings are called breach, and an ominous power that is called Breach itself ensures the separation of the cities.

Story and Plot
The novel follows the Besź inspector Tyador Borlú who investigates the murder of an American PhD student named Mahalia Geary, who has been investigating the legend of a third city that lurks in those spaces which neither Besźel nor Ul Qoma claim for themselves: Orciny. Since Mahalia's body is found in Besźel but the murder has been committed in Ul Qoma, Borlú crosses over, supporting the local police (called *militsya*), loosely working together with an officer called Dhatt. As it turns out, Mahalia's murderer is Dr. Bowden, a foreign scientist who, many years ago, published a much-criticised book on Orciny that ruined his career. In the end, Borlú himself breaches in order to take down the murderer of a friend of Mahalia's, Yolanda Rodriguez. Breach take Borlú, and a man called Ashil makes him part of their group, so the inspector has to give up his former life.

Narration and Perception
The City & The City is told by Borlú in autodiegetic fashion. His perspective is the only one given, which goes together with the novel's configuration as a postmodern detective story. The readers see what Borlú sees, but may come to their own conclusions. However, Borlú knows a good deal about the two cities and the practice of unseeing as well as the delicate political situation, and the reader does not; again, the framing of the novel as a detective story is helpful. After a startling beginning in medias res at the first murder site (where the reader has a hard time making sense of a first description of unseeing), the reader is taken by the hand as Borlú tries to find out what happened, never tiring of providing the reader with detailed observations. Thus, the way of leading the reader into the story world is quite different from the one in *Perdido Street Station*, where Yagharek as the first main protagonist is just as clueless as the reader.

Due to its mode of a typical detective story, the novel displays the topography of a crime novel or a political thriller: as Borlú works the murder case, he enters a web of political groups, suspicions, witnesses, and police work. This topography is spatialized by resting upon another one, namely the topography of the divided but overlapping cities, heavily influenced by unseeing, as described above. While the city is split into Besźel and Ul Qoma, the crosshatch zones provide an overlap. Furthermore, the city is split between the mythical, non-existent city of Orciny on the one hand and Besźel and Ul Qoma as actually existing places on the other. Lastly, Besźel and Ul Qoma are placed against the equally elusive, but nevertheless existing Breach.

Dystopian Turn and Development
The dystopian origins of *The City & The City* can be traced back to the time before the existence of Besźel and Ul Qoma as they are in the story-now, a time that is called 'pre-Cleavage'. The coming about of the Cleavage is unsolved, however: "All we know is nomads on the steppes, then those black-box centuries of urban instigation" – no town history has been recorded (*TC&TC:* 61). Two theories, split theory (one town dividing into two) and convergence theory (two formerly separate towns coming closer to each other), are identified without being further explained, so one does not know whether the cities have ever been one unit.[15] The only remnants of pre-Cleavage are the artefacts dug up by archaeologists on sites such as the Bol Ye'an dig, the work place of the Canadian delegation that includes Bowden, Mahalia, and Yolanda.

Since pre-Cleavage, the two cities fought two open wars against each other. In World War II, they were "noncombatant supporters of opposing sides" (*TC&TC:* 73). Politically speaking, the two cities are quite different. Besźel's constitution is democratic, but ever quarrelling, and even an apparent social democrat such as Mikhel Buric turns out to be a hidden nationalist. The city is also not free from prejudice or racism, and partly in the hands of an ultranationalist paramilitary called the True Citizens who stand outside the political system. Ul Qoma is run by a national party with totalitarian tendencies including censorship and the ban of other parties. Since the so-called Silver Renewal, however, Ul Qoma tries to show a sense of cosmopolitanism by opening up to the world and foreign investors. Yet, it has its own bunch of not explicitly legal ultranationalists called Qoma First. When it comes to international politics, Ul Qoma's prestige suffers from the existence of its refugee camps. The city is avoided by the USA but favoured by Canada, whereas Besźel has connections to both countries. Some attributes of dystopian states are obvious: xenophobia, censorship (espe-

---

[15] For a sociological discussion of this question under the heading of *methodological urbanism*, see Schroer (2006: 238).

cially of books), CCTV, illegal splinter groups, to name but a few (see Meyer 2001: 35–90). Although geographically interwoven with each other, the cities only come together to speak in the so-called Oversight Committee (a telling name in a city dominated by indoctrinated unseeing, as chapter IV will show), which is made up of twenty-one delegates from each city.

Living in Besźel or Ul Qoma, despite the dystopian elements, does not seem too bad – in comparison to other dystopias, that is. Information on institutional terror, isolation of the individual, or collectivism is rather scarce. The only field where absolute compliance is not only demanded but excessively described – and thus the dystopian key element – is the practice of unseeing in order to not breach. Relations between the cities certainly have improved since the wars, but it is a fragile peace, the Oversight Committee being a place where the cities have to come together while avoiding it elsewhere as much as possible. The cities, in order to keep up their status quo, need a certain exchange of goods and information because they are so close to each other from a grosstopical point of view and because they cannot let go from each other in a material sense. Breach and the enforced unseeing are a desperate attempt to keep apart what is materially speaking not only close, but interwoven.[16] In the context of dystopian thought, Breach's status is fairly ambivalent: during Borlú's hearing in the Oversight Committee, Breach are introduced as a mysterious force. Then, by the introduction of Orciny and the rumour that Breach and Orciny might be identical, Breach acquire the image of an evil secret society. As they take on Borlú and make him part of their group, they almost seem to become the good guys. Only at the end of the story, this apparent positive image is thwarted again: firstly, because Borlú cannot get out again and is not allowed to contact anybody from his former life; and, secondly, because Breach is still in charge of keeping the balance between the two cities – and of keeping them apart.

II.2.3 *City of Bohane* (2011)

Spaces
Kevin Barry's *City of Bohane* (2011) tells the story of an Irish city (named after the river Bohane that runs through it) in the year 2053, characterised by a gangland topography of pubs, drug parlours, run-down alleys, gambling dens, and whore

---

[16] Mysterious third parties who stand above the common order are – again – a running theme in dystopian novels. See, for example, John Christopher's *The Guardians* (1970), or the Controllers in *Brave New World* (1932).

houses. Different gangs (called Fancies) inhabit different quarters as they struggle for control. These quarters are contrasted with some gang-free, upper-class areas, but the lower-class, crime-ridden ones dominate the overall mood of the city which exhales violence, whoring, and drugs, combined with a strong urge for nostalgia. At the same time, the city as a whole is in stark contrast with the vast swamps of Big Nothin' surrounding it. The novel comes with a printed city map, which will be analysed in chapter III.2.3.

Characters often remember the good old days, the Bohane "lost-time" (*CoB*: 3). They go back there by walking contemplatively, by taking drugs, by watching old film reels and photographs and by singing or listening to old songs. Thus, numerous spaces in the city are highlighted as bearers or triggers of memory. The spaces of the lost-time gain importance by adding a second temporalized topographical layer of nostalgia to the city space. Remembering Bohane is at least as relevant as living in it, or better: remembering Bohane's lost-time enables living in or escaping the present. The novel's narrator plays a crucial role in this juxtaposition of past and present because he, as the owner of the Ancient and Historical Bohane Film Society, provides access to Bohane's lost-time for the characters (by running a one-seat cinema) and the reader (by compiling the overall story). The Bohane lost-time is present in songs, stories, photographs, films, places, and in personal memories. Barry displays his sense of humour when Macu, Logan Hartnett's wife, enters the narrator's cinema – and instead of films shot for entertainment, the cinema shows old CCTV material, dating back as far as the 2030s (see *CoB:* 179). What is traditionally part of a surveillance state's system of control and oppression has become a precious, nostalgia-charged treasure of memory and history.

Story and Plot
The novel tells five individual stories of seeking and losing power which, put together, tell the overarching story of Bohane as a city. The most dominant individual story is the one of Logan Hartnett, the boss of the ruling Hartnett Fancy, and his descent from a proud gang leader to a sad, lonely man abandoned by his wife Macu. Closely connected are the stories of all his lieutenants (Jenni Ching, Wolfie Stanners, and Fucker Burke) and how they try to profit from Logan's increasing weakness as he is both struggling with his marriage and his legacy as the Fancy's leader. Last but not least is the story of the Gant Broderick, Logan's nemesis, who returns to Bohane after 25 years. Most people assume he wants to take revenge on Logan and win back Macu (who went out with the Gant Broderick in their younger days, but turned him down to be with Logan), but it turns out that

Logan acutally asked him to come back in order to test the loyalty of Macu and all his lieutenants in order to find a suitable successor.

More specifically, the overall story of *City of Bohane* is concerned with the fate of the city in the hot summer of 2053. It is the year of the Feud, of the climactic clash between the Hartnett Fancy and their most dangerous rivals (called Norries). In order to stand a chance, Logan calls on the so-called sand-pikeys (a wild tribe living out in the dunes). Logan's alliance actually wins, but at a steep price: in exchange for their support, the sand-pikeys are given part of the city. The novel ends on the night of August Fair, a grand holiday, when the young celebrate their youth and the old (the Gant Broderick among them) dwell in their lost-time memories. Logan, powerless but still in love, waits for Macu in order to talk things over, but the only person who comes looking for him is his bed-ridden mother Girly. At the same time, a new gang begins to seize control of the city: the freshly formed girl gang of Jenni Ching, the last of Logan's lieutenants.

Narration and Perception

The presentation of the story world is dominated by a heterodiegetic narrator with flexible focalisation. Numerous characters function as focalisers: Logan, all his lieutenants, his mother Girly, Macu, the Gant Broderick, to name but the most important ones. Almost all of these focalisers belong to the Hartnett Fancy or are loyal to it; thus, the story world is presented as a milieu-specific gangland topography of individuals who try to cope with love and gang politics in the present and, simultaneously, with the Bohane lost-time of the past. However, the narrator also appears occasionally in a homodiegetic fashion. In these passages, it is revealed that the narrator is also part of the Bohane story world. He poses as the city's inofficial town chronicler who tries to overcome the fact that he, too, is bound to the story world. By doing so, he mediates between town history and individual memory.

Dystopian Turn and Development

In contrast to most of the other story worlds examined in this study, Bohane lacks certain classic dystopian elements: the City of Bohane is not run as a totalitarian surveillance state in any sense, but by its gangs. The absence of technology from the city is also striking: the only complex machines seem to be jukeboxes and the projector of the narrator's cinema that still uses film reels. Both jukeboxes and film reels, along with the usage of photographs and hand-written letters, give the novel its characteristic nostalgic touch.

Once again, the reader is not told much about how the dystopian story-now came about because the novel rather focusses on the lost-time predating the dystopian turn on the one hand and on the present-day gangland topography on the other. The ruling of Bohane falls to Logan Hartnett's gang, the Hartnett Fancy. The Fancies in general came into power by making horse money (trades and races); in 2053, the gangs are mostly into "herb and dream and hoors" (*CoB:* 221). Although not a dystopian government in the classic totalitarian, utopia-denying sense, there are some dystopian elements. Logan insists that there is only one newspaper in town (the *Bohane Vindicator*) in order to control information. In general, he sees his task as the boss in keeping "the town in check" (*CoB:* 105), to "'keep the place somewhat fucking civilised'" (*CoB:* 248) – a task he has adopted from the men of the Bohane Authority, who are powerless and uninvolved in comparison to the gangs:

> The Authority Men were desperate and ill-paid souls who lived as peaceably as they could in the modest terraces that ascended towards (but did not reach) the Beauvista heights. They always kept to the New Town side of De Valera Street [which is gang-free]. They went nervously about their business in an animal town. Their business was to keep the place in some manner civilised. It was a job of work. (*CoB:* 156)

The Authority Men are supposed to have an ordering function in a crime-ridden city, but the task is taken over by Logan and his gang. At the beginning of the novel, the citizens of Bohane can look back to a period of "Calm" (*CoB:* 30), of ceasefire among the gangs. As the story unfolds, the Calm does not continue and it becomes harder and harder to keep the city and the gangland civilised. Logan finds himself ageing and is torn between running the Fancy and spending more time with his wife Macu; younger lieutenants in his Fancy – Jenni Ching, Wolfie Stanners, and Fucker Burke – develop ambitions of their own (see *CoB:* 167); Logan's nemesis and former leader of the Back Trace Fancy, the Gant Broderick, is back in town; the gangs from the Northside Rises provoke a feud bigger than ever before; Logan himself asks the devilish sand-pikeys for help, and the city is in danger of falling to their brutish customs. Ol' Boy Mannion, a middleman, knows why things go as they do in Bohane: "But there was the possibility, Ol' Boy realised, that too long and persistent a Calm might be no good for the city. A place should never for too long go against its nature" (*CoB:* 30). Others in Bohane, however, have long given up the rough gang life. Whereas the young people (Jenni, Wolfie, Fucker) live very much for the moment and hardly think of tomorrow, it is especially the older characters (Macu, the Gant Broderick, Logan's mother Girly) who think of (and live in) the past to such a degree that they almost forget the here and now. Bohane is a rough place full of drugs, whoring, and gang fights. The dystopian element is not based on a surveillance state of any sort, but on what the people, particularly the gangs, make of the city – a rough and melancholic place. "Happy? Who's happy in fuckin' Bohane? Ya'd be a long time scoutin' for happy in this place" (*CoB:* 58). Only the nostalgic past of the lost-time offers some felicity.

II.2.4 *Lilac and Flag: An Old Wives' Tale of a City* (1990)

Spaces
Lilac and Flag is the final volume of John Berger's *Into Their Labours* trilogy. While the first two volumes focus on life in the country, the third is – as suggested by the subtitle – more concerned with the contrasting living conditions in the city, the connection between the texts being the novel's cast of characters (see below). *Lilac and Flag* as a city tale takes place in the ultimate European "cosmopolis"[17] (Nurmi-Schomers 2007: 263) of Troy some time in the 20th century. Troy, in terms of its location and urban topography, seems fairly vague at first. Excessive name-dropping overwhelms the reader with a vast amount of quarters, shops, and places within the city named after cities and federal states from all over the world as well as from ancient Greek and Roman mythology. Chapter IV.2.4 will show that, despite the first impression of unmappability, the sum of its telling place names translates into a rough topography after all.

Troy has some decent quarters, but the majority of quarters is in a rather bad shape. Industrial areas and slums mostly inhabited by immigrants tell of a city full that fell prey to the negative results of capitalism including hard work, poverty, crime, and economical problems. The country village, on the other hand, figures as a nostalgic place of treasured memory.

Story and Plot
The novel's main protagonists are Sucus (called Flag by his girlfriend Szuzsa, a name initially invented by her for a non-existent lover) and Szuzsa (called Lilac; the name is also the Persian variety of Susanna or Susa), two young people who grow up in the city, fall in love with each other and struggle with their poor living conditions. Sucus takes up various jobs without ever succeeding. As Sucus goes from job to job, and from failed opportunity to failed opportunity, he and Szuzsa constantly dream of fleeing to the countryside and leading a happier life. In the end, they steal passports from a train in order to sell them, and Szuzsa turns to

---

17 The origin of the term can be traced back to Edward Soja.

prostitution. In the aftermath of the train heist, Szuzsa's brother Naisi gets killed and Sucus gets arrested. As Sucus commits suicide, Szuzsa is left alone in the city.

The story of the young lovers is accompanied by traditional immigrant stories of old men who came to the city from the country decades ago in order to make a living. One of these old men is Sucus's father, Clement Gex, a day labourer. He also dreams of going back to the country with his wife, but he never actually makes this dream come true. In the end, he is killed by a malfunctioning TV set. Hector, who is from the same village as Clement, is an aged police superintendent who left the country for the same reasons as Hector: making a living in Troy and becoming rich. He struggles with the fear of being useless after his upcoming retirement and with the impossibility of returning to the country because of his wife (who is from the city and outright refuses to move to the country). After having interrogated Sucus, he commits suicide as well.

Various strands and characters in the novel and in the entire trilogy are interconnected. For example, it is only during his interrogation of Sucus that Hector finds out that the young man's father (Clement) is from the same village as Hector himself. Additionally, several characters from the first two volumes of the trilogy are mentioned or make short appearances. In the end, the aforementioned four men (Naisi, Sucus, Clement, and Hector) are dead and embark on a white ship alluding to Charon's ferry from ancient Greek mythology, which carries them to the country. It becomes clear that the country is somehow located in the afterlife and that the country in the world of Troy is long gone – it is only present in characters' memories and in the old woman who poses as the novel's narrator.

Narration and Perception
Appropriately subtitled "An Old Wives' Tale of a City", the novel is presented to the reader by an old woman from the countryside. Thus, the old wives' tale draws upon the oral tradition of storytelling as well as upon the spatial notion of the Golden Age. The narrative situation appears to be confusing at first or when the novel is read in isolation, but it is a conclusive follow-up to the first two volumes of the trilogy because the trilogy's style of narration evolves (from matter-of-fact reports, poems and short stories to a postmodern style) as the story – stretching over the three volumes – evolves from country life to urban cosmopolis. In *Lilac and Flag*, the old woman narrator presents herself as another character from the country village of Clement and Hector, but the village itself is long gone and only present in characters' dreams and memories and in the afterlife. The old woman oscillates between her personal memories of the country and at-

tempts to make contact with the characters in the city. Since she is unable to do so until these other characters are dead, it becomes clear that the old woman is dead herself, a ghost from the country now haunting Troy.

Dystopian Turn and Development

While the living conditions in *Lilac and Flag* are quite bad for most people, Troy is not a classic dystopian or anti-utopian surveillance state. Also, there is no clear point of time where the story world takes a dystopian turn resulting in the dystopian differences from the actual world. It shares a considerable amount of elements with *City of Bohane*, however. In terms of who is in charge, a President (*L&F:* 64) and mobsters (*L&F:* 13) are mentioned. There is also a police force: Superintendent Hector, who moved to Troy from the country, is rather mild and melancholic, whereas younger colleagues turn out to be corrupt and violent. The land beyond the city is also similar to Bohane's Big Nothin' as an undefined area where people go without ever coming back: "Zsuzsa's father had disappeared five years earlier, without a trace. On the roads between cities people often vanish" (*L&F:* 5). The most important similarity to *City of Bohane*, however, is to be found in the the role of the past. Both novels evoke the past as a positive, even utopian, contrast to the grim present. Whereas Bohane's lost-time focusses on the city life, however, the happy days in *Lilac and Flag* are associated with the past of rural life in contrast to the urban present.

The novel tells the stories of several outsiders – former peasants and foreign workers who moved to Troy in order to make a living (see Welz 1996: 192). The hopelessness of their situation mostly circles around the lack of money and jobs (see *L&F:* 39; 93) while they live in poor, unhealthy conditions (see *L&F:* 28; 124). Berger, as will be shown, joins Henri Lefebvre in his criticism of the city as the embodiment of the dehumanising powers of capitalism. Troy is primarily an economic dystopia. Utopia, on the other hand, is present in the reverberating village life back in the day: returning to the country is impossible in this life and thus figures as a utopian ideal (see Welz 1996: 187). The analysis will show how, in the relationship between dystopia and utopia, one can easily tip over into the other, and that Berger is well aware of the excess of nostalgia usually associated with the country.

II.2.5 *Divided Kingdom* (2005)

Spaces

As the title already suggests, the novel takes the United Kingdom as its template but, due to what is called the Rearrangement, significant changes occur within the story world. The term "Rearrangement" already implies the change of established relations as *Divided Kingdom*'s dystopian core. The new Divided Kingdom is separated into four quarters (red, green, blue, and yellow), inspired by ancient Greek humourism. People are not classified by intelligence, social status, or ethnicity – they are classified on the basis of the four humours or temperaments as proposed by Hippocrates (yellow bile/choleric: Yellow Quarter; black bile/melancholic: Green Quarter; phlegm/phlegmatic: Blue Quarter; blood/sanguine: Red Quarter). Newly built walls, border checkpoints, and the removal of bridges make sure that people stay in the quarter they have been assigned to. Every quarter has its specific mood, inspired by the humour in question: for example, the (phlegmatic) Blue Quarter features many lakes, rivers, and waterways, while the (choleric) Yellow Quarter sees riots on a daily basis.

In contrast to the other dystopian novels in this study, Thomson's novel does not focus on one city in particular, but on many locations scattered all over the Divided Kingdom. On the one hand, there are rather rural locations: the boys' home to which the main protagonist is moved after being separated from his parents, the little house of his new family, a secluded, sect-like community called the Church of Heaven on Earth, and a little village in the Green Quarter. On the other hand, the capitals of the new quarters feature prominently as well: London, the former United Kingdom's capital, is split into four parts, i.e. into four new capitals: Pneuma (capital of the Red Quarter), Aquaville (Blue Quarter), Pledge (Green Quarter), and Thermopolis (Yellow Quarter). The main protagonist starts his career as an employee of the dystopian government in the capital of the Red Quarter and then visits those of the Blue and the Yellow Quarter in course of a conference. Thus, similar to Berlin during the Cold War, the splitting of the city runs parallel to the splitting of the entire country.

Furthermore, the novel text is accompanied by a map of the new Divided Kingdom, which is of particular interest with regard to selection and omission and to how these processes impact on the conception of the story world. An analysis of the map follows in chapter III.2.2 in the context of maps and literature.

Story and Plot
The story starts in medias res with the little boy Matthew Micklewright being taken away from his parents as the Rearrangement begins. He then grows up in a boys' home, indoctrinated with the new Divided Kingdom's idelology. Afterwards, as a teenager, he is moved to a new family, the Parrys, and given a new name: Thomas Parry. Life with the new family is marked by loss: Parry longs for his old family while Victor (his new father) and Marie (his new sister) struggle with the loss of their wife/mother, who was relocated to another quarter. As an adult, Parry is integrated into the government's system, given a job in the Ministry of Health and Social Security, and becomes a relocation officer (a supervisor for other people's relocations). He excels at his work and is sent to a cross-border conference in the Blue Quarter, where officials and researchers from all four quarters meet to discuss the country's development. The Blue Quarter fascinates him; his most striking experience there takes place in a club called the Bathysphere, where he has an intense vision of his lost mother. This vision makes him aware of all the lies and murdered identities upon which the Divided Kingdom rests, and as the whole conference is moved to the Yellow Quarter, Parry is desperate to go back to the Bathysphere. A bomb attack offers Parry a way to spontaneously flee from the conference and leave behind his old life. He hitchhikes around the Yellow Quarter, finally entering a ship as a stowaway. He is then shipwrecked and washed ashore in the Blue Quarter. After a short episode of recovery in the Church of Heaven on Earth, Parry returns to Aquaville, the Blue Quarter's capital.

He is seized before he can enter the Bathysphere again and has to undergo several tests. Dr Gilbert, the responsible scientist, reclassifies Parry as green; as a result, he is relocated to a village in the Green Quarter's countryside. While he is expected to try to settle in, Parry plans his escape. He steals the clothes of one of the White People (a group of marginalised, ignored, and persecuted people who live outside the classificatory system of the four humours), joins up with other White People, and finally makes it back to the Red Quarter. During his trip through all the quarters, he meets a woman called Odell several times, and an affectionate relationship develops. Odell helps Parry to cross over into the Red Quarter. At home, his old boss Vishram from the ministry waits for him; he reveals that Parry has been under observation all the time and that the whole quest's purpose was to see whether Parry would make a good successor. After that, Parry tries to settle in again, but he fails to do so. Finally, Odell contacts him and says that she is in serious trouble. Parry agrees to flee with her, and the novel ends with him waiting for her to show up.

Narration and Perception

Throughout the entire novel, Parry as the main protagonist remains the narrator of the story, and only his thoughts and emotions are conveyed (homodiegetic narration with fixed internal focalisation). In a way, the style of narration suits the dystopian setting as it provides only one perspective of one single person within the system, who then starts to question things as they are and thus becomes a typical dystopian outsider (see Meyer 2001: 94). Parry himself remains a rather flat character, and this makes much sense insofar as he is the protagonist of a novel that is mainly concerned with the fragility and instability of identity anyway.

Two instances stand out in Parry's narration because they are told very coherently and detailedly where one would not expect it. Firstly, there are Parry's childhood memories. It is remarkable how well he is able to remember and present many details from his youth, especially from his time at the boys' home, and these memories may strike one as unexpected or even unrealistic at first glance (how much can one, in one's thirties, remember from the time when one was an eight year-old? Even worse, how much can one remember from one's early childhood if it is contested by a quite different, indoctrination-ridden childhood?). However, the detailed remembering of Parry's childhood goes hand in hand with the novel's overall strategy of placing a strong longing for a past where one still knew who one was against the fragile identity of the present. The second occurrence of a surprisingly accessible narration is the episode of Parry as one of the White People. There, he starts out as an intruder; he is not one of them and thus unable to access their group mind (an image-based, telepathy-like way of communication). Soon, however, Parry loses the ability to speak, just as the rest of the group cannot speak. At the same time, he is later able to detailedly narrate his adventures as a White Person – and this contradicts the way regular citizens see the White People. On the contrary, it is common knowledge in the Divided Kingdom that the White People are simple-minded beings without any identity. So, if Parry becomes part of a group without identities, how is he still able to convey all the personalised details to the reader? This answer lies in the observation that the White People do not have no colour, but *all* colours, and that they are complex individuals indeed who simply cannot be classified by the means of the Divided Kingdom's humour system.[18]

---

[18] For more details on the White People, see chapter V.2.3.

Dystopian Turn and Development

In *Divided Kingdom*, the reader can actually follow the advent of the dystopian setting as the novel opens with the disbanding of the protagonist's family due to the Rearrangement's initiation. The argument for rearranging an entire country draws upon the decline of social values and the family after industrialisation, as Miss Groves, one of Parry's teachers at the boys' home, explains:

> [T]he family had been in serious decline for years, decades even [...]. How could people with little or nothing in common be expected to live together? How could they achieve stability, let alone happiness? [...] In short, the family could be held responsible for society's disintegration, and the politicians who masterminded the Rearrangement had felt compelled to acknowledge the fact. [...] If they rearranged the population according to the humours, then [...] the new family would be a group of people who shared a psychological affinity – people who got on, in other words. Blood ties would be set aside in favour of simple compatibility, and if that wasn't a propitious unit on which to base an efficient and harmonious society, Miss Groves had argued, then she would like to know what was. (*DK*: 14)

It is striking how, even in this compelling explanation, anti-utopian notions shine through: stability is listed before happiness, efficiency before harmony. Blaming the family for weakening society's fabric, and weakening the family in turn, is once again a typical move in dystopian fiction (see Meyer 2001: 46; 51). Taking children away from their families as early as possible and indoctrinating them (as happens to Parry at the very beginning of the novel) in order to win them for the government is also commonplace – and in Parry's case, who starts a career at the Ministry of Health and Social Security, it seems to work perfectly at first. Thus, the Rearrangement obviously changes people's social relations by tearing them apart and putting them together in another constellation. As a long-term strategy, the idea is that Rearrangement and relocation will become obsolete over time since people get used to the new spatial and social structure and adapt to the new psychological scheme defining them. However, the psychological aspect of the Rearrangement is constantly problematized. Melancholics, for instance, tend to commit suicide because they cannot handle the new arrangement, and Cholerics actively and collectively rebel against the new government. As chapter IV.2.5 will show at great length, people are haunted by their former lives. In order not to be relocated again for displaying inappropriate behaviour (getting too angry as, say, an inhabitant of the Blue Quarter), people "become used to lead a double life. The Rearrangement had created a climate of suspicion and denial [...]. People had buried the parts of their personalities that didn't fit" (*DK*: 44). Especially Parry himself as a red relocation officer who becomes more and more interested in the other quarters (and the Blue Quarter in particular) personifies the ambiguity of the psychological Rearrangement.

II.2 Brave New Worlds: Key Coordinates of Five Dystopian Novels — 33

Why rearrange a whole country? The United Kingdom, over time, "had become a troubled place, [Miss Groves] said, obsessed with acquisition and celebrity, a place defined by envy, misery, and greed" (*DK:* 8). Numerous social grievances are commonplace: crime, divorce, racism, violence. "For decades, if not for centuries, the country had employed a complicated web of manners and convention[s] to draw a veil over its true nature, but now, finally, it had thrown off all pretence to be anything other than it was – northern, inward-looking, fundamentally barbaric" (*DK:* 8).[19] The Rearrangement, then, is the government's only solution to the growing problems – "to reorganise the country's population – the entire population, from the royal family down" (*DK:* 9). As a result, "[n]ew borders were created. New infrastructures too. New loyalties" (*DK:* 11). Of course, some classifications of people might turn out to be incorrect, and some might suffer, but the typical dystopian notion of the greater good washes away all doubt: "In times of crisis, [Miss Groves] said, the good of the many always outweighed the misfortunes of a few, especially when the health of an entire nation was at stake" (*DK:* 11). The spatial Rearrangement goes along with a judicial one:

> Throughout the divided kingdom the walls of concrete blocks had been reinforced with watch-towers, axial crosses and even, in some areas, with mine-fields, which rendered contact between the citizens of different countries a physical impossibility [...]. Attempts to cross the border illegally were punishable by prison sentences, and if you defied the guards they had the right to open fire on you. [...] Anybody suspected of 'undermining the fabric of society' could now be arrested on unspecified charges for up to two years. (*DK:* 28)

The new laws follow the classic dystopian rules of isolation, collectivism, and anti-individualism with an underlying ideology (see Meyer 2001: 35–90). A constant unease is the result – people always fear they might be relocated again (see *DK:* 14; 51); suspicious behaviour is to be reported and children, as in *Nineteen Eighty-Four*, are told to spy on their parents (see *DK:* 38). Of all the novels in this study, the historical backdrop of *Divided Kingdom* is most prominent, the reason being that the reader is not simply told how the world turned out after the dystopian turn with brief remarks about how it all came about. The reader, like Parry, witnesses the dystopian turn as the United Kingdom takes a wrong turn in its development and becomes its own dystopian counterpart.

---

19 The remark on the growing distress in British society might well point towards a fundamental conflict which emerged in the Victorian Age: "The Victorian will to preserve public steadiness and decency clashed with the fears brought about by a complex historical and cultural moment where new scientific discoveries and industrial progress were developing, and where the old system was starting to show its incapability of restraining phenomena such as social change" (Di Liddo 2009: 107; see also Botting 1996: 135–154).

Since people's status quo becomes problematic, the past before the Rearrangement is almost presented as a utopian and elusive time. The wish for going back is strong in many inhabitants of the Divided Kingdom – again, Thomas Parry as the main protagonist proves to be exemplary in this respect. The Bathysphere club in the Blue Quarter grants him a pre-Rearrangement experience of his childhood, and he goes through various hardships in order to get back to the Bathysphere after the conference so he can relive that moment once more. In the end, Parry's plan for the future is to live together with Odell illegally, thus "undermining the system" (*DK*, p. 395). As so often in the dystopian tradition, the question remains whether these utopian alternatives can come true.

III Literature and Maps, Maps and Literature

After the introduction and the overview over the dystopian tradition in general and the novels this study is concerned with in particular, it is now time to explore the first important thrust in the context of urban topographies: the cartographic representation of cities and related strategies of mapping. Thus, for the purpose of this study, I will mostly focus on the map as it is presented in fiction. Generally speaking, the excitement of exploring the relations between map and territory in literature lies in the varying constellations between reality and fictionality. I start with a general overview of the interrelations between maps and literature; after that, chapter III.2 provides close readings of cartographic strategies in *Perdido Street Station*, *Divided Kingdom*, and *City of Bohane*, primarily based on the paratextual maps that accompany the texts.

III.1 Maps and Literature: Cartography and Literary Studies

Linking maps and literature as human products is a comparatively old phenomenon, as a look at the history of cartography can show.[1] Basically, four early historical types of maps can be distinguished (see Stockhammer 2007: 14–16): firstly, there are cadastral and early city maps. Itineraries as a second kind were intended for travels along a given route from one specific place to the next. Thirdly, portolan charts, which showed mostly coastlines as a navigation tool for sailors, need to be mentioned. Lastly, and most interesting in terms of their literariness, are the so-called mappaemundi; they represent the world without relying on geography as their primary source.[2] Instead, the focus was on historical events and stories from the bible, which made them highly narrative. The exact location of a town or site was less important than its relevance within the context of salvation (see Schneider 2006: 27). Mappaemundi were also embellished with pictures or travel reports. However, after having figured prominently in the Middle Ages, they were increasingly replaced by topographical maps in the late 15th century. Several factors (a new sense of time and individuality, the continuous exploration of nature and especially the exploration of America, new developments in mathematics, astronomy, and physics) led to a two-fold marginalization of stories and pictures in cartography (see Schneider 2006:

---

[1] For a thorough introduction, see Schneider (2006).
[2] For more details on the Hereford Mappamundi, the best-known mappamundi produced in England, see Brotton 2012: 82–113.

33–34). Hartmann Schedel's map of the world from 1493 shows a shift from maps such as the Ebstorfer map from 1284:

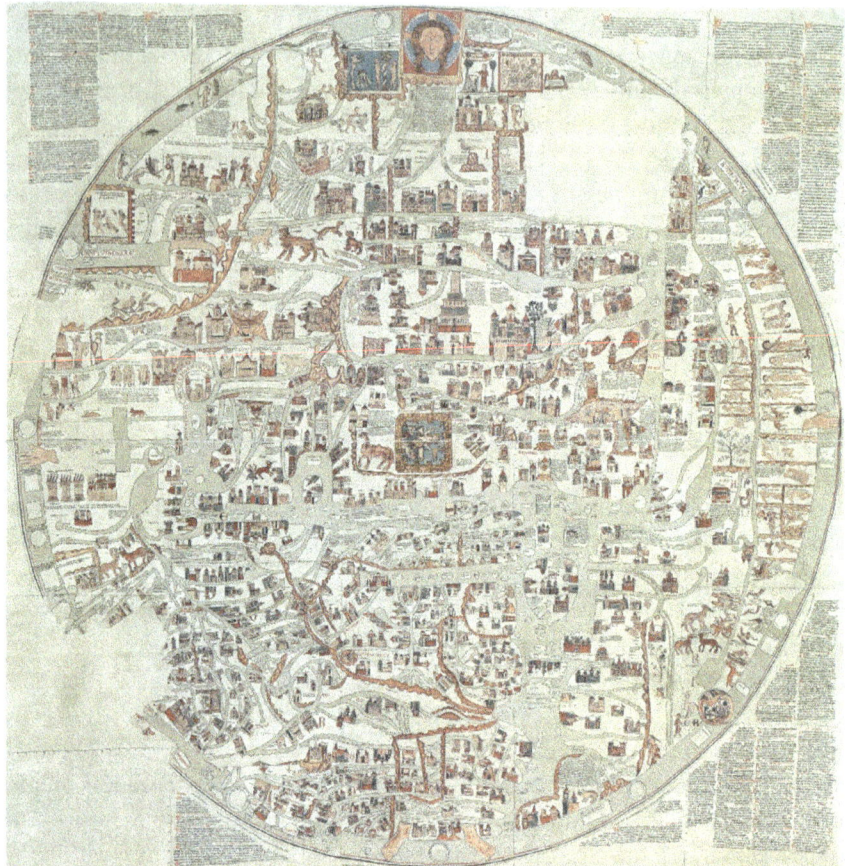

Fig. i: Ebstorfer Map of the World (1284); copyright bpk / Staatsbibliothek zu Berlin / Ruth Schacht

Whereas the older map depicted and located fantastic creatures such as the birdmen on the edge of the world (but still depicted within the map)[3], Schedel put them outside the mapped world on the left:

---

[3] A hyperimage facsimile reproduction can be found on the website of Lüneburg University as the centrepiece of the the so-called *Ebscart* research project (see Warnke 2011: n.pag.).

Fig. ii: Hartmann Schedel's Map of the World (1492); copyright bpk / Dietmar Katz

Similarly, the three sons of Noah, who initially represented the three continents Europe, Asia, and Africa, are placed outside the map. This process of marginalization resulted in maps that became increasingly independent from history. Just as Noah's sons were being gradually removed from their representation within the map itself, the figure of the human being more generally moved beyond the map and humankind gained new ways of looking at the world (see Schneider 2006: 33–34). As de Certeau sums up: at this pivotal moment in cartographic history, the map loses its narrativity, defeats its own illustrative and descriptive value and starts to limit itself to the representation of topographical characteristics (see de Certeau 1984: 120–135). Hence, the history of cartography is part of a greater discourse on objectivity that began in the Renaissance. As the rise of the written alphabet and print media strengthens visuality and weakens other forms of perception, the human being as an observer – or, in this case, a map user – is enabled to take a safe look from a distance. He or she can establish him-/herself as an uninvolved subject objectifying what is being observed while the observed becomes independent from its observer and from the act of observation itself (see Huck 2010: 37–38).

Defining the Map

Thus, what passes as a map today is very different from its ancient or medieval predecessors, one of the most important differences being the grid of longitude and latitude (see Stockhammer 2007: 16). Generally speaking, according to the International Cartographic Association (ICA), "[a] map is a symbolised image of geographical reality, representing selected features or characteristics, resulting from the creative effort of its author's execution of choices, and is designed for use when spatial relationships are of primary relevance" (Ortag 1995: n.pag.). As Schneider observes, this broad definition offers possibilities to deal with different kinds of maps and related artefacts that organize space according to varying criteria (see Schneider 2006: 7). What becomes very clear is that a map does not show the world 'as it is' – it is a *symbolized* image that *refers* to the world out there: "Rather than imitating the world, maps develop conventional signs which we come to accept as standing in for what they can never truly show" (Brotton 2012: 7). Or, as philosopher Alfred Korzybski famously puts it: "The map is not the territory" (qtd. In Stockhammer 2007: 13). Furthermore, it only represents bits and pieces. By and large sticking to the ICA definition, Schneider suggests four dimensions for dealing with maps. Firstly, the predominant feature of maps is their historicity. Maps are always created in a specific context, and for a specific purpose and related to a specific world view, all of which have to be kept in mind in order to read the map in question accordingly. In this respect, Brotton emphasises the reciprocal relation between map and world view: "A world view gives rise to a world map; but the world map in turn defines its culture's view of the world" (Brotton 2012: 6). Mapmaking thus "provides different cultures with particular visions of the world at specific points in time" (Brotton 2012: 13). Secondly, the role of the map producer is of high importance. A map is not as objective as one might think since the appearance of the map is always shaped by an authorial process of creation, selection, and omission: "every map shows one thing, but therefore not another, and represents the world in one way, and as a consequence not in another" (Brotton 2012: 15). Thirdly, one has to keep in mind that maps are creators of space that always attempt to construct forms of projection that are 'close to reality,' but which remain approximations of the actual world (depending on the maps' principles of construction). Thus, maps can also create locations of memory or pose as creators of locations of memory and play a role in terms of spatial identities. Lastly, maps contribute to the creation of specific views of the world, be it geographically, socially, politically or ethically. Thus, "[m]apmakers do not just reproduce the world, they construct it" (Brotton 2012: 7), and their constructions may work as material manifestations of mental maps and spatial imagination (see Schneider 2006: 7–9).[4]

Far Away Is Close at Hand in Images of Elsewhere
In fantasy literature, it is customary to provide the reader with a rather detailed map of the fictional world in order to compensate for the fact that the fictional world has ostensibly little to do with 'our real world' (the measure of all things being Tolkien's self-drawn map of Middle Earth in his *Lord of the Rings* trilogy). In other cases, authors may take the real world as a template and enrich it with fictional elements by, say, placing fictional settlements or whole countries into an otherwise 'realistic' area.[5] Furthermore, a novel's story may take place in an area apparently close to reality and exploit this closeness by means of naming and describing places the reader might recognise from his/her own world-knowledge. This closeness to reality of the fictional world tends to spawn much interest in readers as well as editors, publishers, and scholars, the results being literary tourism (fans of the fictional character Sherlock Holmes visiting the actual-world Baker Street) and the production of specific maps (a map of Charles Dickens' London created by literary scholars, for instance).[6] All these mapping operations raise questions concerning referentiality. How 'real' can a map of an entirely fictional place be, and how fictional is the map of a real-world place when it appears in a work of fiction? What happens when the map's topography is congruent with the real world, but all place names are changed?

In order to come to terms with such questions, I will turn to three names repeatedly. Michel de Certeau will be first. In *The Practice of Everday Life* from the 1980s, he is interested in the subject-oriented double relation between *map* and area (the latter also being called *tour*) on the one hand and the detachedly observing voyeur and the ground-level walker on the other. Secondly, German literary scholar Robert Stockhammer, by relying on some of de Certeau's basic ideas, takes the map as an inherently textual artefact and a human product (see Stockhammer 2007: 53)[7] and emphasises the force field of lust and power in the triangular relationship of the map, the territory it refers to, and the map user or mapmaker. Lastly, Barbara Piatti presents a model operating on three lev-

---
4 For a similar collection of points, cf. Schlögel 2003: 90 ff.
5 Piatti names, among others, the Lost World in Arthur Conan Doyle's novel of the same name (see Piatti 2009: 342).
6 For a canonical overview of maps in literature, see Wyatt (2013).
7 See Stockhammer 2007, p. 53.

els (single text – region – greater area) which, under the label of literary geography, is concerned with the hinges between inner-world (i.e. fictional) and extramundane (i.e. 'real') reality in fiction.

In his model of looking at the world (and especially the city) in *The Practice of Everyday Life*, de Certeau links space and language. He treats walking and the production of linguistic utterances as analogous performances that relate to spatial organisation. Language, according to de Certeau, is in itself highly spatial. For example, deictic elements, i.e. words and phrases such as 'you', 'here', or 'tomorrow', which rely on contextual information in order to convey meaning, help speakers to locate themselves and others in time and space. Thus, reports, stories, and speech acts in general are considered "spatial trajectories" that are essential for everyday life (see de Certeau 1984: 115). He then distinguishes between two different ways of approaching (city) space. First, one can assume the position of an observer, or voyeur, who looks at the city from high above. Distance and passivity allow the voyeur to see the city as a text, "to read it, to be a solar Eye, looking down like a god" (de Certau 1984: 92). However, the voyeur who is reading the city is not reading more than a "facsimile produced" (de Certeau 1984: 92), a "theoretical (that is, visual) simulacrum" (de Certeau 1984: 93). In the very act of detaching himself/herself from the city 'down there,' the voyeur puts himself/herself into a position that leads to a "misunderstanding of practices" (de Certeau 1984: 93).[8] De Certeau's counter-concept to the voyeur's is that of the person on street level walking through the city. Instead of being passive, walkers are actively experiencing the city. In the act of walking they literally create the city space. Walking is made an essential part on the way towards "a theory of everyday practices, of lived space, of the disquieting familiarity of the city" for de Certeau (de Certeau 1984: 96). For the creation of space, de Certeau draws upon Roland Barthes by stating that "pedestrian movements form one of these 'real systems whose existence in fact makes up the city.' They are not localized; it is rather that they spatialize" (de Certeau 1984: 97). People in the city walk, and as they do so, they appropriate the topographical system, a practice which de Certeau compares to the speech act, defining "walking as a space of enunciation" (de Certeau 1984: 98). The spatial order offers the walker a pre-selection of possibilities and prohibitions of where to move and how. Walkers can comply with this pre-selection, modify it, ignore it, trespass, and invent and appropriate

---

8 Schlögel (2003: 23–24; 309; 503) goes even further by stating that the city simply cannot be read as a text because the city *is* no text. Instead, he considers the act of walking in combination with mental operations of perception and reflection (by taking upon yourself the risk of getting lost) similar to the exploration of an unknown continent the only suitable way of experiencing the city.

new possibilities. "He[/she] thus makes a selection [...] [and] creates a discreteness" (de Certeau 1984: 98), his[/her] very own choreography in and in relation to space. Still, the singularity of a walker's movement does not lead to isolation because the walker is part of a whole "framework of enunciation" and thus always to be seen in relation to other enunciations that all "initiate, maintain, or interrupt contact" in "a mobile organicity in the environment, a sequence of phatic topoi" (de Certeau 1984: 99). Walkers thus have an advantage over voyeurs: due to their position within the city, they a have first-order observer position, which enables them to actually experience the city and enter a dialogue with it as well as with other walkers.

The limitation of this apprehension of city space, however, is that walkers are unable to read the text they are creating because they do not inhabit the observer's second-order position and can be observed themselves (see Huck 2010: 37). The walkers are on ground level, where they experience and create the city space without being able to read it since "[t]he networks of these moving, intersecting writings compose a manifold story that has neither author nor spectator, shaped out of fragments of trajectories and alterations of spaces: in relation to representations, it remains daily and indefinitely other" (de Certeau 1984: 93). Walking is an appropriation of the topographic system, a spatial realisation of place, and at the same time a matter of relation between positions. Furthermore walking, according to de Certeau, belongs to a sphere called *tour* which, in "a discursive series of operations," creates space. The opposing perspective, belonging to the voyeur, is that of the *map*, which represents a way of seeing instead of walking, a distanced "knowledge of the order of places" on a "tableau" – a "plane projection totalizing observations" (de Certeau 1984: 119). Just as it can be seen in Hartmann Schedel's map, what is at stake here is an artefact that is a tool for the human being to simulate a look from outside: whereas walking demands movement within the city or landscape, the map is to be looked at from an external point of view. Together, these bipolar phenomena offer an interplay of proximity and distance reminding one of the overall epistemological discourse on objectivity, and one can see that the original understanding of the distanced position from outside (or, in de Certeau's sense, from above) a map becomes complicated on closer inspection: "[i]n a somewhat paradoxical way the observer has to be part and not part of the observed world, and the simultaneity of these mutually exclusive positions makes this stance fragile" (Huck 2010: 47).[9]

---

[9] According to Huck (2010: 82), it is the novel as an innovative form of writing that finds a middle course between these two positions on the field of literature.

Stockhammer's notion of maps points into the same direction when he proclaims that a map links graphic gestures with movements in the particular area. To him, maps are "Zeichenverbundsysteme [...], die ein Gelände darstellen, das als bereisbar vorgestellt wird" (Stockhammer 2007: 13), i.e. composite sign systems which exhibit an area as being travelable. Hence, topographies can be the representations of areas – be it by means of texts or maps – as well as the areas themselves (see Stockhammer 2007: 40). This definition, as Stockhammer points out, excludes certain charts, graphs, and structure trees and paves the way for another field: fiction. The apparent problem that the map of a fictional area cannot indexically refer to the area it represents because this area does not exist in the actual world is solved by arguing along the lines of writer Per Olov Enquist (see Stockhammer 2007: 66). By assigning the fictional area another state of existence, this fictional area is presented as being travelable and becomes presentable as

> a concrete world with a different state of existence [...], a world that is present in the mind of its artist or one that has been created in another medium such as a novel. Maps of fictional worlds possess dynamic objects as well, namely those in fictional worlds. Thanks to these maps one can imagine those areas as if they really existed – without the necessity of their actual existence. (Stockhammer 2007: 67 [my translation])

The effect is, in Barbara Piatti's terms, one of realisation, a "Realisierungseffekt"; by simply having a map depicting the fictional world, this very world acquires a certain state of (possible) existence as its location shifts from nowhere to somewhere and becomes accessible (Piatti 2009: 34).[10] As soon as there is a map of any territory, it taps into the domain of referentiality, and poses questions about the territory presented. A graffiti found by scholar Jerry Brotton along the railway lines close to Paddington Station in London puts it aptly: "'Faraway is close at hand in images of elsewhere'" (Brotton 2012: 14). Thus, in contrast to the comparatively down-to-earth ICA terminology, Stockhammer and Piatti strengthen the fictionality of maps. The reason for paying attention to maps of both fictional and actual places is that both make use of indices that allow its user to refer to places, events or people, and structurally speaking, they are not very different anyway (see Stockhammer 2007: 65).[11]

Thus, it becomes hard to distinguish between maps of 'real' areas on the one hand and fictional ones on the other. In view of the points made by Schneider

---

10 For a similar argument, cf. Dünne 2013: 223.
11 See also Wood and Fels (1986) – an excellent essay on how all maps and signs depend on conventions.

above, it becomes quite clear that the designation of reality or fictionality is at best a fuzzy issue. Again, the following questions arise: how 'real' can a fictional map be? How fictional are 'real' maps? Or better: how 'real' can a fictional map be by relying on fantasy and imagination as the basis of its referential power, and how 'fictional' are real maps when even they render the reality they point to as a symbol (see Mokre 2000: 23)?[12] In this discursive field, the map of a fictional world is an extremely powerful tool because the map is not an abstract philosophical concept, but a concrete textual artefact. In Genette's classic terminology, the map is a device accompanying the actual novel text and can thus be called a paratext (see Genette 1993: 11–12). It is exactly due to this status that the map can, to use Stockhammer's words, present the area it refers to as being travelable – independent from the question whether the area does or does not exist in the actual world. The fact that almost everything – from crime rates in urban areas to one's favourite geocaches – can be mapped (see Schlögel 2003: 89) only emphasises the legitimacy of fictional maps.

Having established that as a base, Stockhammer suggests to explore the interplay between the map, the territory it refers to, and the map user as a highly productive operation. In this triangle, two aspects figure prominently: firstly, a lust for the map as an artefact of outstanding craftsmanship refers to the fascination one may find in its decorative value over a fireplace, in tracing roads on a map with a finger, or in imagining the places the map refers to while reading it;[13] secondly, the map can be treated as a tool of power, i.e. of spatial control and verification usually in the context of institutionalised representation (see Gabaude and Maleval 2013: 140), e.g. the drawing of a borderline on a map which will then exert power over the actual territory in question. Because of its power, and because the area on the map is presented as being travelable, the map is ascribed certain precision, certain permanence and preservation, and therefore certain usefulness – be it a map that refers to the actual world or to a fictional one. Now, according to Stockhammer, if a novel is concerned with maps, it makes implicit or explicit statements about the relation of the

---

12 As mentioned in the introduction, I suggest that these questions are part of a larger issue concerning fictional worlds and their relations to our actual world, touching upon dystopian concepts of (irrealist) fiction, systems-theoretical approaches to literature to negotiate between fiction and reality, and spatio-geographical lines of thought.
13 As already suggested by my explanation of the term (directly borrowed from Stockhammer), lust does not refer to a primarily sexual desire, but to a rather general fascination or desire for the map and the place it refers to. Despite the slightly awkward connotation in English, I stick to the word because I still think it comes closer to the concept than related terms – and, at least sometimes, physical engagements with maps (folding/unfolding, touching, tracing roads with one's finger) carry certain lustful associations. See Parker (2009: 1).

map to its own medium (i.e. the literary text) – correspondences, differences, affinities, or competitive situations may figure in the force field of lust and power (see Stockhammer 2007: 69).

Piatti takes the same line as Stockhammer in terms of what literary texts or maps can do, namely producing the fictional area through the text or map. She also agrees that the maps of literature can never be congruent with those of the actual world but that they can be looked at and examined just as one can look at and examine the imaginary space of a novel text which – as Enquist suggests – also attests a certain state of existence operating according to consistent and coherent principles (see Piatti 2009: 31). However, she also goes a step beyond stating that maps of real and fictional areas are structurally similar. She strives to exploit precisely this structural similarity of the two because it is at the heart of Stockhammer's concept of cartographic lust. The lust for maps originates in the aforementioned effect of realisation and the domain of referentiality: as soon as one faces a map of any place (real or fictional), one is invited to deal with the question of the map's verification. This invitation is the basis for Piatti's entire research project of literary geography as an oscillation between the sphere of the imaginary ("Sphäre des Imaginären") and the pole of reality ("Pol des Realen"; Piatti 2009: 137). The following passages highlight the role of maps and cartography in literary geographical negotiations between reality and fictionality.

Besides the importance of the *Realisierungseffekt*, Piatti stresses that paratextual maps productively contribute to the novel text by providing another perspective or way of accessing the fictional world the text itself does not provide (see Piatti 2009: 50). Thus, the map as a paratextual device can go with or against the main text. The map is also relevant for Piatti's model of the space of action ("Handlungsraum"; Piatti 2009: 23; 126–127). Piatti's model is intended as an instrument for shedding light on the intersections between fictional world(s) and actual world, which is doubly valuable because not only does the actual world shape the fictional world in question, but the fictional world is also capable of having an effect on the actual world (see Doležel 1998: x; 20).

The first component of Piatti's literary geography model is the so-called space of action, which tries to come to terms with the organization of the different spaces, places, locations and references which can be found in a text, the entirety of which is called text space (*Textraum*)[14] or space of action (*Handlungs-*

---

14 All following English terms referring to Piatti's concept are my translations of her terminology.

raum; Piatti 2009: 127–129).[15] The space of action contains two inner layers: the geographical horizon (*geographischer Horizont*) and the figure space (*Figurenraum*), and together, they make up the entirety of spaces accessible by characters within the text. The geographical horizon is concerned with all the locations that are only mentioned by characters without any character ever physically being there; these locations are called topographical markers (*topographische Marker*). Another category within the geographical horizon are projected spaces (*projizierte Räume*), i.e. spaces of memory, dreams, and other physically rather inaccessible spaces (see Piatti 2009: 128). The plot of any text is taking place in the figure space. Therefore, within the figure space, the basic units of any text can be found: the locations (*Schauplätze*) and zones of action (*Handlungszonen*). Locations are a text's smallest units, e.g. a clearing in a forest, a castle, or a mansion. Zones of action, according to Piatti, reveal the macrostructure of texts by abstractly summing up several locations. For example, a county may be analysed as a zone of action by containing several villages (locations). What is important with regard to the zones of action is that they 'stand alone' in a way. They are not placed within a spatial continuum so that white or blank spots are common and their relations (e.g. how far it is from one zone of action to another, and how one gets from one zone of action to another) are not clearly defined (see Piatti 2009: 129).

This first component, the space of action, is relevant for the organisation of any novel's spatiality, and will recur in later chapters in this study, but it does not tell us much about the relations between fictional world and actual world. For Piatti, these relations can be examined with the help of her model's second component: the so-called degree of referentiality ("Referentialitätsgrad"), i.e. the extent of actual-world elements, spaces, and references one can find in a text (e.g. the story of a Charles Dickens novel taking place in 'London'). Piatti distinguishes between spaces of fiction without any reference to the actual world[16] and fictionalised spaces, i.e. spaces within the fictional world that have an actual-world equivalent. Spaces of fiction are entirely fictional: the planet Hoth in

---

15 The space of action is contrasted with the geospace (*Georaum*), i.e. with the spatial reality of the actual world (see Piatti 2009: 23).
16 The question is, however, what a space in a novel text needs to be like in order to have no reference to the actual world at all. This may be possible with maps of fantastic places whose topography has nothing in common with the topographies of all existing actual-world places, but does not the simple mentioning of the word "city" evoke a concept known to the reader from the actual world already? Piatti seems to mean that there are no explicit markers, such as known place names; but even in these cases, the question arises as to how precise these markers can (or cannot) be – for example, if a novel is said to be taking place in a nameless town in "Ireland".

the *Star Wars* universe, or Mordor as a country which is said to be located in Middle-Earth, do not exist in the actual world. Fictionalised spaces on the other hand do have their origin in the actual world – but they are not actual because they appear within the fictional world. Parts of Robert Louis Stevenson's *Treasure Island* take place in Bristol, for instance, but no matter how 'realistic', 'mimetic' or 'authentic' the representation is, it is not identical with actual-world Bristol (see Piatti 2009: 132).

Elements within the text space can thus be placed on a scale according to their degree of referentiality. Piatti, relying on Frank Zipfel, describes three categories by stating that text space elements can be either immigrant, surrogate, or native objects. The basic idea of this differentiation is to take the text space as a territory into which objects either immigrate or which they inhabit right from the start (see Piatti 2009: 132). Native objects are non-existent in the actual world – they are invented places and therefore spaces of fiction that are native to the fictional world. Contrarily, immigrant objects have their origin in the actual world; they immigrate into the text space and are therefore fictionalised spaces. The key strategy for 'moving' immigrant objects into the text space is name-dropping by use of toponyms. This is often used in the very first sentences of a text in order to help the reader to 'place' the action: for example, a character might be described as walking down "Downing Street" in "London". However, these two categories are not sufficient for covering all objects. In many instances, objects from the actual world undergo certain more or less significant changes as they find their way into the text space. In these cases, these objects are surrogate objects, i.e. "fictional counterparts of real objects in those fictional texts that substantially modify their descriptions" (qtd. In Piatti 2009: 134). Thus, if one looks at all three categories of objects, a decrease in reference to the actual world (from immigrant objects over surrogate objects to native objects) is noticeable. Objects can then be placed on a scale, ranging from the sphere of the imaginary to the pole of reality. All native objects, without any further graduation, fall into the sphere of the imaginary. Immigrant objects find themselves closest to the pole of reality[17] while surrogate objects occupy the vast space between the two extremes.

How do these categories influence the mapping of certain objects in literature? According to Piatti, mapping immigrant objects is least complicated because one can broadly rely on world knowledge and geographic maps (see Piatti

---

17 'Closest' to the pole of reality, not *at* it, because literature and reality are never congruent or identical. Even the most detailed or 'realistic' representation, be it in a text or on a map, can ever be more than an approximation to reality without ever reaching the pole of reality (cf. Piatti 2009: 136).

2009: 136). Still, as I established earlier in this chapter, every territory can be mapped, including those which are entirely products of imagination. In this context, one should not forget that it is inherent to these categories that they are fuzzy[18] and liable to change. The mappaemundi addressed at the beginning of this chapter can serve as an example. A person looking at one of these maps in the Middle Ages might well have taken some of the depicted countries (or even Paradise) for real while a 21st-century observer will rather classify them as imaginary constructs (while taking, say, a contemporary OS Explorer map 'for granted').

Now that the three approaches to literature and maps have been introduced, it is time to forge them into one model. The following chart shows my model of literature and maps based on de Certeau, Stockhammer, and Piatti:

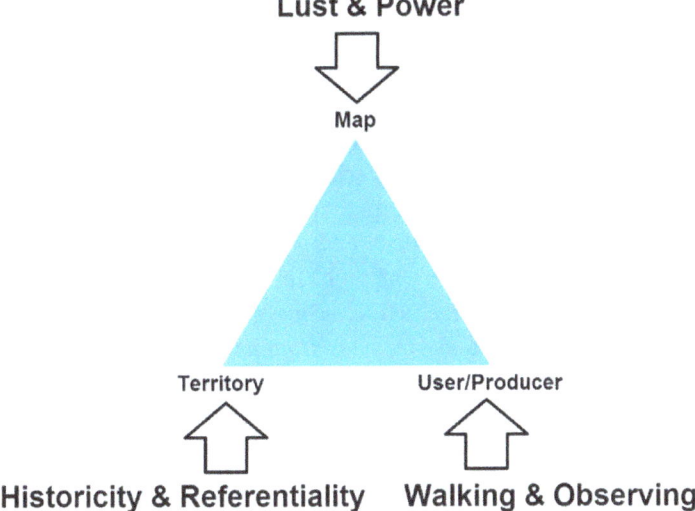

Fig. iii: Model of Map, Territory, and User/Producer

The quintessential triangular relation of the map, the territory it refers to, and the map user or producer is placed at the centre: the map inevitably refers to some place in some way; as a human product, it must have been made by somebody, and it is used by somebody with respect to the territory it refers to. Placed around the triangle are the three force fields or domains which severely

---

18 It is especially hard to differentiate between immigrant and surrogate objects. See Piatti 2009: 134.

influence it. The force field of lust and power is taken from Stockhammer and emphasises the oscillation of maps between being an aesthetic object without any further purpose and being a tool expressing and exercising power over whatever it refers to. Walking and observing as the second force field, based upon de Certeau's basic differentiation of *tour* and *map,* is relevant for the map's status between immediacy and panoptic vision. The final force field is called historicity and referentiality. Historicity refers to the interconnected development of maps and literature, starting with the establishment of highly narrative maps (such as early mappaemundi) and their replacement by more geographical maps and the simultaneous loss of narrativity, followed by a reintegration of maps into literature (as authors and publishers start to add paratextual maps to the texts), finally arriving at the proclaimed *spatial turn* as scholars start to focus on phenomena of spatial representation/imagination, mapping, and maps in literature. Referentiality on the other hand is based on Piatti's notion of the effect of realisation and its connections to questions of reality and fictionality (once again: how 'real' can fictional maps be, and how fictional are 'real' maps?). Although these force fields influence the triangle in its entirety, each seems to have a perspicuous access point: the force field of lust and power is most influential with relation to the map as an object, which oscillates between being an aesthetic and beautiful piece of art or craftsmanship, and an ideologically charged tool of power. The arrow pointing from historicity and referentiality towards the territory demonstrates the impact of Piatti's effect of realisation on any presented territory – be it on a map or in a written text. Last but not least, de Certeau's opposition of walking on street level and observing from high above primarily determines the person dealing with the map and territory in question.

 This chapter tried to show that literature and maps have been going together for quite a while, that they still go well together, and that they do so for some very good reasons. First, both texts (and language in general) and maps are composite sign systems based upon arbitrariness, referentiality, and relations. Second, both texts and maps are products of a specific time, place, and purpose. Third, both maps and literature have an effect on the world and vice versa. Fourth, they share a long history of combination, drifting apart, and mutual reintegration. Last, both maps and literature refer to territories (be they real or imaginary) and present them as being travelable, while both maps and literature suffer from a similar kind of projection problem: despite their vast potential of being able to represent/map pretty much everything, any representation is, as a matter of principle, selective and imperfect.

III.2 Places to Get Lost: Literature and Maps

The following three subchapters elaborate on the notions addressed above by examining three novels which feature a paratextual map printed in the actual book. The first subchapter takes a close look at the status of maps as apparently aesthetic, consistent, helpful, and reliable artefacts in terms of verification and use by showing how *Perdido Street Station* plays with these assumptions by deliberately misleading the reader, luring him/her into a game of recognition, misrecognition, and overall cartographic negation. The second subchapter on *Divided Kingdom* focusses on the map as a tool of power in its strategies of omission, thus supporting the dystopian program of the Kingdom's government. Lastly, the map of *City of Bohane* is examined in terms of its visual design of the city's quarters and in terms of its staging of a touristic lust for a superficial topography (the most striking feature being a city square on the map metafictionally referring to author Kevin Barry as well as the Irish republican who lived in the early 20th century).

II.2.1 "Strange Tricks of Cartography": The Map(s) of *Perdido Street Station*[19]

As shown in chapter III.1, there is a long tradition of embellishing novels with paratextual maps, most prominently in contemporary fantasy fiction. The idea behind providing the reader with a map printed at the beginning of the novel often is to give him/her a means of orientation. Since the story world in genre fiction is usually a world of its own with few or even no similarities to the actual world, the map supports the reader in several ways: it may help him/her to better imagine the story world, to get a feeling for its geography, and to track the movements of the novel's characters from place to place. Maps – no matter whether they refer to 'our' actual world or to an imagined one – are generally considered helpful in terms of orientation and imagination, to be artefacts of precision and preservation. This is where China Miéville and *Perdido Street Station* come in. In the following, I will use Michel de Certeau's ideas from *The Practice of Everyday Life* (1984) to show how the novel plays with the triad of map, territory, and map user in connection with the force field of lust and power inherent to maps and cartography. The novel lures its readers into a game of recognition and misrecognition and presents itself as a meditation on maps, as well as a meditation on

---

[19] A very condensed combination of chapter III.1 and the following chapter was published as a follow-up to the first conference solely dedicated to China Miéville's works (see Zähringer 2015).

spatial imagination itself. *Perdido Street Station*, featuring both a printed map[20] of the city where the action is taking place and many maps within the story world, will prove to be an exemplary case for the most important interplays at work between maps and literature: as I will show, the relations enable the novel to reflect on the maps' power as narrative devices and on literature's own relation to medial means of localisation (see Stockhammer 2005: 323). *Perdido Street Station* as a work of literature and its maps oscillate between the notion of maps being artefacts of power as well as aesthetic artefacts of lust. As one is told in the novel: there are "strange tricks of cartography" (*PSS:* 200) going on in New Crobuzon, *Perdido Street Station*'s zone of action.

For the Reader: the Extra-textual Map
Right before the prelude in which the character Yagharek enters the city for the first time, Miéville provides his readers with a double-paged map of New Crobuzon with a scale and a compass rose. The map shows the names of the city's quarters and its network of railways and skyrails with all of their stops indicated. The bridges and rivers are also named. Compared to early examples of literary maps,[21] this map of New Crobuzon is very sophisticated. Miéville himself explains his use of maps as follows:

> [To write a novel] I start with maps, histories, time lines, things like that. I spend a lot of time working on stuff that may or may not actually find its way into the novel, but I know a lot more about the world than makes it into the stories. That's the "RPG" [role-playing game] factor: it's about systematizing the world. But though that's my method, I don't start with [...] the graph papers and the calculators [...]: I start with an image, as unreal and affecting as possible, just like the Surrealists. But then I systematize it and move into a different kind of tradition. (Gordon 2003b: 357)

Thus, Miéville's imagining of the story world is much bigger and more intricate than the reader actually finds in the novel itself. Exceeding the parameters of

---

20 Unfortunately, copyright permission for the map could not be secured, but there are various fansites where one can have a look at it.
21 To give just a few examples, Eric Bulson mentions "the squiggly line over a map of Spain to indicate the direction of Don Quixote's [...] route" and the "barely legible map of the world to the fourth edition of *Robinson Crusoe*, with a dotted line outlining the course of his protagonist's ill-fated voyage" (Bulson 2007: 20). Stockhammer examines no less than five novels featuring maps (Jonathan Swift's *Gulliver's Travels*, Johann Gottfried Schnabel's *Insel Felsenburg*, Goethe's *Die Wahlverwandtschaften*, Adalbert Stifter's *Der Nachsommer*, and Herman Melville's *Moby-Dick; or, The Whale*) in great detail (see Stockhammer 2007: 89–210).

narrative constraint, Miéville's act of cartographic production is therefore an act of systematization, as well as elaboration, of a single image that I would like to suggest can be read as playing with the notion of controlling the story space. As Stockhammer argues: "all those maps support the spatial imagination of the represented area and ensure 'total control' over it. They enable the author to invent coherent results by means of their 'correct' localisation and they enable the reader to verify these results" (Stockhammer 2007: 63 [my translation]).[22] Here, one can see that the role of the map producer is of high importance. A map is not as objective as one might think since the appearance of the map is always shaped by an authorial process of creation and selection (see Schneider 2006: 8). The fact that Miéville as a writer might be in control of his fictional world's space, however, does not mean that his readers are able to exert a similar level of imaginative control. As will be shown, the focalisation of *Perdido Street Station* reveals that Miéville is playing with the reader, as well as the novel's characters, in terms of spatial control and verification. In the following analysis, I would like to argue that *Perdido Street Station* is not only the novelistic expression of a fictional world that happens to have a map, but is itself a meditation on mapping and imagining space.

Although the streets themselves are not named, the map of New Crobuzon is, at first glance, a useful extra-literary tool for readers to follow the novel's characters as they move from quarter to quarter, since *Perdido Street Station* involves a high degree of movement through its urban space – be it by public transport or on foot. At the beginning of the novel, Yagharek offers the reader an introduction to this space as he enters the city. With his wings sawed off his back, the birdman approaches it on a small boat steered by a man. After several passages describing Yagharek's personal impressions, the man relays some information concerning where we are exactly, in topographical terms. In combination with Yagharek's perception, the description of his arrival can be read in correspondence with the map, as names and urban sites are detailed:

> The river twists and turns to face the city. [...] The man murmurs to me, tells me where we are. I do not turn to him. This is Raven's Gate, this brutalized warren around us. The rotten buildings lean against each other, exhausted. [...] A train whistles as it crosses the river before us on raised tracks. [...] I am in Smog Bend, he tells me, and I make myself look away as he points my direction [sic] so he will not know I am lost [...]. A little to the south two great pillars rise from the river. The gates to the Old City [...]. Behind them, a low bridge (Drud Crossing, he says). (PSS: 1–3 [original italics])

---

22 Cf. also Bulson 2007: 20, who sheds light on the underestimated role of the space-producing reader in earlier times. His example is Charles Dickens and the numerous handbooks and maps of 'his' London that have been produced by his readers.

By using the map, the reader can ascertain that Yagharek enters the city on the River Tar in the northwest of New Crobuzon: the twist of the river as mentioned in the text clearly suggests this. The river flows through Raven's Gate, passes the Verso Line railway that runs across the water, and leads to Smog Bend with Drud Crossing to the left. Although both Yagharek and the reader are strangers to New Crobuzon, the reader has the advantage of the map with which he or she can check the whole arrangement from De Certeau's voyeur's perspective – that is to say, distanced and uninvolved.

At first glance, one might think that Miéville uses the map as a helpful tool that unambiguously establishes the realism of this fictional place. But the closer one looks, the more one gets the impression that Miéville's map – just as the map of an actually existing place (see Dünne 2013: 238) – functions only as a symbolised image: a model that does not show everything and is less helpful than one expects it to be. Although the reader has the advantage of being able to adopt a voyeur's perspective (if s/he chooses to consult the map), s/he is not really superior to Yagharek in terms of understanding this topography/terrain. The map seems to help to a certain extent, but it does not provide all the information required in order to comprehend New Crobuzon's intricate landscape. Not only are some street names missing, but there are also innumerable alleys and passageways referenced within the narrative that the reader cannot locate, not to speak of named individual buildings. Additionally, the map fails to represent New Crobuzon's dirt, pollution, crime, its twisted architecture – in short: its atmosphere.[23] The map therefore reminds the reader of its own imperfectly representational status: it serves as a neat but non-realistic representation for the reader. As Bulson puts it: "spatial representations are products of a particular time and place always partial and incomplete" (Bulson 2007: 39).[24]

Descriptions of movement are of similar accuracy when the character in question is familiar with the cityscape. The second character to move through the city is Lin on her way from Aspic Hole to her first visit at Motley's place, her future employer.

> She walked away from the noisy arguments and the profiteering towards the gardens of Sobek Croix. [...] The cab [Lin had entered] was progressing towards the river. [...] They had turned into Shadrach Street. The market was to their south now [...]. Shadrach Street dipped suddenly. The cab was poised on a high point, where the streets curved sharply down away from it. Lin and her driver had a clear view of the grey, snow-specked jags

---

[23] See below, however, for Miéville's use of place names in order to make up for this problem to a certain degree.
[24] See also Schneider's second point about narrowing down the map to reality above in chapter III.1.

of mountains rising splendidly to the west of the city. Before the cab trickled the River Tar. [...] The spires of Nabob Bridge appeared. [...] Over the river, in the Old City, the streets were narrower and darker. [...] Superstitiously, Lin directed the cab up towards Barquest Bridge. It was not the nearest place to cross the Canker the Tar's sister, but that would be in Brock Marsh, [...] where Isaac, like many others, had his laboratory [...]. [S]he sent the cab to Gidd Station, where the Dexter Line stretched out to the east on raised tracks that stretched higher and higher above the city as they moved further from the centre. (*PSS:* 14 – 20)

Again, one can at least by and large follow the character on the map. In contrast to Yagharek, Lin knows where she is supposed to go. Where the garuda had a guide telling him where he is, the situation is reversed in Lin's and the taxi driver's case – she is giving him directions. Furthermore, due to her knowledge of New Crobuzon, she is able to apply certain strategies and adjust her way to her needs (she chooses a longer route in order to avoid coming too close to her lover Isaac's lab).

Many more detailed descriptions can be found in the novel.[25] Miéville creates numerous occasions where the reader is invited to treat the map as more than just a paratextual decoration. The reader is very much reminded of de Certeau's account of the relation of tour and map, and the important distinction between walker and voyeur. Scholar Dorothea Löbbermann takes these two opposing figures in de Certeau's thinking and compares them with two opposing groups whose traversal of the city space reveals their transient status – tourists and vagrants (see Löbbermann 2005: 263). Tourists, according to Löbbermann, assume the position of voyeurs. To them, all places of interest in a city (be they museums, castles, or famous squares, bridges, or statues) are of equal importance, and they ignore all other (ordinary) places; the unfamiliar is being domesticated, and the world that is created is one that seems to defer completely to their wishes to see what they want to see. Tourists thus produce pleasure-oriented fictions of cities by revelling in the cities' superficial lust. City maps and travel guides enable them to take hold of the city. However, the tourist is only a producer of particular fictions of the city – s/he knows that s/he is only moving at the surface. Hence, the tourist is continually trying to catch a glimpse behind the scenes at the 'true' face of the city – which is the world inhabited by the vagrants (see Löbbermann 2005: 266). Yet, the tourist hardly ever strays from the established routes of main roads and city guides (see Löbbermann 2005: 268). Löbbermann's reformulation of de Certeau's tour-map dichotomy is useful for reading *Perdido Street Station* since Miéville arguably places his reader in the same po-

---

25 See, for example, Derkhan's train ride in chapter XII (*PSS:* 110 – 112) and her walk to the communicatrix in chapter XXVII (*PSS* 272– 273).

sition as the tourist. Stuck with a map that only shows the most prominent streets and with only a rough idea of New Crobuzon's quarters, the reader quickly comes to realise that a map as a paraxtextual device is just one of the textual components that constitute a novel, which sometimes works in opposition to the narrative itself:

> Texts are never able to tell as much as maps do implicitly. Even if every road on a map with all its turns and curves were described in great detail in an itinerary – one would only need to travel in the opposite direction or make a different turn at a junction as it is described in the itinerary, and one would have found a new narrative that is potentially there already. [...] Never, on the other hand, can texts tell as few as maps do explicitly. The geographic map of Ptolemaic kind is, according to a helpful distinction of Lotman, exemplary for a text without a sujet where nothing happens – until a directional line is drawn that denotes a rudimentary action, such as the course of a ship. (Stockhammer, 2007: 76 [my translation])

The map as such does not tell any story because it does not show any action, but it is potentially charged with an endless number of possible stories – provided that one is able to put it to use. Or, to frame this problem in hypothetical terms: if Löbbermann's tourist or Miéville's reader was given this map of New Crobuzon and dropped off in some run-down alley of the city, s/he would be completely lost, stranded with a map that would be absolutely useless. Power and control over map and city space are primarily attributed to the author or map producer.

One might add that 'telling names' on a map seem to contribute to its implicit narrativity. On their own, they do not tell a story either, but they have their share in the potential narrativity inherent to the map. New Crobuzon's characteristics – grim, dark, faecal, dirty, industrial, full of crime – are touched upon in the names of many of its quarters: Spatters, Tar Wedge, Smog Bend, Skulkford, Raven's Gate, Bonetown, Canker Wedge, Lichford, Spit Hearth, Badside, Nigh Sump, to name but a few.[26] Similarly, the two rivers, Tar and Canker, come together in the heart of the city and are named the Gross Tar. These names therefore appear to refute Stockhammer's argument that maps do not tell any story; they in fact constitute what J. B. Harley calls a desocialization of "the territory they represent. They foster the notion of a socially empty space" (Harley 2001: 81). Miéville seems to be aware of the map's tendency towards desocialization and arguably incorporates the sociality of New Crobuzon's space through his im-

---

[26] Note also the central station the novel is named after, which is exemplary for the whole of New Crobuzon: Perdido Street Station (roughly "veered from the right path" or "lost" in Portuguese).

III.2 Places to Get Lost: Literature and Maps — 55

plementation of telling names and, more importantly, by offering detailed descriptions of the quarters and their specific characteristics within the narrative itself, so that map and novel complement each other. In considering New Crobuzon's locations via the notion of telling names, one can also identify a connection to one of Schneider's crucial points: that is to say, the names convey extra information about the place or quarter to which they refer (see Schneider 2006: 9).

Thus, Miéville demonstrates that paratextual maps need not be as 'socially empty' as one might expect them to be. In this way, just from the richly suggestive names alone the reader learns about each of New Crobuzon's quarters, which differ from each other largely in terms of population, architecture, atmosphere, history, and passageways. Still, the question remains to what extent Miéville actually uses the map as a helpful tool for the reader so that one can verify the fictional area and thus help to visualize these spaces when one reads such names within a simplified, cartographic representation (see Pavlik 2010)? Similarly, does it help the reader to notice that the sketch of New Crobuzon – particularly in terms of its rivers' meandering waterways and islets – resembles actual-world London? My argument is that Miéville deliberately lures the reader into the world of New Crobuzon, setting his story within an alternative space whose cartographic similarities to London hint at a possible allegorical tale – which it is not. An assumed connection between the two cities is rather misleading. The fact that there is a map does not necessarily mean that it needs to refer to an actually existing area – on the contrary: as established in chapter III.1 by referring to Per Olov Enquist, drawing and examining maps of fictional areas in particular is a much greater pleasure, an act of sheer cartographic lust (see Stockhammer 2007: 66–67). A map of London, or knowledge about the real city, is just as useless to Miéville's reader as the novel's printed map of New Crobuzon (or of London, for that matter) would be for the characters of *Perdido Street Station*.[27] Thus, the map is less helpful than expected on two levels: on the one hand, the map does not enable the reader to track all movements within the depicted territory or to imagine the space within which the movements take place.

---

[27] Although Miéville stated that New Crobuzon is "analogous to a chaos-fucked London" (Gordon 2003b: 362), I would say that the similar city layouts make it even more confusing. One might expect a connection (analogous!), but again: the map is not the territory. Dealing with maps is primarily related to the lust of dealing with the symbolic (see Stockhammer 2007: 12) – and in the case of *Perdido Street Station*, the map(s) are symbolic for getting lost. See also Piatti (2009: 144), for the idea that sometimes fictional places are not more than simulacra of places (in this case: New Crobuzon might be a simulacrum of London), copies without originals, where concrete reference is merely simulated.

And, on the other hand, the map's strategy of misleading its reader can be located in the domain of referentiality since the expected link to actual-world London does not provide any support either.

I will briefly return to the earlier discussion of Löbbermann and the question of transient urban figures. She associates vagrants with de Certeau's conceptualisation of the walker. Vagrants, in Löbbermann's formulation, lack the ability (affluence, access, leisure time etc.) to view the city as a whole; rather, they see behind the scenes as they translate and appropriate the city space according to their specific needs – food and shelter, for example (see Löbbermann 2005: 266). If one searches for an equivalent in *Perdido Street Station*, one might consider Yagharek as a character whose outsider status within the city can be read as enacting precisely this vagrancy, as he learns how to survive in New Crobuzon as a stranger (see *PSS:* 50 – 52). Obtaining food, finding a warm place to sleep, experiencing other people's disgust and ignorance are pressing issues facing Yagharek – as with a vagrant:[28]

> Looking for a place to hide, looking for food and warmth at night and respite from the stares that greet me whenever I set foot on the streets. [...] We are brethren, the city-winds and I. We wander together. We have found sleeping beggars that clutch each other and congeal for warmth like lower creatures, forced back down evolutionary strata by their poverty. [...] I sleep in old arches under the thundering railtracks. I eat whatever organic thing I find that will not kill me. I hide like a parasite in the skin of this old city that snores and farts and rumbles and scratches and swells and grows warty and pugnacious with age. (PSS, p. 50 – 52 [original italics])

Similarly, after their first encounter with the militia, the whole group around Isaac (Derkhan, Lemuel, and again Yagharek) is forced to lead a similar life. See, for example, Yagharek's thoughts at the end of chapter LI: *"We move by night. We are fearful of the milita and of Motley's men. [...] We watch carefully for sudden movements and suspicious glances. We cannot trust our neighbours. We must live in a hinterland of half darkness, isolated and solipsistic. We steal what we need [...]"* (PSS: 594 [original italics]).

For the Characters: Intra-textual Maps

In addition to the extra-textual map intended for the reader, there are also many maps contained within the story itself which shed more light on the force field of

---

[28] Note, however, that the archetypal vagrant as found in fiction (male, single) is a rather mythological/romanticised construction, as more and more vagrants in 21st-century cities are women with children (see Löbbermann 2005: 267).

lust and power. Before travelling to Motley's place, Lin is given a map in order to find her way. After exiting the cab, her "map directed her to a nameless alley on the south side of the Ribs. She wound her way to a quiet street where she found the black-painted buildings she had been told to seek" (*PSS:* 29). This brief description of Lin's map points towards a general attitude to their city shared by New Crobuzon's citizens. Even if you were born and raised in the city, it seems, you cannot always find your way. New Crobuzon is large and confusing enough that each of its characters quickly becomes lost as soon as they move away from lines of public transport or significant landmarks – they are unable to assume and maintain the position of de Certeau's voyeur.

Although the city's main streets do have names, the reader of the novel is very much reminded of the importance of practices of orientation. The description of Tokyo in *Empire of Signs* by Roland Barthes extends this analogy. There, just like the alley Lin is travelling towards, streets are not even named. "There is of course a written address, but it has only a postal value, it refers to a plan […], knowledge of which is accessible to the postman, not the visitor […]" (Barthes 2000: 33). As in Miéville's novel, Japanese people "figure out the address by a (written or printed) schema of orientation, a kind of geographical summary which situates the domicile starting from a known landmark; a train station, for instance" (Barthes 2000: 33–34). In short: they draw a map. In New Crobuzon, as can be seen in Lin's case, this loss of orientation affects not only strangers and visitors, but also locals. If we stay with Lin a little longer, we realise that the map she has been given leads her to an underground boss's hideout. During his sittings for Lin's commissioned sculpture, Motley keeps on talking about mob crime, a sphere unknown to Lin so far. Thinking for herself, she very much detests his attitude: "Every conversation he had with her wherein he disclosed some hidden details of New Crobuzon's underworld lore, she was embroiled in something she was eager to avoid. *I'm nothing but a visitor*, she wanted to sign frantically. *Don't give me a streetmap!*" (*PSS:* 97 [original italics]). Ironically enough, the map she was given in order to find Motley in the first place was her streetmap towards this underworld, and, as the novel progresses, it will become clear that there has been no way out ever since her first arrival at Motley's. Getting involved with the underworld means that one cannot simply walk away from it again.

In addition to Lin, many other characters make use of maps in *Perdido Street Station,* or produce maps themselves. Derkhan, a friend of Isaac and member of a left-wing political group, checks "the directions she had been given […] in the note" on her way to the communicatrix (*PSS:* 273) and confers with the Construct Council "over a scribbled map" (*PSS:* 523); Lemuel Pigeon, Isaac's underground middle-man, "scribble[s] designs [of the Glasshouse] in the dust" (*PSS:* 424); adventurers and rogues are said to be repeatedly hired for "useful services: research, cartography and the like" (*PSS:* 429); the workers of the Construct Council are "all equipped with maps, torches, guns and strict instructions" as they enter the city's sewers (*PSS:* 537); Isaac draws a rough sketch of the city on a piece of paper: "a jagged sideways Y for the two rivers, little crosses for Griss Twist, The Crow, and scribbles delineating Brock Marsh and Spit Hearth in between" (*PSS:* 511); even creatures of the night and mutants "*crawl from sewers into cold flat starlight and whisper shyly to each other, drawing maps and messages in the faecal mud*" (PSS: 51 [original italics]).

Thus, *Perdido Street Station* is packed with all kinds of characters concerned with maps. It is striking that none of these maps are official or authorised representations of New Crobuzon's city space. Instead, they are quickly scribbled down in accordance with the particular subjective requirements of the user and, taken together, question the map's function as a tool of power. Again, *Empire of Signs* can help to interpret the significance of these many maps in the novel. Barthes describes the remarkable skills of Tokyo's inhabitants and how they

> excel in these impromptu drawings, where we see being sketched, right on the scrap of paper, a street, an apartment house [...], making the exchange of addresses into a delicate communication in which a life of the body, an art of the graphic gesture recurs: it is always enjoyable to watch someone write, all the more so to watch someone draw [...]; the fabrication of the address greatly prevailed over the address itself, and, fascinated, I could have hoped it would take hours to give me that address. (Barthes 2000: 34–35)

In *Perdido Street Station*, however, the "impromptu drawings" are far from being aesthetically pleasing. They are quickly scribbled on scraps of paper, or drawn into dust or mud and are thus narrowed down to the visceral experience of the city – instead of being clean and well-structured they are spontaneous, dirty engravings carved into the city's skin and body. They are not meant to last for eternity or, even, to store the information they contain for a short period. Rather, these maps reveal to the reader that in New Crobuzon's labyrinth of roads, the primary concern is not to record the topography permanently, which raises the question: is the city too confusing and liable to change for anyone to gain power over it by means of measurement? This is reaffirmed by the fact that within *Perdido Street Station*, institutional attempts at mapping and thus controlling the city[29] all fail. Take, for instance, the city meteoromancers

---

[29] Two features which usually go together since maps are tools of power. See Harley 1989: 12–14, and Harley 2001: 51–81.

whose task is to map the weather forecast: "The city meteoromancers in the Tar Wedge cloudtower copied figures from spinning dials and tore graphs from frantically scribbling atmospheric gauges. They pursed their lips and shook their heads" (*PSS:* 177). The dials spin wildly, the gauges are frantic, out of control. And although the meteoromancers are able to copy the information they will never put it to use because the cloud tower quit working long ago: "Half-hearted attempts were made to start the engines in the cellars, but they had not moved in one hundred and fifty years, and no one alive was capable of fixing them. New Crobuzon was stuck with the weather dictated by gods or nature or chance" (*PSS:* 177). The government's attempt to render the slake-moths' nocturnal forays in cartographic form is also futile: "We're plotting a map of the nightmare hotspots, see if we can't see some pattern, track the moths in some way" (*PSS:* 356). The government is unable to map the hunting moths. Whereas the enormous cityspace may be one factor, the very nature of the moths is even more important. "They live in several planes" of existence (*PSS:* 329) – apparently, that is why they are so hard to track down. Another depiction in which the moths roam the city sky is striking in its reference to the history of cartography: "From all the way across the city, from the four compass points, they converged in a frenzy of flapping, four starving exultant powerful bodies, descending to feed" (*PSS:* 557). The four compass points locate the moths at the city margins and therefore at the margins of New Crobuzon's map – or even outside the map, thus reminding the reader of the marginalisation of stories and pictures in maps (see Schneider 2006: 32–33). As mentioned in chapter III.1, the stories of the fantastic creatures of historical maps move from the map to its margins and finally beyond the map. Contrastingly, the slake-moths in *Perdido Street Station* move into the map. Coming from outside with an unknown origin,[30] they function in the same way as the mythical creatures in Hartmann Schedel's map of the world from 1493, but their movement is reversed. They re-import both a fantastic element that remains partly unexplainable and a story element which heavily influences the overall narrative.

Another creature stands out in the novel in terms of its use of maps: the Weaver, a supernatural and powerful spider-like entity beyond human ken. At first, it seems not to be concerned with maps at all. Then, in a later passage, it comes close to the act of map production: "The Weaver was tracing its index finger through the water on the roof, leaving a trail of scorched dry stone, drawing patterns and pictures of flowers, whispering to itself" (*PSS:*

---

[30] Montague Vermishank from New Crobuzon University mentions the so-called Fractured Land as a possible origin, but this is not elaborated on further (see *PSS:* 325).

559). It produces a trace, a trail, a drawing that could pass as a map – but this 'map' consists only of patterns and pictures and thus has no value in terms of aiding orientation within the city (to non-Weavers, at least). The trail seems to be an artefact of aesthetic lust. If one looks at the way the Weaver treats space and planes of existence on a larger scale, namely as an aesthetic web, this makes a lot of sense. It does not need to draw a map of the city onto the city's surface or body because it possesses the greatest map of all: the world weave, a map of all reality and possibility in the shape of a vast web. An impression of this map is provided as Isaac, Yagharek, and their companions are saved by the Weaver from the militia and being moved through the world weave:

> [T]he dancing mad god moved along powerful threads of force. [...] I glimpsed at the reality through which the dancing mad god was treading. [...] Spread across the emptiness, streaming away from us with cavernous perspective in all directions and dimensions, encompassing lifetimes and hugeness with each intricate knot of metaphysical substance, was a web. Its substance was known to me. [...] The plait disappeared into the enormity of possible spaces. Every intention, interaction, motivation, every colour, every body, every action and reaction, every piece of physical reality and the thoughts that it engendered, every connection made, every nuanced moment of history and potentiality, every toothache and flagstone, every emotion and birth and banknote, every possible thing ever is woven into that limitless, sprawling web. It is without beginning or end. It is complex to a degree that it humbles the mind. It is a work of such beauty that my soul wept. (PSS: 347f–348 [original italics]

The web is literally all-encompassing: living organisms, dead matter, emotions, thoughts, history, potential futures. Despite its beauty and eternity, there are torn and broken spots. Especially the gossamer of New Crobuzon, due to the slake-moths, is ruined:

> And there rendering the woven strands in the centre was an ugly tear. It spread out and split the fabric of the city-web, taking the multitude of colours and bleeding them dry. They were left a drab and lifeless white. A pointless emptiness, a pallid shade a thousand times more soulless even than the eye of some sightless caveborn catfish. As I watched, my pained eyes wide with insight, I saw that the rip was widening. (PSS: 349 [original italics])

Weavers have a certain conception of what the web should look like,[31] and by intervening in a world such as Bas-Lag, they are able to shape it according to their own particular aesthetic conception. In the end, the Weaver does not

---

[31] See the incident right before the travel through the world web: the Weaver cuts off the left ears of Isaac, Derkhan, Lemuel, and twenty militia (*PSS:* 346). Rudgutter's only explanation is that "[i]t made the web prettier! Obviously!" (*PSS:* 354).

help Isaac and his group because of some moral obligation or bargain but because the slake-moths' defeat fixes the torn web: "LOOK AT THE INTRICATE SKEINS AND THREADLINES WE CORRECT WHERE THE DEADLINGS REAVED WE CAN RESHUFFLE AND SPIN AND FIX IT UP NICE ..." (*PSS:* 573). At this point, one realises the importance of the slake-moths as the novel's antagonists: they are not simply there because giant mind-eating bugs make great monsters for any Science Fiction or horror setting, but because they figure as enemies of existence as such by tearing apart the world weave. Just as regular moths devour cloth, the slake-moths threaten the fabric of the universe which, in *Perdido Street Station*, takes the shape of an endless web.

Since existence never stands still, the web grows and sprawls continuously and hence needs continuous work. In this labour of the Weaver, one can discern a lust for the map as an aesthetic object, and also the aesthetic exaggeration of map usage. The world weave is not only the most complete map of everything that was, is, and could be but also, in less grandiose terms, the most accurate map available to any of the species in Bas-Lag since it is as up to date as possible, never ceasing to be a work in progress,[32] an eternal impromptu drawing that comes intriguingly close to the map as a rhizome in the sense of Deleuze/Guattari: it is "open and connectable in all of its dimensions; it is detachable, reversible, susceptible to constant modification. It can be torn, reversed, adapted to any kind of mounting" (Deleuze and Guattari 2009: 13). But even a map as powerful as the Weaver's web is not without its flaws: the Weaver continuously moves both around the web as well as various locations within New Crobuzon in order to keep the web in order, to maintain it, and keep it up to date. As a result, the Weaver finds itself subjectively located within the map, losing the objective sovereignty of an exterior observer. In de Certeau's terms the Weaver, by stepping into the city and back to the world weave, continuously oscillates between the position of the voyeur and the walker, between map producer and map connoisseur, between power and lust. The Weaver is ever busy to adjust the world and consequently its map according to its own preferences. The aesthetic lust is so strong that the map can never be finished.

Lastly, I turn to mapping strategies which go beyond the production of maps as tangible objects. Yagharek, for example, is mapping the cityscape – but he is doing so without the use of actual, material maps, making use of his bird eyes instead. In the Glasshouse, for example, where he, Isaac, Derkhan, Lemuel, and three hired adventurers try to discover the moths' nest, it is him who finally spots

---

32 In so doing, a serious problem of ordinary maps is solved: the problem that they are out of date very quickly – sometimes even before their publication.

it. However, he is not aimlessly looking around, but he makes use of sophisticated perceptive practices: "Yagharek had not pinpointed [the moth's] nest, and that was critical. His eyes batted inconstantly between the insidious creature itself and the patch of domed darkness from where he had first seen it rise. And as he watched intently [...], he won his prize" (*PSS:* 460). In a way, he seems to be able to re-track the moth's way "through a foggy filter of the hunting trance" (*PSS:* 460) that is characteristic for his (garuda) species. In general, he seems to get along quite well in the city after a short time of settling in; in the following excerpt, he surveys New Crobuzon and its landmarks with precision, control, and understanding:

> At the top of the Glasshouse, the city seemed to be a gift to him [...]. Everywhere he looked, fingers and hands and fists and spines of architecture *thrust rudely into the sky.* The Ribs like ossified tentacles *reaching always up*; the Spike slammed into the city's heart like a *skewer*; the complex mechanistic vortex of Parliament, glowing darkly; Yagharek mapped them with a cold, strategic eye. (*PSS:* 451 [my italics])

While other characters need a physical map, Yagharek requires only his "strategic eye" in order to map the cityscape. It becomes clear that his way of mapping – and, thus, the map he produces – is very different from those of other characters. Looking down on the city, his perception is marked by a strong dynamic of verticality that manifests itself in the choice of words ("thrust rudely into the sky"; "reaching always up"; "like a skewer"). The choice of words also shows that Yagharek is aware of the brute forces lurking behind this architecture of verticality – almost as if he had read Lefebvre: "Verticality and great height have ever been the spatial expression of potentially violent power" (Lefebvre 1991: 98). Note the discrepancy between this panoramic view[33] and Yagharek's earlier experience upon arriving in the city, when the wingless bird-man did not possess the ability to enact this way of seeing or, rather, surveying: "*I wonder how this looks from above, no chance for the city to hide then, if you came at it on the wind you would see it from miles away [...]. I could ride the updrafts [...], sail high over the proud towers [...], ride the chaos, alight where I choose*" (*PSS:* 2 [original italics]). Instead, at the start of the novel, Yagharek is lost: he is displaced by

---

[33] Yagharek's mapping from above should not be confused with the reader's perspective in the sense of de Certeau's voyeur when s/he looks at the map. One could say that Yagharek comes closer to it than other characters, but besides the fact that he is looking at the city from the Glasshouse, he does not exactly look at it from above. In addition, his mapping is strongly structured by height and vertical extension – which the reader's map is lacking. Furthermore, he still needs the urban experience of the walker in order to be completely absorbed in the city (see chapter IV.2.1).

his nocturnal entry into New Crobuzon, as well as the unusual mode of transportation, by boat (for him as a flying creature).

While Yagharek's way of mapping relies on visual impressions, the slake-moths seem also to operate by means of sound and smell: "New Crobuzon steamed with the rich taste-scent of prey. [...] Vibrations in a hundred registers and keys beckoned the thing, as forces and emotions and dreams split and were amplified in the brick chambers of the station and blasted outwards into the sky. A massive, invisible flavour trail" (*PSS:* 222). As with Miéville's extra-textual map of the city, this 'smell map' also proves to be misleading.[34] As Schneider (see 2006: 19) puts it: while moving through space is a universal feature that constitutes human beings (and other thinking life forms, as one might add now), and while mobility presupposes means of orientation, the ways how different cultures (or life forms) perceive space and relate to it can be very different and are, especially in Yagharek's case, also reflected in the use of language. The uselessness of printed maps in *Perdido Street Station* could also be read as exploiting Marshall McLuhan's paradigm shift towards visuality (sse McLuhan 1962: 125) – not so much in its dwarfing of aural/oral culture, but in terms of strengthening different kinds of visuality as ways of accessing the world. Lastly, in the interplay of diverse maps, mapping strategies, ways of perception, and movement through the city, it already transpires that the city space is constructed in the productive force field of materiality and discursivity, i.e. between what is out there in the urban space and how its inhabitants interact with it. The body in *Perdido Street Station* becomes a projection screen for a dialogic and intersubjective understanding of construction and continuous reconstruction of identity and alterity, a location of conflict between self and other, individual and societal discourses and their inherent ascriptions of difference.[35]

Recognition and Misrecognition

As demonstrated, maps in *Perdido Street Station* are very diverse. In addition to the extra-textual map that prefaces Miéville's narrative, designed for a systematization of the story world which easily tricks its readers, the novel is also packed with various maps, as well as different modes of map production within the story

---

34 The moths blindly follow their smell map that Isaac exploits by means of his crisis conductor – and they get killed. Before, their smell map made them superior, they dominated New Crobuzon while any other organism was only prey. With the crisis conductor as a decoy, they only voraciously stare at the map without paying attention to their actual environment of which the map shows a fake and misleading representation.
35 See chapter IV.2.1.

itself, most of which are obscure, non-scientific and non-institutional. As shown above, even the government is unable to establish order and therefore to execute administrative business in the broadest sense, which is mostly reflected in its lack of control over the city space and the movement through it. The preceding analysis of the way in which maps inform and misinform highlighted that New Crobuzon is nothing like a functional city ("funktionelle Stadt") as it is described by Martina Löw (2008b: 97–102), i.e. a well-planned and well-ordered city featuring a strict separation between housing, work, and recreation as its three main functions. The moths cannot be mapped, the weather cannot be regulated, the Weaver is a supernatural force beyond any control, and scientists and adventurers go rogue – underneath the surface of an iron fist government, Miéville leaves his readers in no doubt that there is a whole web of competing structures and movements where mobsters, underground newspapers, rogue scientists, numerous other groups and *"ruder forms of life struggle and fight and die and are eaten"* (*PSS:* 265 [original italics] in a city caught between industrial decay and organic sprawl.

The central point is that two very different levels of observation are at stake when it comes to maps in *Perdido Street Station*, both of which are deficient. On the one hand, there is the reader, stranded with the abstract map of New Crobuzon printed in the book which, as I have suggested, does not help the reader as much as one would expect in terms of orientation, imagination, and referentiality. On the other hand, there is the level of the characters within the story world, whose numerous impromptu maps and different mapping strategies based upon different ways of perception, thwart our general expectation of maps functioning as cultural artefacts of preservation and precision. Together, these two levels play a game of recognition and misrecognition[36] with both the reader and the novel's characters in terms of spatial control and verification. Miéville thus forces his readers to mentally map the city at the same time as they produce the city space. Whilst their process of reading imaginatively moves through the complex world and maps the locations Miéville names, readers are also obliged time and

---

[36] A game that Miéville also pursues in other novels. In *The Scar* (2002), he confronts his reader with the nothingness of the ocean where maps are not useful at all, and the constantly changing layout of Armada, a floating city consisting of numerous ships bound together. In *The City & The City*, maps do exist, but in the murder case of Mahalia, it is the traditional flaw of maps that brings down David Bowden, who ordered her assassination: Yorjavic, the hitman who was supposed to make Mahalia's body disappear, was given an outdated map by Bowden. Thus, instead of being dropped into the estuary, the body ended up in a more recently built skate park, ready to be found by a group of teenagers (see *TC&TC:* 359–360). Urban renewal, Besźel's changing topography, is what thwarts Bowden's plan.

again to interrupt their process of reading, flicking back and forth between the pages of the story and the para-textual map that precedes the narrative:

> The chain of spatializing operations seems to be marked by references to what it produces (a representation of places) or to what it implies (a local order). We thus have the structure of the travel story: stories of journeys and actions are marked out by the 'citation' of the places that result from them or authorize them. (de Certeau 1984: 120 – 121)

Miéville, though, seems to be devious enough to allow his readers to make reality checks by offering citations of places without the possibility to, in Stockhammer's words, verify them. In fact, the maps of *Perdido Street Station* are deliberately unsuitable in every respect. The printed paratextual map is a non-realistic representation that neither invokes the characteristics of the city's quarters in the process of naming them; nor is it of much help when one tries to track a character's movements through the city, and it would not be very helpful for characters if they had this very map at their diposal; the apparent analogy to real-world London is misleading as well. The intra-textual maps are equally misleading and not helpful: most of them do not exercise power over the territory they refer to – and if they do, they are no artefacts of lust. In short, the maps perfectly fit the setting of New Crobuzon as a dark and confusing city where hardly anything is permanent except change and disorientation. Reading *Perdido Street Station* literally means getting 'perdido' – lost.[37]

III.2.2 X Marks the Spot – Not: *Divided Kingdom*

The second map to be scrutinised is the one of the hardcover edition of *Divided Kingdom* (some paperback editions come without the map, others with a black and white version). In contrast to the city maps of New Crobuzon and Bohane, this map shows the entire nation. Every quarter is shown in its corresponding colour (see below).

The Red Quarter covers the southeast and the west of England (the area in the triangle of actual-world London, Bristol, and Liverpool); the Blue Quarter is made up of Wales and southwest England; the Yellow Quarter covers the whole of Northern Ireland, the Isle of Man, and the English west coast from actual-world Glasgow to Liverpool and the area in the triangle of Liverpool, Leeds,

---

[37] A pun that is not always recognised. It is not without irony that Bastei Lübbe, who published the two-volume German edition, not only changed the title to *Die Falter* ("the moths") and *Der Weber* ("the weaver"), but also omitted the map.

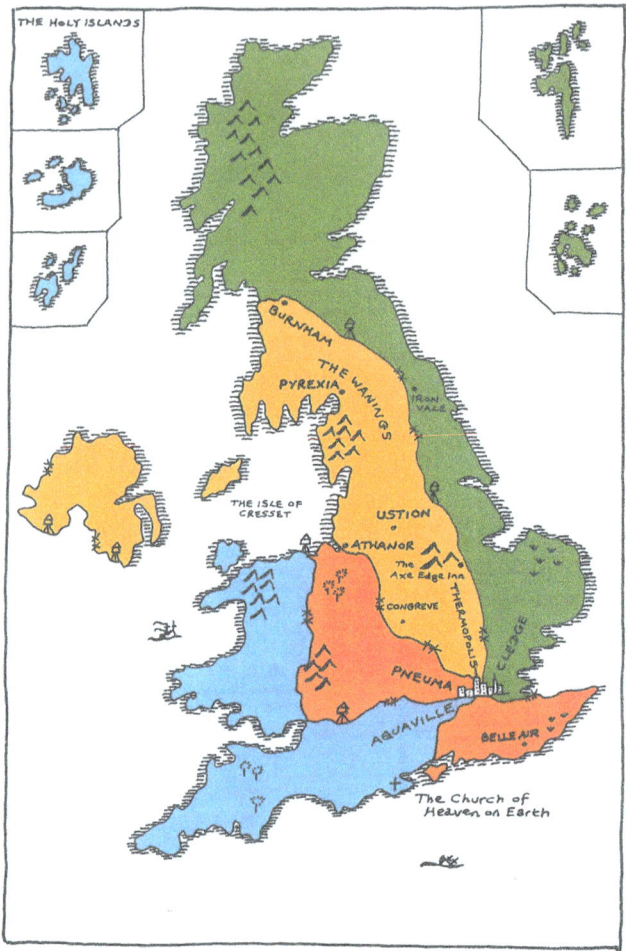

Fig. iv: Map of the Divided Kingdom (Bloomsbury Publishing); reproduced by permission of the author c/o Rogers, Coleridge & White Ltd.

and London; lastly, the entire east coast and the whole of Scotland belong to the Green Quarter. Ireland, not being part of either the United or the Divided Kingdom, does not show on the map, and neither does the French and Belgian coastline on the other side of the Channel, a fact which will be become important later on. Stylised trees, plants and mountains indicate forests, swamps, and mountain ranges without providing any details (e. g. how high the mountain ranges are). A few areas and major cities are indicated by name and can be attributed to their actual-world counterparts by comparing their locations on the maps (e.g. Iron Vale: Newcastle; Athanor: Liverpool; Burnham: Glasgow), but in general, topographical markers reminding the reader of the actual-world United Kingdom are scarce. Three more elements obviously stem from the fictional Divided Kingdom. Firstly, official border posts for crossing from one quarter into the other are marked by a double X along the borders. Secondly, the existence of watchtowers along the borders is also indicated. Lastly, the Church of Heaven on Earth has been placed on the tongue of land south of actual-world Bournemouth, marked by another X. The map does not show any roads and only a handful of cities, thus exemplifying the selectiveness of every cartographic representation. "[E]very map shows one thing, but therefore not another, and represents the world in one way, and as a consequence not in another" (Brotton 2012: 15) – the following pages will show that this is particularly true for the map of the Divided Kingdom as the map not only represents the story world's territory, but also embodies the Divided Kingdom's dystopian thrust.

What is the map's status as a hinge between fictional world and actual world? A map of the Divided Kingdom is nowhere mentioned in the novel. Additionally, the map only shows some of the locations (in the sense of Piatti's model, see chapter III.1) actually visited by Parry while leaving out others which are undoubtedly 'there,' but do not play a major role in the story. What is more, the representation of the Church of Heaven on Earth's location as an inoffical (and even illegal) settlement suggests that this is not an official map existent in any way in the very story world it refers to and intended for rubber-stamped use there, but a help for the reader – a paratextual device in Genette's sense. In contrast to the deliberately misleading map of New Crobuzon, this map can actually be helpful at times.[38] Since the novel itself is rather short on detailed descriptions of places (and if they are described, the focus is rather on their dominating mood rather than on the actual topography; see chapter IV.2.5), the map of the Divided Kingdom intends to highlight both the remnants and traces of the previously United Kingdom and the significant changes ("In which quarter would my home town be in the Divided Kingdom?").

A Fictional Silhouette on an Actual Canvas
Mapping the fictional world by using an actual-world map or area as a blueprint usually ensures a strong link between fictional and actual world which, however,

---

[38] This first impression of helpfulness, as will be shown later on, is nevertheless severely shattered at second glance due to the extent of the authorial process of selection and omission.

is comparatively weak and marginalised in *City of Bohane* or, in the case of *Perdido Street Station*, a trap. In the case of *Divided Kingdom*, attention is drawn to the fact that the map refers to a fictional world (the Divided Kingdom) which is nevertheless heavily based on an extract of the actual world (the United Kingdom). To be more precise, the fictional world takes the actual one as a starting point; then, at some point in the story world's history, the course of history diverges from the actual world's, the result being the dystopian and fictional Divided Kingdom.

Examples such as *Divided Kingdom* are the reason for Piatti's differentiation between zones of action (*Handlungszonen*) and locations (*Schauplätze*):[39] in many cases, only the locations undergo change, while the space of action or particular zones of action might be maintained as a geographical, reality-based frame of reference. With regard to the dimension of referentiality, one could say that Thomson took the map of a real country and maintained its topology (i.e. the relative position of its elements) and 'natural' geography (the Isle of Man has not switched places with the Isle of Anglesey) while modifying its surface (i.e. its topography) by placing a new socio-political overlay of borders, watchtowers, and town/area names over it. Thus, the overlay imposes a fictional world on the actual one, its origin being the dystopian turn caused by the Rearrangement, and the resulting diverging history. In Piatti's terminology, the geographical and topological layout of the actual world as a space of action is an immigrant element against which the surrogate (the renamed cities being the most obvious examples) and native locations (the Church of Heaven on Earth, which does not have a real-world counterpart) are positioned. In fact, such a reliable actual-world background is necessary in order to show and recognise the subordinate modifications (see Piatti 2009: 140–141). Piatti's primary example is *Fatherland* by Robert Harris, but her conclusion can as well serve for describing Thomson's novel, paraphrased with slight modifications in the following: the charm of this contrafactual or prospective location, which is inaccessible or non-existent in the actual world, lies in the fact that it is silhouetted against what actually exists (see Piatti 2009: 142). Thus, the reader can pick up the fictional world's map and become aware of both the similarities and the differences

---

39 As a reminder, *Schauplätze* are, according to Piatti, the smallest spatial units of a story, e.g. the house of the Parry family. *Handlungszonen* are defined as abstract macrostructures containing these locations. A story's space of action or *Handlungsraum* is the outermost layer of narrated space which contains all zones of action as well as the so-called geographical horizon (*geographischer Horizont*) which in turn contains all places and areas which are only mentioned in the story without any character actually being there. See Piatti (2009: 128 ff.), and chapter III.1 of this study.

to the actual world (another facet of Stockhammer's notion of readers' lust for maps) – and by doing so, the notion of the dystopian alternative world in reference to the actual world is evoked: if the United Kingdom in the actual world actually took a wrong turn, what could it be like?

Dystopian Omission

Maps, however, do not only show – they also conceal and omit, and they do so not only because of technical limitations but because of authorial production processes. *Divided Kingdom* uses a strategy of omission for enhancing its dystopian thrust both in the map and in the novel text. Like many paratextual maps, the map of the Divided Kingdom does not show any directional lines of movement, and it does not show any roads or possible itineraries for travelling either, leaving a handful of cities as insulated and (im-)possible destinations. Thus, as described in the former chapter, it implies Lotman's notion of a text without a sujet (see Stockhammer 2007: 76; also see chapter III.1 of this study). Although one could still draw a directional line and thus infuse the map with a route (and therefore with a sujet as an event of travel), the map itself attempts to deny the possibility of travelling and a sujet because the routes presented in the novel text cannot be mapped properly. To summon de Certeau's dichotomy of *tour* and *map* once more, one could say that the map, by omitting geographical landmarks, roads, and other signs of passage, refuses the possibility of a tour. At the same time, it emphasises de Certeau's notion of the map as the totalising sphere of a detached, omniscient observer gazing down at the map like a god – or, in the dystopian context, like a totalitarian government eager to keep things as they are. If there is no possible means of passage, there is no movement, no event, and no sujet; without a sujet, there is no change; without change, the Divided Kingdom and its citizens remain in check. Erecting fences and walls along motorways, then, is a fairly devious move: while roads used to connect cities and people prior the Rearrangement, they now determine the outline of strictly separating borders which make travelling almost impossible. The new monochromatic territories are slapped onto the map and equalise the topography by annihilating opportunities for potential sujets. The watchtowers and the double Xs along the borders only enhance this totalising impression by showing where one *could* cross the border if one were allowed to and if there was a passage to a potential destination. Just as the cities unreachably dangle in front of the inhibited traveller's nose because of the lack of proper means to get there, the Xs undergo a semiotic change: where an X or a cross on a map usually refers to a destination of some sort ('X marks the spot' or 'this is where you need to go'), their purpose in the map of the Divided Kingdom is reversed, and the meaning of the sign is changed. The Xs cross out transit entirely.

Another look at the map reveals that the Divided Kingdom is shown in full while neighbouring countries have been left out. Continental Europe's coastline (France and Belgium) south of the English Channel cannot be found; even more strikingly, Ireland is not represented either, giving the impression that Northern Ireland is an island in its own right. The effect of these omissions is that the Divided Kingdom appears to be completely isolated and detached from all external influence – as if it were an island in the middle of nowhere, even more isolated than, for example, Thomas More's Utopia as illustrated in the 1516 edition (see Piatti 2009: 35). Thus, the map emphasies both the *non-place* meaning in the ambiguous term of utopia as well as the classic (anti-)utopian program of the state which is anxious to keep things as they are. No interaction with the rest of the world ensures the survival of the Divided Kingdom's status quo, and the map as an artefact of power (in this case: the power of omission) plays an important role in this strategy. Not only does the map display the country's self-conception as insular – it also suggests that there is no other conception available. If citizens are not told what is going on beyond the borders, or if they are left in the dark whether there is actually anything beyond the borders, they will accept their fate in the Divided Kingdom because there is no other place to go to anyway. The strategy of omission on the map well corresponds with the strategy of omission in the novel text: no places or countries outside the Divided Kingdom are ever mentioned, and neither are imported goods or reactions of other countries to the Rearrangement. The world beyond the borders is neither mentioned nor imagined; thus, *Divided Kingdom* does not have a geographical horizon (see Piatti 2009: 128) beyond its borders, but only an interior one pointing back to the past, namely to the happy places prior the Rearrangement. Two small details on the map further support the country's isolation: besides the landmass, the map also depicts two ships, or better: both ships represent the same ship which enables Parry to flee from Athanor (depicted in the west) and then sinks south of the Divided Kingdom, from where Parry is washed ashore and rescued by the Church of Heaven on Earth. The ships do not look like contemporary freighters, but rather like sailing ships as they can be found on many older world maps from the days when the earth was not entirely explored and mapped yet. There, these ships usually used to be placed somewhere in the open sea and functioned as placeholders for a vast unknown nothingness. *Divided Kingdom* seems well aware of this tradition: from its isolated point of view, the dystopian Divided Kingdom is the cradle of civilisation without anything worth mapping beyond its borders.

However, close examination of the map reveals that the Divided Kingdom is not as isolated as it seems; it is not the last place on earth either, and the map itself gives away the secret by the way it presents the Northern Ireland coastline. All coastlines on the map are indicated by black shading – except for the south and east of Northern Ireland. Why is there no shading? The answer is simple: because this is where Northern Ireland, in the actual world, borders on Ireland. By omitting the shading, the map suggests that something has been left out, i.e. that there is an Ireland in *Divided Kingdom* as well. Furthermore, two watchtowers and double Xs in Northern Ireland are the only ones placed at the (assumed) coastline, while all other watchtowers and double Xs are placed along internal frontiers. This placement leads to the conclusion that there actually is something on the other side that needs to be watched and kept out – namely, the only non-coastal border of the Divided Kingdom. Thus, the map demonstrates its own deficiency as well as the oscillation between selection and omission of mapmaking in general by bluntly showing that it has something to hide (see Parker 2009: 168 – 171).[40]

III.2.3 The Metafictional Square: *City of Bohane*

A look at the map of *City of Bohane* completes the perspectives on literature and maps in this study.[41] Like the map of New Crobuzon, it is a black and white city map. The map features a compass rose, but no scale. Although the white background of the urban area contrasted with the grey-shaded Big Nothin' wilderness suggests a certain insularity, Bohane is less isolated from the rest of the world than Thomson's Divided Kingdom. The directional arrows in the river, which point to Big Nothin' and the Black Atlantic, imply the travel opportunities via stream navigation and thus a possible sujet in Lotman's sense and the railroad tracks leading from Yella Hall Station into the dark tunnel underneath the Northside Rises suggest another. Although all of them do not explicitly refer to a specific location (in the sense of Piatti's *Schauplatz*), they denote possible destinations and faraway places behind these first vague directions towards the sea, the vast swamp, and the dark tunnel. In short, they expand the geographical horizon of the story world beyond Bohane as the novel's zone of action, and this strategy

---

40 Parker describes how military bases used to be blanked out from the Ordnance Survey maps from 1927 until the end of the Cold War, the result being vast and (and thus highly suspicious) blank spaces of nothingness on those maps.
41 Unfortunately, copyright permission for the map could not be secured, but the map can be found online.

can also be found in the novel text. England as a faraway land (a topographical marker according to Piatti's model) is mentioned as well as a Nation Beyond (which might refer to England as well, or to Ireland). While these faraway lands as topographical markers are not too overt in the text and they are not evoked as important places either, projected places in the form of nostalgic remembrance of Bohane's past play a crucial role. Characters in Bohane constantly remember and try to relive their past, revel in glorious stories and old songs, all of which are bound to Bohane – and thus, similarly to *Divided Kingdom*, to a temporal distance, not a spatial one.[42]

Dublin, Limerick – Bohane...
Bohane itself is clearly an Irish city according to several references in the text,[43] but the scarce references make it hard to pin down its actual location. The first actual-world Irish city which comes to mind is Dublin, simply because it is the country's capital, because it is also located at the coast – and, last but not least, because of its connotative weight concerning the Irish literary tradition, mostly shaped by the works of James Joyce. His short story cycle *Dubliners* refers to the city in the title already, and a connection between *Ulysses* and *City of Bohane* has been put forth by Barry's publisher: on the back of the book, *City of Bohane* is summed up as "Joyce meets Anthony Burgess." Does the comparison work for the cities' maps, i.e. is Bohane's map a fictionalised version of Dublin's? The map of Bohane hardly matches any historical or contemporary map of Dublin. One desperate way of approximating the two might be to turn the former upside down in order to see some similarity in the course of the cities' rivers and reveal some more parallels to actual-world Dublin by doing so. Upside down, Yella Hall Station would roughly coincide with Dublin's Tara St. Station; Bohane's dunes could pass as some of Dublin's numerous parks, and the Kevin Barry Square (!) might be taken as the fictional counterpart of Fitzwilliam Square and/or Merion Square. However, the reference to the Black Atlantic places Bohane somewhere on the Irish west coast instead of the east coast (Dublin). Thus, any congruencies between Bohane and Dublin seem to be even more far-fetched than potential connections between New Crobuzon and London.

The mentioning of the Black Atlantic brings Barry's native city Limerick into play, which actually *is* located on the west coast – but now, a comparison be-

---

42 See chapter IV.2.3 of this study.
43 De Valera Street, for example, alludes to the Irish politician Éamon de Valera. Additionally, Fenians as a crucial part of Irish history are mentioned (see chapter IV.2.3 for more details).

tween the Bohane map and a map of Limerick shows no similarities at all (the river and the main station being the two most prominent features which stand out as not matching). One could probably go on and try to match more buildings, parks, or important roads, but I agree with Piatti that although these attempts are part of the fascination of every mapping game, one should not overdo such attempts of localisation.[44] Bohane can be placed somewhere in the west of Ireland, at (or close to) the sea – and this is all one needs in order to understand it. Ultimately, Bohane's status as a fictional city seems similar to that of Gottfried Keller's Seldwyla or Friedrich Glauser's Randlingen, which equally defy precise localisation: it is not about where Bohane exists exactly or which town it represents exactly. It simply is a typical Irish city without any striking reference, giving the novel a location because the story has to take place *somewhere* (see Piatti 2009: 124–125; 152–153). Thus, according to Piatti's system, it is suffice to say that Bohane as a city can be classified somewhere between a strong surrogate (thus emphasising the fictionalised elements) and a pure native object. The surrounding space of action with England and Big Nothin' as Bohane's geographical horizon is fairly elusive, which makes it even harder to determine its status between the immigrant and the surrogate category.

Mapping Residential Milieus
After this brief digression, the remaining topographical markers on the map deserve some attention. Bohane's quarters can be identified easily – each of them is marked by a flagpole spelling out the quarter's name. Additionally, the quarters are clearly separated, be it by De Valera Street and the El Train railway line (between New Town and the Back Trace), by an area of dunes and cliffs (between the Northside Rises and the Back Trace/New Town as well as between New Town and Beauvista), or by the Bohane River (between Smoketown and the Back Trace). A few buildings stand out from the rest of the city's topography: the railway station, the Ho Pee Ching Oh-Kay Koffee Shoppe, the editorial office of the *Bohane Vindicator*, the Café Aliados, and the Ancient and Historical Bohane Film Society building are all depicted fairly largely, three-dimensionally and in sharp focus in comparison to the rest of Bohane. By doing so, the map partly takes over the job of literary geography – it maps Bohane's locations, i.e. the smallest units of space where characters meet, act, and interact, and where the actual story is taking place (see Piatti 2009: 129). I say partly because the map does not show all

---

[44] See Piatti's (2009: 137) comment on an equally desperate attempt to locate Tolkien's Middle Earth on a map of Europe.

locations, but omits private spaces such as Girly's bedroom. This inconsistency is, as I will explain later on, due to a somewhat touristic thrust in the map's conception.

Besides showing public locations and the city's quarters, the map also tells the reader a lot about Bohane's residential milieus and distribution of wealth. The towers of the Northside Rises rather look like an industrial area. Smoketown and the Back Trace are presented as a wild and unstructured accumulation of small houses not organised in straight city blocks. Contrastingly, New Town does have rather standardised city blocks and its houses seem to be slightly larger than in the crime-ridden areas mentioned before. Furthermore, Beauvista's roads appear to be elegantly curved, the quarter's houses are even larger than the ones in New Town, and the streets are lined with trees. As in *Perdido Street Station*, the quarter's names are 'telling' names. Beauvista poses as Bohane's show-piece while the Back Trace (back streets being typical locations for various crimes) and Smoketown (either referring to soot or to drugs) can well be imagined as dark, dirty, and dangerous. Thus, the names of the quarters and the quarters' visualisation on the map go hand in hand and exceed the implicit information of the map of New Crobuzon where the telling names rather stand alone without much visual support. More than most maps, the map of Bohane illustrates both social and monetary distribution and establishes its stereotypical quarters before the reader even turns to the novel's first sentence.

Bohane Tourism
For the next point, I briefly need to summon again Löbbermann's opposition between tourists and vagrants as avatars of de Certeau's domains of *map* and *tour* which I already outlined in chapter III.2.1. According to Löbbermann, the tourist and the vagrant are two postmodern indices which, in their extreme opposition, constantly negotiate ambiguities of conspicuity and invisibility, between what is visible and what is meant to be overlooked (see Löbbermann 2005: 264). Her examples are mostly taken from paratextual maps or from novels which are concerned with cartography in other ways. One of her map examples, however, stands out: it is a touristic city map or leaflet published by the New York Apple Tours company, which is a map of New York depicting the routes of the company's double-decker bus tours for tourists. The map, obviously, is not a 'complete' map of New York. Touristic sites and important buildings, presented in an isometric (i.e. the map itself is two-dimensional, but tries to represent these buildings three-dimensionally) style, are contrasted with the – for tourists – unimportant remaining city blocks of New York of which no houses are shown and which remain flat. Thus, the only topographical markers on the map are

those considered worth visiting by the company by means of an authorial process of selection and visualisation.

Comparing the New York Apple Tours map with the Bohane map reveals some stunning similarities, which I will take as an invitation to deal with the map of Bohane in similar ways as Löbbermann does with the one of the Big Apple. The beginning of this chapter already hinted at the prominence of various public locations on the map of Bohane (the railway station, the Ho Pee Ching Oh-Kay Koffee Shoppe, the editorial office of the *Bohane Vindicator*, the Café Aliados, and the Ancient and Historical Bohane Film Society building) due to their status as locations in Piatti's terminology. Additionally, the way they are represented in sharp focus and with an isometric perspective and with the flags spelling out their names, their similarities to the touristic sites on the bus tour map are striking. Thus, the fact that the Bohane map does not highlight any private buildings makes much sense: as a tourist map, it emphasises the locations of historical sites and points of interest (the 98er Square and the 98 Steps), places to eat and go out (the café and the Ho Pee drug parlour), culture (the one-seat cinema), and of course the most prominent place of transit (the station). The arrangement, as in the bus tour map, expresses reification and intimacy. The faceless towers of the Northside Rises and the nasty streets of the Back Trace are pushed to the background while the novel's more shiny and important locations stand out, presented in an enticing, manageable layout (see Löbbermann 2005: 273). Thus, the readers of *City of Bohane* are put into the tourists' position. They are invited to enter the city and to interact with the prominent elements of its topography (as well as with the events taking place in the story) without getting lost. According to Löbbermann, this kind of invitation is an attempt to find a middle ground between de Certeau's *tour* and *map* (see Löbbermann 2005: 272–273). By giving up the godlike perspective onto a flat, totalised surface to a certain extent, the touristy reader moves away from the *map* in its most extreme form. The isometric perspective then suggests that the city becomes more tangible while the feeling of being in control as an elevated, detached observer is retained. Simultaneously, the reader does not come too close to the (vagrant's or character's) domain of the *tour* in its purest form either because the range of locations which are actually made tangible only accounts for parts of the city and is limited to the flashy scaffolding while missing out opportunities to look behind the scenes.

Occasionally, the characters in the novel also seem to assume the roles of tourists. In most cases, they do not act out their lives and stories in private places, but in the isometric, touristic locations found on the map. As they visit these locations, the characters indulge in whatever these places have to offer (drugs, films, music). However, they are not interested in looking behind the scenes as such – instead, they could be called nostalgic tourists because they use the touristic locations and their attractions to summon their memories of the Bohane lost-time (see chapter IV.2.3 for a more detailed analysis). Thus, these characters let themselves be guided by their city's nostalgia-ridden locations, and give up their controlling grasp on the city to a certain extent. Logan, for example, drowns his pain and love-sickness in Bohane's drug parlours, and completely neglects his responsibilities as the leader of his Fancy.

Since the story world is obviously presented by its narrator, he can be connected to *City of Bohane*'s touristic strategies, too. After all, the narrator provides Bohane's relevant locations in the first place, which are then backed up by the map. He is thus able to show around his readers who, as tourists, are unfamiliar with the city and its specific gangland topography. The narrator is quite eager to point out Bohane's attractions: for example, he explains August Fair, Bohane's most important holiday (see *CoB*: 244). He also emphasises that he is a local and thus familiar with Bohane's oddities, mood, and inhabitants, as his characterisation of Logan shows:

> [Y]ou wouldn't make eye contact with the Long Fella if you could help it. Strange, but we had a fear of him and a pride in him, both. He had a fine hold of himself, as we say in Bohane. He was graceful and erect and he looked neither left nor right but straight out ahead always, with the shoulders thrown back, like a general. (*CoB*: 4)

His insistence on "we" and his knowledge of typical Bohane collocations enable him to assume an expert position and to function as a tourist guide for his readers. Thus, when readers pick up the novel, they immediately face a two-fold touristic pre-selection as both the narrator and the map point them into a certain direction of what will be interesting and important. It is striking, though, that the narrator does not focus on the flashy, Beauvista side of town, but on the gangland. Thus, his city tour rather feels like some kind of insider or special tour ('the Bohane gangland experience!') that attempts to look behind the scenes of ordinary tourism – and the readers, by taking the tour, get quite close to the gangland experience as they witness the rise and fall of the Hartnett Fancy and its alliances.

The Metafictional Square
Last but not least, the Kevin Barry Square printed on the map is worth a few words. Before talking about possible references to the novel's author, the historical reference should be pointed out. The Irish republican Kevin Barry (1902– 1920) is, up to this day, portrayed as a martyr in Irish history due to his execution

during the early stages of the Irish War of Independence. His fate also inspired a rebel song by the same name that has been performed by numerous Irish musicians. Despite the fact that there is no actual Kevin Barry Square in Dublin, there is a Kevin Barry Memorial Hall, and the reference to Barry ties in with many other references to Irish history and celtic mythology which can be found in the novel (see chapter IV.2.3).

The reference to the historical Kevin Barry, however, is just a starting point, since the author of *City of Bohane* bears the same name. How about possible a reference to the novel's author? Being named after a historical figure offers a nice way of dedicating a metafictional square to oneself on one's own novel's fictional map without showing off too much. The fact that the story of the novel takes place in 2053 may help to account for this self-confident placement. Following the idea that many dystopias take the actual world as a starting point, then take a wrong turn and bring about the dystopian status quo, and following the idea that Bohane is rendered as an aggregation of all Irish cities, one can imagine that Barry stages himself as a (formerly) famous writer from the lost-time. He anticipates his success as a writer (*City of Bohane* being his first novel) at some point of time before Bohane's dystopian turn – as a writer to whom a square is dedicated, which then figures as another leftover from the good old lost-time before the dystopia came about.

The arrangement is not without a good deal of self-mockery, which becomes clear by looking at the way cliché tourists deal with historical sites. According to Löbbermann, they treat all sites equally without accounting for the particularities; everything is potentially interesting if made accessible commercially; the tourists pay the entrance fee, walk around, take a few pictures – and move on to the next site presented to them in order to satisfy their neverending lust for indulgence. By moving from site to site, tourists create fictions of the city they are visiting and thus create a simplified and superficial image of it by means of booked tours, neatly presented and held together by the touristic map (see Löbbermann 2005: 266–267). In this sense, the historical and metafictional Kevin Barry Square is just another site which the tourist ticks off on a must-see list without really being interested who the person behind the name is or was, or which role the square has played in the course of history (and the role of a public square usually is an important one – be it as place of declaration of human rights and freedom or as a place of revolt and rebellion). The Bohane tourist is unable to look beyond the haze concealing the lost-time from foreigners' eyes. Barry's square, and with it his legacy as a brilliant writer (already anticipated by publishers and reviewers by comparing him to Jocye, Burgess, and by all the other eulogies printed on the back of the book), is reduced to an almost empty relic from 'back then' which, in 2053, does not refer to anything tangible anymore. Therefore, Barry does not stage himself as an unforgotten, eternal literary genius, but precisely as someone who, after the chorus of praise fell silent in the course of the dystopian turn, was forgotten again. Thus, Barry seems not to place himself too much in the tradition of the historical Kevin Barry, but rather – and this, again, is a fairly self-confident move – in the tradition of those writers who intertextually appear in dystopian classics: unknown to the general public within the story worlds (i.e. the tourists), but either re-encountered sometimes by exceptional individuals (the works of Shakespeare in *Brave New World*) or well-kept by an exile community (as in *Fahrenheit 451*).

IV Urban Spaces: Taking a Stroll

In this chapter, I provide a model for analysing the dystopian novels' spaces and urban topographies. Analysis of the novels will then follow in individual subchapters. The model primarily relies on Lefebvre's triad of perceived, conceived and lived space in *The Production of Space*. Two quotes that are to be found fairly early in *The Production of Space* provide a suitable starting point. First, Lefebvre claims that "every society […] produces a space, its own space" (Lefebvre 1991: 31); and second, he claims that "(social) space is a (social) product" (Lefebvre 1991: 26). The dystopian city and its status as an alternative and fictional world, just as Lefebvre's philosophical concept of urban space, not only highlight constructedness and the productive aspect, but also show that the constructedness is due to numerous interwoven processes. Lefebvre's triad of social space is then complemented by Martina Löw's sociological approach to city space, the so-called intrinsic logic of cities, and by Sonja Altnöder's exploitation of the body metaphor in the force field of materiality and discursivity. Analysis of the novels shall provide clear results which go beyond Lefebvre's remarks (see Engelke 2009: 98–108). In short: the model will use some of Lefebvre's terminology without sticking too close to his approach's details. By doing so, I am aware that I am not following Lefebvre and Lefebvre scholars in places – a price I am willing to pay for making Lefebvre's socio-philosophical construct productive for literary studies.

IV.1 From Lefebvre to the City as a Body: A Model for Topographic Analysis

When reading Lefebvre's *The Production of Space*, what appears to be most important is his conceptual triad of spatial practice/perceived space, representations of space/conceived space, and spaces of representation/lived space.[1] These three interwoven dimensions provide the basis for analysing (social) space on the whole.

---

[1] In the following, I will only refer to these dimensions as perceived, conceived, and lived space, while Lefebvre seems to differentiate between a transsubjective triad (spatial practice, representations of space, spaces of representation) and a subject-centered figuration (perceived, conceived, lived; see Engelke 2009: 54–55). Since I am mostly concerned with individual characters and their ways of coming to terms as they walk through the city, I will use the subject-centered terms only.

Perceived Space
The first dimension, the perceived space, is what "secretes [a] society's space [...]. It embodies a close association [...] between daily reality (daily routine) and urban reality (the routes and networks which link up the places set aside for work, 'private' life and leisure)" (Lefebvre 1991: 38). Questions such as the following are at stake with regard to perceived space: when a character's walks in a city are described, what does he or she see and how? How does one get in touch with what one sees, or how does what one sees get in touch conversely? Hence, perceived space refers to the materiality of the city.[2]

The material aspect of perceived space also brings the body into play. In Lefebvre's words, "social practice presupposes the use of the body: the use of the hands, members and sensory organs, and the gestures of work as of activity unrelated to work. This is the realm of the *perceived* (the practical basis of the reception of the outside world [...])" (Lefebvre 1991: 40 [original italics]). He states a very bodily relation between the human being and space right from the start which also manifested itself in the way space used to be measured: by means of the body. Fingerbreadth, feet, and other body parts were the tools of measurement of many peoples for ages, while the size of the body part in question varied from person to person. For Lefebvre, the standardisation of measurement due to the decimal system marks the first severe loss of humanity's unity with nature (see Lefebvre 1001: 110–111). Still, the living body remains the crucial force behind the production of space as it produces it while being subject to it simultaneously: "it produces itself in space and it also produces that space" (Lefebvre 1991: 110). The "'distinct body'" keeps interior and exterior separate as its borders interact between self and the outside world, and it helps to incorporate what is going on in social life in particular and outside the body in general (see Lefebvre 1991: 176). The discursive aspect of the interaction between body and city is already foreshadowed here and will be taken up later on again. For now, it is sufficient to say that the idea of perceiving and getting in touch with the city is the mainspring for the body, and the ways of perceiving and getting in touch will vary from character to character.

When looking at the process underlying perceived space, a fragile stance between conscious and unconscious appropriations becomes apparent. On the one hand, it seems at first possible to keep perception innocently on the material surface. On the other hand, in systems-theoretical terms, one is always observing.

---

[2] I thus follow Engelke's attribution of perceived space to materiality, whereas conceived space belongs to the dimension of discursivity. See Engelke 2009: 45; 61. However, I will place lived space in the middle of materiality and discursivity (which Engelke puts on the discursive side).

By observing, one differentiates, and differentiation is the primary means of accessing the world 'out there' in the first place. What is left out remains as an "unmarked space" in opposition to the defined or specific (Luhmann 1997: 232). Continuous first-order observation and differentiation as attempts to further move the border of the unmarked space, however, never manage to incorporate the unmarked.[3] The unmarked is always present in opposition to the defined, without finally being accessible. If a bridge is built between first-order and second-order observation and the materiality of the city, a game of surfaces, of topographies opens up. What does one perceive at first glance? What is behind it? How can it be accessed? Differences in terms of perception and thus perceived space present themselves when it comes to different narrative perspectives – a point worth considering, given the fact that one can take the figure perspective as a first-order observation and the superordinate narrator perspective as a simulated or artificial second-order observation (which the reader can in turn observe on a superordinate level).

Conceived Space
The second dimension is conceived space, the "conceptualized [...] space of scientists, planners, urbanists, technocratic subdividers and social engineers" – and cartographers, one should add (Lefebvre 1991: 38). Maps, statistics, laws – they all provide possibilities of dealing with the world in specific ways. The conceived is concerned with "intellectually worked out", i.e. conscious, conceptions of space (Lefebvre 1991: 39). In contrast to the materiality of perceived space, conceived space has to be placed in the field of discursivity. Questions such as the following will turn up in this study: where do these intellectually worked out concepts come from, and how do they acquire their power? What kinds of mindsets concerning space do they provide, and how do these mindsets influence the dimensions of the perceived and the lived? Conceived space may provide regulations for the configuration of materiality (e.g. the strategies of placing the shelves in supermarkets in such a way that the customers stay as long as possible in the store, passing as many goods as possible) or provide a model for looking at (and walking through) perceived space (a sign may indicate a one-way street, or the rules of tennis may indicate whether a ball which hits the line is 'in' or 'out'). Due to the discursive aspect, this information is usually

---

[3] It is, of course, possible to partially 'get at' first-order observation if the observation is observed itself (second-order observation). However, second-order observation produces its own unmarked space; a final horizon always remains untouched (see Reinfandt 2000: 101–124).

mediated. Perceived space (or people's way of dealing with it, to be more precise) can in turn either comply with the conceived or go against it (e. g. driving down a one-way street the wrong way) because it is materially possible although the intention behind the conceived might be completely different. In terms of narration, the conceived will usually be attributed to heterodiegetic narrators outside the story world, as narrators of this kind seem to provide the world, which is being presented to the reader as an intellectually worked-out construct in which the characters move around. The way of presentation then heavily influences how the fictional world is perceived and/or imagined (readers' understandings of the world's materiality, for instance).[4] It needs to be pointed out, however, that this providing-of-world happens twice in a way: on a first-order level, the story world created by the narrator is created for the characters. This story world is equipped with an inherent logic and certain rules to which the characters are inevitably bound. On a second level, the narrator also creates this story world for the readers, who can thus access the story world through the narrator's mediation which is unavailable for the characters within the story world. Thus, Lefebvre's triad seems to have two layers. The first layer of perceived, conceived, and lived space operates on the story level, while the second one operates on the level of discourse. This discrepancy between first-order and second-order representation of the story world is especially visible in cases of unreliable or subversive narration: the representation for the reader is heavily influenced by the 'how' of the discourse, while the story level is unaffected by any disconcordant narrative perspective (the story world – the 'what' – does not change for the characters just because the narrative voice mediating it becomes subversive).

Lived Space

The last dimension of the triad is lived space. In Lefebvre's words, this is "space as directly *lived* through its associated images and symbols, and hence the space of 'inhabitants' and 'users', but also of some artists [...]. This is the dominated [...] space which the imagination seeks to change and appropriate. It overlays physical space [and, due to their congruence, perceived space], making symbolic use of its objects" (Lefebvre 1991: 39 [original italics]). In lived space symbols, memories, imaginations, and dreams are located (see Engelke 2009: 49; Lefebvre 1991: 41). Thus, questions arise as to what can be disclosed if a novel shows char-

---

[4] Character and narrator perspective are put in brackets in the model at the end of this chapter in order to indicate a tendency rather than a fixed opposition.

acters walking through the city. How do they feel and why? How do specific routes or buildings trigger their imagination? How do their memories affect what they see and how they deal with it? What kinds of artistic and symbolic uses do they impose on the city space? The materiality might remind characters of something or the location itself might be charged with meaning and memories beyond the surface. The triggering process related to these locations can either be conscious (as a character tries to actively invoke his/her past tied to a specific location) or unconscious (the memory pops up involuntarily). While lived space overlays perceived space, perceived space in turn triggers the imaginative associations. The relation between lived space and conceived space, as Lefebvre puts it, is one of domination, as the latter's patterns of thought provide or deny specific lived patterns (one's emotions might, for example, vary greatly when walking through a space in which one is allowed to move in contrast to a space where one is not allowed to, or when walking through a space of which mere knowledge is illegal). Lived space, on the other hand, is able to reappropriate dominated spaces – the term "reappropriation" derives from *The Production of Space*, and it describes the process of an inhabited space that outgrows its original purpose and becomes available for something new, for a new function (Lefebvre 1991: 167).

Due to the established labels of conceived (conscious, dominance) and lived space (unconscious, reappropriation), their relation – as already hinted at in Lefebvre – is mostly based on ideology (from which representations of space, and therefore conceived space, often derive; see Lefebvre 1991: 44). Although apparently objective, these conceived representations, being the space of capital or the state, are always conceived with a specific ideology, power, knowledge or intention behind it (which again ties in with the point about power being expressed in maps, documents, and other means of representation) (see Merrifield 2006: 109). Ideology itself is nothing "without a space to which it refers, a space which it describes, whose vocabulary and links it makes use of, and whose code it embodies," and is thus highly discursive (Lefebvre 1991: 44). For the model below, ideology can refer to a conceived set of (often political/institutional) principles as well as to a personal frame of reference. Especially the discursive distinction of people according to their humours and the resulting spatial separation in *Divided Kingdom* will illustrate this notion. Narrative strategies also accommodate the relation of dominance. Since heterodiegetic narration is attributed to conceived space (because the depicted world is conceived itself), the figure perspective tends to be attributed to lived space, since the characters inhabiting the fictional world in question in turn have to come to terms with the supremacy of heterodiegetic narration.

The Intrinsic Logic of Cities, Materiality and Discursivity

Lefebvre's triad shall now be complemented by Martina Löw's intrinsic logic of cities and Sonja Altnöder's extrapolation of Löw's model. The former will be helpful in understanding the relations between the city and the body (since this study is concerned with the reciprocal effects of city and body anyway), whereas the latter will sharpen the opposition of materiality and discursivity, turning the opposition into a productive force field. The intrinsic logic of cities is part of Löw's layout of a sociology of the city. As with *The Production of Space*, I will only borrow what seems to me most important. Löw understands cities as spatial forms of socialisation which constitute themselves along three parameters: size, density, and homogeneity/heterogeneity[5] as spatial markers that provide specific spatial principles for the material structure (see Löw 2008a: 69).[6] Size refers to the city's population. The larger the population, the wider the range of individual varieties of urban life, and the greater the potential differences between them. A large population also entails that urban people, due to the agglomeration of numerous people in one place, know just a relatively small percentage of those people whom they encounter in the city day by day – in contrast to the village where one meets comparatively few people, but knows most or all of them (see Wirth 1974: 51–52). A high density, i.e. a high number of people per square mile of city space, enhances certain effects of mere size, most importantly differentiation and specialization. People also tend to move to areas where other people of similar status and needs live (see Wirth 1974: 54–55). Heterogeneity and homogeneity refer to the continuous oscillation between spelling out that the city is *one city* and simultaneously made up of *individuals*. The body, on the other hand, is given the parameters of perception, experience, and performance in its display of individuality and identity (see Löw 2008a: 75).

Altnöder then goes one step further and complements Löw's sociological groundwork by a social constructivist approach. The body is not pregiven, but

---

5 While Löw only uses heterogeneity, I will add homogeneity for several reasons. Since the parameters used by Löw are spatial markers, and since they point towards measurability, it seems more appropriate to highlight the potential instability and thus the degree to which homogeneity has collapsed. Additionally, dystopian cities in particular seem to constantly negotiate between the two extremes: totalitarian authorities tend to aim at making all people equal, while counter-movements of e.g. underground groups emphasise heterogeneity. Simultaneously, dystopian authorities may establish ghettos in order to keep certain groups away from the rest, while counter-movements strive for uniting all the people.

6 I will only use the term "city", whereas Löw works with "städtische Doxa" in the original (Löw 2008a: 75–76). The three parameters were established by sociologist Louis Wirth in 1938 and have been borrowed by scholars ever since.

constructed at the intersection of numerous potentially contradictory discourses – similar to, for instance, the category of gender. In contrast to classic constructivism, the body's materiality is not denied but enforced (see Altnöder 2009: 301). Altnöder, by referring back to Judith Butler, renders the material substance of the human body as both means and effect of the subject's (and society's) discursive practices of appropriation (see Altnöder 2009: 302). The body as a means of discursive appropriation shows parallels to the body in Lefebvre: the body makes experience graspable and it controls both perception and positioning in the world while staging the individual's identity along the three parameters of experience, perception, and performance (see Altnöder 2009: 302). These also retroact on the body and continuously reproduce it as an effect of subjective processes of appropriation. The individual is not alone in this process since it is always observable by others. Consequently, the body becomes a projection screen for a dialogic and intersubjective understanding of construction and a continuous reconstruction of identity and alterity, a location of conflict between self and other, individual and social discourses and their inherent ascriptions of difference (see Altnöder 2009: 302–303). Thus, as the material substance of the city and the human habitus come together, the city constitutes itself both in terms of its spatial extension and the practices of its inhabitants, the result being a productive force field not unlike de Certeau's conception of the everyday established in chapter III.1: it is a force field of the city's body and the human body, of urban life's discursivity and the practices of appropriation on the inhabitants' side (see Altnöder 2009: 303). The following chart shows the model based on the texts by Lefebvre, Löw, and Altnöder (see below).

In short, Lefebvre's three dimensions provide an overall layout for analysing urban topographies. The addition of the city and the body as entities enhances the spaces' subject orientation where Lefebvre stays vague by just stating that social space is created by society. Putting the city and the body in a force field of materiality and discursivity then highlights the topographical aspect of the model – the correspondences and anomalies of what is seen/felt/experienced and what is materially there. The following subchapters, each with a different emphasis, will show how the model can work with regard to the novels with which this study has been concerned so far.

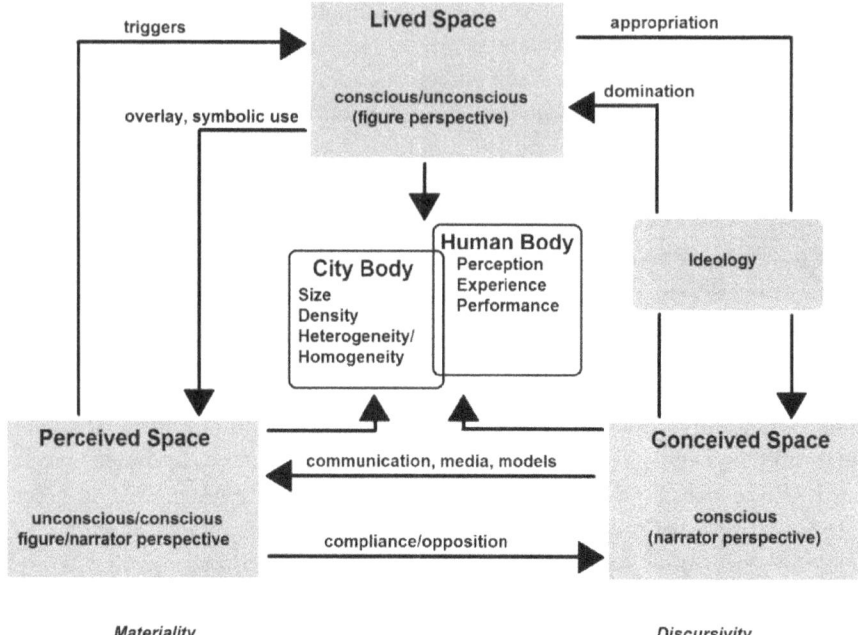

Fig. v: City Space Model

IV.2 Walking the Urban Dystopias

IV.2.1 *Perdido Street Station:* The City as a Body, the Body as a City

The analysis of *Perdido Street Station* in the context of the model developed in IV.1 will consist of several parts. In the first part, after a brief overview of New Crobuzon's quarters, the focus will be on its specific displays of perceived space, conceived space, and lived space. The next part will use Richard Sennett's *Flesh and Stone* (1996) as a springboard for analysing New Crobuzon as a city body beyond mere anthropomorphisation. The chapter will end with a closer look on Yagharek's development as an outstanding case of interaction between city body and human body.

The Urban Spaces of New Crobuzon
In *Perdido Street Station,* many descriptions of New Crobuzon's quarters can be found. From comparatively prosperous and healthy quarters (Flag Hill, Canker

Wedge, Rim, Gidd, Ludmead) and middle-class or open-minded artists' areas (for example Flyside, Salacus Fields, Gallmarch) to poor and industrial areas (Sheck, Sobek Croix, Kelltree) and the nasty slums (Raven's Gate, Smog Bend, Gross Coil, Griss Twist, Dog Fenn, to name but a few) – pretty much every quarter is, at least, given a rough description. Despite the general tendency of the better quarters to be located along the River Canker and in the south and the bad areas along the River Tar and the Gross Tar, some wealthy areas and slums are quite close to each other. For instance, it is just a stone's throw from Ludmead to Bonetown or Brock Marsh and from Ketch Heath to Spatters. Canker Wedge is "[l]ess than two miles from the centre of the city, but a different world" compared to the monstrous and crowded Perdido Street Station itself: "Low, quiet streets and modest housing, small apologetic parks, frumpy churches and halls [...]" (*PSS*: 503). Schlögel's notes on Los Angeles as a city of many fragmented zones come to mind. There, according to him, it is possible to live in one's own world without ever getting out while simultaneously being able to enter a different culture or zone by just moving from one block to another. In short: Los Angeles, not unlike New Crobuzon, is a huge site showing the wonders of people living together and at the same time a vast arena of struggle (see Schlögel 2003: 498). Several quarters in New Crobuzon stand out as ghettoes inhabited by xenians, i.e. by non-humans. The human-beetle hybrid khepri can be found in Creekside and Kinken, the city's bird-men or garuda live in Spatters, only the top third of the cactus people are allowed in the Glasshouse, and the frog-like vodyanoi figure prominently in Kelltree, close to the docks (there are also mixed quarters such as Flyside, Riverskin, and Salacus Fields). Most quarters are very much liable to processes of urbanisation. Here is what happened to Petty Coil over the years:

> A little over a hundred years previously, Petty Coil had been an urban hub for the major families. [...] But industry exploded in New Crobuzon, much of it bankrolled by those very families. [...] Griss Twist, just across the river, enjoyed a short-lived boom of small machinofacture, with all the noise and stink that that entailed. [...] A new landscape of ruin and industrial filth was created, in a speeded-up parody of geological process. [...] Within a few years the local factories had gone but the dumps remained, and the winds that blew in from the sea could send a pestilential stench over the Tar into Petty Coil. The rich deserted their homes. Petty Coil degenerated in a lively fashion. It became noisier. Paint and plaster bubbled, desquamating grotesquely, as the massive houses became homes for more and more of New Crobuzon's swelling population. Windows broke, were fixed roughly, broke again. As small food-shops and bakers and carpenters moved in, Petty Coil fell willing prey to the city's ineluctable capacity for spontaneous architecture. Walls and floors and ceilings were called into question, amended. New and inventive uses were found for deserted constructions. (*PSS*: 272)

Three classic processes as described in urban sociology are at work here. To begin with, segregation takes place, which describes that specific social groups gather in specific quarters (New Crobuzon's major families). Second, invasion is a process where new groups enter a quarter that has previously been home to another group by means of segregation (small shops, bakers, carpenters move in). Last, succession describes the complete conversion of the quarter (from elegant quarter to lower-class; from industry to dump) (see Löw 2008b: 110). Hence, Petty Coil displays a dystopian antithesis to what sociologists call gentrification, i.e. the development from a homogenously poor quarter to a homogenously rich one (see Löw 2008b: 41): decay instead of upswing. Also note the use of the term "spontaneous architecture," which also comes up in *The Production of Space* as a wild form of housing in Latin American slums. Lefebvre describes it as an appropriation by the inhabitants themselves that is brought about in a duality of conflict and contradiction with the dominated space of politics and the state (Lefebvre 1991: 374).

Another quarter named Spatters developed into what sounds very much like a nightmarish "Zwischenstadt" (Löw 2008b: 108 ff.; literal translation: "in-between city") in which the conceived space is remarkably weak:

> The word spread that this was a ghost sector, beyond Parliament's ken, where taxes and laws were as rare as sewage systems. [...] Inhabitation spread like mould. There were no gaslamps to take the edge off the night, no doctors, no jobs, yet within ten years the area was dense with ersatz housing. [...] The suburb was beyond the reach of New Crobuzon's municipality. There was an unreliable alternative infrastructure: a self-appointed network [...]. The only visitors from outside were the regular trains appearing at the incongruously well-maintained Fell Stop Station, and the gangs of masked gunmen [...]. It had acquired a name, Spatters, that reflected the desultory randomness of its outlines: the whole stinking shantytown seemed to have dribbled like shit from the sky. [...] It was simply not part of the city, nothing but a strange little town that had grafted itself onto New Crobuzon without a by-your-leave. (*PSS*: 124–125)

Due to the extension of a railway line, new houses were built until the money ran out. By and by, foreigners started to move in, and the area, only connected to the rest of the city by a railway line, became a marginalised territory quite independent from New Crobuzon and unknown to its authorities. Generally speaking, every demographic change also changes the quarters and their borders (see Schlögel 2003: 499).

Coming back to the model established in IV.1 and Lefebvre's triad of perceived space, conceived space, and lived space, it becomes clear that the conceived space of New Crobuzon is ambiguous. Whereas conceived space in Lefebvre is closely linked to the state, it is – as demonstrated in the chapter on maps – rather in the hands of rogue scientists and social outcasts in *Perdido Street Sta-*

tion. The government is trying to exercise force, i.e. to gain control over the city and fails. The people and groups who actually produce or deal with conceived space are stuck with impromptu drawings that do not offer an efficient means of control either.

Still, New Crobuzon's government does not hand over power so easily, and it struggles for dominance. Sovereignty, according to Lefebvre, implies space that is ruled by violence and force (see Lefebvre 1991: 280) in an attempt to enforce the ideas of a few (i.e. those who are in charge) in such a way that they become undistinguishable from public interest (see Lefebvre 1991: 281) – ideas conceived by the government dominate the lived space and render the perceived space. Lefebvre's point here is reminiscent of Meyer's explanation of the key feature of the typical dystopian government: individual happiness is sacrificed for the good of the state (see Meyer 2001: 42; 356). Control in New Crobuzon is maintained by censure, militia towers, airships, sleepers, and hooded federal agents. Since there is no regular army or police force, the most obvious demonstration of power is the looming presence of institutional buildings, the militia towers:

> Swelling fatly above the low houses before [Lin] was the Flyside militia tower. A vast, pudgy pillar, squat and mean, somehow, for all its thirty-five stories. Thin windows like arrow-slits peppered its sides, their dark glass matt, immune to reflection. The tower's concrete skin was mottled and flaking. Three miles to the north Lin caught a glimpse of an even taller structure: the militia's hub, the Spike, that punctured the earth like a concrete thorn in the heart of the city. (*PSS:* 16–17)

The tower is higher than the surrounding buildings, its windows cannot be looked into from outside and, despite the flaking surface, it appears to be solid and strong. Where governmental control is being questioned actively, the result usually is bloody conflict. Three brief examples from Miéville's novel illustrate this: firstly, the militia's swoop on the hidden editorial office of the *Runagate Rampant* (*PSS:* 261–264) and the arrest of its editor, Benjamin Flex. Secondly, the Kelltree docks strike by the vodyanoi dockers (*PSS:* 255–261), which is put down by the militia. And lastly, the fight of Isaac's group against the militia (*PSS:* 335–346).

As for the first example, the editorial office is located behind a secret door in a slaughterhouse in the nasty quarter of Dog Fenn. The home of the underground newspaper, which one may call an appropriated space (a space modified by a group so that it answers a new purpose), is well-hidden, and it takes much effort for Derkhan to meet with her fellow rebels unseen (*PSS:* 109–121). As the militia raids the place, they not only arrest everybody and destroy all equipment – they blow up the whole building (*PSS:* 263) and thus radically change the location's material aspect. As the reader gets to know later, the government had been informed for years about the secret office and that it had just been waiting for the right moment. The right moment, then, is the *Runagate Rampant*'s shot in the dark about a sinister deal between the government and a mobster (which, as the reader knows, involves Motley and the slake-moths bargain). Thus, as soon as the newspaper poses a threat to the dystopian government with respect to conceived space (a revealing article on the deal might well challenge the government's monopoly on information), Mayor Rudgutter decides to get rid of all resistance and re-establish government's domination of conceived space again.

Example number two is the cover story for this raid: the Kelltree strike by the city's vodyanoi dockers. Again, the militia proves to be quite effective, using hooded agents that pop up in the mass of demonstrants, agents on flying beasts as grim versions of policemen on horses, airships, and gas grenades. The rough intervention is due to the way the vodyanoi dockers try to achieve better pay and working conditions. All vodyanoi are able to perform a form of thaumaturgy called watercraeft that enables them to shape and move water, and the dockers use it to dig a trench into the Gross Tar in order to stop all cargo ships from entering or leaving New Crobuzon: "They had whooped and cheered raggedly, as they lifted the final thin veil of liquid from the great trench they had dug in the river. It yawned fifty or more feet across, an enormous slice of air cut out of the riverwater, stretching the eight hundred feet from one bank to the other" (*PSS:* 255–256). Bluntly speaking, the vodyanoi presume to literally shape and dominate the space of the docks themselves, inevitably resulting in a clash with the government that struggles for domination of the same space. The government organises and regulates the city space; thus, it defends class interests while prioritising itself in contrast to society as a whole; in Lefebvre's words, the dockers develop their own plans and strategies and exercise counter-action, "in the form of counter-plans and counter-projects designed to thwart strategies, plans and programmes imposed from above" (Lefebvre 1991: 383).

The third example sheds light on dominated space breaking into private space. Isaac's colleague, David, tips off the inquisition (the local intelligence, whereas the militia is the executive force), and the militia raids Isaac's warehouse. Since Isaac is not only a threat to the government's control over the city but also possesses valuable information (and, possibly, a crisis engine), the troops want him and his group alive (*PSS:* 338). The fight is described blow-by-blow as the militia make their way through the warehouse (*PSS:* 338–343), wounding Derkhan and catching Lemuel. As Isaac's group loses control over their private space, the Weaver appears and takes them away (*PSS:* 343–346), interrupting the militia's domination process. Without having arrested the group, the militia may dominate the material side of the warehouse's private space, but not the subjects and bodies who constituted it. The escape and the following manhunt are going to change life in New Crobuzon – not only for Isaac, but also for the whole population, as Yagharek observes: "*In the climate of crisis, the militia are to be given extraordinary powers, we read. They may revert to open, uniformed patrols. Civilian rights may be curtailed. Martial law is mooted*" (*PSS:* 592 [original italics]). In short, the dystopian city life becomes even worse as the government establishes means of weakening private space while strengthening its own presence in public space and enhancing its conceived space with stricter laws.

To change life in the city, then, also means to change the lived space of its inhabitants. Yagharek's first days as a vagrant have already been mentioned; with the government and Motley's henchmen chasing him and the rest of Isaac's gang, their experience of the city is greatly changed: "'Every time we move, we're afraid.' [Derkhan] spoke quickly. [...] 'Every time any kind of automaton goes past, we think the Construct Council's found us. Every man or woman or xenian makes us freeze up. Is it the militia? It it one of Motley's thugs? [...] I can't live like this, Isaac', she said" (*PSS:* 599). No more playful dinner in Lin's apartment above the lively market, no more joking around with avant-garde friends in cafés. Consequently, the changes in conceived and lived space also change the spatial practice of the characters. In Yagharek's words:

> We race away. We run as if we are spirits [...]. We clamber over low fences and into narrow swathes of backyards, rude gardens of mutant apple trees and wretched brambles, dubious compost, mud and broken toys. [...] We move roofs, made uneasy by noises from below. [...] We move by night. [...] We cannot trust our neighbours. We must live in a hinterland of half darkness, isolated and solipsistic. We steal what we need, or buy from tiny late-night grocers miles from where we are settled. Every askance look, every gaze, every shout, sudden flurry of hooves or boots, every bang or hiss of a construct's piston is a moment of fear. We are the most wanted in New Crobuzon. (PSS, p. 591 and 594 [original italics])

The new spatial practice also includes living on the city's roofscape with a "quite different ecology" (*PSS:* 544). It demands new ways of foraging, movement, avoidance, and being always on the run.

One of the most striking instances of lived space in *Perdido Street Station* is Lin's return to the places of her childhood. She was born and grew up in the poor khepri ghetto of Creekside, stuck with a mother (called broodma) who was a fierce devotee of Insect Aspect, a khepri religion claiming that "[w]oman had lost the insectile purity of God and male" (*PSS:* 186), a conviction despised by Lin. After an open confrontation with her broodma, Lin ran away to the apparently more open-minded quarter of Kinken. A completely new experience opens up to her:

> [T]here was a part of her that would always remember Kinken as a sanctuary. Now the smugness of the insular community nauseated her, but at the time of her escape she had been drunk on it. [...] She had baptized herself with a khepri name [which is labelled as decadence in Insect Aspect] and – which was vital in New Crobuzon – a human one. (*PSS* 187–188)

Kinken is also Lin's place of sexual liberation as "the most difficult, the most extraordinary transition" (*PSS:* 188). By and by, however, Kinken appears in a new light:

> Her disgust at the squalor of Creekside was joined with some kind of understanding. Then, her five-year love-affair with Kinken drew to an end. It started when she stood in the Plaza of Statues, and realized that they were mawkish and badly executed, embodying a culture that was blind to itself. She began to see Kinken as implicated in the subjugation of Creekside and the never-mentioned Kinken poor, saw a 'community' at best callous and uncaring, at worst deliberately keeping Creekside down to maintain its superiority. [...] Lin realized that she was living in an unsustainable realm. It combined sanctimony, decadence, insecurity and snobbery in a weird neurotic brew. It was parasitic. (*PSS:* 188)

As disappointing as these experiences are – they help Lin to find her way in life. Whereas Creekside is her symbol for maternal and religious oppression, Kinken is at first its liberating counterpart that then turns out to be a disappointment. It is worth mentioning that the moment of change happens in the Plaza of Statues, an artistic space.[7] After a five years' stay, she leaves Kinken. "Lin was never so foolish as to think she could stop being defined by being khepri, as far as the city was concerned. Nor did she want to. But to herself, she stopped trying to be khepri, as she had once stopped trying to be insect" (*PSS:* 188–189). Still, Kinken remains an ambivalent power source. The spaces of Creekside and Kinken, as directly lived bodily experiences and charged with symbolic elements, enable her to feel and find her way although she does not fully understand "the strength she drew from Kinken" (*PSS:* 189); the lived spaces initialise particular spatial practices: passivity under oppression, rebellion, flight, and a new life.

Perceiving and Experiencing the City

In the chapter on maps, different means of perception have already been mentioned, primarily focussing on Yagharek; now, a more detailed look at perception

---

[7] Art in Lefebvre is usually attributed to spaces of representation, and Lin's own art also renders spatiality. During the time as prisoner of Motley, her sculpture becomes the only reference point, "her only escape. Her only means of expression" in a dark chamber deprived of all the other lived and artistic spaces (*PSS:* 584).

and visibility in the sense of Lefebvre's perceived space will follow. Lefebvre is quite clear that the realm of the perceived is not to be confused with mere surface. Looking at the world in just one certain way is not enough (see Lefebvre 1991: 313) and there is an important difference between what is there materially and what one does with it discursively. This is very much true for New Crobuzon. What appears to be a shabby slaughterhouse is also home to the *Runagate Rampant*'s editorial office; an abhorrent brothel serves as rendezvous point for the inquisition (*PSS:* 297); only while moving through Motley's hideout, Lin realises that it not only consists of one building, but "that it must be the whole row of houses, dividing walls destroyed and rebuilt, custom-made, renovated into one vast convoluted space" (*PSS:* 31). Probably the most striking example is Mayor Rudgutter being received in audience by the ambassador of Hell, apparently the literal representative of Bas-Lag's counterpart to heaven. First, after having thaumaturgically established a connection to the ambassador, the ambassador appears as "[a] heavy man in an immaculate dark suit" (*PSS:* 241). Then, as Rudgutter

> stared at the ambassador, the image of the man in the chair flickered for a tiny sliver of a second, to be replaced by... something else. He had experienced this before. Whenever Rudgutter blinked, he saw the room and its occupant in very different forms. Through his eyelids, Rudgutter saw the inside of a slatted cage; iron bars moving like snakes; arcs of unthinkable force, a jagged, rippling maelstrom of heat. Where the ambassador sat, Rudgutter caught glimpses of a monstrous form. A hyaena's head stared at him, tongue lolling. Breasts with gnashing teeth. Hooves and claws. The stale air in the room would not allow him to keep his eyes open: he had to blink. (*PSS:* 242)

It is only by "snapping [his eyes] immediately open" that he can see "that monstrous vista" and "[catch] a glimmer of the ambassador's other form" (*PSS:* 244).

A completely different way of perceiving her surroundings is Lin's. As a khepri (a human body with an entire scarab beetle instead of a human head), her biological preconditions are different and lead to different practices and results:

> Lin's bulging mirrored eyes saw the city in a compound visual cacophony. A million tiny sections of the whole, each minuscule hexagon segment ablaze with sharp colour and even sharper lines, super-sensitive to differentials of light, weak on details unless she focussed hard enough to hurt slightly. Within each segment, the dead scales of decaying walls were invisible to her, architecture reduced to elemental slabs of colour. But a precise story was told. Each visual fragment, each part, each shape, each shade of colour, differed from its surroundings in infinitesimal ways that told her about the state of the whole structure. And she could taste chymicals in the air, could tell how many of which race lived in which building: she could feel vibrations of air and sound with precision enough to converse in a crowded room or feel a train pass overhead. (*PSS:* 14–15)

Her compound eyes enable her to see very differently (and very different things) compared to a human being. They are "weak on details," but strong on colour differentiation. Plus, they enable her to see the structure of buildings and exceed simply looking at surfaces. Her eyes are also supported by her headlegs, and the perception of smells and sounds is added to her compound story of perception which she also tries to explain to Isaac – who, unable to experience it himself, is incapable of understanding her explanation completely:

> I see clearly as you, clearer. For you it is undifferentiated. In one corner a slum collapsing, in another a new train with pistons shining, in another a gaudy lady below a drab and ancient airship... You must process as one picture. What chaos! Tells you nothing, contradicts itself, changes its story. For me each part has integrity, each fractionally different from the next, until all variation is accounted for, incrementally, rationally. (PSS: 15 [original italics])

The fact that what is perceived depends very much on the perceiver, and that perception is more than just visual impressions, is exemplified here in Lin's beetle-like way of perception. These differences in experience and perception – and varying biological preconditions in general – lead to different spatial performances.[8]

Narrative switches tend to accompany these perceptive differences. Whereas the novel mostly relies on a heterodiegetic narrator with Isaac as the focaliser, Lin's way of seeing the city features her as another internal focaliser (cf. the upper quote starting with "Lin's bulging mirrored eyes"). Even more strikingly, Yagharek's exceptional perception of New Crobuzon's topography dominated by verticality is – in addition to all his thoughts – told by himself. Yagharek, not only a xenian, but also the character who is new in the city, an outcast, and the utmost stranger even among other strangers, is the novel's only homodiegetic narrator with fixed internal focalisation. As far as examples of heterodiegetic narration in *Perdido Street Station* are concerned, the xenian (non-human) quarters and housing are the most striking – or, as Isaac puts it: "Important to learn how other races live in our fair city" (*PSS:* 127). The khepri of Kinken eagerly appropriate the space of the former human buildings, turning them into cocoon-like residences:

> Houses oozed the white mucus of home-grubs. Some were completely coated in the thick stuff: it spread across roofs, linking different buildings into a lumpy, congealed totality. [...] The walls and floors that had been provided by human architects had been broken away in places, and the massive home-grubs allowed to burrow their blind way through

---

[8] Here, Löw's parameters which define the human body reverberate again.

the shell, oozing their phlegm-cement from their abdomens, their stubby little legs skittering as they ate their way through the ruined interiors of the buildings. (*PSS:* 183)

The houses are turned into an interconnected hive. As is typical for insectile hives, and in line with the organic sprawl of New Crobuzon as a whole, it is always changing as the inhabitants constantly work on new chambers and passageways. Other xenians dwell in their own residences, but focalisation remains restricted to the human Isaac in these cases. The cactacae (cactus people) are given their own habitat in the Glasshouse, a massive dome of steel and glass in Riverskin quarter. It is strictly separated from the rest of the city. As in the case of Kinken, there used to be human residences in its place, now violently replaced by the massive dome as "the cactacae had simply enclosed an existing clutch of New Crobuzon streets" (*PSS:* 447):

> A little rim of land, about twenty feet wide, had been cleared all around it, beyond which point the streets of Riverskin had been left. The cartography was a snarled puzzle, a collection of road-ends and the rumps of avenues, here the corner of a park and there half a church, even the stump of a canal, now a trough of stagnant water, cut off by the edge of the dome. Lanes criss-crossed the little township at odd angles, segments cut from longer streets where the dome had been placed over them. (*PSS:* 452)

Inside, visitors face some aggressive appropriation. Ceilings are modified in order to suit the size of the new inhabitants, lush lawns and vegetable gardens have been planted, desert birds imported. The resulting landscape is a sandy desert dotted with green oases. Its climate is quite independent from the rest of the city due to the installation of "a single globe of limpid glass" (*PSS:* 448–449) at the very top which intensifies the sunrays from outside. The illusion of a desert is almost perfect. The only things that still have to be added manually are the sastrugi of the dunes: "Here in this tightly closed space, bounded on every side, there were no gusts to carve patterns, and the desert landscape had to be wrought by hand" (*PSS:* 453). Natural phenomena are mimicked as closely as possible, the most striking change in a desert landscape being the ever-changing topography of the dunes and their patterns.

The homes of the frog-like vodyanoi are not described in detail, so the birdmen or garuda in Spatters remain the last xenian group to turn to. Outsiders among outsiders, they live in and on the upper stories of the towers: "The bottom half of the buildings looked deserted. From the sixth or seventh floor up, however, wooden boughs poked at odd angles out of crevices. The windows were covered with brown paper, unlike the empty sockets" (*PSS:* 126). The reader is not granted a look inside the homes, however, since Isaac as the focaliser does not go in. Here, the appropriation is not as all-embracing as with the other xenians, but it is still happening. In contrast to *The City & The City*, what is being highlighted is not the everyday practice of ignorance, but the cognitive preconditions as such. Xenian appropriation and the different quarters in *Perdido Street Station* exemplify the multiplicity of lifestyles in a densely populated area that is inherent to every metropolis.

The City as a Body, the Body as a City

As already suggested, the analytical focus will now switch from the Lefebvrian part of the model to the interplay of human body and city body. Among numerous attempts to approximate the city and the body, Richard Sennett's approach can be categorised as one which, in contrast to Lefebvre's idea of treating the city as a social fabric that only comes into being through its inhabitants' practices and their interrelations, rather anthropomorphises the city. The city is given a body, it moulds limbs and organs and it is given a life of its own. Despite Altnöder's scepticism concerning the anthropomorphisation of the city (see Altnöder 2009: 300–301), Sennett's account comes in handy for dealing with the bodily discourse in *Perdido Street Station* where, as will be shown, the city as a body is ascribed a life of its own to a certain extent after all.

Flesh and Stone closely links the history of cities to bodily discourse and experience, the fundamental hypothesis being that the fortune or fate of the human body is intimately connected to the fortune or fate of the city it lives in (see Sennett 1996: 369). Sennett's primary examples are ancient Athens and Rome, then Paris and London in the 18th and 19th century, ending with 20th-century New York. He is not alone when he proclaims that the inhabitants of the ancient city where literally much more 'in touch' with their city. The custom of public nakedness in ancient Athens draws upon the "people [feeling] entirely at home in the city" (Sennett 1996: 33). Similarly, Lefebvre notes the unity of representational spaces and representations of space in the ancient Greek city as a state of order "of the world, the order of the city and the order of the house [...]. This unity was not a simple or a homogeneous one, but rather a unity of composition and of proportion, of embracing and presupposing differences and hierarchy" where "knowledge and power, social theory and social practice, were commensurate with each other" (Lefebvre 1991: 247).

Going through the ages, Sennett notes the significance of technological progress. A first sense of detachment features in the symmetrical architecture and city planning of ancient Rome analogous to the symmetry of the human body (see Sennett 1996: 90). Still, there is a close connection, but it is not as symbiotic as in ancient Greece. As technology enables the human being to move faster and in more comfortable ways, "[s]pace become[s] a means to the end of pure motion

– we now measure urban spaces in terms of how easy it is to drive through them, to get out of them" (Sennett 1996: 17–18). The result is a general tendency towards a "'tactile crisis,'" a crisis of opposition, of touching: moving freely through the city goes along with a loss of sensitivity, a loss of connection with the places and spaces one is moving through (see Sennett 1996: 256). Thus, the connection between body and city as well as between bodies is considerably weakened as they become more and more estranged. Sennett's ultimate example for the estranged city is New York: planned on a grid, but without a proper city centre, New York is a city of equalisation. Every block is just as unimportant as the next one, so they all can be knocked down with ease in the course of new projects and penetrated by new streets (see Sennett 1996: 359–360). "Of all the world's cities, New York has the most destroyed itself in order to grow; in a hundred years people will have more tangible evidence about Hadrian's Rome than they will about fiber-optic New York" (Sennett 1996: 360). Despite the tactile crisis, the body and the city have always been quite close to one another. Terms such as the 'heart of the city,' a city's gardens as its lungs, its streets as veins or arteries are commonplace nowadays both in everyday language and in literary texts. Miéville, however, goes way beyond established imagery in his descriptions of the city body.

To begin with, the sewers in *Perdido Street Station* are described as the "veins" (*PSS:* 535) of the city, pipes that run in the sewers are called "arterial clutches" (*PSS:* 538). Also, the parliament's mail delivery and transportation system has "mechanized veins" (*PSS:* 89). The relation to urbanist planning is to be found in the idea that the city, just like the human body, needs to breathe freely. According to Sennett, a new sense of bodily hygiene (bodily practice) is accompanied by the instalment of sewers and means of waste disposal in the 18th century (see Sennett 1996: 261 ff.). Besides that, veins and arteries in Sennett's work are primarily examined by turning to urban planner G.E. Haussmann's system of street networks for Napoleon's Paris. Haussmann himself follows in the footsteps of 18th-century urbanists who applied medical insights about breathing and blood circulation to the city (see Sennett 1996: 256) and systematises the city's streets according to three networks, or maps, classifying them as follows. In the first network, there are high-traffic streets (intended to replace narrow passageways in order to make way for carriages) within the city which are called veins; these connect important sites around town and make accessible the medieval old town in the centre. Streets belonging to the second network are primarily intended for leaving the city or moving towards its periphery and called arteries. Lastly, the third network consists of both arteries and veins which function as connectors between the other two networks (see Sennett 1996: 311).[9] The analogy of streets and blood circulation is obvious: the veins move blood to the heart which in turn pumps it through the arteries, thus supplying the rest of the body. Accordingly, the streets move people to and from the heart of the city. Turning to New Crobuzon, similar imagery can be noticed: streets originating from Perdido Street Station are called "main arteries" that "burst out in all directions" (*PSS:* 293), while the station itself is called "the city's heart" (*PSS:* 512).

However, in *Perdido Street Station*, many more details can be found that anthropomorphise the city in general and the station in particular. The latter is said to have "bowels" (*PSS:* 539) and an "underbelly" (*PSS:* 540) and is located roughly in the centre of the city. In many ancient cities, a so-called umbilicus can be found in the city centre, a starting point for city planning and construction, which is also referred to as "the navel of the [city's] body; from this urban belly button the planners drew all measurements for spaces in the city" (Sennett 1996: 106–107). The station in Miéville's novel even has "[f]ive enormous brick mouths" (*PSS:* 56) and "brick like jutting teeth" (*PSS:* 542). Houses in Dog Fenn are "rusting, bleeding with the rain and the damp, staining the skin of the buildings" (*PSS:* 112). Miéville adds limbs to the twisted urban body: Yagharek's view over the city reveals "fingers and hands and fists and spines of architecture" (*PSS:* 451). Even real bones can be found that loom over the houses: there is a place in Bonetown called the Ribs where the indestructible remains of an ancient beast burst out of the ground over a hundred feet high (*PSS:* 29). The Glasshouse contributes to this monstrous image as "the curve of the dome seem[s] to break the surface of the earth like the tip of a bent back, implying a vast body below ground" (*PSS:* 448). In short: New Crobuzon is packed with sites and descriptions that render it "some unthinkable torpid giant" (*PSS:* 592). This giant starkly contrasts with bodies of cities in Sennett's examples. The ancient Athenians' custom of walking nakedly through the streets as a sign of well-being and feeling at home is, to say the least, unthinkable in New Crobuzon. Furthermore, it does not share much with the grid-like arrangement of New York's city blocks either. Miéville's giant is obviously sick, rotten, tumourous. Dog Fenn can serve as a primary example again: "The nodes and cells of brick and wood and palsied concrete had gone rogue, spreading like malignant tumours" (*PSS:* 114). Even governmental sites are affected. In the Diplomatic Zone which houses foreign ambassadors, "[t]he extra rooms jutted like

---

9 In Sennett's book, however, arteries and veins seem to be mixed up: there, the first network of streets (the one moving in) is called arteries, and the second network (moving out) is called veins – while in human physiology, the terms are used the other way round.

ugly tumours from the interior walls of the eleventh floor, bulging precariously over the garden" (*PSS:* 239). Not only are the rooms tumourous – they also threaten the garden as the 'lung' of the Diplomatic Zone. They jut and bulge, they are out of place. The image of the tumour exemplifies the general tendency of New Crobuzon's architecture to grow inconceivably, to sprawl – to literally "ooze out of its bounds" (*PSS:* 539). Urban planning as in the cities presented by Sennett does not apply. There is no grid plan for New Crobuzon as a means of urban planning as it can be traced back to cities in Sumer and ancient Egypt (see Sennett 1996: 106). More typical of Miéville's city is what happened during the construction of Fell Stop:

> The planners and money-men [...] had opened the railway station, Fell Stop, and had started building another in Rudewood itself, before anything more than a narrow strip around the railway had been cleared. There had been plans for another station beyond that, and the tracks had extended into the forest accordingly. There had even been tentative, absurdly hubristic schemes to extend the rails hundreds of miles south or west, to link New Crobuzon to Myrshock or Cobsea. Then, the money had run out. There had been some financial crisis, some speculative bubble had burst [...], and the project had been killed in its infancy. The trains had still visited Fell Stop, pointlessly waiting a few minutes before returning to the city. Rudewood quickly reclaimed the land south of the empty architecture, assimilating the nameless empty station and the rusting tracks. (*PSS:* 124)

If there is any planning at all, it involves bogus deals, speculation, rough ideas and wishful thinking, eventually dooming the project to fail. At the same time, deserted areas rust and decay, others sprawl inconceivably, and the extent of human and xenian control is often far from clear. Thus, although Miéville's giant city (or city giant) is not really breathing freely, it seems to have a life of its own to a certain degree.

Still, there are also reciprocal effects between New Crobuzon and its inhabitants. A mutual sense of decay occurs in terms of symmetry, for example. The tumourous sprawling of New Crobuzon thwarts symmetrical thinking that can also be found in its population. Whereas in ancient Rome people were fascinated with the geometry and symmetry of the human body and transferred them to the city's body, New Crobuzon does not have this symmetry. Consequentially, its people share its fate. Remaking as an extreme form of mutilatory punishment, the urban rebel Jack Half-a-Prayer armed with a mantis claw, the removal of Lin's headlegs by Motley, Motley's deformed body, the wingless Yagharek, the ears cut off by the Weaver – numerous characters are as deformed as the city itself. The shared bodily experience is pain, which brings Sennett into play again: his basic idea of physical crises, of dissonance and unease as prerequisites for compassion strikingly figures in *Perdido Street Station*. It is fairly remarkable that Miéville's main characters suffer both mentally and physically as individuals and still become a team that is going through numerous encounters and fight after fight.[10] They lose their bodily health, their minds, and their loved ones – and still, they experience their city anew and feel alive as never before.[11] Living in New Crobuzon is an endless crisis where one is continuously experiencing resistance and struggle, caught between perishing and feeling alive, between decay and sprawling growth. City and body share the same fate, after all, and are closely intertwined in *Perdido Street Station.*

Not only is New Crobuzon given a body – the interplay of materiality and discursivity also hinges on the novel's characters. Isaac serves as a first example. On his first encounter with Yagharek, the rogue scientist is asked about his philosophy of science. His answer is as follows:

> 'I think of myself as the main station for all schools of thought. Like Perdido Street Station. You know it? [...] Unavoidable, ain't it? Fucking massive great thing.' Isaac patted his belly, maintaining the analogy. 'All the train-lines meet there – Sud Line, Dexter, Verso, Head and Sink Lines; everything has to pass through it. That's like me.' (*PSS:* 45)

Isaac compares himself to the massive station both in terms of the mere physical similarities of size (materiality) as well as conceptually (discursivity). The station that "ooze[s] out of its bounds" (*PSS:* 539) is the city's operational centre of public transport, Isaac's transgressive research is the interdisciplinary fulcrum of its schools of science. "Isaac, like Perdido Street Station [...], is diffuse and permeable, but also central" (Gordon 2003a: 467), not only as far as its location on the map is concerned, but also its role in the unfolding narrative. "Its diffuse, motley, hybrid, chaotic nature is what makes the heterotopian space of Perdido Street Station the hub of the city, geographically and novelistically, since multiple plot lines converge there in a climactic battle" at the end of the novel (Gordon 2003a: 467).[12] Another building can be paralleled to Isaac in the context of materiality and discursivity even more aptly: his warehouse in Brock Marsh. A quick glimpse at the map reveals that its geographical – and hence material – location is even more central than Perdido Street Station. More importantly, it is the place where everything starts in terms of plot. Of course, Yagharek's crime and punish-

---

10 See Joan Gordon's remarkable reading of character connections in *Perdido Street Station* as relations of mateship and hybridity (Gordon 2003a: 468–474).
11 See, for example, Yagharek's section at the end of chapter LI (*PSS:* 590–596).
12 See also Gordon 2003a: 461–462, where the centrality of Isaac for the novel is further exploited in analogy to Miéville himself as a writer of Weird Fiction inspired by a multitude of genres and authors.

ment came first, but it is only due to Isaac's school of thought, his engagement and research which unfold in his lab, that the "Midsummer Nightmares" (*PSS:* 323) come about. He acquires the grub that will turn into the slake-moth and escape from his lab, free its companions and haunt the city, so that Isaac and his group have to fight it at the end. The place of origin is rather his lab in the warehouse than the station. As Rudgutter puts it during the raid of Isaac's place: "It started from here [...]. This is the centre. This is the source" (*PSS:* 342). The warehouse is the true centre, the umbilicus of the plot that inscribes itself into the city's body in a nightmarish fashion.[13] It is *Perdido Street Station*'s narrative navel, the "hellhole" (Sennett 1996: 108) that gives birth to Isaac's ideas, the moths going berserk, and the unfolding story.[14]

Yagharek: From Bird-Man to Man
As a last point on the interplay of human body and city body, Yagharek's development from a total stranger to a man completely absorbed in the city deserves some attention. In the following, starting with his first steps and spatial practices, I will trace his way through New Crobuzon as he struggles to appropriate the unknown urban space and becomes himself ultimately transformed. His arrival in Smog Bend on board of a barge at the novel's very beginning is an encounter of uncertainty: "*My captain leaps ashore and ties up. His relief is draining to see. He is wittering gruffly in triumph and ushering me quickly ashore and away and I alight, as slowly as if onto coals, picking my way through the rubbish and the broken glass*" (*PSS:* 3).[15] Whereas the bargeman easily leaps ashore, Yagharek's very first steps in New Crobuzon are tentative, intent on dodging even the tiniest obstacles. In a first attempt at becoming independent, he "*ignore[s] the man's eager*

---

[13] I take Gordon's point that Perdido Street Station is the location for the climactic battle where multiple plot lines come together, but it is more arbitrary than it seems at first glance. Isaac tells the Construct Council that his crisis engine needs "the city's focal point, where all the lines converge. We have to go to Perdido Street Station" (*PSS:* 511), but at his arrival at the station, it becomes clear that he lied: "'We're not going to get very close to the centre of Perdido Street Station.' [...] *It doesn't matter*, he thought. *Picking the station was just something to tell the Construct Council, to get out of the dump and away from it*" (*PSS:* 543–544). In a way, this looks like another trick by Miéville played on the reader in terms of cartography.
[14] As mentioned earlier, the idea of the hellhole or umbilicus can be traced back to a particular Roman custom related to founding a city, where "'a chamber [...] consecrated to infernal gods' below the earth's crust" (Sennett 1996: 108) was consecreated and sealed with a square stone that marks the centre and starting point for all construction of the new city.
[15] All passages narrated by Yagharek are printed in italics in the novel, all of which will be retained for this study withour further indication.

explanations and walk[s] away through this time-bleached zone, past yawning doors that promise the comfort of true dark and an escape from the river stench. [...] A city light is promising itself in the east." (*PSS:* 3–4). The first promise of a dark hideout is thwarted in this never-sleeping city of wan light. Yagharek lacks proficiency on all levels of Löw's habitus: he is not a creature of the night (perception), he has never been in a human city (experience), and – as a garuda, a bird-man – he never had to walk through it in order to orient himself (performance). Consequently, lost and a complete stranger, Yagharek turns towards the materiality of the city as a means of orientation: "*I will follow the trainlines. I will stalk in their shadow as they pass by over the houses and towers and barracks and offices and prisons of the city, I will track them from the arches that anchor them to the earth. I must find my way in*" (*PSS:* 4). The arches of the train lines become his own anchors, his checkpoints for his way into the body of the city, his desperate means of protection being his cloak and the illusion created by the wooden construction of fake wings under it. Shortly after, in his first encounter with Isaac, Yagharek does not want to enter into a commitment. Asked by Isaac where he can find him, his only answer is: "I do not know where I will be, Grimnebulin. I shun this city. It hunts me. I must keep moving" (*PSS:* 45). The garuda is still a stranger in town. He needs to stay in New Crobuzon because Isaac is his only hope of getting his ability of flight back, but he is still a foreign body, futilely trying to avoid getting sucked into the interplay of materiality and discursivity. The city is his hunter and the habitat in which it hunts at the same time, while he as a newcomer is only prey. After a short encounter with a city-born garuda who mocks and pelts him, he realises that there is nobody to join forces with: "*In this city, those who look like me are not like me. I made the mistake once (tired and afraid and desperate for help) of doubting that. [...] I realized then as the stones splintered my pillow of old paint that I was alone. And so, and so, I know that I must live without respite from this isolation*" (*PSS:* 50).

However, Yagharek begins to change: "*I have taken to foraging alone after nightfall when the city quiets and becomes introspective. I walk as an intruder on its solipsistic dream. I came by darkness, I live by darkness. The savage brightness of the desert is like some legend I heard a long time ago. My existence grows nocturnal. My beliefs change*" (*PSS:* 51). The former stranger and victim slowly becomes an intruder; the former creature of the day becomes nocturnal and thus adopts new spatial practices and mental concepts. The discrepancy is best visible in the difference between the Cymek desert winds and the city-winds and how Yagharek relates to them:

> I share the streets with aimlessly moving scraps of paper and little whirlwinds of dust, with motes that pass like erratic thieves under eaves and through doors. I remember the desert

winds: the Khamsin that scourges the land like smokeless fire; the Föhm that bursts from hot mountainsides as if in ambush; the sly Simoom that inveigles its way through leather sandscreens and library doors. The winds of the city are a more melancholy breed. They explore like lost souls, looking in at dusty gaslit windows. We are brethren, the city-winds and I. We wander together. (PSS: 51)

In the following passages, it is remarkable how often Yagharek uses first person plural, referring to himself and the winds: "*We have found [...]. We have seen [...]. We have watched [...]*" (*PSS:* 51). Yagharek is still without human (or xenian) company. The city-winds are his ersatz brethren for his lost past. He has still not arrived in New Crobuzon properly and is still without a place, but he is trying to get along now by walking.[16] His change is also noticeable in the way he perceives his own body: "*I am forgetting the weight, the sweep, the motion of wings*" (*PSS:* 51). Sometimes he climbs Isaac's warehouse that becomes a temporary shelter and a place of healing: "*The thought of all that energy of [Isaac's] mind channelled towards flight, my flight, my deliverance, lessens the itching in my ruined back*" (*PSS:* 51). It is only by digging his claws into the roof, into the city's body that he can resist the anger of his city-wind companion who wants him back on the ground:

> The wind tugs me harder when I am here: it feels betrayed. It knows that if I am made whole it will lose its nighttime companion in the brick mire and midden of New Crobuzon. So it chastises me when I lie there, suddenly threatening to pull me from my perch into the wide stinking river, clutching my feathers, fat petulant air warning me not to leave it; but I grip the roof with my claws and let the healing vibrations pass up from Grimnebulin's mind through the rumbling slate into my poor flesh. (PSS: 51–52)

Yagharek turns from a stranger to an explorer to a "*parasite*" (*PSS:* 52).[17] Only sometimes, when he climbs a tower, he remembers flight itself, the freedom, and the independence from ground-level materiality that can be found in the desert winds of his past:

> Up in the thinner air, the winds lose the melancholy curiosity they have at street level. They abandon their second-floor petulance. Stirred by towers that poke above the host of city light [...] the winds rejoice and play. I can dig my claws into the rim of a building's crown and spread my arms and feel the buffets and gouts of boisterous air and I can close my eyes and remember, for a moment, what it is to fly. (PSS: 52)

Three different kinds of wind circulate in the city: the melancholy wanderers on the ground, those freely playing over the city, and the angry gusts in between.

---

[16] Cf. also de Certeau's remark: "To walk is to lack a place" (de Certeau 1984: 103).
[17] See also Yagharek's spatial practice as a vagrant (chapter III.2.1 of this study).

They are different indeed because they relate to different layers of the city's materiality and are thus triggering different emotions, discourses and bodily actions in Yagharek. Later in the novel, in the course of the crisis related to the slake-moths, Yagharek unwillingly becomes a member of Isaac's group: "*At first, I felt sick to be around them, all these men, their rushing, heavy, stinking breaths [...]. I wanted the cold again, the darkness below the railways, where ruder forms of life struggle and fight and die and are eaten. There is a comfort in that brute simplicity*" (*PSS:* 265). His first point of reference, the railway, still reverberates. However, he has to adapt:

> But this is not my land and that is not my choice to make. I have struggled to contain myself. I have struggled with the alien jurisprudence of this city, all sharp divides and fences, lines that separate this from that and yours from mine. I have modelled myself on this. I have sought comfort and protection in owning myself, in being my own, my isolate, my private property for this the first time. (PSS: 265)

He has to come to terms with the city's materiality which is rendered by the discursivity of jurisprudence, by the power of conceived space that goes along with the differentiation of private and public property marked by fences and walls, in short: the (material) pre-selection of possibilities as described by de Certeau, which shape his practices accordingly.

Yagharek also has to learn that it is impossible to live in his desired isolation. He is being woven into New Crobuzon's social network, whether he likes it or not. Social space is, after all, a social product: "*The splendid isolation I have sought is crumbled. I need Grimnebulin, Grimnebulin needs his friend* [Lublamai, the first victim of the escaping moth, RZ], *his friend needs succour from us all. It is simple mathematics to cancel common terms and discover that I need succour, too. I must offer it to others, to save myself*" (*PSS:* 265). Getting along in the city is not only based upon the relation between the city body and self, but also upon the relations to other human bodies in the city. Meeting, fighting, and befriending others, in Altnöder's words, continuously constructs and reconstructs identity and alterity with the individual body as a projection screen in the overall process (see Altnöder 2009: 303). Yagharek's acceptance is inevitable and sometimes interrupted by the winds of the past, but hesitant: "*I was once a creature of the air, and it remembers me. When I climb to the city heights and lean out into the wind, it tickles me with currents and vectors from my past*" (*PSS:* 265–266); in these moments, he feels the burden of not being able to fly anymore: "*But I am earthbound*" (*PSS:* 266). By and by, he learns how to move in the city: "*I walk bent double along the sides of the railways, the trains screaming at me in irate warning as they blast by. I sneak now across the rail bridge, watching the Tar coil beneath me. [...] Looking over to the west I can see over the water and* the swell of Riverskin houses to the tip of the Glasshouse" (*PSS:* 438). He gets to know his environment, acquires new points of reference in the topography of the cityscape and is able to name them. Yagharek, due to his interaction with the city's body, has entered a stage of transformation, though the outcome is still unclear to himself: "*I am changing. [...] Something is welling up under my own skin. I am not sure who I am. [...] I have trailed these humans as if I am dumb. A worthless, mindless presence, without opinion or intellect. Without knowing who I am, how can I know what to say?*" (*PSS:* 438).

In his search for identity, Yagharek retraces his past. First, the retracing takes place in remembrance of his way to New Crobuzon and the different selves he had appropriated: the respected garuda at home, the raging gladiator in Shankell, the tired wanderer in the grasslands, "*the lost thing that wandered the concrete walkways of the city introspective and lost [...]. I am none of those. I am changing, and I do not know what I will be*" (*PSS:* 438). Going back in memory fails. His second attempt is a bodily one:

> I shall wander for a night and a day. I will retrace the steps that once I made in the shade of the railways. I will stalk the city's monstrous geography and find the streets that bore me here, the squat channels in the brick to which I owe my life and self. I will find the tramps who shared my food [...]. They became my tribe, atomized and ruined and broken, but still some kind of tribe. [...] I will find them again for my own sake, not theirs. (PSS: 439)

Yagharek is not going back for the company, but for finding out about his own self. It is worth mentioning that this happens during the preparations for the climactic battle against the slake-moths, and the garuda does not know what the future will bring. He sees two options: either failure and death, or victory and the regaining of flight. In both cases, he anticipates change: "*I feel as if I walk these streets for the last time*" (*PSS:* 439). At the end of the novel, it will become clear that he was both right and wrong (his group will win, but he will not fly again). During his walk, he ponders on the group again: "*If I am to be anything real, something more than the mute, imbecile presence I have so far been, I should stay and intervene and plan and prepare and nod at their suggestions, supplement with my own*" – to be a full member of the group (*PSS:* 440). However, he feels the urge to go out and find himself first: "*I tried to say my sorries, to let [them] [...] know that I am one with them, that I am part of the gang. The crew. The posse. The moth-hunters. But it rang hollow in my skull. I will look and find myself, and then I will know if I can tell them that. And if not, what I can say instead*" (*PSS:* 440). It is striking that he says "one *with* them" instead of "one *of* them" and that he is searching for an accurate description for the group. Still, he feels a need to help them: "*Even if I find myself an outsider, I will not let them die unaided*" (*PSS:* 440). The retracing's schedule is clear:

> The noises of New Crobuzon fill my ears. I will follow them, welcome them. I will let them surround me. I will dive into the hot, city life. Under arch and over stone, through the sparse bone forest of the Ribs, into the brick burrows of Badside and Dog Fenn, through the booming industry of Gross Coil. Like Lemuel sniffing for contacts I will retrace all the steps I have made. And here and there, I hope, among the spires and the crammed architecture, I will touch the immigrants, the refugees, the outsiders who remake New Crobuzon every day. This place with bastard culture. This mongrel city. I will hear the sounds of Perrick violining or the Gnurr Kett funeral dirge or a Chet stone-riddle, or I will smell the goat porridge they eat in Neovadan or see a doorway painted with the symbols of a Cobsea printer-captain... A long, long way from their homes. Homeless. Home. (PSS: 441)

This time, the retracing is not a mental one but one of bodily performance. Revisiting his vagrant times and places shall help him to find out who he is. He wants to learn from his former contacts and other refugees, who all are both homeless and at home in New Crobuzon, how they set up their discourses with the city and its inhabitants. The performance is primarily guided by the senses, as in Löw's triad of perception, experience, and performance, and thus inseparable from both his own body and the materiality of the "mongrel city" which is as unsure about what it is as Yagharek himself. The necessary practice demands continuous reconstruction ("who remake New Crobuzon every day") and surrender to the environment and not only a full exposure of the body, but the interpenetration of Yagharek's body by the city: "*All around me will be New Crobuzon, seeping in through my skin*" (*PSS*: 441). After the fight against the moth in the Glasshouse and the destruction of its eggs, Yagharek's transformation is still incomplete. Again, he uses first person plural multiple times (*PSS*: 497) in reference to Isaac and the others, but he is still too much occupied with his past, as one can see when Pengefinchess tells her story. She is the only survivor of the hired adventurers who fought with Isaac and the others in the Glasshouse. She tells them the story how the three adventurers came together and how they came to New Crobuzon. Then,

> [h]er testimony ends. It demands response, like some ritual liturgy. [...] I try. I open my beak and the story of my crime and my punishment and my exile wells up in my throat. It almost emerges, it almost bursts through the crack. But I batten it down. It is not connected. It is not for tonight. Pengefinchess's story is one of selfishness and plunder, yet it is made by the telling into a valedictory for dead comrades. My history of selfishness and exile resists transmutation. It cannot but be a base story of base things. I am silent. (PSS: 498)

Yagharek still "resists transmutation", just like his story does. After the final battle and the defeat of the rest of the moths, however, the change is expected to happen finally. The city's body is freed, so now Yagharek can be free again, too. Since he did not die, and since Isaac succeeded in building his crisis engine, one expects Isaac to keep his promise: one expects Yagharek to regain flight and either head off or to become a full member of Isaac's group in a joint escape from the government, maybe even leaving the city together. The group moves together, they watch each other's step as they move through the city, hunted by both Motley's men and the milita.¹⁸ They are *"[w]eary and exhilarated. [...] [I]t is hard not to catch each other's eyes and smile or caw softly in astonishment"*, and again Yagharek makes frequent use of first person plural (*PSS:* 591). The expectation is thwarted since the next step in search for identity is the betrayal by Isaac who, after having met Kar'uchai, the victim of Yagharek's crime, refuses to make him fly again and leaves him. Yagharek was not with the group at that time, taking another stroll through the city instead, *"seeking some spurious, faltering freedom in the city. [...] I visited Howl Barrow today. I saw Lichford. I stood before a grey wall in Barrackham, the crumbling skin of a dead factory, and read all the graffiti. I was foolish. I took risks. Did not remain carefully hidden. I felt almost drunk with that little snatch of freedom, eager for more"* (*PSS:* 617). Is this the freedom of a more tourist-like approach to the city (he "visits" Howl Barrow, takes the time to read graffiti, and is not on his guard) or the supposed practice of someone who is finally ready to be earthbound and live in the city?

In any case, only temporal freedom is offered. For resolution, Yagharek needs to take two more steps. First, he not only rethinks his way to the city, but also the events that made him an outcast: the crime and the resulting punishment (*PSS:* 618–619). Second, with healing and reestablishment finally lost, it is again a question of materiality and discursivity directly tied to his body. His wooden contraption that resembles his long-gone wings under the cloak is gone. He climbs a block of houses:

> One hundred and fifty feet or more. There are plenty of taller structures in New Crobuzon. But this is high enough that the block rears out of the streets and stone and brick [...]. I stalk past the rubble and the signs of bonfires [...]. I am alone in the skyline tonight. The brick wall that contains the roofspace is five feet high. I lean on it and look out, to all sides. (PSS: 620)

He takes in the city he has been roaming for so long. Orientation is fairly easy now:

> I know what it is I see. I can place myself exactly. That is a glimpse of the Glasshouse dome, a smudge of dirty light between two gas towers. The clenching ribs are only a mile away [...]. The lights, the lights of all different colours, all around me. I vault easily on the wall, and

---

18 For the new ways of moving and the spatial practices involved, see the beginning of this chapter.

> stand. I am on top of New Crubuzon now. It is such an enormous thing. Such a great wallow. There is everything within it, spread out under my feet. (PSS: 620)

Finally, after arriving in the city's filth on ground level at the beginning of the novel, he is now on top of it at the end of the novel, both physically and mentally. For a moment, the reader is tricked into thinking Yagharek might throw himself off the roof:

> I stretch out my arms. [...] I close my eyes. [...] I can imagine it with absolute exactitude. A flight. [...] I feel the wind force my fingers apart. I am buffeted invitingly. I feel the twitching as my ragged flanges of wingbone stretch. I will not do this any more. I will not be this cripple, this earth-bound bird, any longer. This half-life ends now, with my hope. I can so well picture a last flight, a swift, elegant curving sweep through the air that parts like a lost lover to welcome me. Let the wind take me. I lean forward on the wall, out over the tumbling city, into the air. (PSS: 621)

Instead of suicide, however, Yagharek finds another resolution. He plucks himself; he gets rid of all his feathers, revealing the skin underneath as another layer of his body, stripping his body from everything except its ultimate layer that enables him to get in touch with his exterior and thus the materiality of the city body. A last offer is being made by the 'fReemade' Jack Half-a-Prayer, an escaped Remade, New Crobuzon's deformed version of Robin Hood. He sees a companion in misfortune in Yagharek and wants Yagharek to join him:

> [His offer] is generous, but I must decline. He offers me the half-world. He offers to share his bastard liminal life, his interstitial city. [...] He does not fit in. [...] He sees another broken-down half-thing, another exhausted relic that he might convert to fight his unthinkable fight, another for whom existence in any world is impossible, a paradox, a bird that cannot fly. And he offers me a way out, into his uncommunity, his margin, his mongrel city. (PSS, p. 622–623)

By plucking his feathers, however, Yagharek's transformation is complete. The bird that cannot fly is gone due to his bodily change: "*My face a mass of raw and ragged flesh, bleeding copiously from a hundred little punctures where the feathers left my flesh. [...] I stand before the building in my new flesh*" (PSS: 622). Yagharek does not fit into Jack's life on the margin. With the garuda gone, he is finally able to fully appropriate the city space, to modify the force field of materiality and discursivity between his body and the body of New Crobuzon. "*I must leave this half-breed world alone [...]. I am not the earthbound garuda any more. That one is dead. This is a new life. I am not a half-thing, a failed neither-nor. I have torn the misleading quills from my skin and made it smooth, and below that avian affectation, I am the same as my citizen fellows*" (PSS: 623). Only at the very end, Yagharek finds a way of life, after having found his way through this bastard city:

> I can live foresquare in one world. I [...] turn away, stepping off into the dim lamplight to the east, towards the university campus and Ludmead Station, through my world of bricks and mortar and tar, bazaars and markets, sulphur-lit streets. It is night and I must hurry to find my bed, to find a bed in this my city where I can live my foresquare life. [...] I turn and walk away into the city my home, not bird or garuda, not miserable crossbreed. I turn and walk into my home, the city, a man. (PSS: 623)

Flesh and blood at last, a body made for walking, for producing social space in an overwhelming network of spatial practices. After a long and painful process of inscribing himself into the city's flesh, Yagharek is finally bound to New Crobuzon and ready to overcome Sennett's tactile crisis. Thus, *Perdido Street Station* highlights the interactions of human body and city body. Human bodies clash as they struggle for power; different designs of city bodies clash as they sprawl and fall to pieces; human body and city body clash until they finally come together in Yagharek as the avatar of the overall appropriation. Thus, Yagharek becomes much more than Isaac's sidekick in a story and a city in which he does not seem to belong. Yagharek being a key figure in terms of urban walking and experience is also the answer to the question why the novel starts and ends with his homodiegetic passages: a vast process connects the novel's first passage of Yagharek as a foreigner and the last passage of someone who, turned into a man, can finally find a new home. Furthermore, the reader is going through the very same process (see Moylan 2000: 6): at the beginning, Bas-Lag in general and New Crobuzon in particular are strange, unfamiliar, and bewildering places – and at the end, one has learned a lot about this strange world (and is ready for *The Scar*, the second volume of the Bas-Lag trilogy).

IV.2.2 *The City & The City:* Perceived Space and the Force of Unseeing

The City & The City offers a very distinct idea of urban space in a dystopia. The reader is hardly given any information about particular quarters as in *Perdido Street Station*; instead, the description stays on the surface of the strict separation between the overlapping cities Besźel and Ul Qoma. The novel's fascination lies in the power relations between perceived and conceived space. As already spelled out in chapter II.2.2, what should geographically be one city is actually treated as two because the authorities say so. The city space is accordingly separated (i.e. conceived) by order of the Oversight Committee, who classify every building and every street as either total, alter, or crosshatch. Total and alter areas are areas which are treated as separate, i. e. as belonging to one city only; total always refers to one's own city and alter refers to the foreign city. Thus, both a deictic element and a certain interchangeability of classification are highlighted: to people from Ul Qoma, Ul Qoma is the total area, while Besź people will refer to Besźel as total; both use the same term while referring to a different place. Crosshatch streets and places belong to both cities in the sense that they are used by both. Materially speaking, the cities overlap here, but in terms of performance, they are treated as separate. The performance in question is called unseeing: whenever people from Besźel and Ul Qoma walk on a crosshatch street, they ignore each other as much as they can because, although they are grosstopically close, they still are in different cities.[19] Citizens of both cities are forced to comply; unseeing alter elements is mandatory if one does not want to commit breach and disappear by being taken by Breach, who ensure that the cities stay separate. Hence, the conceived space of the authorities dictates what should be perceived by the people and thus their perceived space, which in turn renders the lived space as the people accept the restriction of their environment. The visual restriction entails a restriction of the discursivity of everday life. It is especially the constructed element of the conceived space in *The City & the City* that shows its connection to dominated spaces in Lefebvre (see Lefebvre 1991: 164).

Unseeing – a (Not So) Social Practice
The relation between materiality and discursivity, and between perceived and conceived space in *The City & The City* hinges on the practice of unseeing. After establishing the city space as an inherently human product that goes beyond mere architectural construction, this chapter's main concern will be how unseeing has an impact on the spaces in question by prioritising discursivity over materiality.

Separation in *The City & The City* is not so much a matter of materialism, but a matter of exceptional perception. Inspector Borlú, the main protagonist, makes it quite clear that other "split" cities such as Berlin or Jerusalem, split by walls and barbed wire, are nothing like Besźel and Ul Qoma: those city splits are "'[t]otally missing the point'" (*TC&TC:* 90) as the separation of Miéville's two cities is primarily a mental one that helps to keep up the spatial or material one. Although the weather is not different in Ul Qoma, Borlú experiences it as different: "It would not be winter for weeks, and though it was no colder in Ul Qoma

---

19 Consequently, crosshatch streets also have two names, a Besź one and a Ul Qoman one.

than in Besźel, it felt colder to me" (*TC&TC:* 231). The weather conditions in both cities are judged differently, for example when Borlú makes fun of Dhatt and the weather in Ul Qoma: "'I like rain. Anyway, this is drizzle. You wouldn't last a day in Besźel. We get *real* rain in Besźel.'" (*TC&TC:* 237 [original italics]). If you stay in your part of the city, the only way of getting to know the alter city is to consume mass media, whose images of the alter city are blurred. Here is Borlú's impression of colours and light after having arrived in Ul Qoma for the first in time in years: "Day, so the light was that of the overcast cold sky, not the twists of neon I had seen in so many programs about the neighbouring country, which the producers evidently thought it easier for us to visualise in its garish night" (*TC&TC:* 162).

The arbitrary separation of Besźel and Ul Qoma is first of all due to the practice of unseeing, which shall be elucidated in the following. The people from Besźel and Ul Qoma are ascribed different gaits, postures, facial expressions, and dress styles, most of which appear to be clichés or even results of propaganda because these behaviours are imposed on the citizens (see *TC&TC:* 161). Citizens of both countries are trained (one might even say brainwashed) to more or less instinctively ignore all input from the other city, both from its alter areas as well as in the shared crosshatch areas. Besides unseeing, there is also unsmelling (*TC&TC:* 66; 303) and unhearing (*TC&TC:* 172), but unseeing as visual (non-)perception is paramount. In some instances, it seems to come as a reflex – or, as Borlú puts it, as a "prediscursive instinct" (*TC&TC:* 93): "The few unseeing Besź pedestrians crossed without probably being conscious that they did so to the other side of the street" (*TC&TC:* 174). Yet, unseeing does not come as an automatism. Firstly, it is something children seem to have to learn (*TC&TC:* 46). What is more, depending on how specific the given information is, unseeing might become a matter of processing, as in Borlú's encounter with the old woman shortly after the finding of Mahalia's body: "An elderly woman was walking slowly away from me in a shambling way. She turned her head and looked at me. I was struck by her motion, and I met her eyes. I wondered if she wanted to tell me something. In my glance I took in her clothes, her way of walking, of holding herself, and looking" (*TC&TC:* 14). Borlú checks the woman's outer appearance as well as her habitus in order to find out where she belongs. Then, suddenly, he understands: "With a hard start, I realised that she was not on Gunter-Strász at all, and that I should not have seen her" (*TC&TC:* 14) – but he has seen her. The solution, then, is to pretend that nothing happened, to unsee her as fast as possible:

> Immediately and flustered I looked away, and she did the same, with the same speed. I raised my head, towards an aircraft on its final descent. When after some seconds I looked

back up, unnoticing the old woman stepping heavily away, I looked carefully instead of at her in her foreign street at the facades of the nearby and local GunterStrász, that depressed zone. (*TC&TC*, p. 14)

The process is fairly intricate: although he looks "carefully" away, thus unnoticing her, he still 'sees' that the old woman is not simply walking away, but in a specific manner – she is "stepping heavily away." Despite the practice of unseeing, Borlú still grasps a detail as if the woman was still visible in the corner of his eye while he tries to ignore her as well as he can. Hence, perceived space in *The City & The City* finds itself in a fragile stance caught between conscious processing and unconscious exposure that becomes most visible in crosshatch zones. There, on the one hand, one automatically knows what one is supposed to see and what not while on the other hand one is continuously running checks and pushing not-belonging elements into the background if the unconscious routine goes wrong. The correction (Borlú unseeing the old woman after having accidentally seen her) then seems to be both an unconscious reflex and a conscious process. The example of Borlú seeing and unseeing the old woman is the first in the novel, and it sets the benchmark for later scenes. Borlú often states that he can first see what is going on in the city he is in, but objects or persons whom he is supposed to unsee are there nevertheless, and one often has the impression that he is not only aware of the fact, but in a way also aware of the objects or persons themselves. A sentence such as: "Most of those around us were in Besźel so we saw them" (*TC&TC*: 21) makes this quite clear. Those around him who are in Ul Qoma while he is in Besźel may be in another city, but they do not simply vanish. A striking instance is Borlú's first unseeing of Besźel after his arrival in Ul Qoma:

> I looked at what Dhatt showed me. Unseeing, of course, but I could not fail to be aware of all the familiar places I passed grosstopically, the streets at home I regularly walked, now a whole city away, particular cafés I frequented that we passed, but in another country. I had them in the background now, hardly any more present than Ul Qoma was when I was at home. I held my breath. I was unseeing Besźel. I had forgotten what this was like; I had tried and failed to imagine it. I was seeing Ul Qoma. (*TC&TC:* 161–162)

Alter areas are still there somewhere, but pushed into the background. Borlú is aware that they are there, but they are supposed to be in another country. One cannot completely shield oneself from alter input, but it is being pushed to the margins of perception. Thus, the entire novel plays with Luhmann's notion of unmarked space. Since observation does not go without differentiation in order to be able to describe something (see Reinfandt 2000), the unmarked space usually refers to what stays beyond the limits of perception as one tries to cross the border to the so far unreached. In Miéville's novel, however, unseeing is the attempt to wilfully deny parts of what you see, hear, or smell, to let perception fail on purpose. Citizens of Besźel and Ul Qoma limit their own observational potential and thus deny themselves the possibility of crossing the border into the unmarked space (i.e. into the alter city) because of the rules established and maintained by the Oversight Committee. The authorities determine what is marked and what is unmarked, which is quite problematic if the unmarked includes an entire city. In contrast to Luhmann's unmarked space, the alter areas in *The City & The City* are intentionally conceived by the authorities and then sold to the people as a naturally unmarked space (which therefore is not supposed to have a discursive presence). Breaching can consequently be taken as an either unconscious (Borlú seeing the old woman in the streets) or conscious (Borlú, while being in Ul Qoma, shooting Yorjavic, who is in Besźel at that moment) advance into the unmarked space. Human perception in *The City & The City* is a continuous battle between what is grosstopically or materialistically speaking there and what is not supposed to be there.

Sometimes, when there is too much input from the alter area, unseeing can also become quite arduous:

> It was, not surprisingly that day perhaps, hard to observe borders, to see and unsee only what I should, on my way home. I was hemmed in by people not in my city, walking slowly through areas crowded but not crowded in Besźel. I focused on the stones really around me – cathedrals, bars, the brick flourishes of what had been a school – that I had grown up with. I ignored the rest or tried. (*TC&TC:* 44)

When the alter input is too much, unseeing does not come as easy as on other occasions. Also note the attempt to focus on what is "really around" Borlú, which, to him, refers to a specific, mentally differentiated section of reality, whereas foreigners would refer to the wholeness of materiality. For people not from Besźel or Ul Qoma, it becomes almost absurd when locals dodge masses of people who, to foreigners, are on the same street, whereas they are a country away for the locals (*TC&TC:* 54), or when locals routinely dodge, unhear and unsee something as large, loud and unavoidable as an alter police car with lights and alarm switched on (*TC&TC:* 282).

Non-unseeing Tourists
The practice of unseeing in the novel can also be related to the parameters of Löw's intrinsic logic of cities (size, density, homogeneity/heterogeneity of the city vs. perception, experience, performance of the human habitus and body; see chapter IV.1). Due to the special perception of the locals, *The City & The*

City has a specific intrinsic logic that foregrounds differentiation as the absence of homogeneity to such an extent that it renders one city into two. From a sociological perspective, the novel alludes to the tendency of judging cities in our time not as a unified whole anymore, but as patchwork cities (see Schroer 2006: 237), with diverging parts. The outcome is a formation of several cities on the same territory which either ignore and do not care about each other or even become enemies (see Sieverts 2000: 171). The parameters for this separation are humanly constructed and are thus also a matter of the human body. In contrast to Yagharek in *Perdido Street Station*, however, characters in *The City & The City* – except for the unificationists – do not strive for an all-encompassing way of getting 'in touch' with the city, but for a superimposed partiality. The separation can only be kept up because people's experience enables them to continuously let perception go wrong, because they do not long for the unmarked space, which in turn enables the specific performance. When one switches the focus from locals to visitors or tourists, it is on the side of the habitus attributed to the body where differences occur. Of course, people not from Besźel or Ul Qoma are not used to unseeing. In order to prevent them from breaching and the resulting expulsion, they usually receive special instruction:

> [T]hey would have had to undergo mandatory training and passed the not-unstringent entrance exam, both its theoretical and practical-role-play elements, to qualify for their visas. They would know, at least in outline, key signifiers of architecture, clothing, alphabet and manner, outlaw colours and gestures, obligatory details – and, depending on their Besź teacher, the supposed distinctions in national physiognomies – distinguishing Besźel and Ul Qoma, and their citizens. [...] Crucially, they would know enough to avoid obvious breaches of their own. (*TC&TC*: 93)

However, fooling your own perception, or forcing it to suddenly ignore what you have been seeing for years or decades, to suddenly make a selection of what to see and what not, is not that straightforward. Borlú acknowledges that, despite some training, it is impossible for foreigners to unsee properly:

> After a two-week or however-long-it-was course, no one thought visitors would have metabolised the deep prediscursive instinct for our borders that Besź and Ul Qomans have, to have picked up real rudiments of unseeing. But we did insist that they acted as if they had. We, and the authorities of Ul Qoma, expected strict overt decorum, interacting with, and indeed obviously noticing, our crosshatched neighbouring city-state not at all. (*TC&TC*: 93)

People not from the two cities, in their routines of observation and differentiation, are used to advance into the unmarked space. Unable to unsee, tourists are supposed to pretend that they actually can unsee in order to avoid breach, in order to keep the spatial order intact – at least on the surface. Again, the novel displays differences in patterns of perception that render the urban topography. One can see how – literally speaking – superficial the cities' characteristics are to tourists. They stay at the material surface without the locals' deeper indoctrination. To put it according to Löw's parameters, they lack the experience in order to adjust their perception, but they are expected to behave (perform) as if they could. Locals are in turn not only aware of the superficial performance of tourists, they also have to play along – they have to pretend that the tourists' unseeing works, as in the case of Mahalia's father, Mr. Geary, who is from the USA:

> So long as they do not point and coo [...], everyone concerned can indulge the possibility that there is no breach. It is that restraint that the pre-visa training teaches, rather than a local's rigorous unseeing, and most students have the nous to understand that. We all, Breach included, give the benefit of the doubt to visitors when possible. In the mirror of the car I saw Mr. Geary watch a passing truck. I unsaw it because it was in Ul Qoma. (*TC&TC:* 94)

Borlú has to play along and pretend he has not seen Mr. Geary's illegal seeing of the truck in what one could call a second-order unseeing. Here, at the very latest, the degree of construction becomes apparent. The body continuously runs a discursive operation that separates the city space into here and there (and into here and not here) according to instilled rules. The body positions itself against the city's materiality in its wholeness and selects a section. In the light of de Certeau's notion of walking, it also wilfully reduces the given pre-selection of passages, creates detours (channelled through Copula Hall as an official location for crossing from one city into the other) by putting up mental or cognitive borders where there are no material ones and thus ends up with a self-denied unmarked space. What is more, some areas are materialistically speaking still shared (the crosshatch areas), but conceptually they are as separated as possible. *The City & The City* pushes the notion of separated cities to its limits so that it becomes almost impossible – utopian – to treat them as a unified whole. How does one access what one wilfully denies by pushing it into the unmarked? Grosstopically close areas can belong to completely different patterns of order (see Schroer 2006: 239) as it is spelled out in the *The City & The City* in general and in the cities' tales in particular:

> How could one not think of the stories we all grew up on, that surely the Ul Qomans grew up on too? Ul Qoman man and Besź maid, meeting in the middle of Copula Hall, returning to their homes to realise that they live, grosstopically, next door to each other, spending their lives faithful and alone, rising at the same time, walking crosshatched streets close like a couple, each in their own city, never breaching, never quite touching, never speaking a word across the border. (*TC&TC:* 160–161)

Spatial proximity and neighbourship do not entail social closeness anymore. Individual discursivity and patterns of perception shape individual excerpts of reality.

The selective reduction of perception is also reflected in the novel's mode of narration. The whole story is told by Borlú as a first-person narrator who finds himself within the story world. Consequently, he is unable to transcend the indoctrinated way of (un)seeing the two cities while an external and unmarked narration lingers beyond his own perception and narration. Thus, in a way, his limited focalisation displays another unmarked space – a narratological one – until the point where Borlú becomes a member of Breach and starts to learn to see truly. At this point, one might anticipate a new sujet (Borlú's life in Breach), but instead of a switch of narration to a totalising mode, the novel ends.

To what end does Miéville present all these facets of unseeing? His exploitation of urban ignorance is well applicable to the way human beings in general see and do not see things. From everyday life, we well know perceptive patterns of unseeing: for example, whenever we see a homeless person on the street and look away or pretend to see nothing; whenever we do not want to notice a person smoking in a non-smoking area on a station platform because we do not want to cause any trouble. *The City & The City* reflects on our everyday urban practices of unseeing by taking them to extremes.

IV.2.3 *City of Bohane:* The Back Trace of Memory

The City of Bohane feels much smaller than the other examples talked about so far. In comparison to New Crobuzon, it has fewer quarters and places, but they are presented in more detail. Additionally, in contrast to the faceless masses that need to be unseen in *The City & The City*, everyone seems to know everyone else.

Two areas are gangland: the realm of the Hartnett Fancy in 2053 called the Back Trace, and the Northside Rises with the rivalling Norrie gangs. Smoketown is the novel's hotbed of sin, full of drugs and prostitution. New Town might pass as a more or less gang-free middle-class area, Beauvista as upper-class. The novel reduces the quarters to stereotypes so that they can be distinguished from each other. The transitions and borders of quarters are clearly marked: Smoketown is connected to the Back Trace by a footbridge over the Bohane River; in order to move on to the Northside Rises one needs to go up the 98 steps; and De Valera Street separates the better quarters (New Town and Beauvista) from the nastier ones. Several buildings gain importance as the story unfolds: the Ancient and Historical Bohane Film Society, the Ho Pee Ching Oh-Kay

Koffee Shoppe, the Café Aliados, and the editorial office of the *Bohane Vindicator*. In the south, just outside of town, the sand-pikey savages live in the dunes. If one leaves the city in any other direction, one ends up in Big Nothin', a vast area "of thorn and stone and sudden devouring swamp-holes" (*CoB:* 43) with scarce population except for some hamlets.

Conceived space, as in Lefebvre's triad, does not seem to figure prominently at first glance because Bohane is hardly technocratic or scientifically contrived. Yet, the quarters themselves structure the city authoritatively since the borders between them are clearly defined, and the quarters are clearly separated in people's mindsets. The people in Bohane consistently emphasise the tribal social structure – whether people are, for example, from the Back Trace in "blood and bone" as the Hartnetts (*CoB:* 65), from Big Nothin' (the Gant Broderick), or whether they have a share of pikey-blood in them, such as Fucker Burke. Origin is important because in Bohane, belonging to a certain family or bloodline entails certain practices, characteristics, and a certain habitus. Sand-pikeys are said to be primitive brutes, Big Nothin' people to be simple-minded, the Norries are described as "a skittish, temperamental people with a tendency towards odd turns of logic" (*CoB:* 25). Ironically, "Trace and Rises families [as the two main rivals] are almost all blood-related, if you go way back, and this perhaps explains the depth of bitterness between them" (*CoB:* 25) – the racial attributions are unmasked and revealed as human constructions. Obviously, the ascriptions are not free from prejudice and stereotypes and might well pass as ideology in the sense of a personal frame of reference.[20]

Of paramount importance in Bohane, however, is lived space: "Each of our districts has a particular feeling, a signature melody" (*CoB:* 18). People walk through the city and sense or feel a vast panorama of urban aspects: first, "the taint of badness on the city's air [which] is a taint off that river" (*CoB:* 3), and which is blamed for having infected the people, has an effect: the "Riverside feeling" (*CoB:* 214), "that odd swoop in the spirit [...] is a frightening sensation – one senses an odd lurch within, a movement that can feel almost nauseous" (*CoB:* 212). Moreover "[t]he city's mood [...][is] a blend of fear and titillation" (*CoB:* 79), especially before the Feud between the Hartnetts and the Norries; "the city simmered now with bitterness, rage, threat" (*CoB:* 89), and the "Trace had an odd, nervous shimmer to it this evening" before the clash of the two gangs on the following day (*CoB:* 94); people note "a great thrumming on the air" (*CoB:* 101). The night of August Fair drawing close similarly triggers a certain feel and mood: "The atmosphere generally was riverine and as Wolfie

---

20 See also the model in chapter IV.1.

walked the wharf there was no small amount of poetry mingled with violent intention" (*CoB:* 202). In these instances of city moods, it is remarkable that most of them cannot be attributed to specific characters directly. On the contrary, it seems as if the city itself in a Sennettian way of personification is able to generate the particular feelings and thus dominate Bohane's lived space. Where do these feelings come from, then? In contrast to New Crobuzon, Bohane as a city is not given an actual or metaphorical body, but the city buzzes with old memories and feelings which can be traced back way into the past. This so-called Bohane lost-time is present throughout the novel as the most powerful force in terms of rendering city space and shall be paid attention to in the following.

Narrating the Bohane Lost-time

City of Bohane will be identified not only in terms of its ways of appropriating the city space of the story-now (as in most novels examined so far), but in terms of its inquiries into spaces of the past. Therefore, the focus of the chapter will be on the novel's lived space, its placement between materiality and discursivity, the relations between conscious and unconscious remembering, and the corresponding narrative perspectives. Walking in Bohane hinges on what the locals call the lost-time: a nostalgic remembrance of days long gone, either tied to good old times of living in Bohane in general or to one's own youth, triggered while walking through Bohane and entering a discourse with it.

Numerous characters are drawn back to the lost-time, some of whom will be scrutinised on the following pages. In this respect, the novel's way of conveying its story to the reader is of high importance since, as established in the city space model in chapter IV.1, whenever one is concerned with space in fiction, the fictional work's configurations of perception are at stake as well; therefore, it can be very revealing to have a look at the narrative perspectives used in the text. *City of Bohane* uses a fairly subtle approach when it comes to narration. Most of the time, the reader is facing heterodiegetic narration featuring numerous characters as focalisers. However, starting as early as in the first chapter,[21] the narrative voice switches into a homodiegetic mode time and again. Therefore, narration in *City of Bohane* is always part of the story world as the homodiegetic passages frame the overall narrative while compiling the heterodiegetic ones. The homodiegetic narrator's identity is mostly obscure – as it turns out he is fair-

---

[21] The homodiegetic narrator's first appearance actually occurs in the very first sentence of the novel: "Whatever's wrong with us is coming in off that river" (*CoB:* 3).

ly old, he is the owner of the cinema, i.e. of the Ancient and Historical Bohane Film Society, and he likes to pose as the city's inofficial chronicler. It will become clear at the end of this chapter that the role of the homodiegetic narrator defining the frame narration of the novel is part of an intricate narrative strategy which strives to tie the novel's overall mediation to one crucial scene where the homodiegetic narrator becomes most overt (see *CoB:* 180).

Wolfie Stanner's remembrance of his deceased mother can serve as a starting point for an analysis of the lost-time as a narrative device. A pickpocket always living on the edge, she simply disappears one night when Wolfie is still a child. It is striking that Wolfie does remember her as a somewhat caring person, yet without the domestic context of a family's home:

> And nightly, then, their roaming of the Trace. The way she'd drag him close to her when she was boozed up and croon old songs, the tunes of the lost-time. He felt yet the beating of her heart and the way she nuzzled his neck. Later in the night she'd disappear for a while. The night came that she didn't come back. (*CoB:* 113)

Mother and son roamed the streets together. Wolfie's journey back to the lost-time evokes the bodily closeness to his mother on the one hand and her old songs on the other,[22] both of which are embedded in the urban materiality of the Back Trace. The Hartnett Fancy's lieutenant's memory is exemplary for the two ways of evoking the lost-time: either as a bodily issue (walking or touching) or as the result of mediatisation (songs,[23] film reels, newspaper articles, conversation, hand-written letters). If it weren't for his burning desire for Jenni Ching, who replaces his mother as his female confidante, one might suggest that it is the loss in his lost-time that has made Wolfie so tough and free of emotions in the story world.

Narrating the Bohane Lost-time: Girly
Girly, Logan Hartnett's bedridden mother, has her very own version of the lost-time which she calls the "lightness," a vision-like delirium. Lying in bed all

---

22 As far as the songs are concerned, one might even speak of a double lost-time, since Wolfie remembers his mother's old songs as his lost-time, which are in turn called up by her in memory of her own lost-time further back in time.
23 The presence of songs and associated dances is emphasised throughout the story. To name but a few besides Wolfie's mother's songs, there are the whistled tunes of the Norries (*CoB:* 95–96), the song sung by Blind Nora on August Fair (*CoB:* 258; 268; 273), and the penultimate scene where Logan "select[s] a slow-burner of an old calypso tune from the lost-time" on the jukebox as he waits for Macu: "She'd know this one" (*CoB:* 275).

day, drugged to the eyeballs with pills and whiskey, there is not much left to do for her except for thinking of her better days a long time ago. Yet, Girly has a high opinion of herself. Each single movement is painful, but "[i]t was Girly's opinion that she still had a fine pair of pins on her" (*CoB:* 87). Her experience of being an old lady displays a material facet of urbanity as her frail body is compared to a building: "Girly felt like a derelict house. Strike that – a derelict mansion. No panes in the windows and no fire in the grate and crows in the attic but there was grandeur yet, even so. A stately ruin was Girly" (*CoB:* 89) – and she displays another facet of Sennett's treatment of the ancient city's body. Just as the building's construction is inspired by the body's characteristics, building and body also share each other's decay (see Sennett 1996: 90; see also chapter IV.2.1). As we can see in her efforts to get out of bed and look out of the window, Girly is deprived of walking on foot as the usual means of getting in touch with the city. After having swung her legs out of the bed, accompanied by excruciating pain, "[o]f course the next thing was the walking. Girly considered the vast Sahara of the beige-tone carpet that opened out between herself and the far window overlooking the Dev Street drag" (*CoB:* 88). The window to the outside world is one desert away, and her crossing this desert is a quest of unimaginable effort:

> The great tragic armies of history had made it over storm-whipped mountain ranges quicker than Girly made it across that carpet but she persevered, and she reached, after an epic struggle, the drapes. She clutched, wheezing, at their long folds of blue velvet – dizzying, the flow of the fabric – and Girly whited out for a moment – the lightness! – and then re-gathered. (*CoB:* 89)

Finally, she is able to look down at the city. It seems as if the mere glance at the urban materiality triggers her journey back into the old days: "Wistfully Girly looked on De Valera Street – ah, that she might have the strength for a good ruck yet herself – and the box windows of the El train zipped past then, the flick and yellow flashing of them, and the street blurred, and her mind went with it – the lightness – and Girly travelled to the lost-time" (*CoB:* 90). Girly's lost-time, triggered by mere looking, is presented as a fairly unconscious phenomenon which takes her over. The blurriness leads to a clear vision of the time when she had been in charge of the Fancy: "The Gant Broderick she saw as a ten-year-old gypo child. [...] Girly returned; she left old Bohane to itself, at least for the time being, but the past, she knew, was never still in this city, it continued to seethe and brew back there, and it gave taint to the present" (*CoB:* 91). The last bit is crucial for understanding Bohane and its inhabitants. City and body are not only intertwined in the story-now, but also in their mutual historicity. Over generations, bodies have been both means and effect of the discursive appropriation of the city's body, into which the discursive practices have been inscribed (see Altnöder 2009: 303), and these practices reverberate. It already transpires that the ways of reverberation are not only bound to persons but also quite individual in terms of access and quality.

Narrating the Bohane Lost-time: Macu
Macu's lost-time, then, turns out to be quite different, both in terms of its triggers and its performativity. Caught in an unhappy relationship with Logan, she "walk[s] each evening in the Bohane New Town, as if every step might bring her further from the life she had made" (*CoB:* 51). Like so many other characters, Macu assumes the role of a walker on street level. In contrast to de Certeau's conception of walking, however, Macu's walking is rather a going away than an appropriation. Walking as such is Macu's trigger for the "mapline *to* her lost-time" (*CoB:* 52 [my emphasis]) and simultaneously away *from* the present – she strolls without a destination, and the images of the past come back: "A twist and a turn, a feint. A twist and a turn, and the pathways of her thoughts were intricate as the Trace, and as indeterminate" (*CoB:* 264). An unconscious practice of walking serves the conscious wish of running away from the present. Materialistically speaking, her feet take her nowhere in particular, but in terms of discursivity, she always ends up in the Café Aliados of her youth, where she and the Gant Broderick, the young and vigorous leader of the Fancy back then, met 25 years ago for the first time: "Oh these were good-looking young people, in a hard town by the sea, and the days bled into the sweet nights, and it was as if the summer would never end" (*CoB:* 53).[24] The second episode from Macu's lost-time is her happy time with Logan. Again by walking, she ends up in a square that does not seem related to her relationship with Logan in particular (it is not mentioned that they have ever sat there), but it is symbolic for the tender beginning and the later disenchantment of the relationship:

> Then it was night-time in the Trace. She walked the wynds, and she came at length to a small, deserted square, and she sat for a while on the wrought-iron bench. Dead lovers' names were scratched into the wooden seat back. [...] Sometimes, in the good times, they didn't even have to speak to know what the other was feeling. [...] [A] child never came, and the space was filled by his jealousy. (*CoB:* 218)

The square with the bench exemplifies the relation of place, person, and memory. The place's function as a memorial support is not 'given' – its potential for

---

24 At the end of each day, however, "always she circled home again" (*CoB:* 51).

storing memories only unfolds in connection with a narrative (e.g. the one of a lost love) which gives the place its meaning (see Rupp 2009: 186). On the other hand, the place is not completely random either. With the first lovers' names scratched into the bench, the place starts to accumulate memories as more and more couples inscribe their story into the square's materiality.

To go even further, Logan's jealousy also projects into the city space. He wants to stay in control of Macu's movements as she starts her walks: "Were you out at all? Did you see anyone? What have you been doing? [...] Where did you go? [...] He had the Fancy boys follow her" (*CoB:* 219). After the Gant Broderick's visit, she leaves a note for Logan and, once again, goes nowhere in particular, and being away from her husband is her single goal: "The jealousy is poison. [...] I can't be with you any more. [...] I don't know where I'm going to go but I'm going" (*CoB:* 151). After she leaves him, no one is following her anymore indeed since Logan is too depressed, drugged, and caught in his own lost-time. In a letter to Macu, he suggests the Café Aliados on the night of August Fair as a place for a possible reunion: "He would be waiting at midnight in the Café Aliados. She did not yet know if she would go to him there" (*CoB:* 264). At midnight sharp the door opens, and instead of Macu, Girly enters. Since this event is described on the penultimate page, and since Macu is not further mentioned, it is suggested that Macu finally managed to walk away. Girly on the other hand finally manages to overcome her confining frailty and walk the city at least one more time. The fact that she meets her son Logan at the café might foreshadow what becomes of him. Logan has lost his leadership of the Fancy; he has also lost his lieutenants and his wife – and then his mother shows up in order to take him to the one place where men can hide after they have failed in the world out there: back home to Hotel Mum.

Narrating the Bohane Lost-time: Logan
Logan's walking starts out rather independently of the lost-time. The beginning of the novel establishes him as the unquestioned boss of the city who is in accord with the surrounding materiality of Bohane: "He walked the docks and breathed in the sweet badness of the river. [...] There was an evenness to his footfall, a slow calm rhythm of leather on stone [...]. The water's roar for Hartnett was as the rushing of his own blood [...]" (*CoB:* 3). Both the way people behave in his presence as well as his way of walking make it clear that he is the one in charge, a most proficient walker:

> Dank little squares of the Trace opened out suddenly, like gasps, and Logan passed through. All sorts of squarehawks lingered Trace-deep in the small hours. They looked

down as he passed, they examined their toes and their sacks of tawny wine – you wouldn't make eye contact with the Long Fella if you could help it. Strange, but *we* had a fear of him and a pride in him, both. He had a fine hold of himself, *as we say in Bohane*. He was graceful and erect and he looked neither left nor right but straight out ahead always, with the shoulders thrown back, like a general. (*CoB:* 4 [my italics])

The quote is from the second page of the novel, and the narrator (see the italics in the quote) clearly mediates the scene. The "we" (just as the "us" in his very first overt occurrence on page 3) points towards the narrator's self-conception – he is no genius mastermind behind his very own narrative, but a town chronicler and thus part of the city collective working on the city's collective memory. Describing Logan as having "a fine hold of himself, as we say in Bohane" embeds the story told by the homodiegetic narrator into the city's mythology reaching far back into the past.

Besides the narrative situation, the quote is also relevant in terms of Logan's relation to the city space. A comparison with Yagharek's steady but slow learning process of moving through the city as a foreigner makes it clear that Logan is not only familiar with the city space but its superior. The boss of both the city and its inhabitants walks upright and straight without any need of being cautious. What is more, he knows the city to its heart: "Yes and Logan was in his element as he made progress through the labyrinth. He feared not the shadows, he knew the fibres of the place, he knew every last twist and lilt of it" (*CoB:* 4). Logan is able to look behind the scenes just like the vagrant archetype as outlined by Löbbermann (see chapter III.2.1) [25] while at the same time being the boss of the place, de Certeau's "solar Eye" exercising power.

So far, Logan is the only character who seems to be able to reconcile the two distant spheres of tour and map. Yet, even within him, they are in a fragile balance. His lieutenants become ambitious and his jealousy finally drives away Macu. As a result, Logan loses control of himself, the Fancy, and the city as well. His thoughts still circle around Macu: "Logan Hartnett on an April morning walked the stony rut of his one-track mind: Where does she sleep now? [...] He crossed the S'town footbridge. He walked the Bohane front. He was dreamsick in the morning, and his nausea fed on the squalling of the gulls, the slaughterhouse roar, the clanking of the meat wagons" (*CoB:* 173). The loss of information concerning his wife's whereabouts goes along with the loss of control over the Fancy, the loss of his superior performance of walking, and the loss of unity with the city space. The calm rhythm from the beginning is replaced by nausea;

---

[25] Note the remark that he knows "the fibres of the place"; Logan's hold on Bohane does not stay on the surface, as is the case with de Certeau's voyeur.

the sweet roaring of the water that had been aligned with the rushing of his own blood gives way to sounds of the city which are not his anymore. Drugs and walking take him to the lost-time. Riverside Boulevard is presented as a place where

> [t]houghts come loose. Souls hang on the air. Warps occur. And Logan Hartnett, dream-sick in April, sold to the pipe and heartache, had begun almost daily to haunt the place. He walked it; he fed on the weird. He chased with clouded eyes the flight of the demon sukas. Hummed softly. And he made – with pale lips moving – his dark reckonings. (*CoB*: 212)

Interestingly, with Macu gone, his lost-time memories do hardly circle around her. His walking back into the past rather sheds light on his Fancy than on his marriage: "Each turn of the Trace that he took signified – there he'd had a knee-trembler, there he'd bled a foe" (*CoB*: 245). Different places function as memorial stones for personal encounters that were inscribed into the city's body years ago, and Logan's walking retraces and reilluminates them. His lost-time also exceeds his personal discursivity of gang life and goes further back into the past of the Hartnett Fancy mythology: "Corridor sang with old spirits. Logan as he followed the fat polis closed his eyes – he was tapering yet from a Ho Pee dream – and heard the screeches of age-dead Fenians seep from the walls. No shortage of ghosts in this place" (*CoB*: 191). As in Girly's example, the past is not silent in Bohane as it seeps into the present. The sudden mentioning of Fenians is one of the very few instances where Bohane can be identified as an Irish city (the High Boreen being another example), and it is so in two ways. Firstly, it refers to Fenianism and the related organisation in the context of the establishment of an Irish Republic. Secondly, it can also refer farther back to the so-called Fenian Cycle by the poet Ossian, also known as the Ossianic Cycle, a collection of prose and verse and one of the most important sources of Irish mythology. In this context, the Irish word *fian* commonly refers to "a larger or smaller band of roving warriors, who had joined for the purpose of making war on their own account" (Meyer 1910: ix) and thus perfectly matches the Bohane gangs. Furthermore, these warriors' actions tap into local historicity: "their deeds and adventures were celebrated in songs and stories, and their existence was even considered essential for the welfare of the community" (Meyer 1910: ix). Bohane thus never forgot its Irishness although it might be hidden deep in the past while the gangs, descendants of the Fenian warriors, still keep the city in check. Nevertheless, the tribal structure of Bohane's population, the songs and memories, and the cross references to Irish history go well together. The gang mythology, evoked by memory and inscribed into specific places, secures a place for all those long gone:

All the old faces were in their own time fabled in the Back Trace universe, he said. The Trace was a world within a world, he said, and each of these dead souls had a power in the world once, was known for his swiftness with the shkelp, or his knack with the tush, or his canniness with a buck. Each was in the boneyard now, he said; Logan Hartnett, reality instructor. (*CoB:* 248)

The last sentence, however, already points towards the sad part of the arrangement. "[T]he Long Fella shook his head sadly; there was no going back" (*CoB:* 213). The lost-time is what it is – a sweet memory of blurry, misty-eyed images, unseizable despite its reverberation in the present. The lost-time is hanging over Bohane like a veil. As the novel draws to its end, Logan realises that moaning over the lost days is a waste of time, and he turns back to the present and acts on two fields. Firstly, he takes care of the business of the Fancy. Logan knows that his days as the general are over. Over the course of the novel, all his lieutenants and possible successors have been tested: Fucker Burke airily sold him out; Wolfie Stanners turned to be too much caught up in his love to Jenni; Jenni herself had also been tested and, luckily, proved to be "no gommie lackeen" (*CoB:* 222).[26] Hence, she would make a decent successor in his eyes.[27] In order to weaken the Norries, Logan also hires a little child as a fake avatar (including fake stigmata) of the Sweet Baba Jay, Bohane's version of Christ (see *CoB:* 190–194; 223–227). Secondly, there is his attempt to win back Macu. The Gant Broderick reassures him that she didn't fall for him on his return to town. A letter (see *CoB:* 228–229) and the suggested meeting in the Café on August Fair may make her give him another chance.

Narrating the Bohane Lost-time: the Gant Broderick

Lastly, I turn to the Gant Broderick, who returns to Bohane after 25 years of exile. Besides homesickness, his second reason for coming back is to see whether he still has a chance with Macu with whom he only went out for three weeks before she left him for Logan – and the Gant went down the High Boreen into Big Nothin' and beyond. His lost-time is narrated in his letter to Macu and in his walks

---

[26] For testing them, Logan hires the Gant Broderick who, homesick, is granted free passage to his beloved city in return. The Gant talks Fucker Burke into giving away Logan's walking routines and tracks (see *CoB:* 172; note again the spatiality – knowing the movements of your enemy as a tactical advantage since you can simply follow or ambush him; see *CoB:* 72–74 and the murder of Cantillon by Fucker Burke and Wolfie).

[27] In his meeting with the Gant, Logan states that he wants "to go on for a while yet" (*CoB:* 235), but still his first priority seems to be saving his relationship since he does not intervene when Jenni is about to take over the Back Trace at the novel's end.

around Bohane and Big Nothin' after his return. Right on his arrival by train, it all comes back to him: "[T]he flush of heat brought to him a charge of feeling, also [...]. The tang of stolen youth seeped up in his throat with the rasping burn of nausea and on the El train in yellow light the Gant trembled" (*CoB:* 12). As soon as he is back, the bittersweet lost-time inherent to Bohane kicks in, this time in an in obviously unconscious fashion: "The Gant had come back in early August. At once, he had fallen victim to our native reminiscence. In the Bohane creation, time comes loose, there is a curious fluidity, the past seeps into the future, and the moment itself as it passes is the hardest to grasp" (*CoB_* 60). Again, the homodiegetic narrator makes himself heard and he describes the lost-time as an inherent feature of Bohane. The Gant's lost-time, in contrast to Logan's, always circles around his three happy weeks with Macu. It is a painful remembering: "He walked on into the night and he shook his great, bearish head against memory, and he briefly wept, and he chortled at himself then for the weeping. Oh this is a nice package you're presenting, Gant" (*CoB:* 60). The Gant's pain, in this self-evaluation, is again tied to the lost past. Once again the reader is made aware of the fact that the lost-time is lost indeed: "He closed his eyes and tried to bring himself to the lost-time, but it could never be regained. He would never take back the true taste. He had known it just once and it was Macu's" (*CoB:* 59). More information is given in his letter to Macu in which the day of departure still reverberates after 25 years. The Gant writes: "It only seems like weeks ago that I walked out of the place. A lot has happened to me in that time as you can well imagine since I took to the High Boreen that was a hard day believe me that day marked me" (*CoB:* 75). The Gant's lost-time is filled with all the little things young lovers say and do. Here is another section from his letter: "You said that no matter what happened we would end up together. Do you remember that? It was probably just something a young girl would say and she was in love but I believed it for years it kept me together for years it kept me from the lip of the grave Macu" (*CoB:* 76). The performativity of the act of remembrance is again highlighted in the Gant's remembering of shared walks, which he remembers as he is walking after his return:

> He walked the Nothin' plain. The hardwind by 'n' by walloped a little sense into him. [...] The Gant willed himself to straight thinking. He felt the tread of their shared past underfoot. Your step there, he thought, and my step here. That's your step there, and my step here, on the days that we walked out, Macu, in the noonday of the lost-time. Nostalgia, on the peninsula, was a many-hooked lure. (*CoB:* 60)

A conscious retracing of steps leads to the lost-time. Walking is further elaborated on in the metaphorical choosing between different paths of life. Macu chose the Back Trace with Logan, whereas the Gant chose the High Boreen and left town, as he explains in his letter to her:

> We used to walk on those nights in the Trace and go down to the river. I can hear again the river on the summer nights and the way we'd sit on the stone steps and you would lean your head back onto my chest and rest it there. I thought that nobody could ever come between us Macu. I tell myself that to come back here might be a way to break the hold on me you have still. The touch that I have felt on me these years in my dark times always it is your touch. I see you at seventeen, eighteen so perfectly clear every detail [...]. I believe they were the wrong paths we took and what I have seen of your life here with Hartnett does not change my belief. [...] There are places that you would remember I'm sure from our own time when sometimes we'd walk out here. [...] As much as things change in Bohane things stay the same on Big Nothin'. (*CoB:* 77)

It is striking that the Gant's lost-time not only refers to the city of Bohane but also, or even more, to the bog plains of Big Nothin', where he was born. He first settles in a small cabin out in Big Nothin' after his return in order to find his peace of mind – once again linked to walking:

> He walked the October night its length through. He came into a white space of mind and it was restful. He circled the plain. Towards dawn, he walked across the splintered boards of an old jetty by the small lake – the boards gave and groaned as he walked, the birds sang – and he crouched there, and he felt the looming presence of the Nothin' hills beyond. Dark shadow of mountain against the waking sky. He felt a presence; he felt it as a great tenderness. And then he heard its voice. 'Oh Baba?' the Gant pleaded. 'Oh Sweet B?' (*CoB:* 63)

The loneliness and calm of Big Nothin' also offers some sort of religious experience. City and countryside are presented as ever-changing and never-changing, busy and calm, rough and tender.[28] And yet, the Big Nothin' calm is not to be confused with peace of mind or happiness in a natural or religious experience, as another passage of his letter can show:

> I am living back on Nothin' now and it is my intention to settle here for as long as I have left may the SBJ [= Sweet Baba Jay] grant that it is more than a season or two. I cannot say that I have known happiness since I came back here a few months ago I cannot say that I will ever know that again but there is quiet out here all the same that suits me and is a comfort to my old bones. You know that Nothin' has been a special place for me always. You know my feelings for this place and you will understand it was painful for me to be away from it so long. (*CoB:* 76)

---

28 This opposition will be problematised in the context of *Lilac and Flag* and the dystopian tradition. It is also worth noting that the Gant's conception of the city as an ever-changing place is not entirely correct, as the end of this chapter shows.

Big Nothin' is the Gant's special place because of his origin, but it does not stop him from going back to the city. His lost-time is not the never-changing calm of the countryside, but the vibrant relationship with the city girl Macu – hence the inability of Big Nothin' to give him back happiness. "And so, quietly, he had taken a room in the Back Trace. It was a place to breathe in the city and see what feeling he could take from it" (*CoB:* 181). The night Macu left him figures most prominently; it is not a blurry vision induced by a dream pipe, as in Logan's case, but a very clear image: "It was just three weeks they had been together. The night she left him he remembered in a visceral way. He could summon it at will. The colours of the lonely street that night; the nausea of defeat. He experienced again every moment of it. He saw it so clearly" (*CoB:* 182), and the experience is truly bodily ("visceral") – the conscious summoning of memory as a reliving permeates the body's surface just as the event did back then. The city then becomes his place of purging the old demons of his lost love. As he seeks out Macu in order to fulfil his part of the deal with Logan (testing whether she would leave Logan for running away with the Gant), he realises that his love for her has in fact burned out: "The firelight traced out the lines of her aged skin. She was no longer what he needed or wanted. Reality infected him with its sourness and truth" (*CoB:* 145). Macu is not seventeen anymore and neither is he. Her bodily presence in the present eats up the nostalgic past as they clash. He then attempts to make her want him, to hurt her where she cannot hurt him anymore, and fails. "There in the attic room the Gant came back to the moment and he seethed again with youth's intensity. [...] In the glare of spring, he was seeing things plain. [...] [O]n the longest night of the winter, on Beauvista, he saw that time had already from Macu taken its revenge" (*CoB:* 183). With the affection gone in both of them he is free of his personal lost-time pain and able to tap another lost-time: the lost-time of the city collective.

The Gant's development takes two further steps after he is done with Macu. Firstly, he gives an interview for Big Dom Gleeson and Balthazar Grimes from the *Bohane Vindicator*. The city is at the brink of self-destruction at this point in the story: Logan is lost in his lost-time and drugs and thus unable to lead the Fancy; the girls of the Back Trace form a new gang in the footsteps of Jenni Ching; and the sand-pikeys roam the streets after they have been called in to support the Hartnett Fancy in the Feud. Gleeson and his newspaper provide a distraction from all the fighting: "'All Our Yesterdays' was by far the most popular and prestigious column of the *Bohane Vindicator*. It was penned by Dominick himself, in a limpid and melancholy prose, and its stock was reminiscence and anecdotes of the Bohane lost-time" (*CoB:* 196). Shortly after the meeting with Macu, the Gant agrees on an interview for a special issue of Gleeson's column. The interview is on the one hand a retracing of the Gant's steps (from Big Nothin' to Bohane to

England, then back to Big Nothin' and, finally, Bohane) and of the lost-time 25 years ago on the other. "He spent long nights, he said, walking the backstreets of strange cities. Skunk hours in the demon mist. The Gant walked every street of every city and they were never his streets and when the streets are not your own they are not for dreaming" (*CoB:* 199). Again, the contrast to Yagharek's appropriation of New Crobuzon is apparent. The garuda, in a city that is much larger, stranger, and more confusing than Bohane, manages what the Gant cannot. The city of Bohane is charged with a back-breaking amount of memories and dreams that leaves no space within the Gant for the appropriation of another city. Yagharek, at the end of *Perdido Street Station*, makes the formerly strange streets his own; for the Gant, there are only the streets of Bohane while "England's cheerless marches" and "the dark cities of the north" remain behind inaccessibly (*CoB:* 198). In the setting of Barry's novel, one cannot make a home just anywhere. Each city has its own intrinsic logic and, what is more, its own story, and one cannot weave oneself into every one. As the Gant admits himself: "'I was drawn back to the lost-time,' the Gant said. 'And did you find it a dangerous place to linger?' Big Dom showed his skill. 'Yeah,' said the Gant. It's too sweet back there'" (*CoB:* 200). Now, freed from his personal lost-time demons, he is able to relish in the broader lost-time of Bohane. As in Logan's lost-time of gang mythology and tribal structures, the people long gone haunt the city like ghosts: "They spoke at length of the Bohane lost-time. They talked of the great feeling for it that had drawn the Gant to the creation once more. They talked of those who had passed, and of how their spirits persisted yet and carried always on the air of the city" (*CoB:* 198). In the reactions of Gleeson and Grimes, the Gant's function after coming to terms with his own past is foreshadowed – he becomes a conductor for other people's takes on the lost-time:

> Dom would be happy to talk about the old Bohane until the clock came down the stairs, and there on the hardback chair he rocked to and fro, rhythmically, as he made notes from the Gant's powerful recall, and the hunchback Grimes, too, was set adrift on memory bliss – ah, youth; he'd been a puckish spirit in his youth, Balt Grimes; [...] and the three men cut across each other, and riffed; when a reminiscence got going in the Back Trace, nights, it worked like a freestyle morphine jazz. (*CoB:* 201)

Secondly, then, he joins the old men on August Fair. The Gant had been away for 25 years and is now in his mid-fifties, so he does not fit into the target audience of the fair: "Fair Day was a time of massive hilarity, and sentimental music, and it was a most useful pressure valve, for these were hard times in the city, in this hard town by the sea. [...] Fair Day, as we always say in Bohane, is a day for the youth" (*CoB:* 244). What is a big, vibrant party full of drinking, brawling, and loving to the young guns is an opportunity to nostalgically revel in the past for older citizens. Among the latter, the Gant finds his place: "The Gant was among [old lads], and having been gone so long, he was himself a relic of the lost-time, and they prompted him, and he succumbed" (*CoB:* 250–251). However, as mentioned, he becomes more than just another old man: "At the Capricorn Bar, [...] the old-timers worked a whiskey-fed reminiscence, and the Gant was its conductor" (*CoB:* 255). As a living legend from the good old days he triggers the whole conversation that goes on for several pages as names, events and places are being summoned. To give but one example, the reader hears of Wolfie's mother again: "'And there was Candy, do you remember Candy?' 'Candy Stanners!' 'I dunno if there was ever a finer dip-pocket on Dev.' 'Not a one then or since fit to lace her boots.' 'Of course she'd a bad end as well.' 'That's the Back Trace for you.' 'Oh that's the Trace'" (*CoB:* 257). The hilarious ending of the conversation, for one last time, makes clear how to take the lost-time – as something lost and gone:

> 'Taafes were this near side o' Nothin' Mountain. Skinned goats for a trade his people.' 'Was a price paid for goat pelt that time.' 'A fine price. But that's all gone now.' 'All gone.' 'Lots of it gone.' 'Lots of it.' 'Oh we're all getting old now.' 'Old, yes.' 'Oh, old.' 'Old!' 'Oh.' The Gant slid from his stool at the Capricorn Bar and stumbled to a corner and vomited. (*CoB:* 263)

Travelling back to the lost-time is always temporary. Sooner or later, the drug trip, the story, or the song is over, and one is back in the present. The lost-time and the associated past may still shape the city, but they are not coming back.

Narrating the Bohane Lost-time: the Narrator and the Media

The media and related products in *City of Bohane* have their share in conducting the lost-time. Songs, the newspaper, hand-written notes and letters provide storage for the city's memories which, as mentioned at the beginning of this chapter, can be summoned, for example by starting to sing or selecting a song on the jukebox. The one-seat cinema stands out since it also sheds some light on the novel's narrative strategy. Most of the time, *City of Bohane*'s homodiegetic frame narrator, the town chronicler, is fairly covert and heterodiegetic passages with flexible focalisation dominate the narrative.[29] However, when Macu seeks out the Ancient & Historical Bohane Film Society, the homodiegetic narrator who runs the cinema (see *CoB:* 178 ff.) shows himself more overt than in all for-

---

29 See Reinfandt (1997: 167) for the preference of using the term 'flexible' focalisation instead of 'zero' focalisation.

mer instances where he has popped up without a proper explanation who he might be. Macu asks for the services of the cinema and watches a film showing the street outside the Café Aliados as her favourite place in the city:

> 'De Valera Street? The Trace?' 'Dev,' she said. 'Maybe there by the Aliados?' 'Where it gives onto the Trace,' I whispered soulfully. I picked a favourite compendium; a really lovely reel. It shows the snakebend roll of Dev Street, deep in the bustle and glare of the lost-time, at night, [...] and it was a different world, so glaringly lit. [...] Discreetly, through the hatch, I watched the lady as she watched the screen. She was mesmerised. And though I have watched this reel thousands of times, I was as always drawn into it, I was put under a spell by the roll and carry of the Dev Street habituees. If all had changed in Bohane, the people had not, and would never: That certain hip-swing. That especially haughty turn-of-snout. That belligerence. (*CoB:* 180)

Macu watching the old CCTV material not only shows the power the lost-time exercises over Macu and other characters – the narrator himself is put under its spell as well as the lost-time's temporality is heightened. While the lost-time and "the moment itself as it passes [was] the hardest to grasp" (*CoB:* 60) in other instances, it is intensified to a hypnotising concentration ("mesmerised") of nostalgic admiration in the cinema.

At this point, the narrative strategy of *City of Bohane* is highlighted. The fact that the homodiegetic narrator, in spite of his covert tendencies, is indeed framing the narrative is quite plausible. He can thus function as the aforementioned town chronicler controlling and presenting the narrative by selecting appropriate passages and perspectives in order to convey the story to his audience. He is in the story world and employs various media in order to transcend this status. The reel he is showing to Macu is supported by music accompanying the silent CCTV footage and the reel itself is a compendium, a customised composition (see *CoB:* 180) – just like the overall narrative where the homodiegetic narrator compiles different focalisations accompanied by various songs, letters and so on in his attempts to mediate story, memory, and town history. Furthermore, the homodiegetic narrator becomes most overt when he is himself most fascinated by his own composition – he is so fascinated that he cannot maintain his usual way of heterodiegetic storytelling with flexible focalisation, but shows himself as a fairly overt homodiegetic narrator. The second-order observation and the underlying message are remarkable: Macu is watching the reel; the narrator watches her watching the reel, both of whom fall under the reel's spell; and the reader is watching the narrator watching Macu watching the reel. The arrangement invites the reader to join this chain of watching: just as Macu is falling under the spell of the reel, and just as the narrator is falling under the spell of her watching it, the reader is invited to fall under the overall narrative's spell by watching the narrator watching (and telling) his composite story. The scene of Macu and the narrator in the one-seat cinema (another hint towards the invitation for a mesmerising journey into fiction, since reading is usually done alone and in private as well) is thus closely tied to the narrative as such and the way it is presented to the reader: sit down, watch, and have your very own lost-time experience.

If the lived space in the shape of the lost-time is so strong and so overt throughout *City of Bohane*, the question arises why Barry emphasises it that excessively. As shown, different varieties of lost-time shape the lived space of Bohane: personal and individual journeys on the on one hand and the city collective haunted by ghosts from better times long past on the other. At first glance, it seems sufficient to attest the typical dystopian topos: Bohane's past was wonderful, the story-now is horrible, and the narrator seems to pick a crucial phase of Bohane's history worth telling as it might change the city forever. However, based on the narrator's remark that the people in Bohane never change (and never will), the Bohane lost-time can also be considered an ironic comment on what people all over the world have always been saying and probably will keep on saying until the end of the world: "Everything was better in the old days." Was it better indeed? If the old days are always considered as better, does it matter whether the fight for control over Bohane is carried out between the Hartnett Fancy and the Norries or between Jenni Ching's gals and the sandpikeys if each conflict will be eventually be replaced by another and pass away into the lost-time itself only to be nostalgically summoned on August Fair? In a way this very attitude, by glorifying the past, is responsible for conversely labelling the present as dystopian – and since one cannot go back to the self-constructed utopian past, there is no way out.

IV.2.4 *Lilac and Flag:* Opening Urban Oysters

The following analysis of *Lilac and Flag* and its opposition of country and city will circle around three interrelated spheres – the numerous place names evoked, the novel's old woman narrator, and the force field of materiality and discursivity as established in the city space model in chapter IV.1. The chapter opens with an overview of the city of Troy and focusses on the place names and other evocative references in the novel which oscillate between actual-world references and ancient Greek mythology as well as between mappability and the impossibility to pin down any location. As will be shown, these references give the city some kind of structure while deliberately denying a clear picture simultaneously. Afterwards, I will highlight narrative situation since it is of paramount importance for understanding the relations between country and city the novel hinges on. The link between the two is the novel's old woman narrator, a heterodiegetic narrator with flexible focalisation who does not seem to be part of the urban story world but who is able to know many characters' thoughts and feelings. The narrative situation is particularly striking because the old woman narrator, as will become clear, is long dead and haunts the city as a spirit anchored in the country. Lastly, the unattainability of the country linked to the peculiar narrative situation is identified as part of an essentially utopian and anti-utopian program which draws upon established literary idealisations and constructions of the opposition of country and city and is quite present in *Lilac and Flag*'s characters' attitudes towards the country. I will base the examination of the latter opposition on Raymond Williams's influential study *The Country and the City* (1973).

Urban Troy – Place Names between Materiality and Discursivity
In order to find a way into Troy, I start with a rather long quote from the novel in which the old woman narrator points out the potential universality of Troy as a city:

> IT IS POSSIBLE you have been to Troy without recognising the city. The road from the airport is like many others in the world. It has a superhighway and is often blocked. You leave the airport buildings which are like space vessels never finished, you pass the packed carparks, the international, a mile or two of barbed wire, broken fields, the last stray cattle, billboards that advertise cars and Coca-Cola, storage tanks, a cement plant, the first shanty town, several giant depots for big stores, ring-road flyovers, working-class flats, a part of an ancient city wall, the old boroughs with trees, crammed shopping streets, new golden office-blocks, a number of ancient domes and spires, and finally you arrive at the acropolis of wealth. (*L&F:* 170)

The narrator's focus is on Troy's urban elements which can be found in many other cities: an airport, a highway, traffic jams, adverts, housing and so on. All these interchangeable elements of materiality render Troy a metropolis as well as a cosmopolis; it is a big city, and it could be found anywhere. At the same time, though, some historical and mythological elements seep in: the word "ancient" is used twice in connection with constructions which do not fit a 20th-century metropolis, or which at least stand out; in addition to that, the name Troy itself is highly discursive, creating images of a prehistoric, vaguely European city packed with stories and remarkable characters. Furthermore, the "acropolis of wealth" combines the famous fortress/temple district from ancient Athens with capitalist economy. Thus, the quote makes one wonder how the urban and the ancient, the capitalist and the mythological go together in Berger's

Troy. In order to shed light on these connections and interrelations, Berger scholars mostly concentrate on the excessive name-dropping occurring in the novel. In the following, I will also focus on the novel's place (and some character) names and try to come up with some kind of systematisation, and by doing so I will show that most of these scholars give up too easily.

When reading *Lilac and Flag* for the first time, one is overwhelmed by the sheer number of place names Berger throws at his readers: St. Pauli, Las Vegas, Alexanderplatz, Escorial, Chicago, Swansea, Cachan, Park Avenue, Tenochtitlán, to name but a few – all these names refer to quarters of Troy, to specific buildings, or to other cities more or less far away from Troy. As in *Perdido Street Station*, all these place names are expected to trigger something in the reader. However, the place names are more irritating than helpful at first for several reasons. Firstly, there are too many in order to take them all in. Secondly, the names are an extremely wild mix: mythological and biblical names occur alongside names of actual 20th-century places, and names of cities are jumbled with those of federal states and nation states from all over the world. Lastly, a good deal of them requires expert knowledge because not all names are as evocative as Las Vegas. Thus, most scholars (at least those publishing in English or German) have concluded that this disruption of actual-world hierarchies in combination with the sheer overkill of place names makes it impossible to pinpoint or imagine any of the locations. Troy, they argue, cannot be mapped. As Nurmi-Schomers suggests, for example, what is at stake here is "a spatially indeterminate/indeterminable cosmopolis 'somewhere' – or 'anywhere' – in Europe [or even the world] as in some way issuing from and/or referring back to the ancient city of Troy" (Nurmi-Schomers 2007: 264).

The city of Troy is thus usually seen as a 20th-century cosmopolis charged with mythological place names to such an extent that the locality collapses under the sheer amount of place names evoked. Each single name or reference "is in fact only one of many proper nouns which putatively name districts, edifices and institutions of Troy, creating a tenuous frame of reference" (Nurmi-Schomers 2007: 270). The accumulation of all these place names results in "coordinates of an opaque spatial configuration, evoking in their implied connectedness the image of a polyglot, polylocal cityscape whose excessive over-determination renders it completely indeterminate and indeterminable as a concrete geolocality" (Nurmi-Schomers 2007: 270). Names appear to remain mere surfaces without anything behind them; they are not part of any tangible materiality while the discursive aspect struggles with the overkill of names, which does not help to create any reliable frame of reference either. In contrast to Bohane, where the locations themselves are able to create a discursive response in the characters at least, Troy is classified as a city of an empty and superficial present (see Welz 1996: 197). Localisation (the relation of the places to each other) and temporality both seem to refute analysis in *Lilac and Flag*. "Troy resists cartographic objectivization; it proves to be as unmappable as it is undatable" (Nurmi-Schomers 2007: 270). The city, according to Nurmi-Schomers and others, is both time- and nameless, an every-city; the names both refer to everything and nothing. *Lilac and Flag* may take place in the city, but the characters are not emotionally bound to it; instead, one has the impression that Troy is presented as an urban non-location with a superficial materiality that defies the discursivity of its places names.[30] There is nothing to cling to in the city and there is (in contrast to Yagharek's development in *Perdido Street Station*) no process of appropriation.

Further proof for Troy's urban emptiness can be found in a passage where the novel's characters struggle with the disruption of the city's materiality and discursivity: Zsuzsa, while visiting her uncle Dima in prison, wears a shirt that says "STANFORD UNIVERSITY," thus evoking the famous Californian university which is in itself almost a mythological entity due to its international reputation. It is nowhere mentioned in the novel that there is a Stanford University in Troy; furthermore, Zsuzsa herself cannot read and has never been to any university. As the prison guards see Zsuzsa wearing the shirt, they "quizzed each letter of the unpronounceable words" and underneath the surface, they only detect Zsuzsa's breasts: "Nice pair of lemons there" (all three quotes *L&F:* 7). Thus, the discursive reference to the university is rendered irrelevant three times: firstly because of its non-existence in Troy; secondly because of Zsuzsa as an illiterate wearing the shirt, and, thirdly, because the prison guards cannot make sense of it. Conversely, the material aspect is highlighted (because the prison guards prefer to look at the breasts underneath the failing discursive surface). In short, it is easy to fall prey to Troy's apparent urban emptiness. The cosmopolis, with its telling names that do not appear to stand for anything anymore, gives the impression of an ultimate surface without anything behind it – of a topography packed with signifiers without any signifieds.

And yet, there is another passage also related to language which provides a strategy for a better understanding of Troy's topography if one digs deep enough and connects the dots. Clement Gex, Sucus's father, has a specific way of reveling in the past – he revels in the origin of words after his wife gives him an etymological dictionary:

---

30 See also Sennett's account of New York (Sennett 1997: 360) as a city erasing its own historicity, which might well fit Troy as well as it is described in the introductory quote above.

For her part, she changed his life with a book: a dictionary that explained the origins of words. Clement read it for the next thirty years, and never forgot a thing he learnt. It became a passion. He opened words, as he opened oysters, to find, within, their real meaning. Through words he listened to the past and to what he believed to be the truth. To migrate, from the Latin migrare, to change one's abode. (*L&F:* 33–34)

His day job (opening oysters) and his passion (etymology) are aligned. Just as the opening of oysters aims at getting at the tasty content (or, possibly, a pearl) inside the hard shell, the etymological dismantling of words overcomes the mere surface of their everyday usage in search of something more profound. The reader, in order to make sense of the overkill of place names, needs to do what Clement does for a living: opening shells, namely the shells of the place names in order to trace the names evoked back to their origins. I will do so in the following while also keeping an eye on the minimalist hints in the text which give away how the quarters and place names relate in order to show how they add up to a topographical sketch.[31]

I will move from outside the city towards the centre (leaving out some names without any hints or connections to other areas). Firstly, there are names which point towards other cities beyond Troy, for example Paris, Tenochtitlán, and Izmir. Secondly, there are industrial or low-class quarters which seem to be outskirts and suburbs a good distance away from the city centre: farthest away seem to be the quarters named Chicago (see *L&F:* 18), Santa Barbara (which is not only a city in California – there is another one in South America), and Tortoise Hill (bearing the same name as a South-African Wine) with Rat Hill as one of its sub-districts (possibly named after a place in New Zealand). Two other areas are mentioned in the context of Tortoise Hill because they can be seen from there (see *L&F:* 7; 95) and thus imply proximity while at the same time implying that the city centre is comparatively far away: Champ-de-Mars (numerous references are at work here)[32] with the city's prison (usually far away from any city

---

[31] By doing so, I will mostly focus on the place names occurring in the novel, but it is worth mentioning that the names of some characters are charged with referential potential as well: Naisi, Zsuzsa's brother, bears the same name as a small community in Malawi; Zsuzsa's name is a Hungarian version of Susanna, which has a Persian origin – and there actually was an ancient Persian town named Susa (both the first name as well as the city name in turn refer to the lilium flower).

[32] Firstly, Champ-de-Mars can refer to a vast public greenspace in St. Petersburg, in Paris and another one in Montreal; secondly, the two latter cities also have metro stops bearing the same name. Thirdly, a part of a quarter in Munich is called "Marsfeld." Fourthly, there is a Champ de Mars racecourse in Port Louis, Mauritius. Lastly, there is the Campus Martius, which used to be a parade ground in ancient Rome, and which nowadays is a public square called Campo Marzio.

centre), and Eddington (which can be traced back to several towns in England and in the USA) with the city's tanneries, suggesting that this quarter is busy with craft, but not too industrial. Additionally, there is also a single building close to Tortoise Hill: the Patrai Hotel, named after a Greek town (see *L&F:* 106). Moving in further, industrial quarters can be identified: Gentilly (named after a French town very close to Paris) features a fertilizer factory as another off-centre element, and Swansea – as a typical British industrial city – is said to be an industrial quarter with red-brick buildings (see *L&F:* 24). East of Swansea is San Isidoro, named after several towns in Peru and Argentina, where Yannis, the crane operator, has his home (thus suggesting a working-class area). Further east, the quarters of the city centre can be found: Cauchy Street, named after a street in Paris, is the district of Hector's police department, and Cachan, named after a French community in the metropolitan area of Paris, features an IBM building as well as Sucus's home and a restaurant called Las Vegas. A quarter dotted with lots of trees and inhabited by the rich people, Escorial (named after the residence of the King of Spain), can also be located in the centre.[33] Another central quarter is Carouge (named after a small community in the Romandie in Switzerland), which is connected to Park Avenue as the financial district (thus alluding to the actual-world Park Avenue in Manhattan). Lastly, there is St. Pauli, a red-light district (named after the red-light district of Hamburg in Germany) with the Golden Fleece bar, Budapest Station and Alexanderplatz close by.

Therefore, a certain order is established which can be reconstructed by the reader indeed: the quarters in Troy parallel the equivalent actual-world locations, thus retaining a certain amount of their specific characteristics (Swansea and Escorial may both be quarters in Troy, but their properties – location, mood, inhabitants – are very different). Even if a good deal of expert knowledge is required for some of them, the place names of actual-world locations and cities above directly translate into a topography: the city centre consists of Middle-European places (French, Swiss, German, Hungarian) and becomes more international the further one 'zooms' out (UK, Greece, Africa, USA, New Zealand). Thus, by dismantling Troy's place names like oysters, one is actually able to simultaneously reveal their origin (discursivity) and their placement within the city's topography (materiality).

Admittedly, there are some irritations. For example, numerous French towns are mentioned (see above), and the Métro is mentioned as a means of public transport in Troy, but Paris itself as *the* French/Métro City is established as an-

---

33 In Escorial, there is also the upper-class café where Zsuzsa and Sucus are, according to some rich ladies, completely out of place (see *L&F:* 14).

other city that has nothing to do with Troy while other cities from other continents are explicitly part of it. Furthermore, Troy's currency is the Polish zloti, but no other Polish influences can be found. Thus the names, after having been cracked open like Clement's oysters, provide a rough topographical sketch, but it is impossible to say where Berger's Troy is located exactly. The reader, like Clement with his etymological dictionary, can only discern one pattern of truth, a hidden topography beneath the surface, but not 'the truth.' However, I am hesitant to call this a mistake on Berger's part. Instead, I suggest that by decoding the place names connected with Troy, one is not only reminded of Clement's job, but also of the historical and archaeological debate on Troy's exact location in the actual world and its status between fact and fiction. Archaeology, as etymology, goes beyond mere surfaces, hoping to reveal structures underneath which, when analysed and interpreted, make sense and explain something – and Berger is well aware of this connection. Around 1990, when Berger was about to complete *Lilac and Flag*, historians and archaeologists were still debating whether the town which archaeologist Heinrich Schliemann found in Turkey in the 19th century was Troy indeed. To be more precise, some scholars believed that the city found at the digging site was Homer's inspiration for the *Iliad* while others went further and claimed that Schliemann's discovery *was* Homer's Troy (i.e. that the events described in the *Iliad* were more than fiction).[34] Berger, it seems, exploited this debate by feeding mythological elements into his novel by not only calling his city Troy, but also by using other names from ancient Greek mythology (e.g. Hector from the *Iliad*, or the Argonaut supermarket and the Golden Fleece bar which allude to the tales of Jason and the Argonauts). Berger, by rendering his version of Troy as associative and as fuzzy as centuries of storytelling and wild debates have rendered Homer's Troy, also seems to play on the connections between etymology and archaeology – but while the former offers a rather flat topography (connecting place names), the latter adds a vertical dimension (by digging into the ground and revealing layers lying upon another). Thus, Troy in *Lilac and Flag* is not only shaped according to Clement's opening of oysters, but also according to the contemporary debate on Troy – some structures can be made visible, but many fuzzy edges remain.

An Old Wives' Tale of a City
Unfortunately, Berger's use of narration in *Lilac and Flag* has been misunderstood even more than his excessive use of place names. In order to understand

---

34 For more information on the debate, see Schweitzer and Kienlin (2001/2002: 7–38).

the novel's narrative situation, one needs to see it in connection with the rest of the trilogy. Without going into too much detail here, the development is striking. While the first volume, *Pig Earth* (1979), starts out as a fairly descriptive work with many short stories and poems (the very first 'story' being a factual report about slaughtering a cow), but without many characters or much action, *Once in Europa* (1987) features longer stories, fewer poems and more inhabitants of the country village as narrators. *Lilac and Flag* features only one poem and, as mentioned earlier on, a postmodern style of narration with a dead narrator. Additionally, the focus switches from tales related to the country to those of the city. Scholars have observed this development before, but what they seem to have ignored so far is the interdependency between style of narration and the story world (see Hertel 2005: 29–30).[35] Strikingly, the trilogy maps the unfolding of its modes of narration onto the progress of modernisation in the story world: the story world evolves and is being modernised, and so is the style of narration. *Lilac and Flag*'s narrative style has received harsh criticism; Welz, for instance, describes it as contradictory and – especially in the novel's closing chapters – as an outright failure on Berger's part (see Welz 1996: 197). As with the reduction of Berger's use of place names to a confusing overkill, I will show that these conclusions are a bit short-sighted and that the fuzziness of the narrative situation is due to a deliberate construction of transcendent narration. In order to do so, I will examine the narratological status of the old woman narrator in closer detail on the following pages.

The old woman narrator, as mentioned above, can be classified as a heterodiegetic narrator with flexible focalisation. She switches between overt and covert passages, interspersing her own stories and memories from the country with the main action taking place in Troy. What is so peculiar about the old woman and her techniques of conveying the story to the reader is her unclear relation to the story world. On the one hand, she explicitly states that she has always been living in the country without ever having been to Troy:

> I HAVE LIVED all my long life in the village. What I know of Troy comes from *The Messenger* – the provincial newspaper – from television, from my dreams, from my broken heart, and from what those who come back tell me before they disappear for good. I have seen countless men go. They take the noon bus outside the Republican Lyre and they wave through the back window as the bus winds its way down the hill past the dairy. This is the first and easiest step they take. Once they have left the valley and are far from the blue waters

---

[35] Similarly unaware of the interdependency, Welz accurately identifies the trilogy's varying styles of narration, but simply traces back the changes to Berger's increasing identification with the country, where he spent a good deal of his life (see Welz 1996: 194).

> of our river – until they become Trojans, if ever they do – there is nothing in the world they can trust or depend upon. (*L&F*: 120)

She is clearly contrasted with those who actually take the bus and head for the city and she highlights the difficulties of truly becoming a city person, thus displaying an understanding of 20th-century consumer society and the challenges it poses for underprivileged foreign workers who usually have a rural background (see Welz 1996: 185). The narrator's story of her grandmother teaching her how to scythe (see *L&F*: 120) similarly seems to anchor her in the rural sphere.

On the other hand, as the subtitle of the novel has it, she tells an *Old Wives' Tale of a City*, and she does so as a narrator who does not seem to be part of the urban story world while being able to know many characters' thoughts nevertheless. Did someone who made it back to the village tell her the stories of Sucus and the others and she retells them, mixed with her own stories? It may seem so as long as she tells the reader about the characters within the city tale, thus positioning herself in the here and now of her village so that one may take the tale of the city as a story of and from the past: "I want to rock Sucus to sleep now. I have a cradle-bed in the barn that would be almost large enough. It was made many years ago by the great-grandfather who left behind the stone sabot. I want to rock Sucus to sleep in the cradle-bed and sing him a song" (*L&F*: 138). Many other passages are startling or irritating. For example, the sound of a hunting horn heard by the narrator at first seems to originate from a rural position:

> I can hear the sound of a hunting horn. The hunting horn is strange, always leaving, its back turned, speaking over its shoulder. Everything about it announces departure. [...] I hear the horn beneath the high glass roof of Budapest Station, on platform 17, and it's like the howling of a wild animal. I can almost touch the animal's fur, warm, sweaty, golden burrs lodged in it, thick as felt. The bellowing of its voice bruises itself against the iron-cast pillars, crying for the wounds and the wounded to come. (*L&F*: 100)

At first, one has the impression that she hears the hunting horn in the country and connects it with the station as an inherently urban element. The following scene then takes place exactly on platform 17 of Troy's Budapest Station where Zsuzsa and Sucus steal passports from a train. How can the narrator interpret the hunting horn so urbanely if she has never been to the city at all? Therefore, one needs to reverse the situation: the narrator actually *is* at Budapest Station and hears the horn of a leaving train which reminds her of a hunting horn from the country. The connection between the two horns works because of the similarity of the sounds as well as the associated departure. Thus, the narrator hears the train leaving, and similarly departs from the story-now briefly herself, remembering what goes together with the sound of a horn in a rural context: the howling of an animal (again by the similarity of the sounds) and the materiality of the animal itself.

The idea of the narrator being placed in a rural story-now while the city is only a long-gone tale ultimately ceases to be an option as soon as she seems to be present as an invisible narrator in Troy herself. She overhears Sergeant Pasqua interrogating the arrested Sucus after the stealing of the passports and it is implied that she is present at the scene: "I heard grunts, footsteps and a voice. The voice belonged to Sergeant Pasqua although it was shriller than his everyday one. The grunts came from Sucus" (*L&F:* 146). However, via flexible focalisation, she is not only able to listen but also to know what is going on in Sucus's body and mind: "The grief Sucus felt in his heart made him practically immune to the pain being inflicted on him by the sergeant. Each shock winded him, and smashed mercilessly against the inside of his skull. But between the shocks, the other pain was worse" (*L&F:* 146). She also overhears the conversation between Hector (Pasqua's supervisor) and Sucus. The narrator's perception is limited to hearing as she positions herself outside the interrogation room: "At this point Hector probably made some sign with his hand" (*L&F:* 150); "There was no reply, and it seemed that neither of the men made any effort to break the silence. For a moment I asked myself whether they had both gone, taking the inside lift like Sergeant Pasqua" (*L&F:* 152); "It was impossible to be sure which one of them it was who asked the question" (*L&F:* 156). Obviously, the narrative situation switches here from internal focalisation to external focalisation as her impressions of the scene are suddenly limited. In another passage, she directly speaks to Hector and tells him a longer story which makes clear that he grew up in the same village as she: "Do you remember your aunt who kept goats, Hector? One day in the tall grass behind her house she found a dead fox [...]" (*L&F:* 133–134). Hector does not hear her or answer. The narrator is a ghost of the village past that cannot make herself noticeable in the city.

At the close of the novel, the transcendent quality of the old woman's narration is spelled out even clearer. After the deaths of Naisi, Sucus, and Hector, the three men travel on a huge white ship, "a floating palace" (*L&F:* 159) for the dead.[36] It is a first-class ship with individually furnished cabins, but without any lifeboats or lifebelts. The narrator claims that the ship is actually hers (see *L&F:* 159) and it is she who receives Sucus and Hector "among the last to embark" (*L&F:* 160). In contrast to the meeting in Troy, they are now also able to see and hear her. Thus, as soon as the other characters have died and begin

---

36 The chapter is appropriately named "Voyage" (*L&F:* 159).

their journey to the afterlife, the former heterodiegetic narrator is now part of the characters' story world – or, to be more precise: the three characters leave their own story world and enter the narrator's world of transcendence. At this point, Berger once again turns to mythology. The old woman owning a luxury liner is connected to Charon, the ferryman on the river Styx whose ship, since the resurrection of Jesus Christ, carries the dead to the afterlife every third day instead of daily as before in the ancient Greek tradition, as the conversation between Naisi and Sucus shows: "'I never thought you'd be on this ship', said Sucus again. 'She leaves every third day.' 'I thought every night.' 'Once, long ago, she used to. The schedule changed in Jerusalem at the time forgiveness began.'" (*L&F:* 160–161 [my quotation marks]).

Thus, the narrator functions as an entity from an afterlife country which can in turn only be accessed by death. The story as such, however, takes place in the city. Both are linked by the narrator who haunts Troy without being able to contact the characters there. These characters living in the city conversely remember the country, idealise it or dream of going back there one day – but they will only access it by dying. Therefore, while the two spheres are clearly separated, they are also closely linked, and it is worth looking at some characters' perpectives against the background of Berger's historical afterword, against the background of Raymond Williams's account of the constructed relations and oppositions between country and city, and against the background of utopian and anti-utopian notions.

Utopian Country, Anti-utopian City?
Raymond Williams's *The Country and the City* (1973) identifies the generally accepted opposition between country and city as a construction which, as will be shown, is particularly prominent in literature. Furthermore, the opposition ties in nicely with the equally constructed opposition between utopia and anti-utopia.

The opposition between country and city as such, Williams claims, is fairly old, especially in England. In pretty much every century of English history, one can find a critical voice claiming that it is 'now' that country and city have really drifted apart. (see Williams 1973: ch. 2) However, proclaiming a drifting apart of country and city in whatever century is as much an oversimplification as is the mere reduction of the country and the city to two self-contained and opposed domains (see Williams 1973: 1). The country is not a happy place because it has its own power structures which, in the context of agriculture, lead to the exploitation of day labourers by wealthy landowners from the *country*; thus, the "idealisation of a 'natural' or 'moral' economy on which so many have relied, as a contrast to the thrusting ruthlessness of the new capitalism," is questionable (Williams 1973: 37). Furthermore, as these wealthy landowners became richer and richer, it was them who actually contributed to the rampant growth of cities and thus to another relation of exploitation, i.e. between city and country: "[t]here is then no simple contrast between wicked town and innocent country, for what happens in the town is generated by the needs of the dominant rural class" (Williams 1973: 53; also see 39). The relation between country and city has always been a story of exploitation, but people, it seems, imagine and construct a better, earlier, and uncorrupted age of a country life without landlords and without power structures of domination. To Williams, the most important origin of this so-called mystified Golden Age is Virgil's *Georgics:* there, peasants happily work together for the gain of the entire community without even separating one field of crops from another by landmarks (see Williams 1973: 42). In a way, it is only natural to construct such an image of an innocent country past if one perceives one's own present as being affected by severe changes (see Williams 1973: 293) – and if there are so many voices from so many centuries who do exactly that, it becomes clear why the notion of the glorified and idealised Golden Age countryside is so persistent. Furthermore, when taking this Golden Age and the opposition between country and city for granted, it is fairly easy to acknowledge a development of modern England from a rural to an industrial society, to use it as a projection screen for the nations' descent into disorder and loss of humanity, and to blame capitalism for it. The fact that the opposition between country and city is a construction does not weaken its power, and the construction of the opposition (see Williams 1973: 293) continues to influence heavily perspectives on country and city.

Literature, as Williams and also Richard Lehan show, tends to exploit the constructed opposition outlined above. To name but a few examples, "Wordsworth's poetry was founded on an opposition between the natural and the artificial, between a spirit of humanity and a spirit of fashion" – and thus between country and city (Lehan 1998: 76). Charles Dickens's *Dombey and Son* portrays, according to Lehan, "a man whose life is ruined by commercial greed. And never before had Dickens so clearly focused on the way the new city had been taken over by commerce and technology – by the forces of money and industry" – in short, by the rise of industrialisation and capitalism (Lehan 1998: 40). According to Williams, T.S. Eliot is another writer who, especially in his later works, solidifies the opposition by highlighting the Golden Age of the long-gone country: "the rural settlements – isolated and remote, visited from the city – acquire, if only by default, a traditional significance. This regular association of rural living with the past and with tradition [...] became commonplace" (Williams 1973: 240).

Berger seems indebted to this literary tradition, as a look at his historical afterword to *Pig Earth*, the trilogy's first novel, can reveal. However he, with a few exceptions, has not fallen victim to some prominent traditional oversimplifications,[37] and he is well aware of the economic interrelations between country and city (see Berger 1979: 199–200). In the historical afterword, Berger acknowledges the phenomenon of "deserted villages" as peasants abandon the country in order to become wage earners in the city (Williams 1979: 199). Consequently, *Lilac and Flag* is full of characters who do exactly that. Clement Gex and Hector left the country in order to find a job and a wife in Troy, and Clement, as pointed out earlier, became a day labourer there. While Hector became a police superintendent, Yannis similarly left behind his village on Samos and ended up as a crane operator on the same construction site as the character Murat, who emigrated from a Turkish village. All these characters, along with those who were born in the city but whose parents stem from the country, constantly dream of the country as a happier and better place. In the following, I present a couple of examples in some more detail.

Hector, the police superintendent, poses as the archetype of the village boy who moves to the city to make his fortune, but ends up unhappy. The narrator remembers him as an enthusiastic boy: "When he first left the village, age fourteen, Hector wept. [...] Then he ran down the steps to get into the bus and he shouted to his friends: You'd better lock up all your chicks and chickens when I get back!" (*L&F*: 72). The fact that "[h]e only came back twice" (*L&F*: 72) does not mean that he did not want to come back. On the contrary, he keeps on dreaming of returning with his wife, a city person whom he met in Troy:

> The last time he had tried to persuade Susanna that when he retired they should build a house in his village, on the land he had inherited from his aunt above the Republican Lyre, Susanna had finished her glass, put her swanlike arms round his neck, and said: You must be out of your mind, darling, I've told you a hundred times I'm not going to end my days living with a nag-who-has-a-broken-leg! (*L&F*: 74)

The quote shows the contrasting attitudes of Hector and Susanna and thus of a former country person and a city person. Hector draws upon the country's materiality as an inherited piece of land which could be made arable and where a house could be erected. Simultaneously, the pub named the Republican Lyre evokes the discursivity of Greek folklore music by alluding to the Cretan lyra

---

[37] One simplification on Berger's part can be found indeed, namely in his usage of the umbrella term of the peasant which does not seem to take into account Williams's differentiation between peasants as landowners and peasants as day labourers.

on the one hand and the political system of classical republics (their power resting with the people governing themselves rather than a monarch) on the other. Thus, the pub functions as a focal point: it brings together people both in terms of music and politics (the pub being a place where everybody can have one's say about current events), but it is also a place of transition (one dreams of going back to it while it is also a place of departure because of the bus leaving to the city from its doorstep). Susanna, conversely, ridicules the name of Hector's village (lucky-horse-with-a-broken-leg)[38] and by doing so, she ridicules the overall idea of living in the country.

Furthermore, Susanna has ambitions of her own. Her dream is not to stay and keep on living her life – she dreams of another variety of city life superior to what Troy can offer: "After a number of years in the city, Hector married Susanna, the daughter of a disgraced army officer. [...] And one day he would take her away, she dreamed, from sprawling Troy to a nobler city such as Tenochtitlán, where nobody would have to handle anything except chalices and anointing oils and flowers, flowers..." (*L&F:* 72). Her imagination of city life proper evokes the Aztec metropolis as a utopia with people dwelling in glamour and idleness and is oriented towards the future, whereas Hector's is – similar to the old lads in *City of Bohane* – caught in the past: "We all want to go back... just for a moment to look around. No, to look for something, really. Something lost. We think if we find it, we'll die happy. In my experience nobody dies happy" (*L&F:* 153). Hector wants to go back while at the same time telling himself that it is impossible – his village of old figures as a utopia, a beautiful non-place. The impossibility of returning is never spelled out explicitly, tough. The reader is never told that he cannot afford it and Hector is to be retired soon – a perfect opportunity to abandon the city which he nevertheless dismisses airily. Being 'too old' is his ostensible argument for not going back, while his wife and his inability to take his life into his own hands, to make a change, are the only obstacles preventing him from at least giving it a shot. As his retirement threatens to take away his job as the last thing he has been living for, Hector interrogates the arrested Sucus and finds out that Sucus's father is from the same village. At this point, Hector has already accepted that there is no going back for him, but he encourages Sucus to return to the village so that he may take Hector's spirit with him:

---

[38] The name again interrelates materiality and discursivity because it refers to how the village was founded. Clement tells Sucus the story of a tribe wandering through the mountains. Their chief's horse broke a leg and "[i]f your horse breaks a leg, you have to stay where you are. [...] That's how our village was founded centuries ago" (*L&F:* 40).

> We'll go back together, we'll find the village, we'll climb up the steps to the Republican Lyre – we'll order champagne, we'll sit on the terrace. I'm too old, Hector is too old, but you're not, you're Clement Gex's son. Shout out for us both! We're back! Hector Juaradoz and Clement Gex's son are back... back for good, back for ever. (*L&F:* 157)

Hector shoots himself after this conversation. The hope remains that the younger generation may accomplish what he could not do.

Sucus's father Clement Gex is, just as Hector, a former village boy who came to Troy at the age of seventeen. Thirteen years later, he married Wislawa, a fish warehouse worker. In contrast to Hector and Susanna, the two do actually visit the village before Sucus's birth, and Sucus himself is "conceived" in Clement's parents' house (*L&F:* 34). Then, however, capitalist inflation kicks in and takes away the possibility of travelling:

> From Troy they were always promising to come back to the village to show Casimir and Angeline their grandson, but, after the birth, Wislawa's health got worse and Clement's earnings became feebler and feebler as prices in Troy increased a hundredfold. So they put off coming and both grandparents died without ever having seen their grandson. (*L&F:* 35)

In the hospital, shortly before his death, Clement has one final conversation with his son about going back to the village in which he evokes numerous stories from the two preceding volumes of Berger's trilogy:

> 'I want to show my village to you, my son. I want to show you the house where I was born, the church where your mother and I got married, the chapel where Jean seduced the Cocadrille, the factory where they make molybdenum, the pass of St. Pair where the ravens fly, the blueberries and the bollets... Promise me, Sucus?' 'What do you want me to promise?' 'Promise me!' [...] 'Promise me to go to Park Avenue', whispered his father, and bit his under lip. (*L&F:* 41 [my quotation marks])

As in Hector's memory of the country, Clement's memory of the village is packed with stories which keep it alive.[39] The returning, however, is once again thwarted. Sucus does not understand right away what he is supposed to promise Clement – and Clement, utterly disappointed, only bites his under lip and sarcastically sends him to Park Avenue, Troy's financial district. Then, however, the nurse enters and Sucus has to leave – without making any promise.

Lastly, Sucus and Zsuzsa as the younger generation deserve some attention. Both have grown up in Troy without ever having been to the village. Still, the far-

---

[39] Again, the country interconnects the materiality of a place with a discursive aspect ("the church where Jean seduced the Cocadrille").

away village can function as an alternative to Troy for the two lovers. After Clement's death, Sucus plays with the idea of going to the country with Zsuzsa and his mother:

> Is it true? asked Sucus, his eyes shut. Are there people in the village who live on a mountain so high up, so far away, that when they whisper they can hear an echo from the rocks? [...] Why don't we go back to the village, Maman, the three of us? [...] You, Zsuzsa, and me. Father always said there was a wooden house on the mountain and a pine forest that still belonged to us. (*L&F*: 94)

Sucus highlights the materiality of the country: rocks, mountains, and the pine forest, without any names, render the country a tangible place in contrast to the elusive surfaces of the city. Sucus's mother, however, answers in the same vein as Hector: "There's no way, my boy, there's no way", without providing a good reason (*L&F*: 94). As they fall in love, Zsuzsa and Sucus imagine numerous futures together. In the first one, they build a house together (*L&F*: 28–29). As they build castles in the air, the element of leaving someone or something beloved behind comes in already:

> 'And ZSUZSA written in gold [on the door].' 'That's right, so the postman knows where to deliver the letters', she said. 'Who's going to write?' 'You, when you go away, you're going to write!' 'Why do I go away?' 'To find something else, something you can't find here. You steal a car.' 'I don't take you in the car?' 'I wait for you [...]. And I stay awake praying.' 'Praying for me to come back.' 'I'm expecting you back and I'm angry.' 'I don't come.' 'I can't believe it.' 'I have to be rich to come back.' 'I leave and I start looking for you.' 'You find me on the day I make twenty million.' [...] 'Then we take a ship', Zsuzsa said. 'A white ship.' 'We have a cabin to ourselves.' [...] 'We're locked in the cabin.' (*L&F*: 29–30 [my quotation marks])

The playful imagination also foreshadows the ending of the novel, where all the dead travel back to the country on a white ship, their cabins resembling tombs (see *L&F*: 167). After having stolen the passports from the train, Zsuzsa and Sucus have a little money; their first purchase is a night spent together in a hotel. The scenario of actually leaving Troy by train is toyed with: "'We could take tomorrow's train.' 'We could, yes.' 'We've got the cash.' 'First-class?' 'If you want, Lilac.' 'What would we do when we got there?' 'I've got a wooden house on a mountain. [...] My father's house. [...] We could live in it'" (*L&F*: 105 [my quotation marks]). As they keep on dreaming of a better place, however, it becomes clear that it will remain a dream:

> 'Shall we go?' 'We could, you know.' 'Take a sleeper to Paris.' 'No, no, the big sleeper out.' 'Far, far away.' [...] 'One-way tickets!' 'First-class, and not in a shanty train.' 'Nobody'll notice.' 'We can't yet. Your mother! Give me time to fill our wardrobe.' 'Wardrobe my arse!' 'It's too soon.' 'You want to be older? When I saw my dad in hospital I said- [...] There'll be noth-

ing better.' 'Better than what, love?' 'This.' 'They'd separate us and take everything away from us.' 'I'd find you in secret and pass you things through the bars. [...] If not now, when? If not here, where?' (*L&F:* 118 [my quotation marks])

The young lovers mentally construct an alternative world, or worlds, including stories, all of which remain unfulfilled and are dismissed quickly. Sucus and Zsuzsa, just as the others, are hesitant, since they have families which they would leave behind if they left and since they are afraid of being disappointed in the country.

It is striking that money, in their dreams, is not a problem, while it has been a massive problem in their real lives. As Sucus is told by the legless Michael who lives in a broken-down Cadillac:[40] "In dreams money's abolished. Everywhere. Maybe you dream of money. But you never dream of paying! Nobody in the world dreams of paying. This is what makes waking up so terrible. This is what makes waking up worse than hunger" (*L&F:* 145). As soon as they wake up, they are back in Troy where nothing works out nicely. In Sucus's words: "There's never any, any, any, going back, policeman" (*L&F:* 151). The alternative world-building of the lovers, then, is another failing attempt to make life in Troy worth living.

While all these characters in *Lilac and Flag* constantly dream of the country and revel in its nostalgic past, not a single one of them actually makes it back to the village. In fact, they do not even try. Why is that so? Several reasons are outlined above: they do not dare to go, they are afraid, they have other characters making them stay in Troy – but deep inside, they might know that the country they are dreaming of and the life associated with it is not even there anymore (or has never been there in the first place) without ever spelling it out explicitly. I suggest that this has to do with Berger's general attitude towards idealisations of the country as a happy place in his historical afterword which strikingly coincides with Williams's observations. Berger, like Williams, sees the history of country and city as a history of continuous exploitation. Thus, "any idealisation of their [i.e. the peasants'] way of life becomes impossible. In a just world such a class would not exist" (Berger 1979: 211). To Berger, the peasant is a "survivor," "a person who has continued to live when others have disappeared or perished" (Berger 1979: 199). The peasant class, while changing, has outlived all other societal traditions which came and went with the centuries (see Berger 1979: 197). However, Berger points out, it would be too easy to simply classify the peasant as "backward, a relic of the past" (Berger 1979: 200). Instead, it is more precise to associate the peasant class with certain timelessness. Their overall attitude to-

---

[40] Michael is another character who was introduced earlier in the trilogy. See Hertel (2005: 30).

wards life hinges on "a cyclic view of time" with the seasons coming and going (see Berger 1979: 201–202).[41] This does not mean that the past is not important to the peasant, but it is so again in terms of a cycle. If the peasant dies, there is no future awaiting him in the afterlife – instead, he goes back: "After his death he will not be transported into the future – his notion of immortality is different: he will return to the past" Berger 1979: 201). A corresponding passage can be found in *Lilac and Flag*. The narrator at one point explains the difference between the dead of the village and those of the city:

> When people die here they are all buried in the village cemetery. With time, their names, cut in marble, are effaced by the frost, the sun, and the rain; eventually they are forgotten, as the dead have been from the beginning. Yet, nameless, they are still remembered in the course a road follows, in the placing of a bridge over a river, in the way a wall runs, in the paths that lead over the mountains. In Troy it is different. There the names of the dead are forgotten more quickly. The only ones remembered are those with streets named after them. Otherwise, millions disappear without trace, leaving behind no landmark. In the city the bereaved alone carry their dead in their heads. The only memorials are private choices. Here we have so few choices. In Troy they need the dead to help them, because they face so many. (*L&F*: 44)

In both cases, the dead themselves of course stay dead. In the country, however, traces of them remain embedded in nature's capacity for remembering and the landmarks which the deceased have walked through or erected in their lives. Thus, the landmarks can function as discursive memorials while the dead are re-absorbed in the country's materiality. The dead of the city die without leaving a discursive mark; memories of them are at best reduced to the private sector of mourning. Exceptions are again those who profit from capitalism: the rich and the famous, after whom streets are named. The link is not as strong as in the village, though, because their names are not remembered personally, but merely join Troy's sketchy topography of place names.

Life, to the peasant, is thus just another part of the cycle, "an interlude" (Berger 1979: 200). Therefore, Berger's way of pointing out the importance of the past for the country has much in common with the traditional image of the Golden Age which cannot simply be traced to a specific time 'way back in the past,' but which is beyond any spatial or temporal anchoring. When taking into account the mystified Golden Age in this line of thought, the idea of utopia is close at hand. Williams, for example, uses both terms in the same context. The constructed ideal of the village comes close to the idea of utopia as it can be

---

41 Cf. also Berger 1979: 204–205 for the difference between how cultures of survival and cultures of progress perceive the past and the future.

found in the literary tradition: both are concerned with a simultaneously beautiful and imaginary place which can never be reached, has been lost, or is denied in some other way. However, I would like to argue that this apparently utopian program in *Lilac and Flag* is heavily overshadowed by a dystopian thrust (with a strong tendency to the anti-utopian end of the scale), and I base my argument on what the narrator leaves out in the long quote above, namely what happens to the dead themselves after having died.

Sucus, after his journey on the ship of the dead, arrives in the country, where he meets the old woman narrator in person.[42] Again, the notion of a Golden Age utopia is evoked in terms of both space and time: the old woman idly sits under a pear tree in an orchard, alluding to the Garden of Eden as a spatially detached primitive state – and thus to the archetypical Golden Age place. After having realised that Zsuzsa is not with the old woman and therefore still alive, Sucus weeps "for a millennium" (*L&F:* 169) which adds a temporal detachment to the spatial one; the country, it seems, is beyond place and beyond time. Thus, Sucus's arrival highlights that the country is his final destination: he will remain for eternity in this rural rendition of the afterlife. The spatial and temporal transposition of the country seems to render the rural afterlife a utopia, while the city of Troy poses as an anti-utopia as in classic texts of the tradition (in the attempt to escape to the country in Orwell's *Nineteen Eighty-Four,* for example, or in the literary community in Bradbury's *Fahrenheit 451*). However, with Berger being aware of the constructedness of country and city, it would be too simple to just stick to the opposition of utopian country and anti-utopian city. The denial of utopia is fairly strong in *Lilac and Flag* because the country is not even there anymore in the world of the living. Contrastingly, there still is a country in *Nineteen Eighty-Four,* and although Winston's and Julia's attempt to escape fails, they can at least try and even manage to spend some happy hours in the country. In *Lilac and Flag*, by placing utopia in the afterlife, the very idea of a utopia tips over into an anti-utopian hopelessness without many chances for a dystopian oscillation between these two extremes. Only death can bring you back to the Golden Age country. What remains of the dead are stories, stored on the white pages of Berger's novel, metaphorically present as the narrator's white ship.

What Berger does *not* do, then, is idealise the country as such. On the contrary, judging from the historical afterword in *Pig Earth*, he knows only too well that the actual-world history of the country does not offer a happy place or time. Instead, the ideal of the country needs to be traced farther back and farther

---

[42] Naisi, on the other hand, is going to Aleppo. Apparently, one always returns to the home of one's father (see *L&F:* 161).

away – namely to the utopian Golden Age, which is congruent with the afterlife in *Lilac and Flag*. However, if the only way of accessing this Golden Age country is to die in the city, the apparently obvious opposition of rural utopia and urban anti-utopia itself is questioned. The present in *Lilac and Flag* is fairly anti-utopian; the future is anti-utopian, and the utopian past is a mere construction and therefore highly unstable or even non-existent. The only utopian solution in *Lilac and Flag* is a return to the country which is only made possible by dying first. Thus, while the novel's utopia is a utopia in the true sense of the word (it *is* a beautiful place and it *is* unreachable in life), an anti-utopian element blackens the utopian ideal and thus stands as an excellent example of how blurry the borders between the two are (see also Meyer 2001: 91). Thus, Berger also manages to bring together two domains of constructedness, namely those outlined by Meyer and by Williams: the opposition of utopia and anti-utopia is as constructed as the one between country and city, and assimilated into an emphatic understanding of storytelling at different historical stages, determined by different narrative styles (from matter-of-fact reports to post-modern narration). The trilogy thus progresses from sketch to tale to story/novella and, ultimately, accomplishes its completion and perfection in the form of the novel.

IV.2.5 *Divided Kingdom:* Conceived Space, Ideology, and Identity

The title *Divided Kingdom* already gives away that the spatial separation affects the whole country instead of a single city. In fact, both run parallel: London as the former capital of the United Kingdom is divided into four capitals of the new Divided Kingdom. The analysis on the following pages will, after a brief overview of the four temperaments according to Hippocrates, concentrate on the strategies and processes of the Rearrangement in the context of conceived space and the emergence of ideologies (both institutional and personal ones, and according to the loose definition introduced in chapter IV.1) which work for or against it. Afterwards, the relations between the dominating conceived space on the one hand and lived space and perceived space on the other are taken into account.

Humourism
What is most striking in terms of conceived space in *Divided Kingdom* is, obviously, the Rearrangement according to the four humours from ancient Greek philosophy as a consciously conceived (in Lefebvre's terms: an intellectually worked out) project. Humourism is relevant on two levels in *Divided Kingdom:* firstly, it is

relevant for the classification of individuals; secondly, it is relevant for the overall image of the Divided Kingdom as a body.

Historically, the model of the four humours or temperaments became popular through Hippocrates (ca. 460 BC – ca. 377 BC) and several unknown authors, whose writings are usually attributed to Hippocrates as well (see Arikha 2007: 6). What was so revolutionary about the model was its concern for the whole body: "'every part of the body, on becoming ill, immediately produces disease in some other part'" (Arikha 2007: 7). It is fairly straightforward to analyse the ideology in *Divided Kingdom* along these lines: the "body politic" (*DK:* 10), i.e. the Divided Kingdom as such, can be taken as a body in which the humours are all mixed up. The four humours are, according to Hippocrates, blood, phlegm, yellow bile, and black bile. Blood is considered the "most neutral" and is "associated with springtime and childhood, with the sanguine temperament; and its prevalence within the organism was generally correlated with health and mental balance, serenity, sensuousness, and optimism" (Arikha 2007: 10). Phlegmatic temperaments, on the other hand, are said "to be sluggish in action and reaction" (Arikha 2007: 10). Phlegm is associated "with the winter and old age; many common illnesses, such as headcolds, were also attributed to its actions" (Arikha 2007: 10). Yellow bile, attributed to cholerics, describes "quick-tempered, sometimes resentful or envious, generally argumentative" behaviour and is "associated with summer and adolescence or youth" (Arikha 2007: 10). Lastly, black bile is said to be the "humour of maturity," autumn being the corresponding season. "Melancholic people tended to be introspective, and so this humour could be useful for creativity, although it was also instrumental in delirium, madness, or conditions associated today with depression" (Arikha 2007: 10). The corresponding descriptions of the four humours in *Divided Kingdom* are strikingly close to the ancient Greek paradigm:

> Choleric people were known for their aggressive qualities. They led lives packed with action and excess. Melancholic people, by contrast, were morbid and introspective. What interested them was the life of the mind. Phlegmatic people were swayed by feeling. Empathy came naturally to them, as did a certain spirituality, but they tended to be passive, a little sluggish. As for sanguine people, they were optimistic, good-humoured and well-meaning. (*DK:* 11)

While the novel does not bother to describe each single detail (for example, the tasks the humours do fulfil in order to keep the body healthy, where they are produced exactly, and how lack or excess can make people sick), the emerging archetpyes of citizens are easy to imagine.

According to Hippocrates, every human being is made up of all four humours and cannot be reduced "to one element or one humour [...]. All the elements and substances were present in each individual, from birth to death" (Arikha 2007: 8). If all are present in one's body, one's condition hinges on the humours' relations in the body: "the preponderance of some [humours] over others [...] determine[s] the temperament of each individual" (Arikha 2007: 9). Therefore, one is not necessarily sick if one is, say, more phlegmatic than others. However, in order to be healthy, the humours need to be in a proper balance called *eukrasis*; conversely, "[d]isease was understood as a state of imbalance or *dyskrasia* between the humours that made up the body's *krasis*, its general constitution or *complexion*" (Arikha 2007: 8 [original italics]). Therefore, in the terminology of humourism, "illness was a matter of excess or lack, of the exacerbation of one quality over another" (Arikha 2007: 10). In order to rebalance the humours, both internal and external factors come into play, as will become clear later on. Again, the novel proves to be fairly analogous; even eucrasia as the ideal balance between the humours is not only mentioned, but used for describing the ideal state of the nation in healthy balance – just as the individual body. The paradigm shift from the human body to the body politic is made explicit by Miss Groves, Parry's teacher at the boys' home: "'the theory of the humours is built on notions of harmony and equilibrium, and these were the very qualities that were lacking in the country prior to the Rearrangement. [...] All of a sudden, it was the body politic that needed treatment'" (*DK:* 10). Here, it is visible for the first time that Thomson rather borrowed the overall idea of humourism instead of striving for an entirely congruent adaptation. The body politic may be out of balance; disease, crime, corruption and so on may keep it out of balance; which humours does it lack, though, and by which quality is it dominated? Too much violence may point towards an excess of yellow bile and choleric behaviour, and the increase of diseases may point towards too much phlegm. Yet, the state of imbalance, of dyscrasia, is not clearly spelled out according to the humours.

Rearranging People
The title of the novel and of the new country has been mentioned already: the kingdom is divided instead of united. "Rearrangement" or "Ministry of Health and Social Security" (Parry's employer) are terms which sound reasonably neutral at first, but generate their own considerable momentum in a dystopian or nationalist context: the ministry is mostly concerned with "relocating" (another euphemism) citizens, i.e. with tearing apart families,[43] which is generally what

---

[43] It is hard not to be reminded of Orwell's terminology in *Nineteen Eighty-Four*, where the Ministry of Truth, for instance, is responsible for propaganda and lies.

the Rearrangement does. Rearranging here means to separate people spatially, mentally, and emotionally. The term is part of a fully-fledged institutional concept, and it is presented as such as well to the citizens. While the reader fairly early cannot deny a bit of unease about the overall idea, the Rearrangement was "masterminded" (*DK:* 14) by politicians in a long process:

> [T]he government had not flinched from its responsibility. The Prime Minister and the members of his cabinet had met in secret chambers, far from the eyes and ears of the electorate. Down there [...] they talked, they argued, they even wept, and in the end they reached a decision: they were going to do something bold, something extraordinary... (*DK:* 8).

The quote shows how the citizens are supposed to take the Rearrangement: as a necessary reaction of a caring government which assumes responsibility for the nation's health, as a reaction against the social grievances. The Rearrangement is sold to the people as a well-conceived long-term project worked out by a small elite circle far from those whom it will concern.[44] Making use of the four temperaments from ancient Greek philosophy as the basis of the new kingdom is of course a clever move; borrowing ancient concepts projects their respectability onto the Rearrangement. Thus, the Rearrangement becomes an attempt to reconfigure the state's present dyscrasia and to heal the body of the nation. Taking the analogy one step further, the families as the malfunctioning part of society could be treated as the sick body part which then affects the whole body and therefore needs treatment (i.e. they need to be disbanded and relocated).

The Rearrangement seems to work out fine at the beginning: Parry remembers how he and the other boys, after the first indoctrination, were "excited without knowing why. It was the effect of flattery" (*DK:* 6). The "Children of the Red Quarter," according to their teacher, are "to be admired" because they are of a "significance [which] cannot be overestimated" (*DK:* 6). Sanguine boys are, according to the ideology established by their teacher, the best there are because red people are "optimistic, good-humoured and well-meaning" and often inspire others (*DK:* 11). The reader is only given the indoctrination of future red children as the new elite of the new nation, but it is well imaginable that the children of other quarters are similarly addressed so they will be satisfied with their place in

---

[44] To give but one example for the extent of the system's constructedness: melancholy is originally associated with black bile and therefore the colour black. The authorities in *Divided Kingdom*, hoewever, choose green as the melancholic colour because black "had too many negative connotations" (*DK:* 12). The mere change of colour does not restrain people from negatively-connotated melancholic behaviour (such as committing suicide), of course.

the Divided Kingdom.⁴⁵ Still, a look at at the history of humourism reveals that the sanguine temperament is traditionally considered the most neutral, healthy and balanced one (see Arikha 2007: 10). Therefore, it is well possible that, in the setting of *Divided Kingdom*, red is actually superior or at least striving to be superior. The novel's ending also hints at the possibility of a red elite pulling the strings (see the end of this chapter for more details).

Miss Groves's indoctrination seems to be successful as the boys pick up her way of speaking: "'A little too much phlegm this morning, don't you think?'", says of one the boys – "'He had learned his lessons well,'" as Parry states retrospectively (*DK:* 14). It is not without irony that Miss Groves as a (red) propaganda teacher is said to have a phlegmatic (and therefore blue) touch. Making use of bodily imagery, such as the "body politic" (*DK:* 10), and letting the human body's balance of humors run parallel to that of the state's body, can be identified as a typical governmental move for rendering an abstract entity such as a state more concrete or organic (see Lefebvre 1991: 274) and thus as another piece of the authorities' strategy. The Rearrangement is a construction, a model, and its instability concerning classification will become apparent later on. The theory may have been made known to all citizens, but not all citizens do believe it to be true.

The Impact of Conceived Space
How does the conceived space in *Divided Kingdom* dominate the lived space and how does it render perceived space? Obviously, the Rearrangement and the resulting separation have a material impact. The newly arranged quarters develop individual styles of architecture, the waterways in the Blue Quarter being the most striking examples. The new topographies are tailored to the new quarters' particular needs. In the Blue Quarter, for instance, tall buildings are pulled down to prevent people from throwing themselves off and committing suicide, and special graveyards are built for the vast number of suicidal persons who are buried separately from the rest of the dead (see *DK:* 28). Furthermore, the four quarters are related to specific atmospheres, moods, and therefore the dimension of lived space. In Parry's words (during his stay in the Blue Quarter): "It wasn't just the architecture or the dialect; it was something much larger and more abstract,

---

45 *Brave New World*'s hypnopaedia as indoctrination springs to mind. There, the elite Alphas are made happy with their lives because they can work on intellectually challenging things; conversely, the simple-minded Epsilons are equally satisfied with their place in society because they are given simple tasks and short working shifts.

like the look on people's faces, or the atmosphere itself. The citizens of Aquaville seemed to equate existence with peril" (*DK:* 13–14).

The spatial Rearrangement creates new identities and affiliations which can then be subverted or confirmed. Being part of a particular group ties in nicely with the overall idea of the Rearrangement; in order to be happy with the group one is in, there must be other groups one does not want to belong to. Fernandez, a colleague of Parry's from the Yellow Quarter, identifies psychological racism as a phenomenon emerging in the course of the Rearrangement:

> "It's like racism, really, if you think about it," [Fernandez] went on. "I don't mean the old racism. That's dead and gone. I'm not interested in the colour of someone's skin. It's their thoughts that bother me. The new racism is psychological. What's strange is, we seem to need it – to thrive on it. If we don't have someone to despise, we feel uncomfortable, we feel we haven't properly defined ourselves. Hate gives us hard edges. And the authorities knew that, of course. [...] They took the worst part of us and built a system out of it." (*DK:* 195–196)

Four new countries make up the Divided Kingdom, all of which share a psychological racism, while the overall composition of the Divided Kingdom is still described as balanced or harmonious. If one listens to Fernandez, the reciprocal aversion truly seems to stem from nothing but the very construction; in order to be somebody, the four quarters' citizens need something which they are *not* part of. By separation and difference, it becomes possible to identify oneself as belonging to one particular quarter while scorning the other(s); prejudice is commonplace. Fernandez wears his heart on his sleeve:

> "What was so clever about the way they divided us," [Fernandez] said at last, "was that it more or less guaranteed that we would hate each other. I can't help feeling a kind of contempt for you, for instance. It might be because of what you're doing, and the effect it has on others, but it might simply be because of who you are. I'm from the Yellow Quarter, and you're from somewhere else. That's probably enough. And yet, to answer your question, I'm one of the few people who believe in the great pipe dream, that we should be able to live in the same country. [...] Then I see myself succumb to prejudice, and I realise how insidious it is, how easy..." (*DK*, p. 195)

While the authorities proclaim a harmonious equilibrium, they bargain for the citizens to perpetuate the ideologies they have internalised. It is not necessary to openly make one quarter hate another one if the Rearrangement leads to it anyway. Fernandez' remark on being torn between the "great pipe dream" and prejudice should be kept in mind for the question whether the quarter makes the people or the other way round. First, however, the eradication of people's pasts as another part of the Rearrangement deserves some attention.

Giving People New Identities

In order to create new identities in a dystopia, the past has either to be falsified or to be erased completely. In *Divided Kingdom*, the most important act of erasing the past occurs right at the beginning: the family is torn apart; Matthew Micklewright is relocated to another family and given the name Thomas Parry. All that remains is a mental image of his half-awake parents as he is taken away (see *DK:* 23) and in fact, he can hardly remember his old life afterwards. By doing so everywhere in the country, the government makes sure that the new identity is not tied to blood relations as in traditional families, but to the four temperaments, and therefore to the government's ideology. In other words, the government wants to have more control over people's private lives and to make people feel more loyal towards the system than to their families; in the dystopian tradition, the key word for this shift of loyalty is totalitarianism. The officially proclaimed ideology is supposed to influence all aspects of life (see Meyer 2001: 14–15). Being asked by Marie, his new sister, whether he remembers anything, Parry only recalls his old name, which sounds "like gobbledegook," and wishes he "hadn't said [it]" (*DK:* 47). His new name, his new life, and the underlying ideology are so strong that they shrink his former name and identity to nonsense. The old name is without context, without place. Nevertheless Parry, among others, cannot deny a certain "border sickness" – he is aware of the fact that something from his past, from his former lived space, is missing (*DK:* 23). He compares his state of mind to the torn-down bridges which help to keep the four quarters materially apart:

> [W]here the river itself had become the border all bridges had been destroyed. The roads that had once led to them stopped at the water's edge, and stopped abruptly. They seemed to stare into space, no longer knowing what they were doing there or why they had come. During my early twenties I was gripped by the sense of history that emanated from such places; they were like abandoned gateways, entrances to forgotten worlds. Also, of course, I felt I had stumbled on a physical embodiment of my own experience. There were bridges down inside me too. There was the same sense of brutal interruption. (*DK:* 82)

Just as the actual bridge as a material connector across a material river has been destroyed, the bridge to his pre-Rearrangement lived space is missing as well – he cannot access it discursively anymore, which is also highlighted by the "sense of history." Just as the bridges, the people used to have a history prior to the Rearrangement. In the story-now, however, one can only "stare into space" unhinged from the historic context. Just as the torn-down bridges lead to unknown places nowadays, people's pasts are equally "forgotten worlds." Although Parry feels the loss of the past as a "brutal interruption" in his early twenties, it seems to hurt less as time goes by. Years later, memory and interest have faded; he is not only detached from his former name, but also from the identity associated with it: "Once, I had been Matthew Micklewright, but that person no longer existed, and I wasn't even curious about him now. It was just too long ago, too remote – too *unlikely*. [...] That old name had become as hollow and empty as a husk. A name deprived of breath, of meaning" (*DK*, p. 82 [original italics]). On the other hand, the night when he was taken away from his parents now figures as the true beginning of his true life: "And then the night when my life began again..." (*DK:* 82). Parry even goes so far as to compare it to the birth of a baby: "A strange beginning. Soldiers, bright lights. The cold. And me being lifted, as if by surgeons, into a new world – and crying probably, though I couldn't remember that. But every birth is merciless, perhaps" (*DK:* 82). The Rearrangement rearranges Parry's ways of accessing the outside world and his entire biography, straight down to his day of birth. Since Parry is unable to access the past prior to the Rearrangement, he is eager to assign meaning to the present and the more recent past which is still accessible. Bereft of his old identity, he is looking for a new one (to inscribe himself into), which is his ultimate motivation for working so hard for the new authorities (see *DK:* 75).

The cross-border conference, then, to which he is sent on behalf of his ministry, is part and parcel of Parry's crucial change. He visits a club called the Bathysphere in the Blue Quarter, and the name speaks for itself, "suggesting immersion in a foreign element, a descent into the deepest, darkest depths [...]" (*DK:* 112), "a probing of the latent, the forbidden, the impenetrable" (*DK:* 136). The Bathysphere club becomes a device which allows Parry to descend into his early past by means of a vision-like trip. By simply choosing and opening a door inside the club, Parry re-encounters people and places from his past: his former best friend in the boys' home, a car ride with another version of his new 'sister' Marie as a lover, and, most importantly, fragments of the time prior to the Rearrangement present themselves to him in the Bathysphere: "A few brief glimpses of the buried past – the house I had lived in, my mother's voice, my face pushed against her skirt" (*DK:* 254; see also 130–131). It is not all clear which parts of his trip are real and which are not, and to Parry, it does not matter. Fact and fiction blur and evoke "painful nostalgia," a longing for the past which, despite the ontological fuzziness, feels real: "Had I been finding out about myself, or just imagining things? I didn't know. Whatever the truth was, it had felt more real than anything had felt for ages. *I* had felt more real. Or more alive, perhaps" (*DK:* 152 [original italics]). What has been eradicated comes back as the only authentic experience in a world full of artificial, ideologically charged restructuring: "The point was, the fragments *felt* authentic. They felt *real.* In the absence of so much, they were something I could turn to when I needed to, something I could count on" (*DK:* 254 [original italics]). Only then does Parry realise that his rebirth as Thomas Parry could only take place because of the death of Matthew Micklewright: "The authorities had deprived me of a life that was mine, and mine alone. [...] They'd just taken it. By force. In a sense, then, I had been murdered" (*DK:* 266). The great realisation concerning the rift between past and present follows shortly after: Parry and the few people he talks to about the past are by no means the only ones to experience this rift. The conversations, riots in the Yellow Quarter, the Bathysphere, and many more hints point toward the fact that "[t]here were very few who didn't live in the shadow of some separation or other. The united kingdom was united after all, by just one thing: longing" (*DK:* 276 [lowercase in original]) – both temporal and spatial.

Ascription and the Crisis of Identity
If all citizens feel the "rift between past and present" (*DK:* 23), between their former life and the one superimposed by the authorities, between the United Kingdom and the Divided Kingdom, it becomes apparent that the separation according to the four humors is not 'given' but merely constructed. Fernandez's attitude – being torn between a sense of unity on the one hand and hating everyone who is not from the Yellow Quarter on the other – already hints at the ambiguous (Re)arrangement. As described in the following, the conceived classification, and thus the resulting conceived space of the Divided Kingdom, is continuously questioned.

To begin with, the lived space of the four quarters' citizens is dominated by the instability of their own identity. The mere possibility of being (re-)relocated, of being deprived of one's identity a second time (the Rearrangement having been the first time), is a burden: "You never knew who was going to be taken next" in "this uncertain climate" (*DK:* 14). The atmosphere in the house of the Parry family can serve as a good example. One day Victor, Thomas Parry's new father, senses the death of his wife, who had been relocated years ago. He and his daughter Marie become deeply depressed and therefore quite 'unred.' The resulting atmosphere projects itself onto the domestic space of the family's house: "Grief ran down its walls like condensation, and the silence that lay in all the rooms had become so profound, so treacherous, that I feared I might sink into it, as one might sink into a marsh, and never to be seen again" (*DK:* 51). The sinking into a marsh runs parallel to the threat of relocation – it could happen any moment and would make one disappear. Victor and Marie, despite their untypical behaviour, are never taken, but the paranoia is – for Parry at least – always there: "I was always waiting for that unfamiliar and yet predictable knock on the front door" (*DK:* 51).

As a result, if one is afraid of being relocated, one consciously tries to behave as stereotypically as possible while hiding those traits which do not fit: people in the Red Quarter try to be properly sanguine, and so forth. Parry summons the image of a Russian doll: "my lives concealed neatly, one inside the other" (*DK:* 76). The fact that the classifications are not set in stone is fairly apparent and is exemplified by the concept of "psychological contamination" (*DK:* 95). Whatever is beyond one quarter's border is not necessarily disliked or hated. The other also emanates a certain fascination, which for example results in tourist settlements such as the "Border Experience" in the Red Quarter; there, right on the border to the Yellow Quarter, there are "theme hotels, fast-food restaurants and souvenir shops. Sanguine people came from far and wide to climb the viewing platforms, each hoping for a brief taste of life on the other side" (*DK:* 69). The border may be impenetrable materially, but something from the other side might seep through nevertheless. Not only *can* people from the Red Quarter buy all kinds of souvenirs (for example, a t-shirt saying "*I came I saw I lost my temper,*" [original italics] and thus suggesting that sanguine people can become choleric after all) – they actually *do* so and display choleric behaviour by doing so. The Border Experience as such, in its overtly touristic fashion, gives away that "some of the cholerics' notorious materialism had seeped over the wall" discursively (*DK:* 69). Vishram, Parry's supervisor at the Ministry of Health and Social Security, discards psychological contamination as an "old superstition about the border-crossing itself, that one might be mysteriously depleted by the experience, that one might lose part of oneself – that one might suffer injury or harm" (*DK:* 85). For the relocation officers, however, the superstition turns out to be painfully true. Parry, being a relocation officer himself, is extremely influenced by his changing surroundings as he travels from quarter to quarter,[46] and he is by no means the only one: "The old joke about relocation officers was that they themselves often had to be relocated. They crossed too many borders. They burned out. It was an occupational hazard" (*DK:* 88).

Obviously, people's humours and therefore the people's temperaments are liable to change in *Divided Kingdom* as well as in the ancient Greek paradigm: "The temperaments formed by humours were not fixed entities: they were rather an aspect of nature's variability" (Arikha 2007: 14). It is precisely at this point, however, where Hippocrates and Thomson's adaptation diverge. Variability is inherent to the humours and temperaments, but this is exactly what the govern-

---

[46] For a more detailed analysis of Parry's crossings and transgressions as he walks through all four quarters, see chapter V.2.3. Although chapter IV bears the subtitle "Taking a Stroll," it is more appropriate to elucidate his walkings and the search for identity which goes with them in the later chapter because they are closely tied to border-related performances.

ment of the Divided Kingdom does *not* want. By means of the Rearrangement and the strict separation the government wants to make sure that the four quarters and the people within remain stable with as little change as possible in order to keep the body politic in equilibrium and to maintain the classic dystopian status quo. The fact that the citizens are not happier or healthier after the Rearrangement is unimportant as long as the body politic is healthy, and the government does not flinch from keeping its people in an environment where they deliberately become choleric, phlegmatic, or melancholic, i.e. where one humour unhealthily prevails over the others. It is, of course, quite devious to sell this strategy to the people by saying that it is in fact better for them to live among people with similar psychological qualities.

Parry himself is affected by psychological contamination as well. On his return to Aquaville in the Blue Quarter, he seems "very much at home," as Odell observes (*DK:* 231). Gradually, he begins to question the classifications superimposed on the people by the authorities. Not only may the classification go wrong with relocation as a consequence – the whole scheme of classification as such might be misleading: "perhaps, in the end, the four countries didn't vary as much as was commonly believed. Perhaps our famous differences were no more than convenient fictions" (*DK:* 179). The question to what extent the quarters are inherently different indeed hinges on Fernandez' remark quoted earlier: "I'm one of the few people who believe in the great pipe dream, that we should be able to live in the same country. [...] Then I see myself succumb to prejudice, and I realise how insidious it is, how easy..." (*DK:* 195). Each citizen is torn between unity despite the four humors and psychological racism, between what he or she wants to be and what he or she is being made by other forces. The question of identity in *Divided Kingdom*, both on an individual and on a national level, hinges on ascription.[47]

Who attributes what to whom? Firstly, Thomson's novel is packed with passages of self-ascription. The way of identifying oneself in *Divided Kingdom* is inevitably tied to the one thing all citizens have in common: the rift between the pre-Rearrangement past and the present as a unifying longing. The rift, the longing, and the fear of relocation create a state of constant unease, rendering identity dangerously unstable. When Parry is back in the Red Quarter at the very end of the novel, he realises that he cannot simply switch back to his old sanguine

---

47 The term ascription, for the purposes of this study, is borrowed from sociology in the context of classificatory social stratification (see Barker 2004: 436) and slightly modified; it shall describe processes where people are either assigned certain qualities and characteristics (i.e. an identity) by others (external ascription) or where people assign themselves certain qualities and characteristics (self-ascription).

life after having been to all other quarters: "I fell back on my usual routine that morning [...] – but I had the constant, niggling sense that I was only pretending to be myself. At times I could even detect flaws in my own performance. [...] Everything felt familiar, and yet the notion of familiarity was, in itself, strange" (*DK:* 385). The return to his old routine is an attempt to return to his life before his first border-crossing, but he is not the one he is supposed to be anymore. "Performance" functions as a key word for displaying the fictional character of his routine – it is a mere show, a hollow performance of his former days which has nothing to do with him. After having been to all four quarters, he does not feel like the old Thomas Parry anymore – just as he did not feel like the old Matthew Micklewright anymore after the Rearrangement. Who one wants to be is not congruent with who one is supposed to be. The question of identity is always answered according to the four humors.

The incongruities shine through many times. Vishram, Parry's supervisor, openly "admit[s] to a streak of melancholy" (*DK:* 76), while others have to bury such tendencies deep inside them; Parry's imagery of identity being like a Russian doll comes to mind again. Dr Gilbert, a scientist from the Blue Quarter, can serve as another example of such a crisis of identity. Gilbert's task is to reassess Parry after his arrest by running numerous tests on him and evaluating them with the help of some obscure machinery. While reassessing Parry, he explains how the results of the personality test run by the machine and people's self-awareness can differ: "I've often thought that I belonged in the Red Quarter, but the results never came out quite right" (*DK:* 248). The same thing happens to Parry, who wants to return to the Blue Quarter (phlegmatic); however, he is (re-)classified as melancholic (see *DK:* 253). He may feel at home in the Blue Quarter, but the tests say he is supposed to be green. Who is correct? Gilbert spells out the situation: "'It sounds strange to say it, [...] but we know ourselves, don't we? Surely we know ourselves better than all this' – and he looked around the room – 'all this cumbersome machinery with which we surround ourselves'" (*DK:* 248). The resistance group which Parry meets in the Yellow Quarter puts it even more straightforwardly. In a ritual where the four papier mâché animals associated with the four quarters are burned, the leader of the group calls out: "We know what we are [...], and we know what we are not [...]. And what we are not [...], we shall now, ceremonially, destroy" (*DK:* 169). The resistance group clearly opposes the authorities' ideology of the balance of the four humours while proclaiming its own ideology: "All people were different [...], but if one looked beneath those differences, all people were the same. We had to be allowed to live together, to complement one another. That was where true freedom lay" (*DK:* 166). In short: people's impressions of themselves, figuring as personal occurrences of ideology, which stand in stark contrast to the machine's results and the strict separation of the four quarters, question the superimposed systems of classification. Yet, the question is: do the people in the Divided Kingdom really know themselves better – not only better than cumbersome machinery, but also better than all the other discursive ascriptions out there?

Parry feels comfortable as a sanguine person – until he travels to the Blue Quarter, where he immediately feels at home. Conversely, while staying in the Yellow Quarter, the Red Quarter "didn't seem well tempered so much as over-sanitised, devoid of warmth and feeling, bland" (*DK:* 166). Obviously, people and their mindsets are liable to change. Fernandez points out the irony of his time in the Yellow Quarter: "I was classified as choleric [...], which is something I dispute, of course, something that I resent as well, and yet I seem to be getting more and more choleric every year that passes" (*DK:* 196).[48] His environment determines him, the quarter or space seems to render the person.[49] The example of Fernandez seems to validate Parry's theory "that the divided kingdom was self-perpetuating, and that the need for transfer and relocation would eventually die away," the reason being that "[e]ach of the four quarters had already developed its own unique character and identity. In other words, although the idea of four types of people was fundamentally simplistic, there was a certain amount of self-fulfilling prophecy involved. Place someone in an environment for long enough and he starts to take on the attributes of that environment" (*DK,* p. 114).[50] Once again, ancient Greek humourism has its share in this idea in *Divided Kingdom*; the theory takes "into account not only inborn temperaments but also the environmental context within each person lived [...]. [F]actors such as climate and vegetation shaped the human organism and had a direct effect on its humoural constitution" (Arikha 2007: 12). Parry, too, is affected by this kind of environmental adaptation. The Blue Quarter captivates him right at his arrival; furthermore, in the Yellow Quarter, his behaviour is aggressive – choleric (see *DK:* 164–165; 183; 338). It may not always be that clear whether the quarter renders its people or the other way around – the importance of one's environment is beyond question, though. Take the following short passage on health and climate in the blue capital, for example:

---

48 Ironically, the mere act of disputing and resenting one's situation could be described as a display of choleric tendency.
49 Thus, *Divided Kingdom* appears to place itself on the 'nurture' side of the 'nature versus nurture' debate (i.e. whether innate qualities or personal experiences are more important in terms of rendering one's identity).
50 A similar way of thought can be found in the ancient Greek paradigm of humourism: "the course of an illness was in fact a process of natural readjustment of the organism to its environment" (Arikha 2007: 13).

> Aquaville had never enjoyed a healthy reputation. In recent years it had been ravaged by flu epidemics, and locals were always falling prey to arthritis and pneumonia. Some argued that the maladies originated in the phlegmatic character itself, its innate quality being cold and damp, but others believed that the Blue Quarter's administration should shoulder the blame. In adding some two hundred miles of new waterways to the canals and lakes that existed prior to the Rearrangement, it stood accused of actually altering the city's climate. (*DK:* 99)

People's health and their environment go together and fit both the ancient Greek description of phlegmatic temperament as well as the one by Miss Groves. Athanor, the capital of the Yellow Quarter, reveals similar traces of choleric temperament in its topography:

> Athanor shocked me with its brazen air of dereliction. [...] I saw stretches of barren land sealed off by wire-mesh and wooden hoardings, whole sections of the city laid to waste, whole streets demolished, gone. At one point I passed a pub that stood entirely on its own, defiant yet piteous, like the last remaining tooth in a punch-drunk boxer's mouth. (*DK:* 187–188)

It is no wonder that riots remain visible in the country's most choleric city. The analogy goes further still: the city is about to break down completely, it barely stands and, like the "punch-drunk boxer" with one remaining tooth (and like the choleric stereotype who is always in for a drink and a brawl), it is far from being healthy.

Are the people sick/aggressive because they adapted to their environment's natural conditions or because the environment has been designed as to make them sick/aggressive? Both would support Parry's theory of self-perpetuation, but the second possibility would add another layer of complexity in terms of conceived space and ideology. In this case, authorities would not rely on self-perpetuation alone but alter the default situation by conceiving and producing an appropriate space in order to support the self-perpetuation of the four temperaments. Thus, the inherent effect of a quarter's environment on its inhabitants is one thing;[51] external ascriptions and expectations from others are another. The door seems to swing both ways and again, the ancient Greek paradigm reverberates: one text by an unknown Hippocratic writer describes that "nature, climate, and therefore temperament determined culture, that is, political and social structures – although culture also affected nature and could compensate for its effects" (Arikha 2007: 12) – or enhance them. Just as a cold and damp climate

---

[51] Unfortunately, detailed descriptions of the environment are rather scarce in *Divided Kingdom*.

may render people prone to corresponding maladies and therefore sluggish or passive in the Green Quarter, one may conversely tear down or block motorways in all quarters except for the yellow one because motorways are considered extremely choleric (see *DK:* 40; 79). Inhabitants of the Blue Quarter are expected to be phlegmatic because they live there. To give an example from Parry's working routine in the ministry:

> I had to deal, on a regular basis, with people who held equivalent positions in other parts of the divided kingdom, and despite all the obvious differences in temperament and perception it was important to try and maintain good working relations. If I disputed one of their initiatives, it could be regarded as an example of Red Quarter impatience or naivety. If they disputed one of mine, I could just as easily see it as Blue Quarter dithering, Green Quarter cynicism or Yellow recklessness. (*DK:* 75)

One does not even need to listen properly to one another in order to ascribe someone certain behaviour. The governmentally superimposed rhetoric itself is a machine which subverts proper collaboration. The Divided Kingdom is a state of contestation. It is easy to take people's classifications for granted: if one is from the Red Quarter, he or she is simply expected to behave as the archetypical sanguine person. People want their prejudices to be valid, and all actions and utterances are interpreted accordingly. In such a network of internal and external ascriptions, clashes between the two are inevitable.[52] *Divided Kingdom* refuses to reveal which ascriptions are correct; both ways of pinpointing identity are problematic. Hence, the questions raised by Dr Gilbert remain: do people know themselves? Can technology do better?[53]

Another part of the puzzle, besides whether identity is rather to be dealt with by means of technology or human reasoning, the (humanly) conceived system of the four humors as such is highly questionable concerning its legitimacy. As mentioned, Parry considers the arrangement simplistic but effectively self-perpetuating; Fernandez, besides his bitterness, acknowledges the cleverness of the authorities' approach. Gilbert, however, questions the teachings of the four

---

[52] To give one final example, Parry, while at Dr Gilbert's, expects to be classified as yellow (while wishing to be classified as blue), but he actually is ascribed a green affiliation (see *DK:* 253).
[53] Handing evaluation over to machines, and preferring their results to human judgment, is precisely the kind of technological criticism which is characteristic for so many dystopian works of art. Firstly, one's affiliation to one of the four humours matters more than the traditional family; secondly, the continuous unease and fear of being relocated again is equivalent with the estrangement of mankind with its own products – especially if people begin to turn to machines for apparently objective results (see Meyer 2001: 14–15).

humors and their equilibrium in eucrasia: "But perhaps it's *too* perfect [...]. Perhaps one craves a little discord, a little mess. Perhaps, in the end, we tire of harmony" (*DK:* 248 [original italics]). The authorities, with the idea of eucrasia in mind, crave harmony. The citizens of the divided kingdom, however, crave a certain amount of discord.[54]

A quick glance at the etymology of "harmony" sheds some more light on the underlying tension. On the one hand, it can be derived from Harmonia, the Greek goddess of concord in the sense of congruence (see *CDCM:* 170). On the other hand, harmony can also be traced back to the ancient Greek concept of homonoia as the "personification of Harmony" with a slightly different meaning: the unification of opposites to a whole in the sense of an "agreement finally reached between patricians and plebeians," i.e. between different social classes (*CDCM:* 204–205). These two different meanings can show the overall problematic of eucrasia, of the harmony of the four humours in *Divided Kingdom*. The authorities seem to understand harmony according to the first meaning; they strive for harmony in the sense of psychological congruence within each specific quarter, the idea being that people who share psychological attributes should be able to get along (see *DK:* 14). Keeping the four quarters separate, however, leads to discord on the higher level where the four quarters are supposed to form an organic whole despite their opposites (as in the concept of homonoia). Discord, it seems, is inevitable; the people need it and it also projects itself on the model of the four humors and its apparent equilibrium. The idea of the Rearrangement with eucrasia as its philosophical basis is a model which nicely suggests (almost utopian) harmony which it will never reach. As shown in this chapter, nobody is more happy, congruent, or in tune with his environment after the Rearrangement than before. On the contrary, discord is present on all levels: individual people are in discord with themselves as they are not as stable in their psychological ascriptions as estimated; the four individual quarters are in discord because their citizens are liable to 'change colour' and do not necessarily get along better than before in the traditional family system; and the Divided Kingdom made up of the quarters on the whole is in discord as well, psychological racism being the strongest evidence. Being faced with so much discord, it is highly questionable whether Parry's theory of self-perpetuation will turn out to be true. In the novel's 27 years of story time at least, the most striking discord is to be found between the expectations towards the conceived, superimposed system and the way it is

---

54 This opposition can be identitified as another classic dystopian theme, most present probably in *Brave New World*. True individual happiness needs a streak of discord beyond institutional reglementations ensuring stability (see Meyer 2001: 36–37).

supposed to dominate lived space on the one hand, and the actual outcome on the other.

Even apparently non-dystopian places in the Divided Kingdom are not free from ideology and discord. After being shipwrecked, Parry finds himself in the Blue Quarter again, in a close-to-nature community called Church of Heaven on Earth, which displays another facet of ideology. At first glance, it appears to be a rural, utopian counter-design to the rearranged Divided Kingdom. The community and Owen, its founder,[55] understand themselves along these lines: "Owen had created a place in which he could try and redress the damage wreaked by the division of the kingdom. Losses could be overcome there. Injuries could heal. [...] [I was identified] as a casualty, not of the shipwreck, but of an earlier catastrophy – the Rearrangement" (*DK:* 223–224). The Church of Heaven on Earth is about regeneration, while the Divided Kingdom makes use of eradication. Furthermore, it does not appear to be conceived. Owen started out on his own without any particular vision in mind, and people simply started coming: "It hadn't been planned, or even thought about. It had happened organically. And, purely by chance their way of life was perfectly in tune with the phlegmatic temperament" (*DK:* 219). At last, people seem to be in harmony with their environment and their social relations. Yet, even the Church of Heaven on Earth is not free from ideological tendencies: firstly, it also relies on Greek philosophy as its basis by defining happiness, along the teachings of Epicurus, "negatively as freedom from distress and pain" (*DK:* 213). Furthermore, even in this happy community, someone committed suicide – with a negative effect on the community's mood, of course. Being thus put on the spot, Owen makes a prophecy: the community will be given a sign from outside concerning its future. Parry's arrival, then, is interpreted as a positive sign, and the community can continue (see *DK:* 218). However, Owen himself just makes up the prophecy without actually believing in it; he simply needs it in order to keep the community going by tricking it. Even in the Church of Heaven on Earth, the ends justify the means at times.

Divided Kingdom opens up a network of ascriptions of machines, people, internal and external ascriptions in the context of utopia and anti-utopia by paying particular attention to the conceived space and its effects on the fabric of society. An important role in this field of discourse is played by the question of identity. Internal ascriptions (everyone wants to be, say, sanguine, or smart, or funny) and external ones (be it by personality tests run by machines, or by other people's judgment with a dash of prejudice on top) clash – as do subjectivity and

---

[55] An allusion to Robert Owen (1771–1858), one of the founders of utopian (!) socialism.

apparent measurable objective results. The apparent danger of losing oneself is ridiculed by the sheer amount of ascriptions, none of which can provide an ultimate answer. What piece of identity can one actually lose if one's identity consists of contradicting ascriptions from numerous sources?

Two possibilities are hesitantly shown at the end of the novel. On the one hand, Parry's return to his home and the meeting with Vishram there suggests that there might be

> some higher authority – a committee made up of representatives from each of the four countries, for example, that would convene in secret and oversee the running of the divided kingdom. It would be a natural extension of the clandestine meetings that had resulted in the Rearrangement. A rainbow cabinet... It seemed logical – even necessary. (*DK:* 381)

Although one is not necessarily sick if one is comparatively melancholic, phlegmatic, or melancholic, one could allege that the primary purpose of the Rearrangement is that the people feel ill deep inside, and treat the others as ill as well by means of ascription. A dystopian government would well dare to insinuate sickness where there is none in order to make the people feel too weak or otherwise occupied in order to protest. Humourism and the Rearrangement could thus function as both a diversion and a weakening of precisely those elements which could threaten the totalitarian-dystopian system: the families and individuals who think outside the box. While the former are being torn apart, the latter are either being disposed of as well or – as in Parry's case – integrated into the system. On the other hand, Parry's and Odell's plan to secretely continue their love affair while ignoring all other (external) ascriptions may pose as an insecure alternative.[56] The related action or spatial performance is border-crossing, the transgression of both material and discursive borders – which is again a typical dystopian strategy, in particular of the dystopian outsider-protagonist. The following chapter will elaborate on these kinds of border-crossings as an array of transgressions, with examples from several of the novels discussed so far.

---

[56] Odell's boss is being disposed of, and she is afraid she might share his fate. Thus, Parry decides to accept Vishram's job offer so he can forge papers for her. She is late for the meeting with Parry, and the novel ends with Parry waiting for her. The reader is left in the dark whether she will show up or if she, as Claire Allen remarks, only exists in Parry's mind (see Allen 2008: n.pag.).

V Against the Grain: Borders and Transgressions

Characters in this study's novels do not simply walk through the dystopian city. They interact with it, change it, oppose it, and become changed by the city in return. From a spatial studies' point of view, the most striking displays of performativity are those where established spaces, borders, and boundaries are challenged. Especially in the oppressive or dominant spaces of dystopian settings, characters go against the grain; as they walk, they sound and cross borders of various kinds. These performances – be they mental, individual, material, bodily, or physical – shall be explored in the following. While V.1 focusses on different ways of coming to terms with various kinds of borders by building a bridge between Yuri M. Lotman's accounts of transgression as a narrative device and other models of borders and transgression, V.2 provides a detailed analysis of borders and border-related performances in *Perdido Street Station*, *The City & The City*, and *Divided Kingdom*.

V.1 Interdisciplinary Approaches towards Transgression

The following chapter consists of two parts. In the first part (called "Drawing the Line"), the problem of defining the term "border" will be addressed; also, some light is shed on what borders do, where they come from, and how one identify different types of borders. Part two ("On the Border – Across the Border") then fleshes out different kinds of performances, mainly by differentiating between border-crossing and transgression, in order to end up with a toolkit for the analysis in V.2.

Drawing the Line
When it comes to pinpointing the term "border", most disciplines pay more attention to political and social borders than to apparently natural borders such as mountain ranges and seem to agree that those borders are the result of (see Gehrke 1999a: 18; 23) – or part of – sets of conceptions of identity and alterity (see Hallet 2009: 87) and therefore inherently 'made' social constructs (see Gehrke 1999b: 27; also see Frank 2009: 70). As social constructs, borders have to be seen as inevitably intertwined with cultural codes of ascription within nations, societies, and communities, but also families and other (sub)systems (see Fludernik and Gehrke 1999: 18). Since these systems, which rely on and create borders, do change, borders themselves are obviously liable to change as well.

However, changes are not restricted to the properties and qualities of borders, but may also range from border-related modes of perception and description to the means of medial communication (see Gehrke 1999a: 23). In this context of vicissitude, 'givenness' of apparently natural borders such as the sea, rivers, or mountain ranges, has also been questioned (see Gehrke 1999b: 31) since those can equally be conventional and constructed in a way (with regard to territorial waters, for example).

Unfortunately, the term "border" itself remains quite vague. The term's fuzziness across the disciplines stems from the problem that, on the one hand, it is unclear what a border is exactly, while on the other hand, the term's relation to others from the same semantic field (such as *limit*, *boundary*, or *frontier*) is equally blurred – particularly in the English language (see Waldenfels 1999: 138; see also Wokart 1995: 275–278). The larger the amount of effort spent on clarifying the term, the more other terms are generated (see Ehlers 2007: 11). Also, more and more functions of borders are described. A border can refer to a small transitory step or a considerable jump (see Gehrke 1999a: 17); it can separate and connect; it can be a thin line or a zone of its own; it can be physical or mental, on a map or in someone's head. Borders can, according to Monika Ehlers,

> *confine* and *limit*, while referring to something ungraspable simultaneously. They shut down *access* points while conversely provoking their opening. As *thresholds*, they *mark transitions* into new phases of life; as taboos, they ban unacceptable areas from the cultural *order*. On the other hand, cryptic *inclusions mark inner borders*, an inaccessible *exterior* within the *interior*. (Ehlers 2007: 12 [my translation, my italics])

Even Ehlers, who is aware of the tangled terminological mess, cannot avoid using equally fuzzy terms (see the italics above). The border as well as its functions remain uncontainable, it seems.

Yet, numerous attempts of classification have been made. For example, Hans-Joachim Gehrke, as a historian, differentiates between demarcation as practice, the border as a space, and the border as a scientific concept (see Gehrke 1999b) with an emphasis on the question of the naturalness and constructedness of borders, which will play a role later on. In the same volume, sociologist Wolfgang Eßbach presents two different origins and metaphorisations of the term "border." First, there are "erdbezogene Grenzen," i.e. borders in terms of areas and landscapes 'out there' *between* one and the other; this umbrella term covers geographical borders, borders of settlements in the broadest sense as well as borders of influence and possession (see Eßbach 1999: 87–90). Second, there are organism-related borders *of* something (e.g. of societies and individuals) which will play a crucial role in the analysis of *Perdido Street Station* in chapter V.2.2 (see Eßbach 1999: 92–94). Waldenfels similarly lists spatiotemporal borders, bodily (in the sense of an individual's internal) borders, interpersonal and social borders, and borders of normalisation (see Waldenfels 1999: 145). Faced with an overwhelming amount of models, this study cannot provide a detailed analysis of all the approaches, and focuses mostly on the one put forth by Monika Fludernik (see Fludernik 1999: 99–108), drawing upon others where appropriate, the reason being that her model is open for a performative dichotomy which will prove to be highly applicable with regard to the border performances found in this study's novels. Note, however, that the systematics of border types here slightly differs from the one put forth by Fludernik.

Fludernik's first border type is the borderline, i.e. the border as an ideational, separating line. Thus, the border utilises a binary either-or opposition which is primarily a political concept (type A in the following) (see Fludernik 1999: 99). The second type elaborates on the first: between the two opposing areas, the border can pose as a zone instead of single line, thus becoming a topological entity in its own right (B). Fludernik's prime example is the political border between Eastern and Western Germany until 1989 – a zone with its own personnel, facilities, and rules (see Fludernik 1999: 99).[1] However, the frequently used term "no man's land" for describing such zones seems questionable; of course, the border zone can belong to no one, but it can also belong to both sides simultaneously and still be a zone of its own. Therefore, Fludernik establishes another type that draws upon mathematical set theory, i.e. intersection (C). This variety of type B takes into account that the border can well be a zone of 'as well as' where the separated areas overlap instead of a binary opposition of 'either/or' (see Fludernik 1999: 99–101). Here, clear-cut separation between territories becomes problematic already. Probably the best-known scholarly piece in this context is Marie Louise Pratt's notion of the contact zone, which "describes the space of colonial encounters, the space in which peoples geographically and historically separated come into contact with each other and establish ongoing relations, usually involving conditions of coercion, radical inequality, and intractable conflict" (Pratt 1992: 6). As Gerhard Stilz points out, contact goes way beyond the tactile sense, i.e. touching – it may involve all senses, it may be active or passive, direct or indirect (see Stilz 2013: 7–8). The contact zone, as well as Fludernik's category of overlap, moves away from the notion of strictly separated cultures marked by strictly separating borders and opens up towards the mutual processes of exchange, influence, and power, which are negotiated both on the level of public norms as well as on the level of individual actions (see Stilz 2013: 13), thus high-

---

[1] Cf. also Stallybrass and White (1986), who focus on hierarchical aspects within a certain culture, where the border between 'high' and 'low' becomes an interstitial zone of movement.

lighting the differentiation between spatio-political and cultural demarcation (see Neumann 2009: 126). This differentiation is paramount to the border paradox of postcolonial literature as put forth by Michael C. Frank: on the one hand, there is a spatial distance between European writers, narrators, and characters, and non-Europe – a distance which must be *overcome* again and again in order to show the cultural difference between self and other. By doing so, the border between self and other is made visible. However, the distance has to be *maintained* so that the border remains visible because otherwise, one would be unable to separate the European self from the non-European other (see Frank 2006: 48). In these transcultural encounters, it is not as clear as one might think at first who is on the active and who is on the passive side: "Indeed, the active and the passive part in establishing contact cannot be reserved to a particular role in these matters" (Stilz 2013: 9).

The name "contact zone" already implies that borders are more than just elements of separation. Accordingly, Fludernik also takes into account the metaphorical level of borders. A border can well be a border between interior and exterior with respect to the deictics of the human body, thus referring to subjective codes of self-constitution instead of geographical elements (see Fludernik 1999: 101). This type (D), as well as the following, owes much to the systems-theoretical processes of selection by means of binary codes which are paramount for constructing identity in the first place (see Eßbach 1999: 92). Type E refers the term border to social processes, i.e. to processes of social assimilation and exclusion (see Fludernik 1999: 101). Both civilisations and social groups need these kinds of borders in order to constitute themselves since they can only do so by separating themselves from others (see Schwengel 1999: 35). By mentioning social groups within civilisations, it becomes apparent that these processes of inclusion and exclusion take place within a larger group or area, i.e. along internal borders. Another paradox shows itself: the more one group tries to separate itself from another one, the stronger the reciprocal reference (see Wokart 1995: 279).

So far, in the types above, the border could be identified as an element between two different, but nevertheless qualitatively comparable areas. However, in the context of thresholds, two final border types emerge with a qualitatively completely different area *beyond* the border. The area beyond can either be an unreachable horizon (type F) – as in the idea of the American *frontier* which is, in Fludernik's words, a spatialised version of the body-deictic type D (see Fludernik 1999: 101–102) – or the border can be the threshold to a completely new "Sinnbezirk" beyond, i.e. a completely new understanding (type G). By moving over the threshold, the individual potentially undergoes a metamorphosis and emerges as a new I (for example, by moving over the threshold as a transitional space towards death; see Fludernik 1999: 101–102). In this context, borders of one's own perception also come into play in terms of how to access what lies beyond one's own horizon of comprehension (see Ehlers 2007: 13). The border may constitute here and there, self and other, identity and alterity, comprehensive horizon and unmarked space.

The following chart provides an overview of the seven border types so far by placing them in four sets according to the types' key aspects (1: strict separation, mostly used in the political/geographical sense; 2: intersection/overlap inspired by mathematical set theory; 3: interior vs. exterior as the crucial means of separating self from other in the context of both groups and individuals; 4: the transgression is due to the entering of a space with a qualitative difference):

Table i: Border Types Model 1

Set Number	1	2	3	4
Key Aspect	Strict separation	Intersection	Interior vs. exterior	New quality
Border Type	A	C	D	F
+ Feature	(ideational line)	(overlap/contact)	(individual's deictics)	(far horizon)
Border Type	B		E	G
+ Feature	(separating zone)		(assimilation/exclusion)	(new "I")

On the Border – Across the Border

The full narrative potential of borders unfolds in combination with a performative act by a character, and most of Fludernik's border types already imply some kind of movement in relation to the border. For Yuri Lotman, an often-cited scholar in this context, performative transgressions of borders are essential for narrative as such. This subchapter, by relying mostly on Fludernik and Lotman, explores different treatments of borders with respect to performativities of crossing, transgression, and treading.

When it comes to borders and transgressions in terms of literature, Yuri Lotman's *Analysis of the Poetic Text* (1976) is usually one of the first sources to turn to. In his study, Lotman refers the border to those spaces which make up the story world of the literary text. Each space constitutes its own semantic field including characters that are unable to move into another field; therefore, semantic separation and spatial separation are congruent (see Frank 2009: 67). Transgressions, i.e. events and movements across the borders of two semantic fields, are the smallest units of plot structure. A spatial transgression triggers the dynamic of the plot (or sujet). This basic idea of the sujet as a revolutionary element in relation to the dominating view of the world is, according to Lotman, at the heart of all narratives (see

Frank 2009: 67), and the analysis of the novels in chapter V.2 will show that this is particularly true for a dystopian view of the world. So far, *Analysis of the Poetic Text* has stood as a definitive book in literary studies. Taking more recent notions of borders into account (such as those presented above), however, Lotman's model is vulnerable to criticism – mostly with regard to its strict separation between – and the binary opposition of – semantic fields (see Frank 2009: 68). Thus, Lotman's model only covers what has been named type A borders above. Shifts of borders and vertical structures such as hierarchies within one specific semantic field are not mentioned either. Especially in the context of the contact zone and other models where individual parameters are of a rather dynamic nature, Lotman appears to be obsolete. Maybe that is the reason why he is not even mentioned in Fludernik's account, as Frank notes to his surprise (see Frank 2009: 68).

Yet, Frank also shows that Lotman did not stop after *Analysis of the Poetic Text*. In "The Semiosphere" in *Universe of the Mind* (1990), he elaborates on borders[2] and transgressions not only in terms of plot, but also in terms of language-related and cultural borders. The following brief overview highlights the parallels to the overall discourse on borders as established above. The parallels start with the notion of borders being essential for processes of self-constitution by separating self and other (see Lotman 1990: 128–129) for both cultures or language areas and individuals. In the latter case, the body-related deictics come into play again. Lotman also explicitly names this clear-cut separation of self and other a "binary division," as in the binary opposition put forth by Fludernik (type A above) and others (Lotman 1990: 131). Within one demarcated area, Lotman now also takes into account internal borders, or "sectional boundaries," with their own mechanisms of inclusion and exclusion: "the entire space of the semiosphere is transected by boundaries of different levels [...], and the internal space of each of these sub-semiospheres has its own semiotic 'I'" (Lotman 1990: 138; see also Stilz 2013: 15). Thus, type E is accounted for as well. The "different levels" also pave the way for internal vertical structures and hierarchies. Lastly, Lotman establishes the domains "centre" and "periphery" as important elements for demarcation and borders.[3] As a result, he is able to show that "all elements of the semiosphere are

---

[2] The English translation of Lotman's text uses "boundary" while I mostly will, as above, stick to "border" in order to emphasise the focus on geographical and political borders (particularly in *The City and the City* and *Divided Kingdom*), while "boundary" rather refers to the limits of "a subject or activity" (*CCAD*). For another project on the debate on the terminology, it might be quite revealing to analyse the Russian terms in the original.

[3] The differentiation between centre and periphery also plays an important role in postcolonial studies and sociological urban studies (see Stichweh 2000: 198–203). For the analysis of *The City & The City* as well as *Divided Kingdom*, maintaining the separation will turn out to be

dynamic, not static, correlations whose terms are constantly changing" (Lotman 1990: 127). The centre of a semiosphere is the driving force behind the semiosphere's self-constitution and the resulting separation from other semiospheres because at the centre, the organisational structure of a semiosphere is the strongest. In contrast, at the periphery, the organisational structure frays. Therefore, the border at the periphery can transcend the idea of simply being a dividing element between self and other and pose as a place of mutual exchange in a semiotic dynamism: "it is the place where what is 'external' is transformed into what is 'internal', it is a filtering membrane which so transforms foreign texts that they become part of the semiosphere's internal semiotics while still retaining their own characteristics" (Lotman 1990: 136–137). Again, Lotman mostly speaks of texts and languages, but the idea is perfectly applicable on a spatial, social, political, bodily or mental level. As in several of Fludernik's types, the border is "ambivalent [...]: it both separates and unites" (Lotman 1990: 136). Even a passage which sounds suspiciously like Luhmann's notion of unmarked space can be found: "However some elements are always set *outside*. If the inner world reproduces the cosmos, then what is on the other side represents chaos, the anti-world, the unstructured chthonic space" (Lotman 1990: 140 [original italics]). In conclusion, considering the development of Lotman's transgressive model from *Analysis of the Poetic Text* to "The Semiosphere," and thus from a static model of strict separation to a dynamic one featuring the border as an in-between space of movement and encounters (see Frank 2009: 69), there actually is a bridge between transgressions and borders of cultures in Lotman's sense on the one hand and concepts such as Pratt's contact zone on the other.

The following chart adds Lotman's key words to the border sets established earlier on:

Table ii: Border Types Model 2

Set Number	1	2	3	4
Key Aspect	Strict separation	Intersection	Interior vs. exterior	New quality
Border Type + Feature	A (ideational line)	C (overlap/ contact)	D (individual's deictics)	F (far horizon)
Border Type + Feature	B (separating zone)		E (assimilation/ exclusion)	G (new "I")
Lotman References	(binary) division	Periphery/centre Ext. →←int.	Sectional boundaries Hierarchies	Inner cosmos/ Anti-world

---

quite productive; cf., however, Jessica Langer's scepticism from a postcolonial perspective (Langer 2010: 172).

What is, in comparison to Lotman, emphasised in the texts by Frank, Fludernik and Gehrke, however, is the differentiation between two kinds of border-related performances, namely between border performances *across* a border and performances *on, along* or *at* the border (see Fludernik 1999: 99; Gehrke 1999a: 17; Frank 2009: 69).[4] The differentiation will prove to be quite fruitful for analysing the novels in the subchapters. Cross-border performances are elaborated on first. I distinguish between the crossing of borders in the sense of legal/tolerated performances and transgressions in the sense of illegal/rule-breaking performances. Not all scholars make this distinction (see Fludernik 1999: 105); in the dystopian context, though, the distinction makes much sense because rules, laws, and sanctions tend to be very strong and thus have an impact on the story world's spaces. Hence, it is useful to distinguish between cross-border performances which play along with established rules and those which do not. What happens to the performer after such a crossing of a border? According to Goetsch, he or she either enters a new order or – with Luhmann's unmarked space in mind – faces a vast borderlessness (see Goetsch 1999: 70). The analysis of the novels will work along the lines of this dichotomy. The second kind of border performance, the one at, on, or along the border, shall be called "treading" in an attempt to cover the idea of the German word "Grenz*be*schreitung" in contrast to the cross-border "Grenz*über*schreitung" (movement *across* a border). The notion of treading shall on the one hand illustrate the notion of walking at, on, or along something and, on the other hand, imply that the movement in the border area is one of careful balancing between "two opposing demands" (*Collins Cobuild Advanced Dictionary* 2009: 1669). The cross-border performances can be said to occur more often while occurrences of treading tend to provide more intricate or intriguing results.

V.2 Transgressive Performances

What are the typical sites of transgression and treading? Jessica Langer, with a postcolonial perspective in mind, speaks of transgressions with regard to the mind, the body, and the city:

> Each of these represents what Fredric Jameson calls a 'frame'of reality, which he suggests are 'radically discontinuous' in the postmodern city. Like layers of an onion, these bounda-

---

[4] While there will be an emphasis on geographical/material borders in the analysis of ch. V.2, other kinds of borders and crossings will be explored as well. They may, for instance, be related to mental or cognitive borders or the borders of the body.

ries are contained within each other, mind within body within city, and so each transgression is echoed doubled and perhaps trebled. (Langer 2010: 174)

Thus, this study has again arrived at the three sites which have already been explored in chapter IV and shall now be expanded upon by a closer look at the transgressive and treading performances involved. The first novel to be analysed is *Perdido Street Station* with its bodily and mental border conception, which Motley, New Crobuzon's underground kingpin, calls the hybrid zone. *The City & The City*, then, mostly stages transgressions with regard to the discursive practice of unseeing. *Divided Kingdom*, the final example, is primarily concerned with borders as strictly separated (and separating) semantic fields, how these borders both shape and inhibit identity, and how transgressions are able to transcend such inhibitions.

V.2.1 *Perdido Street Station* and the Hybrid Zone

While chapter IV.2.1 already discussed New Crobuzon's city space in great detail, the chapter lacked an elaboration on borders and border performances, the reason being that *Perdido Street Station*'s New Crobuzon – in contrast to *The City & The City* and *Divided Kingdom* – actually is an at least loosely knit city state where the external or political borders (Border Set 1 mostly, which contains border types A and B) are not the major concern. Yet, New Crobuzon is also a city where internal border issues are at stake, as already became apparent in the presentation of its quarters. With all its different species and social groups, the city is extremely liable to internal processes of assimilation and exclusion (border type E) as well as performances and effects of the deictics of the body with respect to borders (border type D). Therefore, the following chapter rather focusses on the transgressions and treadings of mind and body in *Perdido Street Station* by selecting a handful of striking characters.[5] For this purpose, Jessica Langer's transgressive sites (mind, body, and city) will be combined with Joan Gordon's reading of *Perdido Street Station* as a hybrid.

Hybridity in Gordon's sense can be taken as a bodily variety of transgression where the body does not only transgress external material or geographical borders, but where the body itself is highlighted as an entity with physical or biological borders, or where the body becomes a physical or biological border itself.

---

5 See Chapter V.1 for more information on the different border types as well as for crossing, transgression, and treading as cross-border performances.

As suggested by Langer's three transgressive sites, this idea can also be transferred to other fields, or better: it is quite revealing to not only talk about bodily transgressions since the body, the mind, and the city are always interrelated with regard to transgression – particularly in New Crobuzon. Therefore, with the close connection between the city and the body in mind (as explored in chapter IV.2.1), the notion of hybridity as an inherent feature of dystopian cities in general and New Crobuzon in particular deserves further attention. Both Gordon and Langer presuppose an overwriting of fixed and established relations, and the combination will lead to the typical character model of the dystopian novel – the outsider.

Gordon reads *Perdido Street Station* as a meditation on hybridity on pretty much every level: individual characters, the city, the novel as such, and Miéville as a writer all draw upon this notion which, originating from biology, has been adapted and modified by cultural and postcolonial studies. Thus, Gordon deals with hybridity in terms of Brian Stross's definition:

> In Latin the hibrida was the offspring of a (female) domestic sow and a (male) wild boar. The semantic range of the word hybrid has expanded in more recent times to include the offspring of a mating by any two unlike animals or plants. The cultural hybrid is a metaphorical broadening of this biological definition. It can be a person who represents the blending of traits from diverse cultures and traditions, or even more broadly it can be a culture, or element of culture, derived from unlike sources; that is, something heterogeneous in origin or composition. (Stross 1999: 254)

Of importance to Gordon is what Stross calls "hybrid vigor" and the superordinate "hybridity cycle." A hybrid starts out with two (or more) "sufficiently unlike parents" or origins and is then taken and "recognized as a new thing." As similar hybrids come into being, "it is refined to a homogeneity which may now be considered purebred. And then the cycle can begin again" (Gordon 2003a: 457). Hybrid vigour "implies a fertile and creative response to environmental pressures and opportunities" (Stross 1999: 263). The quotes from Stross demonstrate why hybridity and transgression go well together: one can well imagine the two "unlike parents" as the two binary oppositions with a strictly separating border between them (border types A and B) which can then, by means of a transgressive performance, come together in some kind of contact zone (Type C) where, due to the "fertile and creative" nature of the encounter, something new can come into being. The following emphasis on Lin, Motley, Yagharek, and Isaac provides a panorama of different kinds of hybridity in relation to transgressions and 'treadings' in the context of Langer's interrelated dimensions of mind, body, and city.[6]

Lin: Hybridity of Xenians, Hybridity of Art

An obvious starting point for hybridity in *Perdido Street Station* is New Crobuzon's vast array of xenians as former hybrid forms that have been accepted as purebred (i.e. combinations of human beings and other organisms who form a race/species of their own). While all of them have a part that human readers will identify as humanoid, the other part in the composition varies. I insist on "a part that human readers will identify as humanoid" because the novel's hybrids seem to be differently hybrid, depending on the point of view. Of course, Miéville as a human writer can only describe what he knows: he, as all writers concerned with the fantastic, writes as a human being about a fictional world which is usually scoio-politically dominated by humans[7] and mediated by human characters and narrators – but one should not confuse his writing position with a false assumption of intratextual human exceptionalism. In fact, Lin herself, whom human readers will describe as a human-beetle hybrid, goes even further by denying having human body parts. From her point of view, "[h]*umans have khepri bodies, legs, hands; and the heads of shaved gibbons*" (*PSS:* 10 [italics in original]). Therefore, the way human writers and readers can come to terms with alien others is necessarily restricted, and this human way of description only works according to what human minds and languages are capable of. Nevertheless, being aware of this limitations can be fairly productive (see Staggs 2011: n.pag.), and the basic strategy of attempting to describe the indescribable is part and parcel of fantastic writing in general and Weird Fiction in particular (see Zähringer 2017). Thus, I will now turn to hybridity, being fully aware that I can only tackle the topic in human terms.

The fact that the parents of any new form can be extremely unlike each other is best exemplified in the cactacae (a human-cactus hybrid, and the only hybrid of a human and a plant). In the following, though, Lin, as a khepri woman, shall serve as a key witness for xenian hybridity. She has the body of a human woman with an entire scarab beetle as a head instead of a human head. It is not men-

---

[6] The analysis of Yagharek is a follow-up to the end of chapter IV.2.1, where his development (from a full garuda to a mutilated half-and-half creature to a man, and from a foreigner to someone who is able to place himself in New Crobuzon) was shown.
[7] One of the rather few exceptions is Barsaive, the fictional world of *Earthdawn*, a pen & paper roleplaying game (first published 1993) which also spawned eleven novels. In Barsaive, dwarves are the dominant species.

tioned how the khepri came into being in the first place, but in the story-now they are considered a purebred form in the sense of Stross, i.e. they make up a species of their own. Human body and scarab beetle, although of formerly different origins, are one body now.

However, despite this established, purebred khepri form, Lin's body still has a physiological hybrid zone, i.e. the spot where her human body and the scarab beetle converge. In Motley's words: "You have the same chords in your neck as a human woman. [...] and then there is... there is a moment... there is a thin zone where that soft human skin merges with the pale segmented cream underneath your head" (*PSS:* 36). It is striking how Motley, searching for an appropriate expression, finally describes the spot as "a thin zone" and thus as a zone of convergence and overlap (border type C). It makes much sense that Motley analyses the composition as a transitory one because it fits the notion of the constitution of self vs. other: if the human body and the scarab beetle were strictly separated (Border Set 1), it would be questionable how they really belong together (as they do, considering the fact that the khepri are to be taken as purebred).

Lin's hybridity is also manifest in her way of life, most prominently in her art and her relationship with the human Isaac (which is mostly focalised through him; hence, it will be analysed later). Her khepri-spit[8] sculptures go beyond the decaying traditional khepri art and owe much to her departure from the narrow-minded slums of Creekside and Kinken in favour of her network of avant-garde artists and friends (see *PSS:* 187–188). Her artistry is therefore a transgression of the old khepri culture with the mind (in Langer's sense) as its location. Still, although the transgressive site in question is the mind, transgression is not a conscious part of her artistry, according to Motley: "*It makes me wonder if we understand each other at all* [...]. It's a wonder you can create such art" (*PSS*, p. 99 [italics in original]). But she can, so Motley assumes that she carries a sense of the hybrid zone anyway:

> [T]his piece before us makes it clear that you *have* a sense of the ruptured moment, even if your question suggests the opposite... So maybe [...] you yourself *contain* that moment. Part of you understands without recourse to words, even if your higher mind asks questions in a format which renders an answer impossible. [...] You too are the bastard-zone, Ms. Lin! Your art takes place where your understanding and your ignorance blur. (*PSS:* 100 [italics in original])

---

8 Khepri-spit is a viscous liquid that the khepri produce in their beetle heads; Lin uses the spit for her art by mixing it with berries of different colours.

Lin's artistic transgressions become her unconscious site of hybridity, taking her somewhere her mind cannot go consciously. Her art is the contact zone not only between tradition and avant-garde, but also between, in Motley's words, "understanding" and "ignorance." One can already see here the interrelatedness of the three sites of transgression and how hard it is to keep them apart. Lin's hybridity as a human-beetle combination obviously has a bodily aspect, but differing conceptions and points of view (her ignorance vs. Motley's deep understanding) of physicality, body borders and deictics, identity and alterity should not be ignored because they render hybridity in different ways. Similarly, the khepri-spit statues can figure as hybrids in numerous ways, be it as an outdated relic from better days (for most khepri), as contemporary art and day-to-day business (for Lin), or as the artistically manifested symbolisation of the hybrid zone as such (for Motley).

Motley: Hybridity of Remaking
Besides the purebred xenian species, New Crobuzon also features more sinister examples of bodily hybridity: the city's Remade, who are no homogeneous group. Former purebreds (mostly humans) are being remade as an act of punishment or created for specific purposes: body parts of animals such as hooves or claws as well as mechanical parts or tools such as sledgehammers are magically grafted to the formerly purebred human body.[9] In terms of borders, remaking immediately evokes those of the deictics of the body (border type D), or rather: their brutal break-up. An individual's body, and thus his/her crucial mode of self-constitution, is merged with parts of another against the individual's will. Sometimes, even two sentient individuals are fused. Remaking, by changing the body as the primary site for getting in touch with one's environment, modifies both the Remade's possibilities of coming to terms with anything beyond as well as his/her self-constitution.[10] The term "remaking" speaks for itself: the 'I' is brutally turned inside out and re-created; thus, it is laid bare that not only the borders of the city's quarters but also the borders of the bodies within

---

9 Note that the term "Remade" for a non-homogeneous, artificially created group is written with a capital letter, while the names of groups which are considered purebred are uncapitalised, thus highlighting the inherent difference between Remade and purebred Crobuzoners. Cf. also Gordon's (2003a: 458–460) analysis of Lin and the Remade as examples of the grotesque.
10 Miéville broaches the issue of identity in the context of remaking in his other two Bas-Lag novels as well. *The Scar* (2002) explores the impact of remaking on the modes of self-constitution of the character Tanner Sack; *Iron Council* (2004) is concerned with socio-political hierarchies in the context of remaking as slavery.

the city are anything but stable (see Langer 2010: 178). Furthermore, remaking has an effect on the construction of identity with regard to social processes of exclusion (border type E) in its most extreme form by turning formerly full members of society into slaves, thereby placing them hierarchically as low as possible and outside 'proper' society simultaneously. Thus, instead of borders separating New Crobuzon from other cities or societies, interal borders (in Lotman's words: sectional boundaries) are more prominent in *Perdido Street Station* (see Langer 2010: 177).

One remade character in New Crobuzon stands out due to both the extent of his remaking as well as his attitude towards his body and his understanding of contact zones: the appropriately named Motley, the underground boss. His body is a wild accumulation of numerous body parts due to excessive remaking, thus more than any other character questioning organism-related borders in Eßbach's sense:[11]

> Scraps of skin and fur and feathers swung as he moved; tiny limbs clutched; eyes rolled from obscure niches; antlers and protrusions of bone jutted precariously; feelers twitched and mouths glistened. Many-coloured skeins of skin collided. A cloven hoof thumped gently against the wood floor. Tides of flesh washed against each other in violent currents. Muscles tethered by alien tense motion. Scales gleamed. Fins quivered. Wings fluttered brokenly. Insect claws folded and unfolded. (*PSS:* 38)

While most Remade Crobuzoners are merged with one foreign element only, Motley has been remade many times and is beyond both recognition of his original body and beyond human comprehension.[12] His body again shows the instability of self by transgressing established anthropological norms – even those of New Crobuzon, which in turn question those of the world of the reader – and thus the borders of the human mind. Again, the mind and the body as transgressive sites are interrelated. While the process of remaking generally functions as a performance of transgression, the result of Motley's remakings is more similar to treading as a performance *on* the border. What makes him special is not only his individual hybridity as far as the extent of his remaking is concerned, but also his

---

[11] See chapter V.1 for details on Eßbach's differentiation between borders in terms of areas and organism-related borders.

[12] The inability of other characters to comprehend Motley's body and identity is also acted out narratologically: the quote above is by the novel's dominant heterodiegetic narrator with the focalisation of Lin in this particular scene. Motley's different body parts are described as above – as an unimaginable mosaic. And just like Lin, the reader can never fully grasp what Motley looks like exactly because the individual body parts, despite being grafted together, never form an integrated whole.

corresponding mindset: "I believe this to be the fundamental dynamic. Transition. The point where one thing becomes another. It is what makes you, the city, the world, what they are. And that is the theme I'm interested in. The zone where the disparate become part of the whole. The hybrid zone" (*PSS*: 37). His world-view is what makes Motley so different from the purebred races and other Remades. He relishes what others despise, fear, or hate. Although he speaks of "transition" instead of transgression and of the "hybrid zone" instead of the contact zone, the parallels can hardly be missed. Motley explicitly refers to his state of being as a "zone"; thus, he renders what is commonly considered a temporal state of transition as the actual state of his existence. Motley thus truly embodies the instability of transgressive characters in Lotman's sense: there is no stability in Motley's mind – there is only an in-between, a transition, spatialised by means of the word "zone." Motley incorporates treading as a border-related performance where everything converges into his mind and his body.

Physically speaking, the xenians as purebred are not dynamic anymore, and neither are their mindsets. Their bodies have been merged once (and only once), and they try to come to terms with their new identity. Motley, however, exceeds the bodily side of hybridity and introduces the mental side that others cannot access. Even an open-minded character such as Lin does not have his understanding. Asked by her what his 'original' body once was, his answer is that it does not matter: "'You still see *this* –' he gesticulated vaguely at his own body with a monkey's paw '– as pathology. You're still interested in what *was* and how it went *wrong. This is not error or absence or mutancy: this is image and essence* [...]. This is totality'" (*PSS*: 99 – 100 [italics in original]).[13] The in-between is elevated to the totality of life. Image and essence, exterior and interior are congruent. His way of seeing himself also corresponds to his view of the world and particularly New Crobuzon with its neverending dynamics of change, of transition:

> 'And what of the city itself? Perched where two rivers strive to become the sea, where mountains become a plateau, where the clumps of trees coagulate to the south and – quantity becomes quality – are suddenly a forest. New Crobuzon's architecture moves from the industrial to the residential to the opulent to the slum to the underground to the airborne to the modern to the ancient to the colourful to the drab to the fecund to the barren...' (*PSS*: 37)

---

13 It is also unclear what came first – his form or "his obsession with the transition zone" (*PSS*: 67).

New Crobuzon, according to Motley, is full of geographical and social contact zones where, in Lotman's words, "all elements are [...] correlations whose terms are constantly changing" and overlapping (Lotman 1990: 127). His model is all-encompassing as it covers the city's ecological and topographical characteristics, its demography, and its architecture. "Miéville's city is a hybrid zone in which each character, each neighbourhood, the massive conurbation itself, is in transition, one thing becoming another, repeating the hybridity cycle like wheels within wheels" (Gordon 2003a: 461). Transition becomes the ultimate state of existence, and Motley is its unimaginable avatar.[14]

Yagharek: Hybridity of Mutilation
Yagharek, as a garuda (i.e. a bird-man), is a purebred just like Lin, but he is no native Crobuzoner. He comes to New Crobuzon because of a severe crime committed back home: "choice-theft in the second degree... with utter disrespect" (*PSS:* 43), which very roughly translates into rape in human terms. Kar'uchai, another garuda and the victim of Yagharek's crime, points out the differences between garuda and New Crobuzon jurisdiction. The garuda are all equal, their society's basis being that every member should be able to make his/her own choices (for more details on the implications of Yagharek's crime and the effect on his friendship with Isaac, see chapter VI.2.1.). By contrast, New Crobuzon authorities, in a garuda's eyes, claim to take into account and take care of all individuals while "crushing them in layers and hierarchies... until their choices might be between three kinds of squalor" (*PSS:* 608). As mentioned before, New Crobuzon, due to all its racism and slavery, can be described with the help of Lotman's internal sectional boundaries and hierarchies. On the other hand, Yagharek's crime against the backdrop of the garuda's social system (based on equality and freedom of choice) severely disrupts the established order by transgressing the rules. His people find him guilty, and the punishmend is a bodily one: his wings are sawed off. While this punishment is an institutional attempt to make him atone for the crime he committed and the damage done, and therefore to re-establish the social order, it also leads to another transgres-

---

14 The question arises why Motley, being obsessed with transition and instability, is equally obsessed with commissioning a statue of himself – a work of art typically considered to be static and unchanging. Motley might remake himself again, thus rendering the statue inaccurate. Does he, as Lin does, attempt to retain the moment? Another answer is offered by the systems-theoretical principle that it is impossible for an individual to observe themselves (see Eßbach 1999: 96). Therefore, the statue could be taken as an attempt to contain the uncontainable, to observe what is beyond one's own borders of perception.

sion. Yagharek's body is brutally mutilated, the result being that he is placed in a completely new state of existence (a transgression according to border type G) – the garuda is transformed both physically and mentally (see chapter III.2.1 for the impact on his perception, and chapter IV.2.1 for his coming to terms with being bereft of his ability of flight as he finds his way into New Crobuzon). The transgression's actual impact on his mind may – depending on the interpretation – range from peace of mind to utter madness.[15]

Throughout the novel, Yagharek's ways of coming to terms with his mutilated body are emphasised. By losing his wings, his home, and his people due to his transgression, he has stopped being a garuda. He describes himself as "*a paradox, a bird that cannot fly*" (*PSS:* 622–623), as neither garuda nor human. His conception of the hybrid zone thus differs from Motley's in two ways. First, Motley even considers purebred xenians as embodiments of the hybrid zone because even their stable form displays a zone where human body and animal body merge. Yagharek, contrastingly, is on a quest of being made whole again, i.e. he considers his unbroken garuda body as a non-hybrid one and compares the mutilated body to living in a "*half-world*" (*PSS:* 622) as a bodily and conceptionally unsound hybrid. Furthermore, while Motley revels in hybridity as the ultimate state of existence, Yagharek aims for the exact opposite: getting his wings and the ability of flight back is his attempt to overcome his enforced hybridity, to become whole again. He wishes to leave behind his incomplete state of existence and to be completely absorbed in a new order, i.e. the one of New Crobuzon. Once more, body and mind as transgressive sites go hand in hand here: Yagharek's bodily mutilation is linked to a conceptual one. It is precisely this link which enables him to free himself at the very end of the novel. By plucking his feathers, i.e. by further transforming his body and by altering his body's borders (type D), he is also able to leave the mind-related half-world. He is "*not [a] miserable crossbreed*" anymore and turns himself into "*a man*" (*PSS:* 623).[16] Yagharek thus explicitly rejects the hybrid zone and the "*bastard liminal life, [the] interstitial*" (*PSS:* 622) on all of Langer's levels. The counter-figure to Yagharek in this context is the escaped Remade Jack Half-a-Prayer, New Crobuzon's self-announced version of Robin Hood, who, as a "fReemade," is

---

15 Cf. Langer (2010: 178) for madness as a feature of transgressive characters.
16 Cf. also Lin as a counterexample to Yagharek with respect to bodily mutilations. Being a prisoner of Motley, her body is mutilated as well, but she is incapable of finding a way out on the level of the mind. On the contrary – as the last remaining slake-moth appears in Motley's hideout, it attacks Lin and "[h]*alf her mind, half her dreams* [are] *gone*" (*PSS:* 594 [original italics]) – a malicious reference to Motley's characterisation that she actually has the hybrid zone in her without being able to access it mentally. Lin ends up doubly mutilated.

both a very suitable inhabitant of the city and its worst enemy. Jack meets Yagharek shortly before the bird-man's final transformation and offers him to join the fReemade, but Yagharek turns down the offer (see chapter IV.2.1 for more details). Yagharek, in contrast to the fReemade renegade, wants to see himself as a man (mind), he wants to walk through New Crobuzon instead of flying above it (body), and he wants to be completely absorbed in the city instead of fighting it (city).

Isaac: Hybridity of Science

Isaac's hybridity as the last example hinges on his transgressive relationship with Lin across social, bodily, and mental borders, and on Unified Field Theory as his field of science. Bodily hybridity and transgression are fairly present in the relationship between a human male and a khepri female partner.[17] It is a relationship not known to many people because it breaks a social taboo; "cross-love," i.e. love among a human and a xenian is considered to transgress established mechanisms of exclusion (border type E) in New Crobuzon. Isaac is very careful not to reveal his partner to people from the university, for example:

> Xenian students had only been admitted as degree candidates in New Crobuzon for twenty years. To cross-love openly would be a quick route to pariah status [...]. What scared him was not that the editors of the journals and the chairs of the conferences and the publishers would find out about Lin and him. What scared him was that he be seen not trying to hide it. (*PSS:* 12)

From his point of view, the relationship is an unspeakable one: the "cross-love," i.e. the relationship which transgresses the barrier between species as well as public norms, might place him in an academic no-man's land (to which it is "a quick route"). In the academic context, Isaac is an outcast who has dropped out once already; another transgression would finally render him untouchable, a "pariah." Only in the avant-garde quarter of Salacus Fields, "his relationship with Lin was an open secret, where he enjoyed being more or less open" (*PSS:* 11). For Lin, on the other hand, the relationship is less problematic. To her peer group, the Salacus Fields artists, "her love-life was an avant-garde transgression, an art-happening, like Concrete Music had been last season" (*PSS:* 11). The relationship, although still a transgression, is accepted due to the trans-

---

[17] Sexuality as an area of transgression also figures in Lin's first experience of pleasuresex with another khepri, which has already been mentioned in chapter IV.2.1 as an act of liberation that is explicitly called "the most difficult, the most extraordinary transition" (*PSS:* 188).

gressive nature of art itself. Different mind(set)s generate different attitudes towards certain behaviour, thus rendering it either fascinating or outrageous.

By shifting the perspective from the mind to the body, it becomes apparent that the first sexual intercourse of Lin and Isaac is also challenging. Here is how he remembers it: "The event had been clumsy and difficult. [...] When he had woken he had felt fearful and horrified, but at the fact of having transgressed rather than the transgression itself" (*PSS:* 381) [in a city full of prejudice, racism, and xenian ghettos].[18] The cross-love "event" here comes closest to the original definition by Stross – "sufficiently unlike parents" (Gordon 2003a: 457) mate and start a new hybridity cycle. Hence, the relationship of Lin and Isaac is not only a transgression of social, but also of biological borders, i.e. those of the bodies (type D). Isaac's reaction, being "fearful and horrified [...] at the fact of having transgressed" points to yet another border type, namely type G which enables him to access a completely new state of mind; it is only after the transgression that he realises what borders and norms he defied exactly – and in New Crobuzon, those borders are well-guarded.

While Isaac hides his relationship with Lin, he is more open with his research. As shown in chapter IV.2.1, he describes it to Yagharek by means of analogy; I repeat the quote here:

> 'I think of myself as the main station for all schools of thought. Like Perdido Street Station. You know it? [...] Unavoidable, ain't it? Fucking massive great thing.' Isaac patted his belly, maintaining the analogy. 'All the train-lines meet there – Sud Line, Dexter, Verso, Head and Sink Lines; everything has to pass through it. That's like me.' (*PSS:* 45)

A building in the city resembles his body; the body contains his mind through which all the city's research passes. Isaac's research thus incorporates Langer's three transgressive sites. As will be shown in the following, Isaac's Unified Field Theory, which is at the heart of his studies, can be called hybrid and transgressive in several ways.

In his attempts at making Yagharek fly again, Isaac, after several failures with other approaches, decides to work with the Unified Field Theory (UFT) and so-called crisis energy. In order to explain the theory to Yagharek, Isaac draws a diagram – a triangle, "'a depiction of the three points within which all scholarship, all knowledge, is located'" (*PSS:* 144): the three points or dimensions are labelled material, social, and occult. Any area of knowledge or study available in the world of Bas-Lag can be placed in the triangle, from magic to

---

[18] For their relationship as an interplay of "repulsion and attraction", see Gordon 2003a: 458–459.

physics and sociology. "'If the subjects are located in one triangle, with three nodes and one centre, then so are the forces and dynamics they study. In other words, [...] there's basically *one* kind of field, one kind of force, being studied in its various aspects here'" (*PSS:* 146 [original italics]). All sciences are to be found within the Unified Field Theory – they meet in the centre of Isaac's diagram, in an academic hybrid zone where all their forces and dynamics overlap. The Unified Field Theory is a scientific extrapolation of the transcultural contact zone.

So far, Isaac's research is hybrid, but it is also transgressive in two ways. Firstly, it is "'not very accepted as a theory [...]. Just about respectable, but a bit crackpot'" (*PSS:* 146). The theory thus transgresses the borders of what other scientists call 'proper' science. Secondly, to make it even worse, Isaac subscribes "to a minority view among UFT theorists. That's over the nature of the forces under investigation" (*PSS:* 146). The nature of those forces leads to the second transgressive aspect. The common opinion among Bas-Lag scholars is that the Unified Field is static and that the essential state of things thus is static as well. This common ground leads to the conclusion that "'falling, flying, rolling, changing your mind, casting a spell, growing older, moving, are basically *deviations* from an essential state'" (*PSS:* 146 [original italics]). By contrast, Isaac believes that "'motion is part of the fabric of ontology'" (*PSS:* 146) – his Unified Field is not static, but dynamic. Changing one's state, and therefore a transgressive impulse, is at the heart of all things – just as in Lotman's account of storytelling and semantic fields. A piece of wood held above the ground serves as his example. All scientists will agree that the wood, held up, has potential energy: "'Potential energy's the energy that gives the wood the power to hurt you or mark the floor, a power it doesn't have when it's just resting on the ground. It has that energy when it's motionless, like it was before, but when it *could fall*. If it does, the potential energy turns into kinetic energy'" (*PSS:* 146–147 [original italics]). On the basis of this physical principle, Isaac explains crisis energy:

> See, potential energy's all about placing something in a situation where it's teetering, where it's about to change its state. [...] The transition from one state to another's affected by taking something – a social group, a piece of wood, a hex – to a place where its interactions with other forces make its *own energy* pull against its current state. I'm talking about taking things to the point of *crisis*. (*PSS:* 147 [original italics])

Isaac thus not only sees switching from one state to another – i.e. transgression – as the essential state of all things, but as a source of enormous energy by means of "interactions with other forces." Different forces come together in an energetic contact zone and provide massive power by bringing somebody or something to the point of crisis: "I'm saying it's in the *nature of things* to enter crisis, as part of what they are. Things turn themselves inside out by virtue of being things" (*PSS:* 147 [original italics]). The only problem is that the peoples of Bas-Lag haven't managed yet to tap these energies properly. Isaac's plan, therefore, is to build a crisis engine which can do exactly that, and to use it against the slake-moths (and to make Yagharek fly again later on). The machine itself is again hybrid in construction, and three quite different entities are connected to the machine in order to feed it with their ways of processing: the Weaver, an extremely powerful, spider-like creature which perceives the world as an aesthetic web (see chapter III.2.1 for more details) for whom "dreams and consciousness were one" (*PSS:* 552), provides input y; the Construct Council, a mechanical being constructed by pure logic, which "thought with chill exactitude" (*PSS:* 552), provides input z; and Andrej, a sick old man abducted from a hospital, provides input x: "Andrej's mind, like any sane human's [...], was a constantly convulsing dialectical unity of consciousness and subconcsciousness" and can thus be described as an "interaction of levels of consciousness [coming together] into an unstable and permanently self-renewing whole" (*PSS:* 553). As the machine starts to process the data streams, the following calculation is the result:

> x, recorded the engines, was unlike y and unlike z. But with underlying structure *and* subconscious flow, with calculating rationality and impulsive fancy, self-maximizing analysis and emotional charge, x, the analytical engines calculated, was equal to y *plus* z. (*PSS:* 553 [original italics])

The human mind is hybrid, namely a hybrid of the Weaver's subconsciousness (y) and the Construct Council's pure rationality (z). The two thus overlap in what could be called a mental contact zone. Thus, the human mind is, in the words of Stross, "heterogeneous in origin or composition"(Stross 1999: 254).

However, as the machine continues, it arrives at a second conclusion that, paradoxically, contradicts the first one, but is simultaneously true nevertheless: "The form of the dataflows under analysis was not just the sum of their constituent parts. y and z were unified, bounded wholes. And most crucially, so was x, Andrej's mind, the reference point for the whole model. *It was integral to the form of each that they were totalities*" (*PSS:* 554 [original italics]). Andrej's mind is not simply the sum of the Weaver's subconsciousness and the Construct Council's consciousness: "What was arithmetically discernible as rationalism *plus* dreams was really a *whole*, whose constituent parts could not be disentangled" (*PSS:* 554 [original italics]). According to the second calculation, then, the human mind is a totality, a purebred, instead of a hybrid. Additionally, "y and z were not half-complete models of x. They were qualitatively different [...]. [T]he crisis engine arrived at two simultaneous conclusions: $x=y+z$; and $x{\neq}y+z$" (*PSS:* 554 [original italics]). The engine, by processing the three levels of consciousness, pits the two different notions of hybridity against each other as already played out between Motley and Lin with regard to their bodies. What is the human mind – hybrid (Motley/calculation 1) or purebred (Lin/calculation 2)? Strikingly, in terms of the UFT, it is both, or rather: it needs to be both in order to uncover and tap the underlying crisis energy. "It was paradoxical, unsustainable, the application of logic tearing itself apart. The process was, from absolute first principles of analysis, modelling and conversion, utterly riddled with crisis" (*PSS:* 554). The paradox finally shows a way of accessing crisis energy. Since both calculations, in spite of cancelling out each other, need to be true,[19] Isaac's crisis engine reveals another level of hybridity: the two contradictory results as "sufficiently unlike parents" (Gordon 2003a: 457) need to overlap in yet another contact zone in order to tap crisis energy.[20] Finally, the crisis engine's calculation and the crisis energy produced can also be read as a transgression of possible-worlds theory poetics. Possible-worlds theory in itself has seen several different models which are "mainly concerned with specifying the relationship between actual, possible and impossible worlds" (Stockwell 2000: 129). Especially the first models provided by Russell (1957) and Strawson (1963) claimed that if statement A is contradictory to statement B in our world, then only one of them can be true. As Stockwell points out, notions of actual, possible, and impossible worlds are crucial for Science Fiction: "[t]he central concern of most of this work seems to be to account for the difference between the logical notion of possible worlds and the looser and more rich notion of fictional worlds" (Stockwell 2000: 129).

Transgressions and Dystopian Outsiders

Whenever the characters in *Perdido Street Station* react towards environmental pressures and opportunities by means of transgression as a particular form of mental, bodily, or urban practice, they become character models for the typical dystopian character – they become outsiders. The closer one looks, the more of them appear; the novel is full of outsiders, rebels, creatures who do not fit in, people who live on the edge. To begin with, Lin leaves her khepri past and adopts a more human lifestyle while reappropriating the traditional, worn-out

---

19 Thus, the calculation is not unlike the notion of doublethink in Orwell's *Nineteen Eighty-Four*.
20 In addition to that, the crisis engine is an outstanding breakthrough in science, a transgression of all established theories on energy and the interplay of different fields of study.

khepri art in transgression. As she starts working for Motley, her secret employer, she even becomes an outsider among her avant-garde friends, which is also expressed spatially in her imprisonment. Isaac leaves behind university as well as his narrow-minded colleagues, finds other eccentric scientist companions just to estrange himself from them as well in his quest for Yagharek's restoration, and more importantly, in his quest for scientific revolution that transgresses not only the boundaries of individual fields of science, but also the laws of nature in general. Lemuel, his contact to the city's underground, works as a middle-man between sellers and buyers of illicit goods and information. He is "the quintessential go-between. [...] Not all of Lemuel's work involved both worlds: some was entirely legal or entirely illegal. It was just that crossing the border was his specialty" (*PSS:* 64). Isaac's three hired adventurers, as so many others, operate in the grey area of escort missions, exploration, and plunder. Jack Half-a-Prayer, as described by Yagharek, is placed in New Crobuzon's "*half world*," leading "*his liminal life, [living in] his interstitial city. [...] He does not fit in*" (*PSS:* 622). The Construct Council and all its related constructs as machines that think transgress the boundaries of technology as "[t]he seemingly spontaneous generation of a conscious subjectivity in an inorganic object represents a hybrid creation, a mind *without* a conventional body" (Langer 2010: 184 [original italics]).

Many more could be mentioned: marginalised xenians, the Remade, Yagharek, Motley, the Weaver, the handlingers... With a city this packed with hybrid forms and characters who are or turn into outsiders, the status of the overall composition is quite paradoxical. First, the sheer multitude of transformed, deformed, plucked, mutated and mutilated bodies questions the reliability of organism-related borders. If, following Lefebvre and Judith Butler, the body is not pre-given, if it can be changed in any way, one is made aware of the unstable relation of interior and exterior as well. Where is the border between the body and what lies outside it? Especially Yagharek's steps towards becoming human (losing his wings, getting rid of his wooden contraption, his cloak, then of his feathers) show the inconclusiveness of borders and the increase of spatial relations which complicate the localisation and adjustment of the variable "*body of flows*" (Schroer 2006: 291 [original italics]). Both space and the body are forced to (re-)construct themselves and the complexity of their relation again and again. Furthermore, the vast panorama of transgressive and hybrid characters gives the impression that hybridity and transgression become the norm again – the characters become equal in their differences. Yet, some Crobuzoners seem to be more equal than others, while others are outsiders among outsiders in a city full of outsiders. And, in many cases, their status as an outsider is due to their transgressive performance related to space, i.e. to their particular spatial practices.

Transgression is, according to Lotman, essential for narratives in general. Additionally, according to Meyer, transgression is also the essential characteristic of the outsider in the dystopian or anti-utopian novel (see Meyer 2001: 121–122).[21] What happens to these characters as they transgress borders? Langer claims that "those who succeed in bridging the boundary [...] are those who are violent and manipulate the power structures to their own ends – or [...] are 'insane', or have thought processes that themselves are beyond a normative boundary" (Langer 2010: 178). All these dimensions can be found in *Perdido Street Station*. Looking at all the mutilations, brutal remakings, and fights, violence as a transgressive act plays an important role. The manipulation of power structures is mostly located in the many conflicts between the dystopian authorities and the numerous counter movements (Jack Half-a-Prayer and his fReemade, Derkhan and the *Runagate Rampant*, and the vodyanoi dockers, to name but three), but also in the force field of material and discursive appropriation in a spatial sense. Insanity and thought processes beyond human capacity are most obviously manifest in two characters. The Weaver, the "dancing mad god" (*PSS:* 347), who, with regard to its abilities of moving through and changing space and existence as such almost at will, is possibly the most powerful, the most transgressive, and simultaneously the most irrational entity in the novel. Surprisingly, Yagharek, whose transformation may be read as a display of utter insanity, can serve as another example. Is his solution of making himself a man at the end of the novel a solution only someone who can well be imagined as utterly traumatised could come to? After all, he himself transgressed social norms by executing violence and in turn suffered brutal punishment; he was torn from his old life and people and wandered about for years, and ended up in a strange, bewildering, and dangerous city. His flicker of hope for recovery is suddenly taken away and he apparently tries to commit suicide by throwing himself off a roof, but mutilates himself by attempting to alter his body instead (in his case: plucking his feathers and attempting to break his beak).

In any case, these transgressive aspects play out on the interrelated levels of mind, body, and city as suggested by Langer, and the borders between the three prove to be extremely diffuse. The characters of *Perdido Street Station*, as well as the city, the novel's genre, and Miéville as a writer (see Gordon 2003a: 461–462; see also Miéville 2009), are all placed (or place themselves) in a hybrid contact zone by means of transgressive acts. These zones may range from tensions be-

---

21 Arguing along the lines of Lotman, Meyer relates the non-developing, stable character to the utopia and its developing, unstable counterpart to the anti-utopia. The outsider does not fit in, sticks out, and questions norms of behaviour and regulations.

tween avant-garde and tradition, art and business (Lin), crime and law (Lemuel), to different fields of science and magic (Isaac), protecting the city and fighting it (Jack Half-a-Prayer), different planes of existence (the Weaver), different bodies (Motley), and so on. The result is a revisiting of the classical dystopian outsider who, starting with Zamyatin's *We* (written in 1920), fails in the end (see Meyer 2001: 386). Outsiders in recent dystopian novels offer a broader spectrum and thus enrich the main characters' profiles. Lin fails, her body is mutilated and half her mind gone. Lemuel is shot by the milita. Isaac, at the intersection of the sciences and magic, manages to transgress the laws of science, but he cannot claim the fame for it, and it is unclear whether his crisis engine will work again one day. He and Derkhan save the city, also shattered, and although they survive and defeat the slake-moths, it is a small triumph since they have lost comrades and friends on the way, and will never be rewarded – on the contrary, they have to leave the city as wanted criminals. They are supported by Jack Half-a-Prayer, who does not leave the city, the result being that he stays on his own in a city that hunts him while he is trying to save it from itself (*PSS:* 622). His position is exemplary of the aforementioned paradox: in terms of his body and his practice, he fits New Crobuzon perfectly, and it is precisely this transgressive practice that makes him an outsider among outsiders. Thus, more recent dystopian fiction features outsiders and heroes who still fail, but the character model has become more complex and variable as the transgressive acts offer a vast variety of – again referring to Stross – "fertile and creative response[s] to environmental pressures and opportunities," thus contributing to the productive repositioning of the tradition. Especially Yagharek offers a striking repositioning. His rape of Kar'uchai as a bodily transgression and the following punishment made him an outsider among the garuda, and he remains an outsider in New Crobuzon. He is neither made whole again nor is he reintegrated in the community of his past. Yet, in contrast to the classic dystopian outsider, he does not fail since in the end, he is flexible enough to transform himself into a man. He resists both Jack Half-a-Prayer's liminal world, thus avoiding the isolated position at the intersection, and Isaac's world of exile, and obtains a new life in its own right. Thus, he adds a new perspective to the spectrum of hybridity as a form of expression of bodily (and, as a result, spatial) transgression that can be found in the genre of the dystopian novel, another expressive reconfiguration of the outsider as the genre's character model, always with the implied danger of becoming insane, of being torn apart, of failure, of belonging nowhere.

V.2.2 *The City & The City*: Once More onto the Breach

The following chapter elaborates on chapter IV.2.2, which presented *The City & The City* as a novel which heavily plays with human perception and everyday ignorance, mostly by means of 'unseeing' as performance. A novel in which two cities occupying the same territory try to keep each other apart as much as possible, to ignore each other as much as possible, and where there is only one place of legal transition between the two, is predestined to be analysed in terms of the borders presented in the text. After a brief add-on to IV.2.2 with respect to Eßbach's area-related and organism-related borders (see chapter V.1), the focus will be on breaching, around which the question of border-crossing, transgression and treading circles.

One Place, Two Places
Besźel and Ul Qoma are two cities on the same territory – materially speaking, they are one, but on the discursive level they are two separate cities. In Eßbach's terms, one can say that the cities construct a "Siedlungsgrenze" for themselves, i.e. they create an artificial border and thus two settlements by means of differentiating between self and other where there is no geographical reason for doing so since they are literally in one place (see Eßbach 1999: 98).[22] As in the border types A and B, the two cities with their total and alter areas proclaim strict separation. However, the separation is neither 'natural' nor obvious, and the specific codes of separation and unseeing have to be learned. And yet, both cities insist on these very contingent settlement borders which, conversely, render geographical borders practically irrelevant.[23] The cities' borders do not run along geographical landmarks, but along – in Eßbach's sense – people's organism-related borders of perception, i.e. unseeing. Three elements can be found under Eßbach's umbrella term "organism-related borders": social borders, subject (i.e. individual) borders, and the problem of excentricity (the fact that the individual's body has both a confining function as well as modes for reaching

---

[22] For the actual-world example of Baarle, a place where the national border between Dutch and Flemish territory runs through one (or two?) towns, and where the national border even runs through individual houses, see Bonnett (2014: 177–182).
[23] The only clear-cut exception is Copula Hall as the bottleneck connecting the two cities and the only place of legal transition. However, it is not a typical border zone of type B, as one might assume – it rather has the attributes of the overlapping type C because "externally it is in both cities; internally, much of it is in both or neither." It is "a juncture, an interstice, one sort-of border built above another" (*TC&TC:* 72).

beyond its own borders; see Eßbach 1999: 92 ff.).[24] Especially the latter two play a crucial role for unseeing in Beszél and Ul Qoma.

In *The City and the City*, the figurations of seeing and unseeing are paramount for numerous issues. If organism-related borders in general are discussed in terms of questions of openness and closedness (see Eßbach 1999: 92), then the construction of identity along the parameters of selection and differentiation can be said to be staged via seeing and unseeing in Miéville's novel. Subject borders, for example, usually refer to the human skin as the ultimate layer, which is open in both directions, between the individual and his or her environment. In *The City & The City*, the skin as a divider and connector is marginalised while the role of visual perception is emphasised. This visual priority is also transferred to the novel's social borders: where the citizens of Beszél or Ul Qoma stop seeing, i.e. where they unsee, their society ends as well. Thus, identity and alterity come into being by means of unseeing. What remains beyond, in the unseen, is the other. This notion is taken to extremes in the cities' crosshatch areas. There, the two cities overlap – theoretically, they should therefore be contact zones (border type C) since they are used by citizens from both sides. However, unseeing prevents crosshatch encounters, and people are strictly forbidden to get in touch with each other. The – in material terms – shared crosshatch areas, in their mutual discursive/cognitive denial, are thus delimited contact zones. Unseeing as a performance also draws upon Eßbach's problem of excentricity: the modes of reaching beyond one's own body, which are closely tied to the sensory organs, are radically trimmed by the enforced unseeing and the marginalisation of other sensory input. Unseeing only works as a collective performance and only because everybody plays along, i.e. as long as all citizens willingly trim their subject borders and thus make themselves capable of preventing contact with the other where the cities overlap. In a way, unseeing presents an important facet of Pratt's contact zone: in order to truly make contact one has to actually *want* to make contact in the first place; there is no fruitful encounter without a mutual willingness for encounters, and there is no encounter without appropriate cognitive preconditions and means of communication (see Stilz 2013: 10).

---

24 It is not all clear, however, why Eßbach lists the problem of excentricity as a subterm for organism-related borders since it is not a border as such but rather highlights one of the features of subject borders.

Breaching as Transgressing, Breaching as Treading
After the description of borders (of (un-)seeing) in *The City & The City*, different kinds of crossings and transgressions as established in V.1 will be at the centre of attention. Non-human occurrences of border-crossing which can be seen or unseen by humans come first. What do citizens of Besźel and Ul Qoma do when they see a dog from/in one city chase a cat from/in the other? The answer is to be found in the concept of protuberances in the following paragraph. Afterwards, several characters are examined. The analysis begins with Yorjavic (the assassin of Yolanda) and the intricacy of his murder (which violates numerous laws without breaching) as a legal crossing and follows with Inspector Tyador Borlú, the novel's main protagonist, and his performances of treading as a barely legal sounding of boundaries. In the next step, I will examine Borlú's treading chase of Yorjavic, which ends with the novel's most striking transgression. After turning towards the consequences of Borlú's transgression with respect to his relation towards the urban space, the analysis will end with David Bowden, the leader of the international archaeological research group and Mahalia's killer, as an outstanding avatar of treading.

Breaching as Transgressing, Breaching as Treading: Natural Occurrences
Border-related occurrences play a role which should not be underestimated. Animals, natural phenomena, human waste – they all cross the borders between Besźel and Ul Qoma without hindrance: "'Rain and woodsmoke live in both cities,' the proverb has it. In Ul Qoma they have the same saw, but one of the subjects is 'fog.' You may occasionally also hear it of other weather conditions, or even rubbish, sewage, and, spoken by the daring, pigeons and wolves" (*TC&TC:* 66).[25] Obviously, cross-border activities or occurrences (for example a Besź dog sniffing a Ul Qoman passerby, or shattering glass on a crosshatched street) usually do not cause breach because, due to a mutual "polite stoic unsensing" (i.e. unseeing), they are considered "protuberances from the other city" (*TC&TC:* 80) – they bulge into the foreign city's space. Materially, they violate the border, but unseeing is too strong a practice, so discursivity once again keeps up the separation. Technically, they could be treated as natural crossings, but in the context of *The City & The City* all cross-border performances which do not go through Copula Hall pose a threat to the social (and spatial) order. People

---

[25] Why is it daring to speak of animals as living in both cities? The reason is that by doing so, one might also start to think about human beings: "If animals are allowed to pass freely from one city into the other, why aren't we?" – a train of thought which any government striving towards maintaining its borders will try to prevent.

may start asking questions if border-crossings were allowed anywhere else but through Copula Hall. Therefore, social (and spatial) pratice does its best to ignore them and, through the idea of protuberance, what could be a transgression is weakened to the self-constructed lie of a bulge. In these cases of protuberance the 'source city' domain is temporarily extended by a bulging of its border, thus questioning ideational lines of separation as in border type A. Rubbish

> is an exception, when it is old enough. Lying across crosshatched pavement or gusted into an alter area from where it was dropped, it starts as protub, but after a long enough time for it to fade and the Illitan or Besź script to be obscured by filth and bleached by light, and when it coagulates with other rubbish, including rubbish from the other city, it's just rubbish, and it drifts across borders, like fog, rain and smoke. (*TC&TC:* 80)

Rubbish bearing script which identifies it as either Besź or Ul Qoman is only incorporated over time when its signs of otherness have gone. Listing all these cross-border elements, it is easy – as in Isaac's scientific paradigm in *Perdido Street Station* – to assume transgression as inherently natural. One can extend this to human beings such as the tourists as explained in chapter IV.2.2. The only people fighting against their transgressive nature and submitting to the imposed unseeing are the citizens of Beszel and Ul Qoma in order not to breach.

Breaching as Transgressing, Breaching as Treading: Yorjavic

Human behaviour in *The City & The City* therefore has a special status that boils down to the question: breach or not breach? Jurisdiction of the local police or of Breach? It is the murders of Mahalia and Yolanda in particular where this question is discussed. The practices of Borlú and of the two murderers, Bowden and Yorjavic, are most relevant in this context. The latter, who is ordered by Buric to both get rid of Mahalia's body and to shoot Yolanda, is particularly eager not to breach. He breaks into three different vans in Beszel, searching for one with a permit for crossing over via Copula Hall, and fills it with junk so the body will be heavy enough to drown. Then he drives over to Ul Qoma, picks up Mahalia's body, drives back to Beszel again, and hides her body in a newly-built skate park. The complication has already been mentioned: Yorjavic was ordered to drop her into the river. However, his passageway to the river is blocked by the skate park that did not show on the outdated map given to him by Bowden; because he is running out of time, Yorjavic drops the body in the skate park. While disposing the body, he crosses the border twice without breaching; his spatial practice complies with the mundane rules of border-crossing – a border-crossing without transgression. As Borlú und Dhatt try to (illegally) escort the frightened and paranoid Yolanda from Ul Qoma to Besźel via Copula Hall, Yorjavic shoots her and wounds Dhatt. He shoots from the Besź side over the border into Ul Qoma:

> *No breach had occurred* though a woman had been killed, brazenly, across a border. Assault, a murder and an attempted murder, but those bullets had travelled across the checkpoint itself, in Copula Hall, across the meeting place. A heinous, complex, vicious killing, but in the assiduous care the assassin had taken – to position himself just so at the point where he could stare openly along the last metres of Besźel over the physical border and *into* Ul Qoma, could aim precisely down this one conduit between the cities – that murder had been committed with if anything a *surplus* of care for the cities' boundaries, the membrane between Ul Qoma and Besźel. There was no breach, Breach had no power here, and only Besź police were in the same city as the killer now. (*TC&TC*: 282 [original italics])

The bullets penetrate the membrane of Copula Hall in its transitive function as a bottleneck between the two cities. Yorjavic's performance in all its intricacy is illegal in terms of mundane jurisdiction (being a member in a paramilitary organisation, carrying firearms, theft, murder), but not in terms of unseeing and breach. The area of influence of the local police ends exactly at the political border, which is in this case congruent with the border of influence in Eßbach's sense (see Eßbach 1999: 90). Yorjavic is – the name of his right-wing group in itself becomes ironic here – a True Citizen who strictly abides by the spatial laws of discursivity and materiality, but within this frame, he violates a large number of laws.

Breaching as Transgressing, Breaching as Treading: Borlú
Yorjavic is, in a way, a counter figure to Borlú. As a cop, Borlú embodies Besź law and order – which he disregards numerous times even to the extent of breaching. Right from the beginning with his delayed unseeing of an old woman (*TC&TC*: 14), he displays tendencies of transgression. It is Borlú's apartment in particular where looking out of the window not only becomes an act of staring outside, but an act of a barely legal sounding of boundaries or even outright transgression: "I turned back to that night-lit city, and this time I looked and saw its neighbour. Illicit, but I did. Who hasn't done that at times? There were gasrooms I shouldn't see [...]. On the street at least one of the passersby – I could tell by the clothes, the colours, the walk – was not in Besźel, and I watched him anyway" (*TC&TC*: 49). Right in front of the window of Borlú's apartment runs a train line – an Ul Qoman one. "[The trains] were not in my city. I did not of course, but I could have stared into the carriages – they were quite that close – and caught the eyes of foreign travellers" (*TC&TC*: 30) – which is what he is doing only slightly later:

> I turned to the railway lines a few metres by my window and waited until, as I knew it would eventually, a late train came. I looked into its rapidly passing, illuminated windows, and into the eyes of the few passengers, a very few of whom even saw me back, and were startled. But they were gone fast, over the conjoined sets of roofs: it was a brief crime, and not their faults [sic]. They probably did not feel guilty for long. They probably did not remember that stare. I always wanted to live where I could watch foreign trains. (*TC&TC:* 49)

Just a "brief crime," but still a provocation and, if one wants to be picky, a transgression; Borlú willingly sees whom he is not supposed to see, and the other way around. So far, Borlú's sounding of boundaries is restricted to cognitive transgression. By revealing his love for watching foreign trains, and by watching foreigners, he displays one of the preconditions for successful encounters in Pratt's contact zone: a fascination for the other, a willingness to make contact.

As it becomes clear that the murder of Mahalia is a cross-border case, Borlú is sent to Ul Qoma and legally passes through Copual Hall (see also the analysis of his first unseeing of Besźel in chapter IV.2.2.). During his stay, he realises that he and his Ul Qoman colleague Dhatt are, grosstopically, almost neighbours (*TC&TC:* 234). After the visit at Dhatt's, Borlú narrates his next provocation, which goes two steps further than staring into Ul Qoma from his appartment. Firstly, knowing that his own place is grosstopically close, he decides to walk past it although he is still in the other city – he extends his sounding of borders beyond his home by transposing it into the urban space. Secondly, he puts his Besź neighbours at risk: "I half expected to see one of my neighbours, none of whom, I think, knew I was abroad, and who might therefore be expected to greet me before noticing my Ul Qoman visitor's badge and hurriedly attempting to unbreach" (*TC&TC:* 238). However, nobody notices him as he comes closer:

> In Ul Qoma I was in Ioy Street. It is pretty equally crosshatched with RosidStrász where I lived. The building two doors along from my own house was a late-night Ul Qoman liquor store, half the pedestrians around me in Ul Qoma, so I was able to stop grosstopically, physically close to my own front door, and unsee it of course, but equally of course not quite, with an emotion the name of which I have no idea. I came slowly closer, keeping my eyes on the entrances in Ul Qoma. (*TC&TC:* 238)

His unspecified emotion gives away that his unseeing, although it kicks in, does not work as perfect as it should. In Löw's terms, one could say that his experience (i.e. his emotional bond to his home) influences his perception (i.e. his unseeing) while he pretends to be fully able to unsee (i.e. performance). Borlú cannot completely relegate his own front door to the background. Then, he realises that he is being watched: "It looked like an old woman. I could hardly see her in the dark [...], something was curious in the way she stood. I [...] could not tell which city she was in. That is a common instant of uncertainty, but this one went on for much longer than usual." Borlú becomes aware that he was about to go too far as more people appear who defy categorisation: "And my alarm did not subside, it grew, as her locus refused to clarify. I saw others in similar shadows, similarly hard to make sense of [...]. The woman continued to stare at me, and she took a step or two in my direction, so either she was in Ul Qoma or breaching. That made me step back" (*TC&TC*: 238–239). Borlú flees from the scene. Only later will he find out that it was Breach watching him, only waiting for him to breach. The examples of Borlú's sounding show how similar border-related treading is to walking on a tightrope: one mistake and it is over.

After the murder of Yolanda at Copula Hall, Borlú breaches indeed in order to hunt down the non-breaching Yorjavic. Since the latter is in Besźel and Borlú in Ul Qoma, and since the border is heavily guarded right after the gunfire, there is no way for Borlú to immediately get his hands on Yorjavic. The Besź inspector is unable to cross legally. What follows is an extraordinary chase: Yorjavic flees on Besź territory while Borlú, grosstopically close but a whole city away, follows him in Ul Qoma. They are on a crosshatched street, so as long as Borlú keeps unseeing Yorjavic, he is able to follow him: "Ul Qomans I shoved out of the way: Besź tried to unsee me but had to scurry to get out of my path. I saw their startled looks. I moved faster than the killer. I kept my eyes not on him but looking at some spot or other in Ul Qoma that put him in my field of vision. I *tracked him without focussing, just legally*" (*TC&TC*: 284 [my italics]). Again, he puts other citizens at risk as they have to dodge him without breaching accidentally. As in the former treading provocations, Borlú sounds the boundaries. In his exhaustion of the practice of unseeing, he comes as close to breaching as possible without the final transgression. While the former examples rather pose as treadings *at* the border (thus poking the fine line between the two cities), he now just legally treads *along* the border of Besźel and Ul Qoma, of breach and not-breach, during the chase – a *Grenzgänger* (someone constantly sounding borders and attempting to extend or cross established limits) indeed. Yorjavic hears Borlú, sees and unsees him: "His eyes widened in astonishment at the sight of me, which, careful even then, he did not hold. He registered me. He looked back into Besźel and sped up [...]. I accelerated too" (*TC&TC*: 284). Yorjavic moves towards the edges of the Old Towns in order to reach a total area where Borlú cannot follow him. "I knew where he was going. The Old Towns of Besźel and Ul Qoma are closely crosshatched: reach their edges, separations begin, alter and total areas. This was not, could not be, a chase. It was only two accelerations. We ran, he in his city, me close behind him, full of rage, in mine" (*TC&TC*: 284–285). To foreigners, the connection between the two accelerations would be obvious; locals, as long as they stick to unseeing, see one movement and unsee a second, separate one – a question of discursivity. Finally, Yorjavic comes to a total street, and Borlú does the only thing that can stop the assassin who was so careful not to breach – he breaches himself:

> He was by a total street, a street in Besźel only. He paused to look up in my direction as I gasped for breath. For that sliver of time, too short for him to be accused of any crime, but certainly deliberate, he looked right at me. [...] He looked at me at the threshold to that abroad-only geography and made a tiny triumphant smile. He stepped toward space where no one in Ul Qoma could go. I raised the pistol and shot him. (*TC&TC:* 285)

By breaching, Borlú takes his non-compliant habitus to extremes. From his general tendency to outsiderism as a non-conformist cop, he develops into someone who walks right along the border of the city and its jurisdiction – and then into a transgressor who not only crosses a border (as he had done by going from Besźel to Ul Qoma through Copula Hall in a legal fashion), but ultimately violates it as he chooses the grosstopically closest passage between the two cities. The border between Besźel and Ul Qoma is breached.

In the following, Breach take him. After being interrogated, Borlú cooperates with Breach in order to find out who hired Yorjavic and why the two female students had to die. In a way, he still works on his former case as a cop, but at the same time he is also obliged to clean up his own transgression. The 'reward' for Borlú's breach is a final transgression. He is made a member of Breach and learns how to move through the cities (mostly through a man called Ashil). His first steps outside after having spent some time inside Breach's buildings are marked by disorientation:

> There were double doors, doors to an outside. We stepped through, and that, when the light ate me up, was when I realised I did not know which city we were in. After panic at the crosshatch, I realised we must be in Ul Qoma [...]. I was breathing deep. [...] I was pleasantly disoriented by all the people [...]. Ashil walked me across a courtyard, below facades of figures and bells, video screens with stock information. I did not know where we were. (*TC&TC:* 302)

Knowing where you are is, of course, of utmost importance in *The City & The City*. In order not to breach by accident, one must be able to place oneself exactly. Borlú, a local with legal cross-border experience, is lost for the first time. The following simple act of buying something to eat and drink becomes a transgressive act by the ultimate performance of stepping from one city right into the other. At first, Borlú is hesitant:

> I tried to unsee them [the foodstands] but there could be no uncertainty: that source of the smell I had been unsmelling was our destination. 'Walk', he said, and he walked me through the membrane between cities; I lifted my boot in Ul Qoma, put it down again in

> Besźel, where breakfast was. [...] Ashil paid with Besźmarques. He put the paper plate in my hand, walked me back across the road into the supermarket. It was in Ul Qoma. He bought a carton of orange juice with dinar, gave it to me. [...] He walked me down the middle of the crosshatched road. (*TC&TC:* 303)

The foodstand is a whole city away in the first moment, a distance undone by a single step. Ashil and Borlú do what Borlú did when he was breaching – they cross the border – but this time, it is qualitatively different. Walking proves its worth as it dissolves the mental barrier. Then, the ultimate experience follows. As both cities come into Borlú's sight, it is described as a bewildering vertigo effect:

> My sight seemed to untether as with a lurching Hitchcock shot, some trickery of dolly and depth of field, so the street lengthened and its focus changed. Everything I had been unseeing now jostled into sudden close-up. Sound and smell came in: the calls of Besźel; [...] they came in a tide with the spice and Illitan yells of Ul Qoma [...]. 'Where are you?' Ashil said. He spoke so only I could hear. 'I...' 'Are you in Besźel or Ul Qoma?' '...Neither. I'm in Breach.' 'You're with me here.' We moved through a crosshatched moving crowd. 'In Breach. No one knows if they're seeing you or unseeing you. Don't creep. You're not in either: you're in both.' He tapped my chest. 'Breathe.' (*TC&TC:* 303–304)

Here, it becomes clear why Ashil's performance is not another breach despite the apparent similarities to Borlú's performance at the end of the chase. Another place unfolds besides Besźel and Ul Qoma: Breach. Saying "between Besźel and Ul Qoma" would be wrong because, although Breach keeps the two apart, it simultaneously *is* part of the two; they intersect in Breach. Therefore, Breach transcends the common crosshatch zones where unseeing maintains the separation – it poses as the ultimate contact zone, or boder type C. If all people lived in Breach, the separation of Besźel and Ul Qoma would be pointless, and everybody could make contact with everybody.

During the following days, Ashil takes Borlú around, both on foot and by public transport. Indicators are given that his experience of the cities has changed forever: "He took us by metro in Ul Qoma, where I sat still as if the remnants of Besźel clung to me like cobwebs and would frighten fellow passengers, out and onto a tram in Besźel, and it felt good, as if I were back home, misleadingly. The feeling of Besźel familiarity was replaced by some larger strangeness" (*TC&TC:* 304). Borlú learns from Ashil how to move in his re-encountering of urban space: "Each day he spent in my company, we walked the cities, in the Breach. I was learning from him how to walk between them, first in one, then the other, or in either [...]" (*TC&TC:* 368).

With the corrupt politician Buric dead and Bowden taken by Breach as well, Borlú finally realises that by breaching he has moved across an ultimate border.

After his breach, after what he has seen and experienced, there is no way back to his former life as a Besź cop. From that angle, breaching also poses as a transgression of a threshold according to border type G. By breaching, Borlú unlocks a completely new field of meaning in an almost divine revelation. Transgressing a threshold/type G border leads, according to Goetsch, to a confrontation with an endlessness which transcends all hitherto existing orders, and/or leads to a transposition of self into an utterly new order. In Borlú's case, both are true. On the one hand, he experiences the borderless (or better: transgressive) aspect of a membership in Breach where he can transcend the previous borders with ease; on the other hand, he is confronted with a new order. He is *in* Breach, and he cannot get out again; contact to people from his old life is strictly forbidden; furthermore, his future performances are restricted in so far as he is unable to unsee – he will have to carry the burden of Breach's borderlessness. Like all the other members of Breach, he committed a crime with consequences that cannot be undone. In Ashil's words: "'You'll never unsee again,'" and Borlú knows that he is right. "I imagined myself in Besźel now, unseeing the Ul Qoma of the crosshatched terrain. Living in half of the space. Unseeing all the people and the architecture and vehicles and the everything in and among which I had lived. I could pretend, perhaps, at best, but something would happen, and Breach would know" (*TC&TC:* 371).

The former cop is not allowed to go back to his former life because he would be unable to stay in it. Thus, he is also denied any contact with it – he is allowed to send farewell letters to a handful of people, delivered by somebody else, and that is it. By being forced to stay in Breach, discursivity is heavily trimmed as his possibilities of social interaction with others are trimmed. Conversely, he is given the ultimate experience of the city's body which, when compared to Yagharek's final experience of the city, shows another facet. In Yagharek's case it is the plucking of his feathers and the resulting transformation into "a man" (*PSS:* 623) that helps him to overcome where he had come from, namely the in-between. The garuda's mental attitude changes as well, but the transformative act as such succeeds through a bodily performance. Borlú on the other hand starts out in a (mentally) strictly separated environment and overcomes the bodily and spatial separation in the course of a mental transgression (i.e. in the course of his breach by stopping to unsee). Thus, he enters the very state that Yagharek leaves behind: the interstitial, the border itself of which he becomes a part. He can now go anywhere, anytime, with ease. Just like Yagharek in the course of his transformation, he acquires new means of getting in touch with his city and new qualities of movement which are again metaphorically charged with relation to the body: "[Ashil] threaded us like a suture in and out of Besźel and Ul Qoma" (*TC&TC:* 370). Ashil and the learning Borlú go back and forth between the skin flaps of the city's body. Whereas Yagharek manages to dissolve the border, Borlú embodies it. Thus, his experience of the city is marked by the continuous alternation and his body performing the alternation. Everywhere else in the novel, the key word in the context of breach was separation. Now, Borlú's movement granted by Breach emphasises the extended possibilities of movement as the metaphorical stitches keep the city together conceptually. Thus, Borlú can rightly say that he may live "in the interstice," but still "in the city and the city" (*TC&TC:* 371). Breach is in both Besźel and Ul Qoma while paradoxically keeping the two apart.

Borlú, as a member of Breach, is also given a new task: it is

> not to uphold the law, or another law, but to maintain the skin that keeps law in place. Two laws in two places, in fact. [...] Inspector Tyador Borlú is gone. I sign off Tye, avatar of Breach [...]. We are all philosophers here where I am, and we debate among many other things the question of where it is that we live. On that issue I am liberal. I live in the interstice yes, but I live both in the city and the city. (*TC&TC:* 373)

By becoming a member of Breach, of an organisation made up of former breachers, his final transgression takes him into an interstitial realm. Borlú becomes a personified part of "the last ditch" (*TC&TC:* 370), of the border itself that he can cross so easily now. The circle is complete as the final words ("I live both in the city and the city") refer back to the novel's title. After numerous issues of materiality and discursivity, of walking along borders and crossing or violating them, one realises that *The City & The City* is not only about the topographical opposition of the two material cities, namely Besźel und Ul Qoma. It is also about the opposition of Besźel and Ul Qoma in their wholeness and Breach on the other side in the force field of separation and simultaneity; about the opposition of Besźel, Ul Qoma, and Breach on the one hand as three places that are given existence in some way and the only constructed urban legend of Orciny on the other; about the opposition between what I perceive and what others perceive; about what I (un)see and what I see and what I am allowed or can be made to (un)see.

Breaching as Transgressing, Breaching as Treading: Bowden

Finally, David Bowden, the author of *Between the City & the City*, the book on the urban legend of Orciny, deserves a few words. Like Yorjavic, he is a murderer (he killed Mahalia in Ul Qoma), and like Yorjavic, he managed to commit the crime without breaching. Thus, Breach have no power over him, only the local police may arrest him. In contrast to Yorjavic, however, Bowden does not simply run away. He provides an outstandingly clever spatial practice related to the title of his book. He does neither stay in either Besźel or Ul Qoma nor does he transgress – he stays in another interstitial fold between the city and the city. He is present at the killing of Yolanda and with all hell breaking loose his whole habitus is focussed on neither belonging to Besźel nor Ul Qoma. Here is Borlú's phone conversation with Dhatt:

> 'Have they [the militsya] got him?' 'Tyad, listen. They can't. There's a problem. […] They *can't tell* where he is. […] He's just… He's been standing there, just outside the entrance, in full view, and then when he saw them moving towards him he started walking… but the way he's moving… the clothes he's wearing… they *can't tell* whether he's in Ul Qoma or Besźel. […] They're fucking terrified that even seeing him and saying *that* [they are seeing him is] breach […].' (*TC&TC:* 349 [original italics])

Both his movements and his clothes (and, as becomes clear when Borlú takes him to task, also his way of talking), do not give away where he is. Thus, no border guard will stop him on his way out of town. Once again, Borlú bends the rules as much as possible. He engages both Dhatt and his Besź colleague Corwi to go for a walk in the area where Bowden was last seen, sending them to tread the borders of unseeing once more. They see Bowden on the streets but have to unsee him in order to not breach. Yet, both keep in touch with Borlú by phone, but they stay extremely cautious in their utterances in fear of breaching. They give him their own positions, but not Bowden's, avoiding to admit that they can see him (cf. *TC&TC:* 352). Still, their locations are sufficient for Borlú to finally meet Mahalia's killer:[26]

> Bowden was instantly visible. That gait. Strange, impossible. Not properly describable, but to anyone used to the physical vernaculars of Besźel and Ul Qoma, it was *rootless* and *untethered*, purposeful and *without a country*. I saw him from behind. He did not drift but strode with *pathological neutrality* away from the cities' centres, ultimately to borders and the mountains and out to the rest of the continent. (*TC&TC:* 353 [my italics])

The whole rhetoric of the passage highlights Bowden's expertise in belonging nowhere – it is literally impossible to place him. Bowden walks a crosshatched street, so the materiality of his surroundings is no help to Borlú. His habitus does not give away where he is either because it does not commit to a specific discursivity. Borlú can only admire the mastership of his performance: "How expert a citizen, how consummate an urban dweller and observer, to mediate those million unnoticed mannerisms that marked out civic specificity, to refuse either ag-

---

26 At this point of time, Borlú has already been taken by Breach so he does not have to unsee Bowden.

gregate of behaviours" (*TC&TC:* 354). It is worth mentioning that Bowden, who masters the urban force field so that he can tread on the thin line in between, is a foreigner. "'Maybe it took an outsider to really see how citizens mark themselves, so as to walk between it'" (*TC&TC:* 368). In a way, the foreigner Bowden manages what other foreigners and Löbbermann's tourist archetype (see chapter III.2.1) fail to achieve: to look behind the scenes. Thus, Bowden, even more than Borlú, exemplifies the careful treading on the border. He does not clearly answer Borlú's question about where he is: "'Inspector Borlú. Fancy meeting you... here?'" (*TC&TC:* 354). The situation is, in the manner of Miéville, weird. Borlú has the murderer right in front of him, the weapon involved in the crime in his hands, two cops from both cities grosstopically close – and yet, Bowden cannot be arrested. He could even shoot Borlú and nobody could intervene or even secure Borlú's body: "'the thing is that if you were killed by someone who no one was sure which city they were in and they weren't sure where *you* were either, your body would have to lie there, rotting, forever. People would have to step over you. Because no one breached. Neither Besźel nor Ul Qoma could risk clearing you up'" (*TC&TC:* 356 [original italics]).

Borlú's solution is, once again, unconventional. Instead of arresting Bowden for a non-existent breach, he lures him into coming with him into Breach. In his study *Between the City and the City*, Bowden had been hunting for the urban legend of Orciny for years, and he never found it. The book ruined his career as an academic, and the urban legend has haunted him ever since. In Mahalia's interest for Orciny, he saw the chance to rebuild the legend, at least for her. However, she outsmarted him without even knowing because in the course of her studies she proved him wrong. Even worse: "Mahalia died because she proved to Bowden that he had been a fool to believe the folktale he created" (*TC&TC:* 359). He has never seen what is really between the city and the city: Breach. Borlú offers to show him, and Bowden consents:

> 'Orciny is bullshit. Do you want to see what's really in between?' [...] Nasty broken man. The only thing more despicable than what he had done was the half-hidden eagerness with which he now took me up on my offer. It was not bravery on his part to come with me. [...] He sagged, with some moan: apology, plea, relief. I was not listening and don't remember. I did not arrest him – I was not *policzai*, not then, and Breach do not arrest – but I had him, and exhaled, because it was over. (*TC&TC:* 362 [original italics])

Bowden is taken by Breach after all. Ironically enough, Bowden entering Breach is another transgression here – not a spatial one, but a transgression of conventions. Bowden violates the last border without violating it: after staying in the interstitial for quite a while, and as masterful as it gets, he is the only person who comes into Breach without ever having actually breached.[27]

In the Breach: Utopia and Crime

Most people in *The City and the City* seem to live in concord with the separation of Besźel and Ul Qoma without being outright nationalists. During the chaotic lockdown after the breaching of a whole bus full of refugees, it is mostly the unificationists,[28] not regular citizens, who can be seen demonstrating in the streets. Dhatt, Borlú's colleague in Ul Qoma, also commits to the idea of keeping the cities separated, laughs about the idea of a unified city, and makes Borlú laugh, too (*TC&TC:* 193). Not only in terms of the practice of unseeing, but also in terms of their mindsets, the characters seem to live too much in their own little worlds in order to appreciate unification. The ideological side of the separatist thinking becomes obvious when even Ashil, as a member of Breach standing above nationalist ideology, describes the unificationists of both cities as "little bands of eager utopians" (*TC&TC:* 239). To him as well as to Borlú and Dhatt as citizens of both cities, unification is utopian in the common negative sense of the word: something to naively dream of instead of facing reality.

How utopian is the unification of Besźel and Ul Qoma? All characters the reader learns about – except for the ridiculed unificationists – are sceptical about it. Citizens as well as the politicians in the Oversight Committee are unable to imagine a life in unison with the other city, and therefore Breach keep the two cities apart, executing the classical motive of the stable utopian/dystopian state that tries to keep up its status quo.[29] The role of Breach is not all clear, however.

---

[27] The question arises whether Breach can hold him. Ashil assures that they will find a reason: ordering Yorjavic to dump Mahalia might count as breach, or "'[m]aybe we'll push him into Besźel and pull him back to Ul Qoma. If we say he breached, he breached" (*TC&TC:* 369). In combination with the fact that Borlú is forced to stay in Breach, this statement adds a bitter taste to the status of Breach. Despite being a powerful force watching the two cities, they also seem to run on certain arbitrariness.
[28] The counter movement to the nationalist groups, the True Citizens and Qoma First. According to members of Breach, Unificationists of both cities work together.
[29] Keeping up the status quo usually goes hand in hand with an authoritarian/totalitarian form of government (here: the nationalist parties) and an institution that ensures that the people obey (here: Breach). See Meyer 2001: 35–36. Indoctrination of unseeing can thus be treated as a variety of classical dystopian methods of brainwashing such as the notion of doublethink in George Orwell's *Nineteen Eighty-Four*. It is a way of seeing the world imposed on the citizens by governmental institutions with the goal to keep the citizens within pre-selected mental boundaries of experiencing reality.

They act independently when someone breaches, but they can also be invoked by the Oversight Committee when an apparent ordinary crime in one of the cities might involve breach. Still, where do Breach come from, and to what extent do they act on behalf of the Committee? What is Breach's own motivation? They seem to celebrate the separation of the cities for the separation's sake, but Breach would be unable to do so if the citizens did not comply. Here is how Ashil describes this silent cooperation:

> It's not just us keeping them apart. It's everyone in Besźel and everyone in Ul Qoma. Every minute, every day. We're only the last ditch: it's everyone in the cities who does most of the work. It works because you don't blink. That's why unseeing and unsensing are so vital. No one can admit it doesn't work. So if you don't admit, it does. But if you breach, even if it's not your fault, for more than the shortest time... you can't come back from that. (*TC&TC*: 370)

The whole practice of unseeing which keeps the two cities apart works because everyone plays along in order not to breach and disappear into Breach. The maintained separation thus perpetuates itself.

What would happen if the people did not comply and ended up in Breach together? Wouldn't they be united, free to walk both cities simultaneously? Wouldn't they achieve what the unificationists long for: utopia in the most positive sense of the word? In the status quo, contrastingly, citizens of both cities are denied this utopian contact zone by the supremacy of unseeing. Here, one can catch a glimpse of the institutional terror: the people of both cities are afraid of breaching because they do not know what will become of them, where they are going to end up, and Breach have the supremacy over the spatial practice. Keeping people in a climate of fear and unknowing, a group of few is able to keep two groups of many under control. Nobody, except for the ridiculed unificationists, can imagine a unified city without making fun of it or considering it dangerous; most people cannot imagine it at all, even Breach itself. Breach, in contrast to other guardian organisations in other dystopias (Mustapha Mond and the world controllers in *Brave New World*, the Guardians in the novel of the same title by John Christopher, the Thought Police of *Nineteen Eighty-Four*, and the political body of *V for Vendetta* come to mind), seem to be caught in the impossibility.[30] All members of Breach are former breachers who cannot go back, and thus somewhat sad figures; is that the price one has to pay for having – in Lotman's sense – a transgressive story? Is that the price for claiming the contact zone as a domain of productive human cooperation, as a place where

---

30 See also Ashil's inability to imagine children being raised in Breach (*TC&TC:* 370).

self and other can meet? Breach remains somewhat paradoxical: Ashil himself admits that Breach needs to become more 'interdisciplinary' in the future, and the novel's story also shows the productivity of cooperation; on the other hand, hardly anybody actually sees cooperation and overlap as desirable for the two cities. If Breach becomes more mixed, its goal will remain the same as before – namely, to maintain and solidify the separation of Besźel and Ul Qoma.

V.2.3 *Divided Kingdom:* **Withour Colour, without Place**

Chapter IV.2.5 showed the constructedness of the Divided Kingdom and the Rearrangement's impact on its citizens' psychology. Here, the borders between the four quarters shall be examined instead, the main point being that *Divided Kingdom* is mostly concerned with rendering its geo-political borders congruent with its psycho-social borders. Afterwards, exemplary border performances will be turned to, in particular those by Thomas Parry as one of the very few persons who travel through all quarters, and those by the socially marginalised White People.

Erasing the Contact Zone
In *Divided Kingdom*, demarcation is based upon three factors. Firstly, seemingly naturally 'given' geographical borders such as rivers determine the separation between one quarter and another. A look at the map[31] printed in the book also reveals that many borders run along former motorways which have become useless in the Divided Kingdom (hardly anybody owns a car anymore anyway): the borderline between the Red and the Green Quarter in the east, for instance, runs along the United Kingdom's M2, and the M3 between London and Southampton becomes the border between a blue and a red sector in the south. Secondly, obvious constructions of areas, such as the borders "of a country, a borough or a parish" (*DK:* 137) become part of the new national border. The borderline between the west of England and Wales, for example, has been maintained and now separates one part of the Blue Quarter and one of the Red Quarter's sectors. Lastly, ley lines, i.e. spiritual lines of force, also play a part: "[the architects of the Rearrangement] had drawn directly and quite deliberately on the land's innate psychic strength, using spiritual power to reinforce political will" (*DK:* 137). By doing so, another reason for not crossing the border (besides

---

[31] See the beginning of chapter III.2.2.

it being a serious crime) comes into being: "Maybe that helped to explain why so many phlegmatics believed that it could be fatal to cross a border, that certain borders could maim or even kill" (*DK:* 137). Therefore, the new borders are far from being arbitrary. Instead, they can be traced back to border constructions prior the Rearrangement, thus suggesting that the Rearrangement is not only necessary, but a natural thing to do.

The country's new borders are created first and the people are rearranged and transferred afterwards according to their humours (see chapter IV.2.5). Thus, the Rearrangement's goal is to not only keep the choleric, phlegmatic, melancholic and sanguine people apart, but to render all the borders congruent: the geographical borders provide the basis for the new political borders, which simultaneously are congruent with the new social and psychological borders. In terms of the border types established in chapter V.1, set 1 (containing border types A and B) is prominent in all these cases. The walls erected between the new quarters aim for strict separation (border type A) while the official cross-border spots are zones in their own right (border type B). Furthermore, border type E also plays an important role in the discursive separation of people and quarters between self and other. The strictness of the separation ultimately aims at erasing border type C, at erasing the contact zone. Nothing shall exist between self and other except for the fear of crossing the border which is said to be harmful both in a physical as well as a psychological sense (see *DK:* 85; 137). The borders of the Divided Kingdom, more than any other borders discussed in this study, both profit from and exist because of the fear of otherness, thus deliberately blocking the initialisation of the "Seven Cs of Contact" starting with communication (Stilz 2013: 9). The result is, as chapter IV.2.5 suggested, a psychological racism nourished by propaganda and prejudice by means of ascription. However, the new borders also create opportunities for forceful transgressive performances, as the following section shows.

Colourful Transgressions, Colourless Crossings
Fairly early in the novel, young Thomas Parry and his friend Bracewell ride their bikes on one of the highways which became useless after the Rearrangement: "There were curving roads with pompous white arrows painted on them, which we delighted in disobeying" (*DK:* 39). The two boys' performance, by being full of delight and disobeyance, points toward the domains of border-related lust and power – not unlike the lust and power of cartography (see chapter III). The fascination of the boys, in contrast to the touristic 'border experience' (see chapter IV.2.5), is not so much due to what lies on the other side of the border; rather, it is about the transgressive act itself. The delight the two boys draw

from disobeying painted lines grows and produces a vast variety of "'border games'" (*DK:* 40) as Parry and Bracewell invent border-related scenarios and playfully impersonate border guards or criminals with a mission to cross into foreign territory. Years later, Parry's new sister Marie tells him about the border performances of her father Victor and herself: "[Victor] had decided to walk round the border. All the way round. He wanted to see exactly where he had been living for the past twenty years. He was curious about 'the dimensions of the cage'. And they had done it, the two of them. They had walked nearly seven hundred miles" (*DK:* 90). Even a comparatively stoic character such as Victor, who lost his wife due to the Rearrangement, who has been unhappy ever since, and who did not care about his environment for twenty years, cannot resist the fascination of the border. The only way to sound his cage, then, is to walk along the entire borderline (treading *at* the border). Sounding the border of his quarter, by walking along it and by seeing what it is like, becomes Victor's way of accessing reality and where it ends, namely at the border he cannot cross. However, Marie and Victor also actually transgress the border once. As they walk round the border, they find a gap in the wall. The fascination is based in the transgressive act itself since the other side "looked the same, of course – but it *felt* different" (*DK:* 91 [original italics]). Even Victor surrenders to the lust of transgression: "'[W]e started laughing.' [...] 'We jumped up and down and shouted things and danced, even though there wasn't any music. We behaved like mad people'" (*DK:* 91). The mere act of transgressing easily through an ordinary gap without any guards or watchtowers bears both joy and madness.

While all these soundings and transgressions are rather mundane, the supernatural ability of Odell, another character, stands out. She was recruited by Parry's boss Vishram as a highly mobile cross-border surveillance agent after having transgressed the border twice illegally. Her ability is called "'escaping notice,'" which is neither camouflage nor proper invisibility, but another kind of ability in accord with her allegedly phlegmatic humour: "In her [...], one could see the true flowering of the phlegmatic character – adaptability, yes, but taken to extremes. [...] [S]he didn't actually *become* invisible. She simply *appeared* to do so" (*DK*, p. 334 [original italics]). Nevertheless, she was caught and more or less forced into the government's service. While Odell's means of transgression are by far the most powerful ones, she and her abilities are also the ones exploited by the predominant power structures and thus stripped of the lust of the transgressive act.

Before turning to Parry's border performances, the so-called White People of *Divided Kingdom* deserve a few words. They are social outcasts who do not fit in with regard to humourism. As Victor explains, "the past had been taken from them, as it had been taken from everyone alive at the time of the Rearrangement, but these were people who had been either unwilling or unable to find a place in the future. They didn't fit into any quarter, he said, or any humour" (*DK:* 125). While other people come to terms with the nation-wide classification according to the four humours, the White People do not. As a consequence, their external ascription (i.e. what others ascribe them; see chapter IV.2.5) stands out: they "were perceived as having no character, they were deemed incapable of causing psychological damage" (*DK:* 125), i.e. encounters with them will not influence other people's psychological balance. Considered to be without character, these people are required to wear white "because white had no status as a colour" (*DK:* 125). They are outsiders in every quarter, excluded from society proper (border type E) with the typical social mechanisms of fear, ignorance, disdain, and violence. In terms of separating self from other, the White People are placed outside the system of the four quarters: "Their existence lay parallel to everybody else's" (*DK:* 281). Thus, they are even more striking avatars of otherness than, say, a yellow citizen might be for a red one.

The White People's status and lives are thus extremely different from the regular citizens', which is also expressed in their relation to the nation's borders. They are free to wander around and across whichever border they want because, as non-persons not bound to the system, their cross-border performances do not affect the fabric of the Divided Kingdom's semantic fields (the quarters).[32] The White People are an in-between group in several ways. Firstly, they are a historical in-between phenomenon because they stem from the pre-Rearrangement era (which has been taken from them) and cannot adapt to the new humourist way of life: "They had ended up marooned between the old kingdom and the new one. Lost in a pocket of history" (*DK:* 125). Secondly, the fact that they can go wherever they want renders them a spatial in-between group with a nomad life of constant border-crossing as they seem, to other citizens, to inhabit their very own "fold of reality" (*DK:* 291). Thirdly, they are an in-between group in terms of what they symbolise for people living in the four quarters. On the one hand, they represent both the marginalised problem cases of society (as mentioned, they are social non-persons who do not belong anywhere) as well as the borderlessness in Goetsch's sense by roaming beyond social borders in terms of the humours (border type E) and by not being affected by those borders' spatio-political manifestations since they can cross the border wherever and

---

[32] Although the White People do not have an official permit for crossing over, their cross-border movements are at least tolerated or simply ignored. Therefore, I classify them as more or less legal crossings instead of transgressions where characters within the system attempt illegal movements across a border.

whenever they want.³³ On the other hand, the White People are not as borderless as it seems at first glance. They may be able to go wherever they want and cross borders at will, but by doing so they easily become victims of bored or sadistic border guards or aggressive mobs (primarily in the Yellow Quarter) and therefore victims of despotism, violence, and abuse (see *DK:* 299–340 and 315–319). This behaviour towards the White People might well point to the border-related question of lust and power. Their cross-border performances are, as mentioned, rather crossings than transgressions since they are not forbidden to move to the other side. Therefore, their performance lacks the subversive element of regular citizens' attempts at illegal crossings (as shown in the examples of Parry and Bracewell, the touristic 'border experience,' and Mary and Victor) and is thus a performance without lust as an end in itself. White People cross borders because they are able to do so, and regular citizens are not; regular citizens hurt and abuse White People because they are able to do so, and White People are not. The White People are a living paradox to others: "although they had been certified as non-persons, they had access to a far wider range of experience than the rest of us. We were limited, imprisoned, but they walked free. Another life indeed…" (*DK:* 281). Underneath the surface of sadism and violence slumbers a deeply-rooted jealousy because the White People, as marginalised and pathetic as they are, can do the one thing regular citizens cannot do.

It is worth to elaborate on this opposition between White People and regular citizens because it resumes the debate of Hippocratic humourism of chapter IV.2.5. The White People are white because they do not fit into one of the four categories of identity provided by the Divided Kingdom³⁴ – but in the original humourism as in Hippocrates, this is not necessary anyway because one needs a proper balance of all four humours instead of one humour desperately dominating or suppressing the others. Furthermore, it is not wrong to say that white as a colour has no status on its own, but what the treatment of the colour white in *Divided Kingdom* leaves out is that white is the combination of *all* colours found in the visible spectrum. White is not a colour in itself, it is a culmination of all colours available. Take this and combine it with the ancient Greek idea of *eukrasis*, and suddenly the White People turn out to be healthier than the rest of the population. Not only are the White People unlimited with regard to their movements, but also with regard to their psychological condition. They do not fit into one of the four categories precisely because their humours are,

---

33 In a way, due to their marginalised status outside the regular order, the White People display a lot of similarities to actual-world gypsies and tinkers.
34 Thus, the exclusion of the White People can also be read as an inversion of actual-world segregation (where especially dark-skinned people were – and still are – marginalised).

in Hippocrates' words, in *eukrasis*. In this light, the agenda of the Divided Kingdom is even more devious than the Rearrangement and its reinterpretation of humourism suggest already: precisely those people who would be balanced (and thus healthy or 'normal') according to Hippocrates are treated as outcasts. Those who live four-square in the world are exiled and banned from society. Thus, the jealousy and prejudices on the other people's part not only result from the fact that the White People are free to cross any border – they are also more deeply rooted in the glimmer of the old life represented by them. The White People, by refusing or being unable to adapt to the new system and adopt a new identity there, retained some of their pre-Rearrangement *eukrasis* and identity which the rest of the population has lost. Thus, the free-roaming outcasts remind the rearranged people of both their forgotten past as well as of the new borders to which they have confined themselves.

Thomas Parry: Walking and Identity

Finally, Thomas Parry's journey of crossings and transgressions is at stake, a journey which is remarkable because Parry is one of the very few people in the Divided Kingdom who actually visit all four quarters – and, by becoming one of the White People, he even manages to step out of the system. In the following, I will trace Parry's steps with a focus on how his cross-border performances are tied to walking and a search for identity.[35]

Parry's first cross-border performance is a legal one, namely his journey from his Red Quarter to the conference in the Blue Quarter (until the end of chapter 3 in the novel) by train.[36] While this crossing by public transport is rather unspectacular, his first steps in Aquaville, the Blue Quarter's capital, deserve some attention. Instead of waiting for a conference member to pick him up, he immediately starts walking to the hotel by himself. It is only after a few steps that he is given a card by a stranger which, it will turn out later, is a flyer of the Bathysphere club, where Parry will be confronted with his pre-Rearrangement past. Therefore, as soon as he starts to sound the foreign territory by walking, his search for identity begins – even though he is not aware of it yet. Starting with his first steps, Parry's walking, travelling, and moving is staged as a "'special act'" concerned with "an inner process of identity reconstruction against the

---

[35] For a basic outline of walking as a way of getting in touch with the world and one's own self, see chapter IV.1.

[36] Before this journey to the conference, Parry goes on one trip as an assistant to two more experienced relocation officers, but he is not allowed to cross into the foreign territory yet (see *DK*: 65–72).

totalitarian eradication of individuality and difference" (Adami 2013: 8) – and this process starts with his first steps in the first unfamiliar quarter. At first, Aquaville and its inhabitants strike him as quite strange, and he does not fit in at all: "I decided to walk [...]. I soon regretted it. I couldn't seem to synchronise my progress with that of the people milling all around me. They moved with so little purpose, with such a lack of certainty, that I kept colliding with them or treading on their feet" (*DK:* 100). Parry's performance as a red person literally clashes with those of the locals. Still, his sanguine determination enables him to continue his walk and to explore the area on his own. Later on his first day, as he is on his way to the Bathysphere, he reflects on his earlier performances. Not only is his fascination kindled – he also realises that his attitude is already changing:

> I found I was in no hurry [...]. During that short walk to the hotel, I had been overwhelmed by the strangeness of the place. It wasn't just the architecture or the dialect; it was something much larger and more abstract, like the look on people's faces, or the atmosphere itself. The citizens of Aquaville seemed to equate existence with peril. They spent most of their time and energy trying to protect themselves – against the present certainly, against the future too, and even, perhaps, against the past. Thoughts of this kind had never entered my head before, but now, as a result of having to negotiate the streets and breathe the air, I was absorbing a little of the local people's trepidation [...]. (*DK:* 113–114)

In contrast to the first performance where he was eager to quickly get to the hotel, Parry finds himself in no hurry now. Additionally, he notices that the phlegmatic surroundings influence his own thoughts – in short, he is aware that he already adopted parts of the Blue Quarter's temperament. Thus, walking as a performance enables an appropriation of Blue Quarter discursivity by getting in touch with the Blue Quarter's materiality. While Parry's initial 'redness' enables him to actually walk and get his journey going, he also becomes a blue person to a certain extent and starts to reflect (and thus mentally operate along phlegmatic lines of thought). Parry is in a fragile stance: his indoctrinated sanguine temperament is strong enough to avoid the typical blue sluggishness and passivity, while the newly-gained phlegmatic aspect prepares him for the encounter with his past in the Bathysphere. This encounter is also characterised by walking since Parry has to choose one out of four doors and walk through it. Parry's walking through the door is thus staged as walking into his past by crossing the threshold. His performance is no transgression because it is not illegal, but the experience has its effect on him because it triggers his memories of what he has lost due to the Rearrangement (see chapter IV.2.5). Walking into his past in the Bathysphere makes him feel more real and alive than his new life within the system (see *DK:* 152), and he is eager to retrieve this living past.

After the Bathysphere episode, the whole conference legally crosses over to the Yellow Quarter by helicopter. This cross-border performance is an official one which is not done on foot, so there is no extraordinary effect on Parry. The experience from the Bathysphere still reverberates, and Parry is determined to go back to the Blue Quarter. A bomb blast provides cover for Parry to flee the conference. He walks away from the destroyed hotel – and again, it is striking how quickly the temperament of the quarter rubs off on him and mixes with his previously gained character traits. Still, his blue temperament enables him to reflect on his plan to return to Aquaville: it is clear to him that there is no direct way back. Instead, he develops a long-term plan: "I would become a student of choleric behaviour, learning rashness and belligerence, but all the while I would be working out how to return to the Blue Quarter" (*DK:* 156). However, he has already acquired some of the yellow temperament without studying it. Just as he ponders over his plan, he also feels an adrenaline rush and the thrill of breaking the rules: "Only a moment ago my hand had been shaking, but now a thrill went through me at the sheer unimaginable magnitude of what I was doing. My thoughts had begun to startle me. Or perhaps I was just discovering new aspects of myself, qualities I hadn't realised I had" (*DK:* 156). These new aspects, then, are due to the influence of the Yellow Quarter, and they shape Parry to a great extent. As he flees the hotel, he is fully aware that this walking away will cost him his career – but he does not care. On the contrary, he is fascinated by the idea of casting all his achievements and his sanguine reputation to the wind: "I would be throwing away my career, my position – all those years. None of that appeared to bother me. I had always been known for my 'integrity' and my 'conscientiousness'. My 'sense of civic responsibility'. A strange, reckless delight swept through me at the thought that I would now be trampling on that reputation" (*DK:* 156–157). He as the narrator puts his previous character traits in quotation marks in order to display how alien they appear to him already. Choleric thoughts are thus with Parry right from his arrival in the respective quarter.

After some hitchhiking and walking, Parry arrives at the wall separating the Yellow Quarter from the Green Quarter (see *DK:* 179) without finding a way to get to the other side. This section of the wall, in contrast to the one Victor and Marie explored, is "both immaculate and unassailable. No flaws or blemishes. Not even any cracks" (*DK:* 180). As a Yellow border guard arrives, he and Parry have a brief conversation about previous clever attempts of other people to cross over and how they failed in the end. As the guard becomes suspicious, Parry, due to his new choleric streak, goes for the most straightforward way of conflict resolutions: he attacks the guard, runs away, and reaches the city Athanor. There, he meets Fernandez (a Yellow colleague from the conference) and talks him into smuggling him aboard a ship as a stowaway. Parry is then shipwrecked and thus reaches the coast of the Blue Quarter and the Church of Heaven on Earth (see chapter IV.2.5 for a description), where his arrival is described as "unorthodox" (*DK:* 214), but he is welcome nevertheless. The performance as a stowaway is, of course, an illegal one, but it does not trigger any new feelings in Parry – illegal as it may be, being a stowaway is not tied to walking as a bidirectional exchange between self and other. He quickly decides to abandon the Church community and move on. He already acquired some blue temperament during his stay in Aquaville – thus, the (blue) Church of Heaven on Earth cannot offer him anything with regard to identity. Leaving the Church behind, Parry takes the train to Aquaville and meets Odell. Their conversation reveals another facet of border-related attitudes. In Parry's words:

> When it actually happens, it's almost impossible to separate all the things you've been told you're going to feel, or imagined you might feel, from the actual feeling itself. [...] [By crossing borders], you're doing something you never thought you'd do. So there's excitement, but there's fear too. I don't think that would ever go away. (*DK:* 231)

Expectations and actual feelings as well as excitement and fear culminate in cross-border experiences. Again, the interplay of fascination and fear with regard to otherness is highlighted – not in terms of a social other this time, but in a spatial sense. The border marks where one's own *Sinnbezirk*, one's own experiential horizon, ends, and everything beyond is both fascinating and scary. While this notion sticks with Parry, the memory of Odell does not. He forgets the encounter on the train – again, there is no walking involved, and the quarter does not have an impact on him either.

Back in Aquaville, Parry is seized before he can enter the Bathysphere again and is reclassified as green (see chapter IV.2.5 for details). He is then relocated to Iron Vale in the Green Quarter (the cross-border performance thus being legal and quite unspectacular) and dropped off at what used to be a hotel and is now a place where relocated people try to settle in again. Thus, he has arrived in the fourth quarter and during this episode, he also becomes more introspective and thus acquires the melancholic temperament. Crucial for his melancholic streak is his visit to the Museum of Tears, a museum in which tear samples of the quarter's inhabitants are stored. There, Parry detects two vials of tears which belonged to his parents. It is then that he truly realises what had been taken from him, and it is the first time that it really hurts: "The grief had been stored inside me for too long. It hurt to bring it out [...]. My whole body jerked [...]" (*DK:* 276– 277). Parry, after having been to all four quarters, realises that the Divided Kingdom robbed him of his only true identity (the one dating back to the time before the Rearrangement):

> I learned something about myself just then. I saw it clearly for the first time. I had never been sanguine – at least, not so far as [sic] I could remember. No, wait – that was wrong. I had been sanguine until the moment I was classified as sanguine, but all my happiness had ended there, and all my optimism too. Ever since that night, the only thing I had ever really wanted was to find my way back. (*DK:* 277)

The Divided Kingdom is finally unmasked as Parry, after the vision in the Bathysphere, is again confronted with his past. Thomas Parry himself, like all inhabitants of the Divided Kingdom, is a mere institutional construction that had been slapped onto little Matthew Micklewright. Underneath, Parry finds what his housekeeper in Iron Vale, Clarise, calls "a common humanity, a common humour" (*DK:* 272). All people are connected not only by longing for the lost past buried deep inside, but also by the basic idea of humourism in the Hippocratic sense: in order to be a human being, and in order to be healthy and happy, one needs all four humours in a proper balance. In order to come to this conclusion, Parry needed to travel all four quarters and to retrieve all four humours. Walking thus figures as a process of making meaning (see Adami 2013: 13) as it expands one's horizon (border type G) by rekindling those humours which had been suppressed since the Rearrangement's initialisation.

However, Parry is still confined by the Divided Kingdom – he might have transgressed its interior borders, but he has never stepped outside. Still in Iron Vale, Parry realises that the White People are his only chance to leave the system itself. When one of them is washing himself in the river, Parry steals his clothes (see *DK:* 283–285) with a new plan in mind: "If I really wanted to step outside the system, if I really wanted to be rid of it entirely, I would have to forget myself – everything I was, or ever had been" (*DK:* 291). Since the system cannot offer him a reconstruction of his old identity, Parry now aims for a shift from retrieving the old forgotten past to acquiring a new I, a new future, by looking at the system from the outside. With Parry as one of the White People, the novel again highlights that the classification according to the humours as propagated in the Divided Kingdom is only an arbitrary construction. As he starts wearing the white clothes, Parry begins to change and to feel different. He unconsciously adopts the White People's apparent inability to speak: "I [...] bellowed, and, much to my surprise, I sounded exactly like the man whose clothes I'd taken" (*DK:* 290; also see 301; 304). The group he joins, after wandering around for a while, moves over the official border into the Yellow Quarter. Walking across a particular piece of land is thus staged as walking in de Certeau's sense, namely as a choreography in and in relation to space (see de Certeau 1984: 98). To Parry, this performance is his first illegal crossing of a border, i.e. his first transgression. It is remarkable that his previous transgression from the Yellow Quarter into the Blue Quarter as a stowaway is not identified as a 'proper' illegal crossing by Parry himself because there, Parry did not visibly cross a border; thus, the performance does not matter. Instead, the performance of walking across the strip of death at the official border, observed by guards, is "the first time I had crossed a border illegally. Actually crossed it" (*DK:* 300). In this quote and the neglect of his illegal arrival after the shipwreck, the significance of constructed borders for the construction of one's reality is particularly emphasised. Parry does not ascribe the sea a proper border between territorial waters, but falls prey to the illusion of apparently natural borders. The more or less coincidental transgression as a stowaway is irrelevant when compared to his conscious, open transgression at an official site that is done on foot.

The fact that Parry describes his cross-border performance as one of the White People as illegal is not only worth pointing out, but deserves some more attention. Through the lens of humourism as interpreted by the Divided Kingdom's authorities, the statement is correct: according to humourism, Parry does not belong to the White People, but is an ex-sanguine melancholic using the white clothes as camouflage in order to get to the other side. Yet, if the entire socio-political arrangement in line with humourism is an arbitrary construction (as chapter IV.2.5 suggested), the illegality of Parry's transgression is questioned as well. If humourism is a mere construction, then Parry is white (and thus one of the White People) while transgressing because he accumulated all fours humours and because he is wearing white in that particular moment. Since the White People can cross borders as they like, his performance could then be named a (legal) crossing instead. Except for the Yellow guards' cruelties, the crossing works out fine. Later on in the Yellow Quarter, however, after a gathering of more than thirty White People at a mass grave, a mob of Yellow citizens attack the group, which scatters during the flight; Parry himself is saved and hidden by Odell (see *DK:* 319). While Odell uses her special ability to escape the guards' notirce in order to get into the Red Quarter, Parry makes use of his white clothes one last time. Again, his plan is to simply walk over, but then he sees the Yellow guards and "the swagger, a casual brutality apparent in both their body language and their speech" (*DK:* 370). In order to avoid the worst, he adds another facet to his cross-border performance. Instead of only walking over as he did with the group, he has an idea:

> It was then that I noticed the piece of dog shit lying in the gutter [...]. What I was about to do would establish my authenticity beyond all doubt. [...] I picked up the shit and examined it painstakingly from every angle, then crushed it painstakingly between my fingers and smeared it on to my cheeks and hair. That done, I began to move towards the checkpoint. The guards stepped away from me, waving their hands in front of their faces. (*DK:* 370)

The performance is so disgusting and convincing that it does not occur to the guards at all that Parry might be trying to hide in plain sight – on the contrary, they see their own prejudices confirmed: "'[The White People] are worse than animals...'" (*DK:* 370), and the guards let him pass. Parry has made himself "untouchable" in two ways (*DK:* 371): firstly, of course, the mere act of dirtying himself makes the guards hesitate. Secondly, it establishes beyond all doubt that he is certifiably one of those others who simply do not belong and are not worth interacting with. Parry thus exploits the guards' assumptions about the opposition between self (as part of the Divided Kingdom) and other (as a non-person not belonging anywhere).

In conclusion, Parry's quest for identity starts in the Red Quarter after his red indoctrination, which left him with a red identity only. His walking as a transgressive performance across strictly separating borders (political, geographical, and mental) enables him to retrieve the other three humours as well. At first, this quest is a search for his old identity as Matthew Micklewright, which had been shattered when he was a little boy, and which he then tries to rebuild by walking, by being a transgressive, "wandering subject" (Adami 2013: 4) eager to regain what has been lost. As he progresses through all four quarters, he moves through all semantic fields offered by the Divided Kingdom. After having reconciled all four humours within himself, the next step is to abandon the system in order observe it from outside. He thus becomes a White Person and transcends the system by means of a second-order observation. As quoted in chapter IV.2.5, his performance back in the Red Quarter is empty because he is not within the system anymore. "The experience of adopting the roaming lifestyle and primitive customs of the White People represents a kind of rite of passage, which allows crossing a border to question one's own identitarian position and inclinations" (Adami 2013: 10). In short: Parry is able to construct a new identity (border type G) with a new goal – and with a new sujet (starting a new life with Odell).

At first glance, Parry's passage towards a new I seems similar to Yagharek's in *Perdido Street Station* since both heavily rely on walking; however, beyond the creation of new identities in both cases, the results could hardly be more different with regard to how their new identities relate to the world: while Yagharek, having started out as an outsider, is able to fully integrate himself into the urban sprawl of New Crobuzon at the end of the novel, Parry develops from an innocent child to a full member of the system and then to an outsider transcending the very system which created him in the first place. Parry's quest for identity can also be compared to Borlú's development in *The City & The City*. As spelled out in chapter V.2.2, the inspector is also transformed. In a way, Borlú seems to occupy a position between Yagharek (full integration) and Parry (abandoning the system completely): his breach enables him to step outside the established order of Bes´zel and Ul Qoma and to look at it from outside, thus achieving a certain borderlessness – but at the same time, he is also confined to the new order of Breach with new rules which amounts to a reintegration of the two contesting city states (since Breach is not between Bes´zel and Ul Qoma, but *in* both). In all three cases, though, "travelling across boundaries becomes an exploration of the inner self, a sort of rebirth leading to a fuller comprehension of life as a necessary step for social and political improvement, upheaval or reaction" (Adami 2013: 10). All three are outsiders in their dystopian worlds, and all three end up changed forever: it is in these outsider protagonists that the subversive potential of dystopian narratives is most prominent (see Langer 2010: 173), and it is poignantly expressed in their border-related performances. Be it the borders of the body (*Perdido Street Station*), of perception (*The City & The City*), or of political ideology (*Divided Kingdom*) – they all not only stage the border itself, but emphasise the border-related spatial aspect and the role of individuals within the border's force field of lust and power, thus also highlighting the construction of identity and alterity. At this point, the model I developed in V.1 by establishing (legal) crossing, (illegal) transgression, and careful (in-between) treading across or at a border comes full circle because the protagonists exactly fall into these three categories: Yagharek ends up integrated (legal crossing), Parry becomes an outsider (illegal transgression), and Borlú is in the balance between the two (treading).

VI Systems Theory and the Fiction of Probable Reality

After the detailed analyses of individual novels in the former chapters, this final chapter aims at a broader contextualisation of dystopian literature. The first section connects dystopian literature with systems theory in order to assess these texts as a follow-up to the realist novel. Section two elaborates on this connection by highlighting the realist thrust of dystopian writing, which Michael Löwy, as a variant of critical realism, calls critical irrealism. The third section, by and large based on Elena Esposito's *Die Fiktion der wahrscheinlichen Realität* (2007), continues the systems-theoretical discussion of dystopian texts by showing how neither probability calculation nor the novel truthfully predict the future or describe the world, but can be helpful nevertheless in both regards. Finally, section four rounds off the chapter by showing how the novel in general and dystopian fiction in particular can function as tools for describing the world in the context of Armin Nassehi's distinction between analogue and digital processes (see Nassehi 2015).

VI.1 Systems Theory, Dystopian Literature, and Complexity

A Systems-Theoretical Draft for Dystopian Literature

Systems-theoretical literary theory's main concern is to examine the placement of literature between its relation to reality and its own configurative principles (see Reinfandt 1997: 7). Its basic assumption is that literature is a part of that very reality with which it is concerned (see Reinfandt 1997: 16), thus overcoming the question why one should bother to examine literature as a phenomenon apparently estranged and detached from the actual world. In fact, literature is written, printed, sold, read, talked about – so it also does exist in the actual world and has an impact on it (see Luhmann 2008: 277). Thus, one can observe the socio-historical conditions of literature's relation to reality and examine the continuity of society and literature (see Reinfandt 1997: 17). Literature thus figures as a social system, which ties in with how modern understandings of reality are generated in and for society in a force field between psychic and social systems in which the individual and society drift apart. As a consequence, systems-theoretical literary studies is concerned with the following basic question: what position can literature in general and the novel in particular assume between individual and society and between actual-world references and self-reference (see

Reinfandt 1997: 19 – 20)?[1] Three categories are relevant for treating literature as a social system: function, performance, and reflexivity; in the following I present these categories in more detail as provided by Reinfandt in the context of the realist novel and extrapolate them with regard to dystopian literature.

The first category, function, i.e. what literature can or should do or what it is 'good for,' is narrowed down in systems theory to a very basic idea. According to Luhmann, art (and literature as one of its subsystems) confronts reality with another (fictional) version of itself, and thus emphasizes the contingency of the actual world and of people's ways of coming to terms with it (see Reinfandt 1997: 25). This notion of fictionality, or of fictional world-building, is tackled differently in different traditions and periods of writing. In dystopian literature, the fictional worlds tend to be designed down to the smallest detail in a mindset which Löwy, as I will describe later, calls critical irrealism (as a Science Fiction-based extrapolation of Realism). These worlds operate by using certain strategies of either highlighting or concealing references to the actual world (e.g. evocation or avoidance of place names or indications about when the story is taking place) as more or less hidden topographies. While art, generally speaking, has been freed of its educational function since the advent of the natural sciences,[2] which are now responsible for explaining the world (see Reinfandt 1997: 28 – 29), dystopian literature retains both aspects of the "delight and teach" catchphrase describing the basic functions of art (Moylan 2000: 45). Dystopian literature is thus "an inherently didactic literature, one that not only demands careful and thoughtful writing and reading but also, at its aesthetic and pedagogical best, offers critical knowledge and awareness of possibilities for change" (Moylan 2000: 45). With regard to the educational thrust of dystopian literature and Science Fiction, its functions circle around three concepts: "compensation, criticism, [and] change" (Moylan 2000: 86). Compensation is concerned with the negation of utopia's promises in the actual world (i.e. these texts problematize how utopian promises fail to hold true in the actual world); criticism turns the utopian disappointment into an attack; and change refers to what Darko Suvin has called the "feedback oscillation": the reader reads and takes in the fictional world and reflects about it, and may then think and/or act differently in the actual world (see Moylan 2000: 5).

Performance is the second systems-theoretical category of literature as a social system. Typically, performance is tied to other social systems on the one

---

[1] In this continuum of literature and world, it is the novel in particular which stands out as the crucial mode of modern literature. See Reinfandt 2012: 236; see also Watt 1995.
[2] Which, in Luhmann's terms, are summed up as the science system at large.

hand and to psychic systems on the other. It is usually acknowledged that literature has an effect on other social systems and vice versa: law, for example, is concerned with issues of copyright and authorship that occur in the context of writing and publishing literature (see Reinfandt 1997: 29). Due to these interrelations, literature as a system becomes more and more interwoven with those systems which make up its environment, while it becomes more and more independent from others to which it maintains no connection. In short: literature as a system forms a stable but versatile network of relationships with other social systems (see Reinfandt 1997: 31). With regard to dystopian literature, one can say that the dystopian label itself is not as far-ranging as Science Fiction. Science Fiction as a broader category has arrived in many other systems: publishing houses are aware of the genre, and some specialize in the respective publications, while others intentionally stay away from it. Science Fiction, similar to (or mixed with) fantasy literature and young adult fiction, has also found its way onto the shelves of bookstores, where it rests as a category in its own right next to horror fiction, crime fiction, or autobiographies. The system of literary studies, on the other hand, has known dystopian fiction for quite a while, and it played an important role with regard to the diversity of genres and categories that has been generated (utopia, anti-utopia, dystopia, Science Ficiton/fantasy as cover terms, and most recently, Weird Fiction and the so-called New Weird [see Miéville 2009]). As far as psychic systems are concerned, the key performance of literature as a social system is the making of meaning ("*Sinngebung*"; Reinfandt 1997: 34), which is possible since both psychic and social systems rely on meaning as their basic medium by which (and in which) these systems constitute themselves. All literature, according to systems theory, produces meaning for psychic systems by generating certain assumptions about how the (actual) world works, mediated by language; this generated meaning can then be incorporated into the process of meaning production of the psychic systems in question (see Reinfandt 1997: 36).[3] As outlined above, dystopian literature does this mostly along the lines of compensation, criticism, and change. On the basis of a conscious fictionality (i.e. all participants are aware of the fact that literature is fiction), alternative and thus fictional models of reality are designed. These models, due to literature's subjectivising parameters (literature is usually read alone and detached from its context of production, thus enabling very subjective experiences in comparison to other social systems), struggle with their limited social relevance – if these fictional models of reality are

---

[3] For example, despite all research in the natural sciences, the most important source for our understanding of love is literature. See Luhmann 1982.

written by one person and are usually read alone without any social interaction, and thus subordinate their own "*Welthaltigkeit*" (Reinfandt 1997: 38) (i.e. their own capacity to respond to the actual world in a meaningful manner) to literary codes and categories, how can they claim cultural relevance and authority? The answer is that literature has two strategies at its disposal: firstly, it can prioritise the private experience while endeavouring to publicly institutionalise it; secondly, literature can provide alternative and fictional models of reality as expectations which offer a space for the impact of other social systems (e.g. in the form of moral questions occurring in systems such as religion or education, which can then be negotiated in literature). Thus, literature negotiates and reflects the relationship between private realm and public realm (see Reinfandt 1997: 40). This is especially true for dystopian literature since it, by providing alternative models of reality which are significantly different, aims at an integration of *Welthaltigkeit* into fiction. The basic question of Science Fiction literature, as outlined in chapter II, is how to negotiate between a subjective I and the world (see Moylan 2000: 3).

The final systems-theoretical category of literature as a social system is reflexivity. It is concerned with "a system's identity by means of self-description and self-observation" and with the "inner-systemic dimension of the exterior dimensions addressed unter the rubrics of function and performance" (Reinfandt 2012: 235). Literature is thus facing constant tension between two different parameters of reference: on the one hand, it is drawn towards environmental reference as it works on a way of how to represent the world beyond its own system (actual-world reference and realism); on the other hand, literature is bound to its own, inner-systemic frame of reference in terms of specific codes, rules, and trends which determine this environmental reference (self-reference and aestheticism; see Reinfandt 1997: 43). For dystopian literature, and for the entire genre of Science Fiction and fantasy literature, reflexivity was greatly enhanced due to its popularity boost and, more importantly, its self-generated code of trivial and not so trivial writings. Moylan also acknowledges a rise of self-reflexivity in utopian writing since the 1960s, primarily in the form of a specific self-awareness with regard to the tradition's limitations (cf. the disappointed voices outlined in chapter II.1, which circle around the discrepancy between literature's promises of a better world and the world 'as it is') while maintaining its basic dream (see Moylan 2000: 83).

If all of the above is true for the realist novel (as shown by Reinfandt) as well as for the dystopian tradition (which designs story worlds quite unlike the actual world and therefore potentially unrealistic ones), it is well worth our while to spell out how and why these features, as established for realist fiction as they are, apply for irrealistic categories of fiction as well. This is attempted in the following section by relying on two basic preconditions for what Michael Löwy calls critical irrealism: the first precondition is that the fictional world and the actual world, even in the most realistic realist novel, can never be perfectly congruent; precondition two is that, if one accepts precondition one, the categories and criteria of what is realistic and what isn't become fuzzy anyway. To be more precise: structurally, realism and dystopian fiction are not very far apart anyway, as they employ similar narrative strategies of establishing a story world since both must be realistically coherent. Dystopian novels, just like realist novels, need to create worlds with a certain logic which must be consistent. Supernatural elements, wondrous creatures and gadgets which do not exist in the actual world can occur, but they still have to succumb to the fixed set of rules provided by the fictional world in question (see chapter II.1).

Critical Irrealism

Whenever one picks up a fictional text, the locations and spaces described in this text are measured against the locations and spaces one knows from the actual world. Chapter III shed light on some of these reciprocal relations between fictional world and actual world and explained how and why these worlds are hardly ever congruent. Through the rise of the novel in the 18th century and the rise of Realism in the 19th century, though, these spatial dimensions have become paramount as markers for what Josephine McDonagh calls the "'sense of place'": in a time of increased mobility, scientific innovation, and a re-mapping of British (and European) territory, realist fiction relied heavily on precise descriptions, references to place names, and other geographical and topographical markers in order to enhance the authentic feel of fictional places (McDonagh 2010: 50). This increased longing for authenticity and accuracy of representation was also expressed in the rise of travel guides and the first steps towards literary tourism (see McDonagh 2010: 53). As in the constant struggle for accuracy in mapping, it became apparent that the relations between fictional world and actual world writers and readers aspired to were riddled with discrepancies, e.g. when literary tourists travelled to locations referred to in their favourite novels by, say, Jane Austen or Arthur Conan Doyle, only to find out that the actual places were quite different (or even non-existent) from what the text had promised them. The 'sense of place,' then, "is not the link to the 'real' place – the index to reality – which it appears to be. Rather it is a supplement, an added accessory that punctures the evenness of homogenous space with a flash that *gives the effect of* familiarity or recognition" (McDonagh 2010: 60 [original italics]). Thus, there is a substantial difference between fictional world and actual world.

The substantial difference between these two domains is further exploited by Michael Löwy and intended as a response to the concept of critical realism as it is presented by Georg Lukács. Löwy sketches how critical realism is often in danger of being too adamant about its applications since it "tends to become exclusive and rigid. Too often – and this certainly applies to Lukács's application of it – realism appears as the only acceptable form of art, and the only one that can have a critical edge in relation to contemporary social reality" (Löwy 2010: 211). Why should critical realism be allowed to monopolise critical power? The answer is to be found in McDonagh's 'sense of place': critical realism appears to be so 'close' to the actual world by implementation of details and a general tendency to fidelity in representation. Therefore, it seems to be the most suitable form of writing to address contemporary issues found in the actual world. As a result of this overconfidence with regard to critical realism, Löwy asks the following questions: "[a]re there not any nonrealist works of art which contain a powerful critique of the social order? In other terms, is there not a category of literary and artistic creation that could be identified as 'critical irrealism'?" (Löwy 2010: 211) The answer is: yes, there is such a category, and dystopian literature can work as a prime example.

Löwy then explains the concept behind critical irrealism. It is defined as an alternative draft to (critical) realism and comprises works of art which do *not* try to represent the world (or create an illusion of the world) 'as it really is' (see Löwy 2010: 212) and which do not aim, in Lukács's words, at "'a truthful reflection of reality'" by claiming a certain objectivity assured by means of details, actual-world references, and accurate descriptions (Löwy 2010: 213). In fact, this realist insistence on the fidelity of representation is beside the point – fiction simply cannot provide a perfect *mimesis* of the actual world.[4] Furthermore, the 'realism' in critical realism is not due to detailed description – any fictional world can be described in endless detail. The difference between realism and irrealism can rather be found in the ontological frame of reference. While realist fiction takes the actual world as its focal point of representative accuracy and logic, irrealism's fundamental frame of reference is precisely *not* that of fidelity to the actual world. Instead, it is founded on the story world's own particular logic of artistic imagination. Miéville's fictional world of Bas-Lag might be quite different from the actual world, so it can be called irrealistic – but, by fol-

---

4 The problem of *mimesis* is usually tied to how stories are told, namely, by a constructed entity usually identified as the story's narrator or narrative voice. See Alber (2013) for an elaboration on how even apparently 'natural' modes of narration, such as the omniscient narration found in realist fiction, are hardly realistic.

lowing its own logic and rules, it is presented as consistent and thus in a realist fashion.⁵

If one accepts this basic outline of critical irrealism, the way is paved for the critical function of critical irrealism, i.e. for the acceptance of the critical potential carried by works of art which do not aim at realism or immediate correspondence with the actual world. On the contrary, criticism can be fairly indirect (see Löwy 2010: 214) due to the spatial and/or temporal rift between fictional world and actual world. As the chapter on the dystopian tradition showed, this is no problem at all because irrealistic texts, by *exploiting* this very difference between the two worlds, possess critical capacities – no matter how different the fictional world is from the actual world, it can address contemporary hopes, fears, and dreams. Critical irrealist worlds in general and critical dystopian worlds in particular, by their very presentation as irrealistic fictional worlds in realistic fashion, are able to teach readers about their own actual world and "about the open-ended ways in which texts [...] can elucidate that world and help to develop the critical capacity of people to know, challenge, and change those aspects of it that deny or inhibit the further emancipation of humanity" (Moylan 2000: 199).

Probability Calculation and the Novel

Above, dystopian literature was established as potentially critical irrealist fiction which conceptualizes fictional worlds with the aim to use these worlds as actual-world criticism and observation. Looking at the broader picture, literature in general is not that far from other ways of looking at the world. Interestingly, as pointed out in Elena Esposito's *Die Fiktion der wahrscheinlichen Realität* (2007), the rise of the novel coincides with the rise of probability calculation (and double-entry bookkeeping). This simultaneous rise is due to the fact that the two, although they seem to be quite different, have a lot in common: both are fictions, and neither is helpful in predicting the future; however, both have an effect on reality (and vice versa) and offer orientation, which can then be used to construct the dream of a better world as you go (as claimed by Moylan). The novel and probability calculation as two world-observing tools intended for coming to terms with uncertainty and contingency which both hinge on differentiation are thus not as different from each other as it seems at first glance. The dystopian novel in particular figures as a very striking and specialised form of duplication of reality because it does not aim at effacing the differ-

---

5 For an argument that is fairly similar to Löwy's, see Moylan (2000: 44).

entiation between fictional world and actual world, but puts the differentiation in the centre of attention. In the following, mostly by relying on Esposito, this subchapter shows how the prioritisation of certain models used for observing the world, especially of probability calculation, is at least an oversimplification; it also elucidates how dystopian literature, as a specialised duplication of reality which hinges on systems-theoretical differentiation, can work in favour of Moylan's 'daring to dream' concept (see chapter II.1).

Models, theories, historiography – there are numerous tools which enable humankind to come to terms with reality by second-order observation. However, with regard to these tools' legitimacy, literature finds itself at the lower end of the scale. In the 20th and 21st century, reliable and thus respectable means of second-order observation are models, statistics, and other scientific means. Not only are they scientific (as in 'natural sciences') – they are also concerned with apparently objective items and numbers, such as birth rates or a nation's GDP. Literature, on the other hand, is often said to be about unreal entities: literature is about people who do not exist, who inhabit worlds which do not exist, and take part in events which are totally uncommon or outright unrealistic. Conversely, probability calculation is fascinating with regard to how it observes the world because it is, or at least seems to be, concerned with the actual world without much (or any) filter or mediation. Probability calculation, as statistics, employs data gathered by methods which produce numbers and which have an objective, exemplary, scientific, and thus reliable and authoritative touch.[6] Numbers 'directly' taken from the actual world by exact measuring are said to provide guaranteed precision. And because probability calculation is said to have this reliable and authoritative touch, it is of utmost importance for explaining the world. Natural sciences, due to their claim for objective truth, have replaced religion and philosophy in this task, and they are quite successful in explaining the past and the present.[7] Statistics, for instance, can gather numbers on the development of economic growth, or on the outcomes of the last 10.000 games of roulette. And because probability calculation can explain the past and the present by means of numbers, people also try to use it in order to make sense of the future: based on the economic growth of the last decade, how large or small will the economic growth of a country be next year? Will

---

6 For the development of numbers from shenanigans towards respectable tools by means of double-entry bookkeeping and their resulting treatment as facts, cf. Poovey (1998: 54).

7 For the historical development of probability calculation from a tool of certainty to a tool of uncertainty in the context of a less and less intelligible world, see Esposito 2007: 7–49. Since the essay, originally in Italian, has not been translated into English yet, this study will always refer to the German edition, translating key terms into English whenever possible and appropriate.

the roulette ball land on a red or on a black field in the next game after it has hit red for the last ten games? Probability calculation seems the ultimate source to turn to. The statement above – that probability calculation is mankind's most reliable tool for observing the world, while literature is one of the worst – is problematized in the following by working on one claim as spelled out by Esposito: that probability calculation does not help to predict the future because the future is essentially open.

Even if probability calculation's numbers are correct in the sense that they are accurately measured, and even if they are not manipulated afterwards,[8] they pose one crucial problem: they are about the present and the past, not about the future. The future holds many possibilities in store, but only one of them will come true. If I toss a coin, I cannot know if it will be heads or tails. In what Esposito calls the present present (*gegenwärtige Gegenwart*, i.e. the world as it is now in this particular moment), both heads and tails are possible as so-called present futures (*gegenwärtige Zukünfte*, i.e. in this particular moment of now, I can imagine both options as viable in the future because the coin has not been tossed yet). However, in the future present (*zukünftige Gegenwart*, i.e. in the future as it will have come about some day), only one of the two options will turn out to be true – heads or tails. How can one predict which result will come true? In Esposito's words (see Esposito 2007: 30), nobody can know whether the future as it will actually come into existence one day (future present) will be the one we imagine today (present future).

The example of tossing a coin assumes a world for which the probabilities are overt before the event in question takes place and in which all events are equally likely. In the actual world, however, this is hardly ever the case, which makes predictions even more problematic: often, the number of possible results as well as their likeliness are unknown. According to systems theory, however, it is particularly important that one is able to select certain elements as relevant for communication while leaving others aside.[9] What is more: the world of probability calculation is a world without observers. In such a world of equally possible events and without observers, probability calculation could provide some guidance. However, systems particularly labour against the actual world's entropy as they continuously create new information and new sources of uncertainty and indetermination. Each single agent can never know what the others will do,

---

8 The proverb "do not believe a statistical study you haven't forged yourself," in a number of different versions, is commonplace today and led to numerous books, articles, and interviews in which statisticians show how to cheat with numbers even if the numbers themselves are correct. See, for example, Beck-Bornholdt and Dubben 2001.
9 Processing of selection as the basis of communication is spelled out in Luhmann 1984: 194 ff.

and vice versa. Ironically, this uncertainty is created by the very decisions that are meant to provide certainty (see Esposito 2007: 51). The role played by observers is the key issue here: every system makes decisions which also affect other systems, and each decision is in turn dependent on other decisions and consequences, the result being a ridiculous spiral of uncertainty. What can be done against this multiplication of uncertainty? Esposito explains that probability calculation can actually be helpful if it is used as an adaptive draft instead of a steadfast plan. Any model or statistic provides some basic guidance and, more importantly, a basis for discussion, development, and modification, which can be constantly reconstructed and thus enrich systemic interaction. Thus, constructions of probability have their limits with regard to future presents: they do not help to predict reality directly or accurately, but they are useful nonetheless because they have an effect on reality. They construct a coherent world on the basis of explicitly imaginary preconditions; they offer a transparent perspective on the world one can share, discuss, and plan with. Probability calculation can work in this way not because it is realistic, but because the consequences of its fictions can be real (see Esposito 2007: 61).

It is exactly this asset that probability calculation shares with literature. Esposito starts by pointing out that, in the 17th century, the novel and probability calculation come into being almost simultaneously as part of a process of massive social change (see Esposito 2007: 7).[10] The 17th century is the first time humanity experiences what Niklas Luhmann called *Realitätsverdoppelung* (duplication of reality): humankind becomes able to differentiate between the actual world or real reality (*reale Realität*) and other realities, such as the apparent reality of novels (which are not false just because they tell their readers about events and people which are non-existent) or the probable (which is not necessarily true just because it is not false); a new relationship of humankind towards reality emerges (see Esposito 2007: 8).[11] The chaos triggered by the new discrepancy between substance and its appearance receives regulation and orientation not only by probability calculation, but also by literature because both work as specific duplications of reality. Fiction, according to Esposito, is usually considered acceptable if it presents a world that is plausible enough that it could be true: the legitimacy of fiction hinges on its apparent realism. The novel, in the course of its differentiation (*Ausdifferenzierung*) strives for a kind of realism that diverges from former ones as exemplified by, for instance, drama and thea-

---

[10] For the rise of both the novel and the civil society from a systems-theoretical point of view, see also Reinfandt 1997.
[11] For Luhmann's notion of the duplication of reality, see also Luhmann 2000: 58 ff.

tre. Readers know that everything that takes place in a novel is just an invention[12] and coherent in the sense that everything in the novel is connected and charged with meaning – in contrast to many events readers are facing in the actual world. Furthermore, the elements in any fictional world (unlike those found in the actual world) are bound to very precise conditions (see Esposito 2007: 19); although he only exists as ink on paper, the character Isaac in *Perdido Street Station* cannot be a little girl. While the reader is aware that the events taking place in a novel are not true, literature provides a fictional world which is highly condensed by focussing on closure and crucial events (see Esposito 2007: 17) – unlike the actual world, which seems to make less and less sense due to the aforementioned spiral of uncertainty. Due to these precise conditions, human beings are enabled to distance themselves from the real world, to look at it 'from outside' in a second-order operation of perception, and to come up with alternatives. The novel, in Esposito's terms, is not a fiction of reality; instead, it is a tool that enables society to reflect[13] on its own contingency in a world that ceases to be preassigned and unambiguous (see Esposito 2007: 18). Dystopian worlds are so fascinating because they are so different from ours and can still be relevant with regard to criticism – and, due to their presentation as coherent worlds which follow a particular inherent logic, they become even more fascinating in their realistic irrealism.

Hidden Topographies, Traces of Urban Reality
Since the spiral of uncertainty started in the 17th century, the world we live in has become fairly complex. Contingency and the openness of the future make it hard to pinpoint the world, as all potential descriptions struggle with the problem that being itself is overly complex. As outlined in the context of the systems-theoretical idea of the unmarked space and individuals' comprehensive horizon, we cannot observe ourselves and have to fall back on second-order observations in order to describe the world – which, merely by being second-order observations, are simplifications and abstractions. Sociologist Armin Nassehi describes these problems of adequately describing the complexity of the world or society by introducing the difference between what he calls digital and analogue strategies. Analogue strategies can be summed up as comparatively immediate, one-to-one operations of transmission. The everyday understanding of communica-

---
12 Cf. Doležel (1998: 24) for fictional texts as a special kind of world-constructing texts (in contrast to world-imaging texts).
13 Note that Esposito speaks of the novel as a mirror for reality – a term I avoided above because of its connection with mimetic approaches to literature.

tion which is based upon the direct transmission of a message from sender to addressee, for example, would fit into this category (see Nassehi 2015: 167 ff.). Applying such strategies makes the world appear to be fairly simple and easy to understand because analogue strategies come to terms with the world by assuming straightforward relations, direct links of cause and effect, and other one-to-one operations. Maps, for example, if taken 'for granted' or as truthful, function as analogue tools for describing the territory they refer to, thus contradicting the "the map is not the territory" catch-phrase (see chapter III.1).

The world, however, operates digitally. Nassehi states that the world, with all its systems and subsystems, is an entity based on distributed intelligence. Between these different operators, there are intersections – but in contrast to analogue readings of the world, these intersections are digital because they precisely do not rely on strict one-to-one links. Instead, they are based on operatively interdependent components. This notion ties in nicely with Esposito's spiral of uncertainty where each agent does not know what the other agents will do, and where choices beget choices: each component only processes signals according to its own rules and only uses those which make a difference for itself. At first, this strategy is quite advantageous because each component can now work for itself, thus ignoring the overarching complexity. Thus, to each component, the world appears to be analogue (because this is the only way we can actually describe/observe it), but it operates digitally (see Nassehi 2015: 159–160). According to Nassehi, this is why this world feels so complex, and why analogue descriptions (which in turn lead to analogue solutions – for digital problems) fall short (see Nassehi 2015: 168–169). Nevertheless, we must rely on analogue descriptions because they are all we have since digital processes can only be observed after having been recoded as analogue.[14] Humankind has developed numerous tools that attempt to either overcome this gap between first-oder and second-order observation, or at least to access the world in an adequate manner, two of which (probability calculation and the novel) were described in the sections above. The discrepancy between analogue description and digital operation as introduced by Nassehi is the reason why these two ways of looking at the world also fall short.

---

14 This basic problem of observation is not only true for larger systems, but can also be found in the very basic way people observe the world: an analogue stimulus (the sound of a car passing by, for instance) is, by means of a digital process of selection, processed by the human brain, and then turned into an analogue signal which makes it possible to identify the sound as that of a car passing by in the first place (see Nassehi 2015: 174). Digital processing is the norm, not the exception.

And still: even though analogue descriptions fail to a certain extent, they are necessary because they are the only means of accessing the world we have – and some of them even exploit the impossible-to-close gap between analogue description and digital complexity. Thus, while (for example) the fictional (dystopian) world does not attempt to mirror the actual world, indirect links exist between the two. This indirectness, which is due to temporal, spatial, and ontological fissures, is productive rather than a problem. On the contrary, it can work in one's favour because it allows one to do certain things even better. Critical irrealism works well, due to the fact that fictional worlds, despite their irrealism, provide a condensed, crisper – and thus analogue – version of reality, bound to a logic which is more accessible than reality itself. These hidden links between fictional world and actual world are most present in various topographies presented in literature. Texts create fictional worlds with more or less detailed topographies, references, spaces, maps, all of which contribute to the fictional worlds' presentation as being travelable, as being realistic despite their irrealism. The more or less hidden topographies found in literature thus function as traces and connections between fictional world and actual world because they, due to the effect of realisation, help to render those fictional places more real; traces seems to be the appropriate expression because they never carry one-to-one mimetic qualities and vary with regard to, for example, detail, form, and focus. What all these hidden topographies do, however, is to refer to our actual world's urban reality in the fashion of critical irrealism and dystopian literature and their capacities to, in Moylan's terms, know, challenge, map, warn, and hope (see Moylan 2000: 196). Thus, the dystopian novel as an analogue description of the actual world and as a specific 'place-making' text can at least hint at what lies just beyond our reach in the digital realm of complexity.

These tasks of literature listed by Moylan provide a link back to the beginning of this chapter because before the postmodern era and the rise of irrealist fiction, these tasks were located in the domain of the realist novel. The rise of the novel, and of the realist novel in particular, is due to what makes it so powerful: modern individuals crave meaning in times of epistemological multiplicities and social problems (in Nassehi's terms: modern individuals crave analogue descriptions and solutions in the face of digital complexity). The realist novel could work on these problems because it reacted to them with an unprecedented immediacy and a stunning focus on reality, which could then be taken up by its readers (who would in turn feed their personal responses into the social system; see Reinfandt 1997: 139). Recent urban dystopian fiction continues in this vein, but employs a different approach. In postmodern times, all historical options for literary innovation seem to be exhausted; therefore, literature today is more concerned with new combinations, new extremes of existing forms, paradoxical forms, and ironic responses (see Reinfandt 1997: 231). Critical irrealism in general and recent dystopian fiction in particular (such as the novels this study is concerned with) does exactly that: it takes the basic uneasy (realist) relation between the individual and the world and, by modification, explores it on new grounds, most importantly by genre-blurring and by focussing on irreal worlds, while at the same time retaining the realist fashion of presentation with a strong emphasis on urbanity as the crucial component of postmodern lifestyle and identity. Topographical place-making strategies contribute to this arrangement by at least hinting at the complexity lurking beyond critical irrealism's borders.

VI.2 Final Readings

The following subchapters elaborate on the theoretical outline above by offering final close readings for all five novels this study is concerned with. With varying focus and emphasis, the chapters explore how all five novels can be read as critical dystopias on a scale between daring to dream (utopia) and utter hopelessness (anti-utopia), and how these readings are influenced by the novels' positioning between fiction and reality. Secondly, the chapters contextualize these critical dystopias with regard to literary history and systems-theoretical studies (dystopian fiction as critical irrealism and its functions with regard to systemic self-reference and actual-world reference). Lastly, the notion of the incalculable future is taken up again; both probability calculation and the novel fail to foresee the future or to adequately describe the world, but both can be used as adaptive drafts which, by employing analogue strategies of description and representation, can at least hint at the world's digital complexity. Such operations are not only provided by the novels as such in the sense of Suvin's oscillation effect (for instance, one might read *The City & The City*, and start to think about its message with regard to ignorance and isolation in 21st-century urbanities), but also on the story levels: many characters are strongly influenced by the openness of the future, and some also reflect this openness, fall back to the past for guidance for the future, and struggle with decisions whose consequences are unknown.

VI.2.1 *Perdido Street Station:* The Dynamics of Transition and Hybridity

The urban spaces presented in *Perdido Street Station*'s New Crobuzon offer a packed, jumbled mess. The city is a highly complex system made up of numerous subsystems (e.g. quarters, organisations, individuals) full of trickery and deceit. *Perdido Street Station*, as the title suggests, is primarily about getting lost, about the cartographic and topographic game of recognition and misrecognition, about dynamic reconstruction torn between urban sprawl and decay – in short, about conflicts and contradictions that nevertheless come together in a multifaceted hybrid zone. A striking dynamics is at work in these relations, and they pose an outstanding deviation from classic dystopias, such as the ones presented in, for instance, *Nineteen Eighty-Four* or *Brave New World*. The traditional attempts of totalitarian surveillance states which aim at stability and the isolation of the individual as well as society at large (see Meyer 2001: 39 ff.) do not apply to New Crobuzon. Instead, it exemplarily shows how the dystopian tradition adapts to what it finds in the actual world: a sprawling urbanity which, due to its extremely complex interrelations, might be even more terrifying than any totalitarian regime. At the same time, *Perdido Street Station* also demonstrates the vast array of possibilities and the inadequate techniques to describe them due to the arrangement's ever-increasing contingency and complexity. Thus, the novel's representation of New Crobuzon as a constantly changing and sprawling city is conducive to the multifaceted panorama of contemporary Science Fiction and its high productivity. Isaac's Moving Unified Field Theory, which is based on the idea that motion and change (instead of stability and being at rest) are the basic state of the world (see chapter V.2.1), goes well together with the critical and innovative potential observed by scholars in terms of the entire genre (see Langer 2010: 186).

Bas-Lag in general, and New Crobuzon in particular, is a place its readers do not know, and it takes time to get acquainted with it. But at the same time, it is also a place readers know only too well – not because of any similarities between New Crobuzon and London, but because 21st-century cities and societies in the actual world are facing very similar problems. The novel thus offers an opportunity to explore actual-world problems on the field of fiction by, in the sense of Nassehi, providing an analogue variant of actual-world complexity and crisis. New Crobuzon is presented as a very grim city: its inhabitants face disorientation, racism, Remaking, slavery, violence, corruption, drugs, and other hardships on a daily basis. The novel's protagonists are all outsiders, and they all have a hard time as they struggle for surivival and acceptance while they are being tricked, hunted, traumatised, and mutilated (see the end of chapter V.2.1). Thus, a strange place in a strange world is provided as the canvas for actual-world criticism with regard to 21st-century problems and challenges acted out in multicultural urbanities. *Perdido Street Station*'s setting, along with its constellation of characters, points toward the hopeless, anti-utopian side of the dystopian scale. And yet, the novel also offers a positive thrust, and this thrust is based on the dynamic characters: even if the world these characters are thrown into is terrible and terrifying, dangerous and unintelligible, they keep on trying and move on, as I will show with regard to Isaac and Yagharek as the novel's main protagonists.

Rationality, Imagination, and the Crisis Engine
While Isaac's group defeats the slake moths and saves the city (which the government is unable to do – or unwilling to do; see Freedman 2015: 19 – 41), he himself also revolutionises science by putting together a working prototype of his crisis engine. Although the city will not remember him and his group as heroes (if it will remember them at all),[15] and although he has to flee, he succeeds on several fields, and that is the vital part of the hopeful, utopian idea of daring to dream: you keep on trying, find your own way, move on, and continue to work on the dream of a better world as you go – even if it is an ideal you will never get close to. Chapter V.2.1 examined the crisis engine with regard to its transgressive qualities; I will elaborate on this machine for a bit in order to also highlight its significance in the context of calculating the future.

Before Isaac puts together the engine, he and his group develop another plan to stop the slake-moths: they plan to locate their nest and take out the moths as well as their eggs. However, there is only one entity in New Crobuzon which is actually able to figure out the location: the Construct Council. Constructs in New Crobuzon are machines designed for serving people's needs very much like robots in other works of Science Fiction: cleaning, carrying or repairing stuff. They usually perform simple tasks without being able to think or learn. However, some people reprogram them so that the constructs are enabled to think. Furthermore, they connect it to an extremely powerful, self-aware construct on the Griss Twist dump: the Construct Council. Born from a mathematical error or virus, it constructed itself "from pure logic, a self-generated machine intellect" (*PSS:* 398). Isaac strikes a deal with the Council: he needs it to do the math for his crisis engine which he needs for destroying the slake-moths. The Council's calculations quickly bring about the location of the moths' nest in the Glasshouse. It explains the operation as follows:

> All of me have tracked the attacks. I have cross-referenced dates and places. I have found correlations, systematized them. I have factored in the evidence of the cameras and the computing engines whose information I steal, the unexplainable shapes in the night sky, the shadows that do not correspond to any city-race. (*PSS:* 417– 418)

---

15 Miéville's two sequels to *Perdido Street Station*, *The Scar* and *Iron Council,* hint at Isaac and the incidents taking place in New Crobuzon, but his fate remains unknown.

A massive amount of data is collected and, as in statistics, numbers are crunched, processed, and evaluated, and then the Council makes a prediction: "'There are complex patterns. I have formalized them. I have discarded possibilities and applied high-level mathematical programmes to the remaining potentialities. With unknown variables, absolute certainty is impossible. But according to the data available, the chance is seventy-eight per cent that the nest is where I say,'" the conclusion being that "'[t]he moths are living in the Glasshouse, above the cactus people, in Riverskin'" (*PSS:* 418). So far, probability calculation appears to be fairly helpful since the collection of data leads to a prediction no human being could have arrived at. However, although the Council clearly identifies the location, the fictionality of the statement cannot be ignored. The Council performs a series of complex operations. Systematisation and formalisation show the fictionality of the overall construction in the attempt to – in Esposito's words – reduce the uncertainty on Isaac's part. He is given a seventy-eight per cent chance that the nest will be in the Glasshouse, so he can talk about the present future of the nest being in the Glasshouse with a chance of seventy-eight per cent. As the Council admits itself, it works with insufficient data because none of his constructs have ever been inside the Glasshouse. Here, the problem that the future is open figures again: Isaac faces a fiction that will come true exactly the way it will – independent from any prediction. Seventy-eight per cent sounds pretty reliable, but it does neither exclude other options nor does it prevent Isaac from eventually regretting his original decision based on the seventy-eight per cent chance. Still, he bases his forthcoming actions on the Council's calculations. Since there is only one correct hypothesis on where the nest can be found, and since Isaac does not know which one is the correct one, he draws on probability calculation. Thus, although in his present present the future is open, he treats the fiction calculated by the Council as if it were already true. The calculation provides a basis for making further plans (hiring the three adventurers, gaining support from some constructs for fighting the moths, figuring out a good way for getting into the Glasshouse) and discussing it with his group. Here one can see Espositio's notion of the reduction of contingency at work as the intransparent future becomes at least fictionally transparent (see Esposito 2007: 33–34). As it turns out, the calculation is correct: the moths' nest is in the Glasshouse indeed.

However, as pointed out in VI.1, one cannot be sure how one will judge events retrospectively because one's criteria of evaluation might change (see Esposito 2007: 51). And, if the criteria of evaluation are liable to change, one may regret decisions retrospectively, as rational as they may have been at the time they were made – especially if one has to cope with negative results. Isaac's group is suffering a heavy blow indeed as they enter the Glasshouse. The calculation of the Council has been correct but still, the resulting action is devastating: two of the three hired adventurers, Shadrach and Tansell, die, the result being that the third one, Pengefinchess, leaves the group again. Lemuel, Isaac's middle-man, is killed during the flight. All supportive constructs are lost, too, the result being that the Council is unable to gather information about the Glasshouse. Cost and benefit are questionable: the eggs of the moths are destroyed, but not the moths themselves, and the price is high. One cannot define reliable guidelines for the future in the present; no calculation provides certainty. Thus, subjectivity finds its way in through the back door: decisions, when agreed on with others, make us think about our own advantages which could emerge if we behaved differently.

As a consequence, Isaac then decides to use the crisis engine in order to take out the moths. As he puts it together, he also guards himself against the Construct Council: he insists on activating the machine on the rooftops of Perdido Street Station, far away from the Council's dump, and he also adds a circuit-valve in order to prevent the Council from gaining information during the process although it is connected to the machine. His reasons are fairly obvious: the Council wants the crisis engine in order "'to increase its own power,'" and "'[i]t's got no empathy, no morals [...]. It's just a calculating intelligence. Cost and benefit. It's trying to... *maximize* itself'" (*PSS:* 546 [original italics]). The Council observes Isaac planning the crisis engine and decides that it is worth having, no matter if some humans are in the way. Isaac observes that the Council wants the engine and prevents it from receiving feedback. If he did not, the results would be, according to Isaac, disastrous for the rest of the city: the Construct Council could do

> [a]*nything.* [...] I'm hamstrung because of all the maths. [...] But the Council's whole damn brain expresses things mathematically. If that bastard links up to the crisis engine, its followers *won't be crazy any more.* Because you know they call it the God-machine...? Well... they'll be right. (*PSS:* 546 [original italics])

Isaac points towards the lack of complete knowledge inherent to humans and other living organisms. Tapping crisis energy would enable the Construct Council to correctly calculate anything it wanted. Basically, the Council would get rid of the crucial problem of probability calculation: the problem that the future cannot be calculated, and that we can never be certain what will happen. Ironically enough, without the crisis engine's power, the Council is also unable to calculate Isaac's circuit-valve trick that blocks it from tapping the engine. Even the most logical, morally uninvolved intelligence in New Crobuzon (and, possibly, Bas-Lag), fails to foresee all eventualities which are due to the multiplication of uncertainty. Here, readers become aware of the limits of the fictional character of probability calculation: it does not help in any way to anticipate reality. The original idea of probability calculation as a calculation tool for the future does not hold due to the skyrocketing increase of uncertainty. We cannot know the future.

Blind reliance on impulses, instincts, and imagination, however, does not work either. In *Perdido Street Station*, these qualities are embodied by the Weaver (see chapter III.2.1). This spider-like entity, who perceives everything as a vast, rhizomic web that stretches across space, time, and possibility, intervenes during the fight in the Glasshouse, and actually saves Isaac and his group. The Weaver attacks without a plan, without calculation – and is unable to defeat the moths and has to retreat eventually (see *PSS*: 487 ff.). As pointed out, only the hybrid zone of rationality (Construct Council) and imagination (Weaver), channelled by a human mind and the crisis engine (see chapter V.2.1), makes it possible to defeat the moths. In this context, Isaac's crisis engine also works as a metaphor for the power of fiction in general and the power of critical irrealism in particular: by combining two mutually exclusive yet interdependent elements in a productive force field (rationality and imagination), he is able to make the impossible possible. Isaac is determined enough to change the world to such an extent that reality itself capitulates and lets him have his way – and if critical irrealists keep on writing, they contribute to a potentially equally world-changing process. It is remarkable that Isaac's scientific revolution is due to his work at a hybrid intersection where multiple lines of thought converge – his success is not based on the blind pursuit of one single path, but on the exploitation of the middle ground offered by the contact zone. It is also worth pointing out that the machine itself was made by a human being (Isaac) and the two consciousnesses of the Council and the Weaver are channelled through a human mind (Andrej) – thus, the role of the human being is emphasised. The human being provides the middle ground between rationality and imagination, between calculating the future and dreaming about it, and it is precisely this middle ground that humankind needs in order to move on – as in Esposito's account of how probability calculation and literature as second-order observations can be made viable for working on the future.

Yagharek and the Benefits of Disappointment
Yagharek, as an equally crucial main protagonist, highlights the novel's utopian tendencies even better. His story, especially in terms of bodily change and physical suffering, is much more painful and traumatising than Isaac's – and yet, he manages to shed his liminal existence as a crippled, exiled bird-man and substitute it with the life of an integrated man, making a new home in New Crobuzon.

However, turning himself into a man is not his initial plan. Instead, his original deal with Isaac is that the scientist will give him back his ability of flight, a promise which Isaac will break at the end of the novel after being visited by Kar'uchai, a garuda from Yagharek's tribe (who tells Isaac what Yagharek's crime was). In the following, I will elaborate on the preconditions for this change of plans by explaining the importance of freedom of choice in the garuda society, how Yagharek's crime of choice-theft makes Isaac reconsider their deal, and how Yagharek's inability to foresee this reconsideration can be read as a crucial instance of the incalculability of the future.

The most valued good of the garuda is freedom of choice. Their society is egalitarian and based on respect for individuality: all garuda are equal, and all garuda are free to do what they want as long as their actions do not violate the freedom of choice of others. Thus, the garuda society not only relies on individuality – it also relies on the fact that all individuals are part of something greater than themselves: a social matrix which holds them all together. Kar'uchai explains the intricacy of this social system: all individuals are "'a node in a matrix [...]. What is a community but a means to... for all we individuals to have... our *choices*'" (PSS: 607 [original italics]). In this network, every action has consequences. If the garuda decide to hunt together, for example, they are able to hunt larger game. If a garuda lies about game, on the other hand, he/she disrespects his/her fellow individuals because they are deprived of the choice to hunt this game: "'[W]*e have all the choices that we can* [...]. Except when someone forgets themselves, forgets the reality of their companions, as if they were an individual *alone*'" (PSS: 608 [original italics]). Thus, actions which would be called crimes among humans amount to what the garuda only know as choice-theft. However, the degree of how choice-theft takes away another individual's choice matters as well. There are severe choice-thefts (with so-called "utter disrespect") which are worse than, say, stealing someone's food. For example, murdering someone obviously takes away another individual's choice to live and not to get hurt. Even worse, murder also takes away all future choices: murder takes away "'*every other choice for all of time* that might be made. Choices beget choices... [...] That is choice-theft in the *highest* degree. But all choice-thefts steal from the future as well as the present'" (*PSS:* 608 [original italics]). Every action within the social matrix has consequences. In systems-theoretical terms: what other agents in a system do influences the range of options of others, and some actions might even completely annihilate certain options.

The information outlined above comprises Isaac's level of knowledge about the garuda society. At the close of the novel, however, new information is revelead by a garuda named Kar'uchai, who visits Isaac in order to convince him not to help Yagharek. Her argument is that Yagharek committed a crime called "'choice-theft in the second degree... with utter disrespect'" (*PSS*: 43). Kar'uchai explains that the closest human jurisprudence could come to an equivalent term would be to call it rape, and that she was the victim of Yagharek's crime. Isaac's head begins to spin as he understands what kinds of choices were taken away from her by being subject to this choice-theft:

> Isaac could not but imagine. Immediately. The act itself, of course, though that was a vague and nebulous brutality in his mind [...]. What he saw most clearly, immediately, were all the vistas, the avenues of choice that Yagharek had stolen. Fleetingly, Isaac glimpsed the denied possibilities. The choice not to have sex, not to be hurt. The choice not to risk pregnancy. And then... what if she had become pregnant? The choice not to abort? The choice not to have a child? The choice to look at Yagharek with respect? (*PSS*: 608–609)

The mere physical act is only the beginning of an entire chain of choices taken from Kar'uchai as choices beget choices. It is remarkable that Yagharek deprives her of "vistas" and "avenues of choice," two terms in which de Certeau's notions of *map* and *tour* reverberate – the effect of his crime inhibits the spatialisation of Kar'uchai's path of life by erasing certain nodes she could have chosen from. Consequently, Yagahrek's actions in the present present predetermine her future present to a great extent. Kar'uchai then demands that Isaac may respect the tribe's decision to punish and exile Yagharek by not helping him to fly again (which would efface the tribe's decision). Thus, the system in which Kar'uchai and Isaac are generates new information about Yagharek's former behaviour and is therefore a new source of uncertainty (is it okay to help Yagharek despite his crime or not? And is it okay to break my promise?). The multiplicity of contingency is apparent. If Isaac had known about Yagharek's past right from the start, he might have behaved differently all along, but the dimensions of time and the social are autonomous, so Isaac gets to know Yagharek's past much later. The reader is shown the difficulties of a world of observations and the observations of observations. In addition to the loss of congruence of social dimension and time as the crucial dilemma of modernity, Isaac is now also facing the disruption of the factual dimension (see Reinfandt 1997: 56–62).

Isaac struggles with Kar'uchai's demand: on the one hand, Yagharek proved to be a friend and a reliable ally who also enabled him to revolutionise science. On the other hand, he is horrified by the fact that he wanted to help a rapist. His crucial problem with regard to coming to a decision is that, in Esposito's terms, he has to base his decision on incomplete knowledge: he is unfamiliar with the garuda way of life. Similar to people who rely on gathered statistical data, Isaac then tries to work with information he *does* have access to: "[s]o it was natural, surely, it was inevitable and healthy, that he should fall back on what he knew: his scepticism; the fact that Yagharek was his friend" (*PSS*: 611). However, Isaac's information processing is also biased because there is another female character who was subject to violence and mutilation – and, possibly, rape: Lin, Isaac's girlfriend, who was locked up and severly hurt by the gang boss Motley. Isaac cannot help but link the two crimes. Finally, his decision is to not help Yagharek: "[i]f withholding help implied negative judgement he could not make, thought Isaac, then helping, bestowing flight, would imply that Yagharek's actions were *acceptable*. And that, thought Isaac in cold distaste and fury, he *would not* do" (*PSS:* 612 [original italics]).

Yagharek, then, has to accept Isaac's decision. The human's refusal is yet another example for the modern-age spiral of contingency: Yagharek could not have anticipated Isaac's decision because he did not know what Kar'uchai would do (i.e. to seek out Isaac and tell him to not help Yagharek). Suddenly, one of Yagharek's options for the future is shattered. Thus, he has to adapt and work out other choices – which is exactly what he does when he decides to leave behind his garuda existence and become a man. Here, Esposito's and Moylan's key strategy for coming to terms with an uncertain future reverberates again: instead of turning to the past, Yagharek learns that he has to look forward, that there is always a new option, and that failure can also result in progress. In short, he is able to re-create his relationship to the world and thus find his place in the world. The narrative perspective is of utmost importance for the overall effect of Yagharek's path: by installing the garuda as a homodiegetic narrator who has the first and last words of the story, Miéville lets Yagharek and the reader enter the city (and the novel) without a clue, and it is a long, hard, confusing, and painful road to understanding – but in the end, both make it, and they both have, in tune with Suvin's oscillation effect, learned a lot over the course of the journey. Thus, Yagharek achieves what all individuals since the Romantic period long for: reconciliation with a dynamic, ever accelerating, unintelligible world (actual-world reference). In order to create this reintegration process, *Perdido Street Station* employs a world that is quite different from the actual world, but its irrealist arrangement comes to life in the detailed description of the city's quarters, characteristics, and places names; in the twisted game of placement and misplacement on its map, which plays out the tensions between map, territory, and map user; and in its overarching notion of conceptual and spatial hybridity. Thus, the novel also stands as an important reconfiguration of critical irrealism, embedded in the subgenres of Weird Fiction and urban fantasy (self-reference).

VI.2.2 *The City & The City:* Caught in Borderlessness

Unseeing as a social and spatial practice, and the resulting delimited contact zones (see chapter V.2.2) are paramount for figuring out *The City & The City*'s positioning in the context of critical irrealism as well as its positioning between utopian and anti-utopian strands. Experience, perception, performance, human relations, and space are subordinated to (and dominated by) unseeing. While the cities of Besźel and Ul Qoma themselves have a touch of a film noir urbanity (the detective story being conducive to the urban spatiality of grey, rainy streets) full of corruption, they are not particularly anti-utopian in either their spatial or their social fabric. Instead, the anti-utopian thrust of the novel primarily hinges on the implementation of unseeing. Without unseeing (a state that could be achieved by, for instance, a collective breach resulting in two entire cities ending up in Breach together), two separated cities would become one. Isolation and limitation would end, as everybody would come together in a utopian contact zone. However, people outside Breach do not dare to see because they fear the unknown. Breach is there, and it will not go away as long as everybody plays along. On both sides of the border, the people are limited to an inadequate way of observing the world (and leading their lives) by succumbing to unseeing and the resulting blind spots. Unseeing can thus be read as an analogue strategy of (not) looking at the world. It assumes that one can simply ignore part of one's surroundings; this ignorance reduces the world's complexity as it suppresses certain elements. Nevertheless, and this is quite remarkable, unseeing as a reduction of complexity not only has its own problems, but *contributes* to complexity, too (see Nassehi 2015: 151–158). The novel highlights the problems that come with unseeing: the danger of breaching, the resulting consequences, and the mere fear of breaching which makes people live in anxiety in a city of delimited spaces. The citizens of both Besźel and Ul Qoma seem to have accepted those highly artificial borders which cripple their perception, performance, and experience every day; to a certain extent, they also seem to need the borders between each other as a means of self-constitution: in order to be someone, they also need to be something they are not. Conversely, it is quite ironic that, if one stops to unsee (i.e. as soon as one begins to see truly) although unseeing is still institutionalised, one ends up in Breach instead. There, people's ways of observing the world and getting in touch with it are still delimited because they are not allowed any bonds to their former lives and relations; on the other hand, breachers face a greater, borderless frame of reference as they start to take in the cityscape in its entirety.

Thus, the positioning of *The City & The City* as a dystopian text depends on the interpretation of Breach. Anti-utopian[16] associations can be identified easily: Breach is a force beyond people's control and ken that makes all citizens live in fear of breaching and lead lives of mutual ignorance by imposing artificial borders onto a potentially cohesive urban topography. The strict separation also spawns ultranationalist groups on both sides who maintain connections with the government. Additionally, breachers are dragged from their lives to which they can never go back to. However, one can also identitfy utopian potential in Breach: being *in* Breach also enables one to transcend the borders generated by unseeing, the result being enhanced possibilities of experience, perception, and performance. Furthermore, all former transgressors come together in Breach as a contact zone without internal borders. These avatars of Breach form a community of equals which does not care about wrongdoings in their former life. Thus, Breach is rather a dystopian than a fully-fledged anti-utopian sphere. The novel's ending in particular shows this fragile stance between hope and hopelessness. While Borlú is fully aware that not everything is fine in Breach, he nevertheless embraces his new opportunities. It seems that human beings, to a certain extent, need borders because they cannot handle any overburdening borderlessness: "The likelihood of a world without borders is not high, and when we think of that world – a utopia of sameness where there is no possibility of escape – we might begin to wonder if it is an attractive destination" (Bonnett 2014: 182). Creating spaces and places is inevitably intertwined with creating borders, and the borders produced also help to create and maintain identity. Here, the benefit of analogue descriptions of the world reverberates again: a world that would be otherwise impossible to comprehend is made readable by being given an order that appears to be analogue (and thus intelligible) by willingly reducing the complexity of the world's digital structures. And there is even more to the borders and places created in this way: "[I]n their unpredictability and sometimes cruelty, these places [which feature striking borders] also impress on us why people find borders so necessary. [...] [T]he reason we keep drawing borders is not a matter of mere utility. Borders can inspire and excite us" (Bonnett 2014: 252). This positive notion is exactly the source of utopian hope in *The City & The City*. Throughout the novel, there are hints that cooperation, communication, and collaboration across borders are productive operations, be they borders of gender (Borlú and his colleague Corwi), nationality (Borlú and Dhatt), jurisdiction (Borlú and Bowden), or others. Breach itself is assumed to become more 'interdisciplinary' in the future (see *TC&TC:* 370). All these operations help to make

---

[16] For the differentiation between utopia, dystopia, and anti-utopia, see chapter II.1.

the world a better place. While the novel's setting itself is dominated by borders and the resulting inhibitions, limitations, and oppositions these borders carry, the story in general (and its ending in particular) rather shows that something has been set in motion. Cross-border performances figure as means to overcome delimited contact zones. Of course, it is open whether all this will actually lead to a better future,[17] and Breach might carry on for eternity – but at least, there is a chance for hope, and Borlú, by his development from an isolated loner to an integrated, transgressive avatar of Breach, functions as this hope's harbinger.

The Intricacies of Crime
With regard to predictions and calculating the future, the most prominent feature in *The City & The City* appears to be its crime novel plot structure; the story revolves around the murder of Mahalia, which actually takes place before the novel starts, and the reader is thrown into the plot by standing next to Borlú at the crime scene. Thus, the plot structure quite stringently follows the typical question of 'Whodunnit?' interspersed with Borlú's reasonings about the state of the society he has to live in. His way of finding the murderer thus functions as an adaptive draft in Esposito's sense. Each crime scene, each new piece of evidence, each witness, and each alibi adds another piece to the calculation puzzle.

In this arrangement, contingency plays a crucial role. New information gathered by the detective provides him with new options (for instance, new suspects may emerge) while shutting down others (a watertight alibi may rule out another suspect). A detective usually starts with a dead body and a crime scene; the possibilities seem endless although there is only one correct solution. In fact, contingency is responsible for getting the entire story running in the first place in *The City & The City*. Yorjavic, David Bowden's partner in crime, fails to foresee the complication arising from the newly-built skatepark which prevents him from making Mahalia's body disappear in the estuary. If the body had not turned up, there would have been no case, no transgression – and therefore no story in the first place. One single difference between present future and future present (see chapter VI.1 and Esposito 2007: 30) makes it possible for Borlú to start his calculation. Another similar difference in expectations also leads to seizing David Bowden, Mahalia's killer: as outlined in chapter V.2.2, Bowden had everything planned out, and even after Borlú correctly identifies him as the murderer,

---

17 According to Nassehi, these open questions would relate to challenges of translation which occur at the intersections between different logics or systems (e.g. between Borlú and Dhatt as two inspectors from different countries and cultures). See Nassehi 2015: 141.

he has a plan for leaving the city which appears to be bulletproof (walking and behaving in such a manner that neither police force dares to arrest him). Then, however, Borlú surprises him by offering him Breach as a recompense for the urban legend of Orciny which Bowden never found – an unknown element appears in Bowden's calculation, and lets him end up in Breach.

Us Versus Them
The City & The City can, if read along the lines of critical irrealism, be taken as a reminder of all the everyday unseeing taking place in our world. Each day, people (willingly or unwillingly) turn their backs on numerous issues, be they self-enclosure by differentiation between groups and individuals (us versus them), inequalities, corruption, or the invasion of private life by authorities. The novel seems to suggest that one should be brave enough to actually look beyond one's own nose, and one might find that there is more to this world – not only in terms of space, but also in terms of people. In fact, the two cities as two distinct spaces hardly play any role in the novel. Although Borlú is staged as a fairly reliable narrator who has been to both cities and who also accesses Breach, he never puts his finger on how exactly Besźel and Ul Qoma as cities, nations, and peoples are different from each other. The detective claims that there is a difference in, for instance, physiognomy, habitus, and architecture – but all descriptions remain at an unconvincing surface without ever spelling out characteristic features. The only clearly marked difference can be found on the level of language since each city has its own street names, own personal names, and its own language. Still – the otherwise superficial descriptions of difference rather hint at the constructedness of these two nations and how these nations conceal similarities that reach beyond national borders, thus constructing the differences in the first place (see Freedman 2015: 85–103). Conceived space in the form of indoctrinated unseeing is able to construct two separate cities on a shared territory by limiting the cities' inhabitants' perceived space and lived space.

The people on the other side of the border might be different – but then again, we are all individuals. Overcoming simplifying stereotypes of us (e. g. Besźel) versus them (Ul Qoma) can lead to the realisation that there are people we can relate to on the other side, and that the simple differentiation between us and them may be inadequate to describe the complexity of 21st-century urbanities. Looking beyond the apparent differences between Besźel and Ul Qoma makes people realise that the group they are in is fairly diverse in itself, and that the other side holds people with whom they might have much more in common (e.g. social status, occupation, world view) than with those who simply have the same passport. Breaching thus figures as a performance that lets people enter a contact zone in the sense of a common ground of what makes us human in the first place. It is striking that the unfocussed attempts for unification by all the factions subsumed under the term 'Unificationists' do not get anywhere. Ashil ridicules them as "'little bands of eager utopians'" (*TC&TC:* 239), and Borlú explains their ineffectiveness: "There were other divisions, between different visions of what the united city would be like, what would be its language, and what would be its name. Even these legal grouplets would be [...] checked up on regularly by the authorities in whichever their city" (*TC&TC:* 53). The unificationists are not unified; some groups are legal, some illegal, and their conceptions of a unification lack common ground. Their basic strategy is to seize immigrants and refugees and to talk them into perceiving the city as a whole because these people are not yet dominated and indoctrinated by unseeing. "The activists wanted to weaponise such urban uncertainty" (*TC&TC:* 53), which is a fairly problematic strategy. They do the exact opposite of what Esposito claims – they increase and exploit uncertainty instead of coming to terms with it or reducing it (besides putting the unknowing refugees and immigrants in danger). Instead of slowly but surely working on the future together with others, they blindly follow one path which cannot hold against the power of Breach and the two cities which feed it. By only taking into account new arrivals, the unificationists' strategy has a blind spot and fails to tackle the cause (Breach).

The novel's irrealist agenda is thus based on the everyday unseeing of common urban and social practices, which is then taken to extremes because it is presented as indoctrinated, almost innate, institutionalised, and enforced without compromise. Besźel and Ul Qoma are staged as representatives for societies or cultures tearing each other apart (actual-world reference); while the nations simplify each other in stereotypes and prejudices, employing these two nations also enables Miéville to reduce urban complexity by limiting it to two (apparently) opposing domains with only Breach between them. Besźel, Ul Qoma, and Breach function as a three-fold analogue description of the complex arrangement one can find in urban topographies. Dividing a city into alter, total, and crosshatch zones equally simplifies the city by reducing the multitude of options walkers usually have at their disposal. As becomes obvious in various examples, e.g. the two cities' way of dealing with tourists and protuberances (see chapter IV.2.2), these analogue strategies cannot properly handle the underlying complexity of urban life, but provide a way of observing urban life that is at least readable.

The Cop Complex(ity)
The hardboiled detective story which plays with its own genre's boundaries (self-reference) also plays an important role in the novel's strategy of, by means of environmental reference, addressing overcomplex actual-world notions in a streamlined (and thus analogue) way. As a detective novel, although there might be some dead ends in Borlú's search for Mahalia's killer, the story of solving a crime is comparatively straightforward to process because the reader just follows the detective by reading page by page. Borlú's quest involves many decisions (where to go when, for example, and whom to interrogate), but these decisions are without any involvement on the reader's part and presented as a chain which the reader can follow. Thus, the plot structure of *The City & The City* reduces the immense complexity of police work (including the not so exciting phases of desk work and filing reports) to the thoughts and movements of one single person following leads which, in the end, make sense and have an easy-to-follow structure. As suggested by Esposito, novels tend to simplify and reduce any story to the most important key components (which is why the reader is, for instance, not told how Borlú brushes his teeth every morning), thus providing an analogue perspective on a complex (and therefore digital) arrangement.

VI.2.3 *City of Bohane:* Bittersweet Memories

Bohane's lost-time is paramount in the representation of the city's urbanity. Places are charged with history, stories, and memories, and they all have an impact on the lived space. Thus, the lost-time functions as a second, elusive topography beneath the city's material topography which, in Nassehi's terms, also functions as an analogue description – not of Bohane as a city in general, but of each individual's past tied to the city. The present is extremely complex; as soon as the present becomes the past, though, it can be made accessible – as memory of individual people, contained in crisp stories or songs, and as history by means of historiography. All these strategies employ similar analogue processes which bring events into a certain (usually chronological) order, make the past events accessible by filing them as historical periods, movements, or personal milestones (and by making them accessible in the first place by observing these events as relevant events), and by exploring causal links between these events. Thus, the lost-time in *City of Bohane* figures as a personalised variant of historiography that suffers from similar problems; memories, just as history, are blurry, retrospective descriptions that can only hint at the past without ever doing it justice. Similarly, the position of the novel's narrator as Bohane's chronicler is problematized: his oscillating between different narrative modes and his eventual admission that he is no superior, exernal observer, but a part of the story world, only highlights what literature in general is always struggling with – how can writing and storytelling as analogue operations describe a complex world of digital structures?

Analogue Lost-time and Urban (Re-)Integreation
And yet – although these lost-time memories may be painful, simplifying, or fuzzy – they play a major part. Analogue descriptions are problematic, but they are all we have. As a consequence, all major and most minor characters in *City of Bohane* struggle with the lost-time, and in some striking cases, they attempt to employ it as a tool for integrating themselves into the city with different outcomes. Logan, for instance, starts as a character who, as Bohane's self-confident gang-boss, is very much in tune with his city. Then, however, after the Feud with the Norries and the breakup of his relationship with Macu, he loses this connection and fails to reintegrate himself again. Here, one can see how important it is to keep working on the future: as long as Logan maintains his role as the leader of his Fancy, he remains in charge – and as soon as he succumbs to his personal problems, his attention is redirected to the past. The decision of offering the sand-pikeys a considerable turf in the city in exchange for their help against the Norries is a difficult decision in itself: is it a good idea to simply hand over parts of the city to a savage tribe as it will weaken Logan's Fancy? Might cutting a deal with the Norries be a better option with fewer losses on both sides? And will the alliance be strong enough to beat the Norries in the first place? In Esposito's terms: in the present present, Logan considers the alliance with the sand-pikeys as the best option, but he cannot know whether he will regret it in the future present. In any case, it is a decision whose consequences could have been controlled if Logan weren't thrown off by his failing relationship. His crawling back into the cozy womb of the lost-time by lamenting in drug parlours is, obviously, not helpful at all because it focusses on the past instead of acting in the present in order to work on the future. As a consequence, he is not only incapable of restoring his marriage – he cannot retrieve his superior status within Bohane's power structure either as he basically hands over his rule to Jenni Ching. Furthermore, he fails to install himself in the hall of fame of Bohane's legendary warriors whose spirits and memories linger in the streets. Finally, after a long period of drug-induced inactivity, after having realised that he has to act in order to save something at least, he starts to act according to an adaptive draft: he works on his gang's future by testing his lieutenants one by one, the final result being that Jenni Ching appears to be the most suitable suc-

cessor. After that, he seems to entirely abandon the urban discourse in favour of a return to the private space (by being picked up by his mother at the end of the novel). Macu, his wife, also fails to find her place in Bohane – close relationships to either Logan or the Gant Broderick are not what they used to be and cannot hold her. Her response, in comparison to Logan's, is quite different, though: she is running away.

The one character who actually manages to reintegrate himself into Bohane is the Gant Broderick after 25 years of spatial displacement. By giving up any social bonds from the past (his love to Macu as well as any feelings of revenge towards Logan), and by offering and opening himself to a greater understanding of urbanity that transcends individual relationships, he becomes a conductor for the city collective, a conductor for others rather than an operator with his own agenda.[18] The Gant Broderick, in contrast to characters who are hungrier for power, helps Logan while having no ambitions himself. By joining the city collective, the Gant succumbs to the past – and thus discards working on the future. Thus, entering the city collective also means that he achieves what Logan does not: the Gant Broderick becomes a living part of Bohane's living memory and history. In fact, he as the only one who ever left Bohane is able to find his place there, while all other characters are stuck in a present deeply infused by the static lost-time. Dynamics, it seems, is as essential for change and a (more or less) happy ending in Bohane as it is in New Crobuzon or in Besźel and Ul Qoma. Nevertheless, the Gant's position is quite different from Yagharek's or Borlú's. Yagharek and Borlú, due to their transgressive performances, figure as fairly active. In Yagharek's case, his ability to now *walk* the city is emphasised; in Borlú's case, his positioning in Breach turns him into a transgressive and transcendent agent. Both, in a way, are granted an eye-opening moment of finding a new I in the confrontation with a vast borderlessness. The Gant's identity rather seems to be diminished after his reintegration into Bohane's discursivity. He keeps his name, of course, and joining the city collective offers him a place – but it is a place and a function that has not much more to offer than simply being there, hanging around in pubs as a part of Bohane's living memory. How much of the old Gant Broderick is still in him when he becomes a living legend that merely triggers other people's charming memories? In the end, he rather seems to be reduced to a fairly passive asset of town history.

---

18 See chapter IV.2.3. The Gant becomes a living legend of Bohane; his mere presence is enough to make people summon the good old lost-time days.

Buck up, that's Life!

How are utopia and anti-utopia played out against each other in *City of Bohane*? All in all, readers face a fairly ambiguous arrangement. Although Bohane is a rough place due to its gangs, the city is not run by a classical anti-utopian government that employs surveillance, control, and collectivism. Similarly, the Gant Broderick's success story of returning to Bohane and finally finding a place there is pitted against a vast number of dead, failing, or simply stuck characters. The Bohane lost-time is equally ambiguous. On the one hand, it can be read as a force that can provide strength, hope, or at least a brief span of happiness in a grim present; on the other hand, the lost-time is also staged as an elusive, blurry, intangible, deceitful, and painful force which, in a dangerous way, blocks those who succumb to it from actually working on the future by acting in the present. Then again, the future is open, and it is easy to succumb to the lost-time: the endless chain of gangs and names and conflicts which come and go points towards the notion that the past was neither better nor worse than the present; all the characters know is that the actors of those conflicts are changing while the issues at stake are always the same. Bohane's history is an endless cycle of fights and truces in which the city is stuck, only to become more and more inscribed with the stories and memories tied to the ups and downs of its inhabitants.

Bohane is shaped by memory, history, stories, and its lost-time, compiled and presented by a narrator who is himself fascinated with the place. In the face of *City of Bohane*'s fine balance between utopian hope and anti-utopian despair, the novel seems to argue for a middle ground. On the one hand, it is fairly critical with regard to the danger of nostalgic blurrings of the past. Thus, it self-referentially also responds to other dystopian writings which rather belong to the utopian side: dwelling in the past all the time is not wise because it prevents you from acting in the present in order to work on the future, and idealising the past further contributes to unhappiness in the present (because the idealised past is inevitably better than the present). On the other hand, the novel is sceptical about exaggerated expectations of future prospects – and again, this can be taken as a response to the utopian tradition where the ideal worlds and the associations tied to them never match the actual result or the course of the actual world. Secondly, by focussing on the successful reintegration of the Gant Broderick, *City of Bohane* also is a charming reminder of how important it is where we come from in order to find out who we are, and where our place is. Thus, Bohane is not only placed against anonymous cities whose inhabitants neither know themselves, their neighbours, nor the city at large, but also against the contemporary fashion to rather emphasise where one is at or where one is going to. The entire novel, it seems, is out of its time – a lost-time in literary form.

Actual-world references and notions of irrealism can be found in Bohane's universality. It is just any Irish city by the sea with a topography that is nevertheless steeped in Irish history. Bohane's universality can be taken as analogue writing of the complexity of Ireland and its history at large. In this process, the map that comes with the novel plays a crucial role because it provides an analogue description of something as complex as a cityscape with rivalling gangs, class differences, and an incredible amount of memories and history. Firstly, the map suggests easy access to neatly separated, easy-to-identify quarters: each quarter has a name, there are clear-cut borders which separate them, and each quarter is unambiguous. Beauvista, as the name, the visual design of the map, and the description in the story suggest, is Bohane's showpiece, a stereotypical area of rich inhabitants in magnificent houses – and although actual-world quarters tend to be broken down to stereotypes in a similar way, such descriptions usually fall short to do justice to urban diversity and heterogeneity. Secondly, the map also employs a touristic strategy (see chapter III.2.3) of highlighting plot-relevant locations (and presenting the rest of the city as a flat, unimportant surface) which simplifies the city considerably. The touristic design of the map functions as a simplifying abstraction that focusses on the most important sights – which is acceptable because tourists (whose trips, in a way, can be taken as analogue walkings of a city) as well as readers are doing okay with superficial, analogue descriptions of the world.

VI.2.4 *Lilac and Flag:* The Only Way Out

In contrast to *City of Bohane*, the dystopian middle ground in *Lilac and Flag* appears to be fairly small; the novel can rather be placed on the anti-utopian side of the scale as not much utopian hope is provided. The present in Troy is bleak and horrible for pretty much every character. This grim present is due to Troy's capitalist topography. Troy's overabundance of place names presents the city as a cosmopolis which, at the expense of day labourers and former peasants, does not live up to the utopian expectations of globalisation and a free market. *Lilac and Flag* cannot come up with any success story in this environment; instead, it points to the many characters who die trying or simply remain in poverty and despair. Behind Troy's shiny place names, there are no jobs, no money, and no future. Staying in the city equals being stuck. However, going back to the country is no solution either – going back is impossible because the country is not even there anymore. And if it were there, people would not dare to go. It is striking how those characters who dream of the country come up with fairly analogue reasons why things do not work out. Sucus and Naisi, for instance, blame the economy (also see Nassehi 2015: ch. 5); there is no real solution: Sucus goes from job to job without ever being successful, and Naisi turns to crime. Their being stuck in the city is potentially a much more complex and thus digital problem they cannot describe appropriately – but within their logic, these characters can only identify analogue causalities. The same goes for all the reasons characters come up with for not returning to the country – being stuck and blaming somebody else is a simple, analogue description of one's situation which puts one in the comfortable spot of not having to act because there is nothing to do anyway if, say, the economy is to blame for everything.

The novel thus provides a critique of capitalism and globalisation (actual-world reference). People tend to have great expectations, but someone has to pay the price for progress at incredible rates. In *Lilac and Flag*, this seems to be a problem of class, not so much of generations, as the character constellation might suggest. The description of Troy's cosmopolitan topography hinges on a wild mix of biblical, mythical, historical, capitalist, and modern associations with other countries and cities. These telling names provide a rough sketch which alludes to a globalised world. Detailed mapping of them reveals that they add up to a topography that is more coherent than it seems at first glance; however, each single name that alludes to another place or city carries a two-fold analogue description: firstly, before the adoption of the name for a quarter in Troy, the mere act of summarising, for instance, the actual-world city Swansea under this one word (including not only its topography, but also its history, inhabitants, its relation to other places, and so on), is a reduction of complexity in itself. Secondly, simply naming one of Troy's quarter Swansea gives the reader an inkling of what the area in Troy might look like, but it obviously fails to account for details and complexity. Taken together, all the place names of Troy hint at the empty surfaces and complex pluralities of globalisation. Additionally, they allude to the archaeological debate on Homer's city of Troy in which the *Illiad* functions as a literary precursor of Berger's Troy (self-reference), embedded in the trilogy's evolution of story world and storytelling.

The Only Way Out
While Troy itself is presented as very anti-utopian, the country is highlighted as a utopian place. It is definitely preferable to the city, so characters should be wanting to return to it. However, the country in *Lilac and Flag* is utopian in a very literal sense: it is the perfect place, but it is also the non-place, and returning to it in this life is impossible. The utopian country suffers from the fact that it is only a potential utopia which can be unmasked as a self-constructed illusion. The only way to get there for a citizen of Troy is to die. Happiness might wait

there, but this glimmer of hope is fairly dim and overshadowed by a fairly anti-utopian mode if one has to actually die in order to reach utopian happiness which cannot be achieved in life. Still, this conception of happiness after death is the only source of hope that can be found in *Lilac and Flag,* and it is rooted in Berger's basic image of the peasant as a survivor with a cyclical conception of life. The peasant, be it as a peasant in the country or as a former peasant who moved to the city, works hard, then dies, and thus goes back to the country, where he has a place after death by being consumed by the country's materiality. In this way, his essence survives death in a way, and he is finally able to dwell in the country that, according to Berger, humanity has always longed for and will always long for. Both in Berger's novel and in people's minds, the country is a utopian concept worth dreaming of. This version of the country is not the historical one Berger was well aware of: the country which is dominated by exploitation, by reckless landowners, by industrialisation, and by interrelations with the city – it is, on the contrary, a secluded, detached, perfect, and therefore utopian, Golden Age country as people have always imagined it. The country as imagined as a utopian place is, consequently, an analogue description of the country. Utopia as a concept can be read as an analogue concept; utopian worlds cannot exist because they are simply perfect, i.e. because they evade the complexity of the actual world.

Lilac and Flag's conception of the country is thus quite similar to the lost-time in *City of Bohane:* both figure as nostalgic visions of the past which block all those who succumb to it from acting in the present in order to make the world a better place and actually get close to utopian ideals. Thus, characters like Szuzsa and Sucus only dream of a better future without actually becoming active in any effective way. As soon as they dream of the country, i.e. as soon as they embed their hopes into a utopian construct from the past, they fail as so many other characters do. The suicide of Hector and the fatal accident of Clement can, in this context, be taken as fatalistic responses to the problem that the future is open – as soon as you are dead, you obviously do not have to work on the future anymore.

VI.2.5 *Divided Kingdom: Eukrasis* Is White

The positioning of *Divided Kingdom* as a dystopian text primarily hinges on the fissures between the nation's overall fate, Parry's personal development, and the interpretation of the White People. A small flicker of hope is provided by the Church of Heaven on Earth (despite the suicide of Kieran, a member of the community, and Owen's false prophecy; see chapter IV.2.5) which offers a communal, nature-oriented retreat where the wounds caused by the Rearrangement can heal – a retreat that is similar to the ending of *Fahrenheit 451*. For Parry, though, the Church does not offer enough. Instead, his utopian thrust is marked by his overall transgressive tendencies. Parry's performances of legal and illegal border-crossings enable him to broaden his horizon and to transcend the simplifying system of the four humours that holds the entire nation in thrall. By travelling through all four quarters as well as to places outside this strict order (visiting the Church of Heaven and Earth and joining the roaming White People, for instance), Parry is a man on an insightful journey which results in a deeper understanding of the world, of himself, and how these two domains are interrelated. In the end, both conceptions prove to be fairly fragile. Parry's final plan to escape with Odell is another facet of his personal utopian design: the system itself may confine an entire country, but one might still get out of it or even undermine it – in any case, this is worth fighting for, and the way the open ending comes about ties in with Moylan's strategies of constructing the future as you go. After Parry's return, he emphasises his dull routine, which is then abruptly interrupted by Odell's call. The escape plan, then, is to simply meet, get going, and the rest will be worked out on the fly. The White People can also be interpreted as fairly utopian: it is exactly their marginalised position as social outcasts which makes them a free group of individuals who nevertheless add up to a greater community; thus, they keep alive the dream of a unified, open, dynamic, border-crossing, all-humours society.

Anti-utopian tendencies suggest a rather equivocal reading of the novel, though. Old identities have been shattered during the Rearrangement, and all citizens tremendously struggle to come to terms with their new ones while still longing for what they have lost. The rift between past and present in *Divided Kingdom* is both powerful and painful, and the new system seems to work well enough to keep everyone in place. Although the system does not seem to perpetuate itself yet, people are isolated, the country's quarters are isolated, and the country itself is isolated from the rest of the world. The Divided Kingdom finds itself in a very static arrangement where the authorities are in almost total control. The idea of the "rainbow cabinet" (*DK:* 381), a silent reunification where the authorities of all four quarters collaborate in order to keep the quarters apart and in check, makes it even worse. Parry's personal ending is also questionable with regard to its utopian aspects: his boss Vishram explains that Parry was under surveillance all the time, and Parry is offered his old superior's job and position. Thus, it is questionable whether one can actually get out of the system at all. However, it is worth pointing out that the exact route was not planned in any way – Parry made all the choices (see *DK:* 382–383). Vishram thus rather expected that Parry might eventually turn out to be a worthy successor – a calculation which proves to be wrong. Parry arguably has the knowledge and all the skills it would take, but Vishram's calculation did not take into account that Parry might decide against the system. In any case, the monitoring of his journey also raises the question whether his choices matter in the end. Furthermore, as Parry is waiting for Odell, it is neither clear whether she really exists nor whether she will actually show up or if she was caught. Thus, Parry's plans and calculation to undermine the system might be thwarted by a serious error; the future is open, and Parry cannot rely on Odell actually showing up or being real.

The White People's status can also be questioned: are they all the shunned individuals who actually are 'fuller' people than ordinary citizens with a strong utopian side, or are they simple-minded outsiders, unfit for any type of community beyond guttural primitivity? Even though the former interpretation is favoured in this study (see chapter V.2.5), the White People are a group which is being hunted and discriminated against – a group without neither a place nor a past to be at home in. All in all, the arrangement is quite anti-utopian, but not as hopeless as in *Lilac and Flag*. It is striking that both novels, and *City of Bohane* as a third one as well, are concerned with a lost past. All three hint at the general problem of how to access this past. Memories are complex, blurry, misleading – and all attempts to think about the past are, therefore, only analogue descriptions which cannot do justice to it. *Divided Kingdom*'s past prior to the Rearrangement occupies a middle ground between the pasts of the other two novels: while the past in Thomson's novel is less accessible than in *City of Bohane* (where it can also have an at least temporary positive effect), it is also less elusive and romanticised than in *Lilac and Flag*.

The Divided and the Digital
A good access point for notions of analogue and digital descriptions in *Divided Kingdom* is provided by the nation's concern with spaces. As outlined in chapter IV, the four quarters come into being as a result of Hippocratic humourism as an overarching and programmatically implemented ideology. The former United Kingdom's topography is changed according to a totalitarian agenda; thus, the new country is heavily influenced by dominated and conceived space, both of which affect its materiality and discursivity, its inhabitants and their emotions. The borders in *Divided Kingdom* are quite similar to the ones in *The City & The City:* in both cases, they figure as an analogue description device for separating what would otherwise be too complex to comprehend. Additionally, borders themselves are more complex because they can be much more than simple, ideational, separating lines since they can also figure as, for example, zones or concepts (see chapter V). The result of the Rearrangement (the four colours and

the instalment of the four quarters) is an extreme example of how analogue descriptions fail to come to terms with a society's complexity. Similar to the simplifying separation of one place into two city states in *The City & The City*, the Divided Kingdom's government's neat four-colour system is a strategy of simplification superimposed on a nation as an (inadequate) description and solution for a digital problem (the plurality and complexity of modernity). Four standardising categories do not adequately describe people, who are much more complex. The four Hippocratic archetypes (which are, to make the model even less appropriate, not adapted in their full complexity; see chapter IV.2.5) are merely analogue descriptions of a society by a government desperately trying to handle social complexity and the problems that come with it.

And yet, how does one describe society appropriately? Everybody sees the world in analogue form and is thus able to perceive some kind of order that can in turn provide a basis for the calculation of further steps. In the actual world, people tend to fall back on the observation of social classes, milieus, 'normal' family structures, and other readable pieces of the social puzzle (see Nassehi 2015: 179). The four humours and the resulting geographical, political, and social borders in *Divided Kingdom* serve the very same purpose: they enable the Kingdom's citizens to comprehend their country as if it was analogue, and this is also the reason why the four quarters work so well. The four quarters provide order in an otherwise complex world, an order that is fairly easy to read: you are either red or green or blue or yellow, and that is it. People from one quarter are thus stuck in their mindset, however, and cannot but help to see people from other quarters as a simplified other, the result being prejudice and superstition towards everything from the other side of the fence. Problems also arise as soon as this self-referential four-colour order is practically questioned which, in the novel, figures as the powerful and painful surge of the citizens' pre-Rearrangement memories and in occasional realisations that the people from the other quarters are not that different and not that stereotypical after all. The principal witnesses for the shortcomings of these analogue descriptions are the White People: these fully fledged individuals, whose white, unifying colour signifies that people are made up of many colours instead of one predominant type of personality, prove to be too complex to be described in the authorities' analogue strategy of simply shelving people as red, blue, green, or yellow. The White People, even more than Parry, show that all people are themselves complex and part of a larger, even more complex phenomenon called society. Parry's quest, the re-acquisition of all four colours, can thus be read as an attempt to regain this human complexity which has been lost since the Rearrangement. Similar to the White People, however, his successful attempt puts him outside the analogue framework – the result being that he then begins to fight the system.

You Got It All Wrong
Divided Kingdom quite clearly spells out that the Rearrangement does not work out as intended by the government. Psychological families do not get along better than biological ones, and in addition, all citizens struggle with their old bonds and memories which are not given a place to unfold. The entire Divided Kingdom is thus based on a wrong prediction. The government's strategy is simply to sit it out: eventually, it is claimed, people will get used to the new order. There is no explicit answer at the close of the novel, but it seems questionable that anyone will be happier in the future. Citizens are assigned to the four quarters after taking some tests monitored by machines; the machines meticulously crunch numbers and process data, so they are usually not doubted – similar to the blind trust in statistics and predictions as explained by Esposito. In a way, the entire, narrow-minded insistence on humourism as the ultimate solution to the United Kingdom's problems is not unlike a blind trust in probability calculation without realising that, once you design a nice and neat model, this model has not as much to do with the actual world as you might think. Furthermore, the novel also demonstrates that going beyond the borders of humourism is beneficial. Parry is the most obvious example that adaptability is desirable because it lets one break free from the simplifying and restrictive four-colour system. In contrast to other citizens who remain in despair because of their lost past, Parry seems to construct the future as he goes by moving from quarter to quarter, thus sounding the world in order to determine his personality and his place in (better: outside) society. At the same time, the novel's main protagonist also exemplifies that succumbing to the past blocks you from working on the future: after the episode in the Blue Quarter, Parry is desperate to go back to the Bathysphere in order to have another vision of his pre-Rearrangement past – and that enables the authorities to seize him because they assumed he might come back.

X Marks the Spot – Not (Again)
The novel's criticism aims at several issues. Actual-world references/criticism can be found in *Divided Kingdom*'s stand against racism; similar to *The City & The City*, it presents self-contained groups which fear the other mostly because they do not know it. Even worse, this 'other' is created by those who pretend to protect the citizens from this other: the authorities. In addition, the novel criti-

cises governmental actions that sacrifice families, the domestic sphere, and private freedom for an elusive greater good of a constructed nation state. Thus, the novel also taps into the UK's crisis of British identity since the rise and fall of Thatcherism. The form of this criticism is, on the other hand, fairly close to the classical works of the dystopian tradition (self-reference).[19]

Finally, how does the novel negotiate notions of critical irrealism? The most eye-catching element certainly is the paratextual map printed in most issues. The map goes hand in hand with the anti-utopian agenda of the Divided Kingdom's government as it provides a visual link between the United Kingdom and the anti-utopian counterpart the UK turns into. Crucial in this shift is the effect of realisation in the sense of Piatti (see chapter III.1 and chapter III.2.5): the cartographic representation of the shift from UK to DK works precisely because of the realist geography (the landmass itself has not been changed) which is given an irrealist overlay with new names and borders. Additionally, the map also functions as an analogue description of a complex world – a way of describing that is conducive to the government's agenda of keeping its citizens in check by constructing a world, country, and British society which nevertheless *appear* to be analogue.

---

[19] See chapter II. When compared to the other four novels discussed in this study, *Divided Kingdom* stands out by drawing most clearly on classical dystopian notions (such as, for instance, the government's methods for ensuring control over its citizens).

VII Conclusion

After all previous analyses, it is now time to bring together the readings of the five novels this study was concerned with. I will do so by mostly relying on the importance of the relation between the individual and the world as established in chapter II, since dystopian readings of dystopian texts hinge on this very relation. The following questions are pursued in this regard: How utopian or anti-utopian are the fictional worlds presented in the novels? To what extent can the development of the dystopian outsider protagonist be taken as utopian or anti-utopian, and how do these positionings negotiate between integration (in the sense of a reconciliation of the relation between 'I' and world) and isolation?

Perdido Street Station arguably presents the most anti-utopian spaces of all five novels in this study. New Crobuzon as the novel's setting is a grim place on all levels, dominated by urban chaos: various groups fight each other and the city's structures, and the city itself seems to fight itself, too. Sprawl and decay create a climate of insecurity, change, and continuous transgression where nobody and nothing can be safe. However, it is remarkable that this very anti-utopian setting is pitted against the fairly successful stories of two main protagonists. Admittedly, Isaac becomes a hunted man at the end, but he accomplishes to revolutionise science and can rely on friendships strengthened by having been exposed to mutilation, despair, and other hardships. A much clearer positive development, though, is presented in Yagharek: as a mutilated, traumatised outcast and utmost stranger, he also goes through various hardships (physically, mentally, and emotionally) but in the end, he achieves his own integration into the city as an individual that is ready to walk and experience the city – a process which is strikingly supported by the novel's narrative technique (the novel starts and ends with Yagharek's homodiegetic passages, while intermittent passages narrated by him document his progress) that puts the reader in the very same position (as s/he also progresses from estrangement to integration into the story world).

The spaces of *The City & The City* are also rather anti-utopian, but not as hopeless as the ones of *Perdido Street Station*. The two split cities certainly have their problems, but there are at least some rules that provide guidance (as arbitrary as they may be). Furthermore, physical aspects of anti-utopia (mutilation, violence) seem to be mitigated in comparison. Nevertheless, unseeing as a (not so) social practice as well as breaching as the result of non-compliance with this practice reveal the anti-utopian thrust of the novel on the character level. Borlú may arguably succeed with regard to integration into the city after his breaching, but the price he has to pay (abandoning his former life entirely) is incredibly steep. As a result, I would argue that his integration is only partial – the ex-inspector may be able to walk anywhere with ease and perceive the two split cities as an integrated whole, but he cannot make full contact with this urban totality. The comparison between him and Yagharek drawn in chapter V highlights two different paths of an individual's integration into the city: while Yagharek finds individuality after having lost it earlier, Borlú loses it by becoming just one more sad avatar of Breach (after having been an unconventional and quite competent cop before with a good understanding of the city). Despite his full view of the city, he is denied full integration due to Breach's role of keeping Besźel and Ul Qoma apart.

Bohane, and thus the entire topography of *City of Bohane*, feels more ambiguous (and thus dystopian) than the two previous examples. It is a fairly rough city full of gang violence, drugs, and prostitution – but at the same time, it is also a place of affection and bittersweet memories of better days, which often rather provide refuge than despair. Thus, the main tension between utopia and anti-utopia can be found in the utopian thrust of the Bohane lost-time constantly pitted against the present – a present which cannot compete with this positive blurring of the past, and which therefore at least gives the impression of being worse than the past; yet, a closer look reveals that this is just the way things go: one idealises the past in order to find comfort in it although the problems of today are not necessarily more serious than before. The cyclical rise and fall of Bohane's gangs very much suits the city's inhabitants; life, it seems, never really changes in Bohane, no matter who is in charge and who is fighting whom – and it feels right that way because citizens and city deserve each other. With regard to character development and integration, *City of Bohane* also paints an ambiguous but nevertheless rather positive image. Several characters' fates are clearly success stories. Jenni Ching takes over the city's gangland with a new gang, carefully chosen by Logan who thus manages to transpose the legacy of the Hartnett fancy to a new, hungrier girl gang under the authority of someone whom he knows and trusts. His personal story is more muted, though: his relationship fails as well as his integration into Bohane's collective memory of gang mythology. The final meeting with his mother Girly seems to hint at a retreat from urban discourse in favour of the comfort of maternal care and family bonds. Lastly, there is the story of the final integration of the Gant Broderick. On the one hand, it is a success story: after more than two decades of absence, he makes his way back to Bohane and is able to make peace with all the old demons that have haunted him (the most prominent ones being the broken relationship with Macu and his rivalry with Logan); even better, he is able to tap into the city's collective memory and become a living legend in Bohane that other people look up to (and that other people can use in order to trigger their own lost-time memories). On the other hand, this role also requires a loss of individuality to a certain extent; while the Gant Broderick basically functions as the focal point for other's memories, he has to give up his own individuality because he becomes an asset of town history that everybody can access. It is an integration into Bohane's urbanity with a rather positive touch (especially when compared to Borlú's in *The City & The City*), but it is more equivocal than, for instance, Yagharek's process.

Lilac and Flag provides a remarkable counterpoint to the constellation of I and world in *Perdido Street Station*. The story world itself cannot really be described as positively utopian, but in comparison to all the other story worlds explored in this study, it seems to be the least negative. Troy is first and foremost an economical dystopia that focusses on working-class problems of day labourers and former peasants in a cosmopolis without jobs – a drawback that can hardly stand up against, say, the physical despair of New Crobuzoners or the psychological yoke of Besź and Ul Qoman citizens. Conversely, the actual story itself is marked by an utter denial of any utopian glimmer of hope. Szuzsa, Sucus, Naisi, Clement, Hector – while some of them at least have dreams of a utopian country they may eventually end up in, they all fail to find any kind of integration or comfort in the urban present. Szuzsa, after the deaths of Naisi and Sucus, remains in Troy without any chance for a better perspective; the male characters, on the other hand, all die over the course of the story after having fought for survival all the time. Utopia, the Golden Age country as imagined by generations of people, is only accessible in death because the 'real' country is either not as utopian as it is always imagined, or not even there anymore in the world of *Lilac and Flag* – a very bleak outlook that transcends other failing integration attempts such as those of, for example, Logan in *City of Bohane*.

Lastly, how do individual integration and urban spaces play out against each other in *Divided Kingdom*? The story world and its spaces can be located on the anti-utopian side of the scale, mostly because of the Rearrangement and the numerous resulting rifts: the rift between past and present, between old and new identity, between the four new quarters, and between the White People and the rest of the population. While *Divided Kingdom* lacks the physical despair of *Perdido Street Station*, the psychological terror seems to have a larger impact than the effect created by unseeing in *The City & The City*. In Miéville's novel, the dystopian turn seems to be so deeply buried in the past that people do not suffer with such immediacy. In *Divided Kingdom*, Thomas Parry's story of an individual finding his place is based on a journey from ignorance and conformity to understanding (of self and world) and opposition, which is a fairly positive process. His new understanding – and this is a striking parallel to Yagharek's story – is not based on a retrieval of his earlier self as Matthew Micklewright prior to the Rearrangement, but on a balanced retrieval of the four humours which, according to Hippocratic humourism, are all necessary in order to be human. The problem, however, lies in the result of this developing understanding of self and world: Parry becomes unable to continue with his dull routine as a red citizen because the four-colour system cannot describe and contain him anymore. As a consequence, he is forced to leave the system behind and fight it. Thus, he finds himself outside of society, but in a potentially more active position than the aimlessly roaming White People.

The following chart sums up the findings above. It tries to place the novels on a scale reaching from utopia to anti-utopia as the extreme ends of the scale with the vast category of dystopia in between. The chart shows the distinctive locations of the novels on the scale according to the interpretation of the development of their major characters on the one hand and the interpretation of the overall urban space on the other:[1] Together, they provide a vast discursive field across which the hidden topographies sketched in this study unfold:

Table iii: The Dystopian Scale

	Utopia	←	←	Dystopia	→	→	Anti-utopia
Character	PSS	CoB	DK			TC&TC	L&F
Space			L&F	CoB	TC&TC	DK	PSS

Perdido Street Station and *Lilac and Flag* pose as two striking opposites: the former features the most anti-utopian space and the most positive character development, and the latter pits the least anti-utopian world against the most negative integrative thrust. *Divided Kingdom* assumes a similar position as *Perdido Street Station* (very anti-utopian space, rather positive character development), but in mitigated form – both character development and setting are not as extreme. Lastly, *City of Bohane* and *The City & The City* almost mirror each other as *Perdido Street Station* and *Lilac and Flag* do: Barry's novel features fairly positive notions of characters' integration, whereas the fate of Borlú in *The City & The City* points

---

[1] The word "interpretation" suggests that these positionings on the scale are my readings based on all the analyses attempted in this study. Again: utopian and anti-utopian readings of texts are in the eye of the beholder, and another approach may arrive at a different distribution (e.g. a preference of protagonists' means of leaving the system behind over the integrative aspect of individual and world would place Thomas Parry's development in *Divided Kingdom* further on the utopian side).

in the other direction. Both story worlds rather occupy the dystopian middle ground of the scale with *City of Bohane* being slightly more on the utopian side.

Taken together, the five novels display a vast panorama of utopian, dystopian, and anti-utopian positionings and interrelations, negotiated in irrealist urban spaces. While these spaces, in all their intricacies, can be placed rather straightforwardly, the question of the 'I' finding a place in these worlds is a bit more complex since the novels feature quite different processes attributed to the relation of I and world which consequently lead to quite different results and constellations of I and world. Some novels and characters show very successful attempts of integration (e. g. Yagharek, Jenni Ching) with a utopian touch; other cases present rather equivocal (and therefore dystopian) developments where integreation/reconciliation appears to work to a certain degree, but it does not lead to full integration or it comes at great personal cost (the Gant Broderick, Borlú). Failing integration attempts as anti-utopian character developments seem to provide two different options: Parry and the White People in *Divided Kingdom* display a greater understanding of self and world, which *should* lead to full integration (Parry finds a new self and discovers how the world works, so he should be able to find his place), but integration is repudiated by the way the society works (Parry's white-colour understanding of self transcends the authorities' four-colour system); the consequence is, inevitably, isolation, exile, and/or expulsion. Other failing attemtps, mostly present in the male characters of *Lilac and Flag*, showcase a total denial of integration that does not merely put these characters outside society or the world, but outside existence itself; Sucus, Naisi, and the other characters only find integration in death. Lastly, Logan Hartnett in *City of Bohane* appears to refuse integration entirely by favouring a retreat from urban discourse.

What Remains
Amy Kaplan, in her book on *The Social Construction of American Realism*, states: "[r]ealistic novels [...] do more than juggle competing visions of social reality; they encompass conflicting forms and narratives which shape that reality" (Kaplan 1988: 13). Literature and the world have a long common history of problematising and commenting on each other. Dystopian novels in the sense of critical irrealism, this study argued, do exactly that, and can thus be placed in the long tradition of works of literature which try to come terms with the relations of I and world, torn between hope and despair in the course of Western modernisation which irrevocably changed the world. Recent urban dystopias, I have argued, continuously highlight "impression[s] of the city and evoke [...] specifically urban experience[s]" (Sarkowsky 2014: 23) as the modern way of life with all

its intricacies and concerns. Recent urban dystopias permanently struggle to find appropriate forms of representation for this urban dystopianisation of the everyday that marks the late 20th and early 21st century: they negotiate the fictionality of reality and the realism of fiction, and shed light on the role paratexts such as maps can play in this discourse; they address the interplay of walkers and observers, of urban materiality and discursive practice, and of border conceptions and border performances; they self-reflexively look for the path dystopian fiction and Science Fiction in general can take between fiction and reality; and, last, but not least, they still pose the ultimate human questions since the Romantic period: "Where in the world am I? What in the world is going on? What am I going to do?" (Moylan 2000: 3) Do I dare to dream?

The next step seems already to be foreshadowed in the quantum leap technological progress has taken in the last couple of years: social networks, game consoles, and smartphones enable us to connect with people all around the globe while a handful of corporations store and sell all these data which can then be used for selling us stuff we do not need (but adverts make us want anyway), for disclosing who we are down to our deepest secrets, or for stealing our identities. Who needs floating camera drones when switching on your phone makes you trackable, and when virtual reality is at our doorsteps?[2] The future, it seems, holds another transposition of the dystopian tradition – not from totalitarian states to urban dystopias, but from urban dystopias to virtual or digital dystopias.[3] For the time being, however, the questions and answers are still out there, in the city – and urban dystopias, in the shape of hidden topographies, constantly figure out ways of coming to terms with them.

---

[2] For example, since 2013, several developers have been working on various head-mounted devices replacing the usual TV screen, providing a completely new gaming experience. Already present in top-notch military research, it is only a question of time until similar devices will not only dominate the gaming industry (the first major releases for end customers have just come about: Oculus Rift hit the stores in January 2016, Valve/HTC released their HTC Vive in April 2016, and Sony's Playstation VR followed in October 2016), but also areas of leisure and entertainment and private life in general, and people's jobs.

[3] While texts and other works of art have been concerned with the role of virtual reality for quite some time (e.g. William Gibson's *Neuromancer* (1984) and Tad Williams's *Otherland* (1996–2001), data accumulation and social networks haven't been explored that much. A remarkable example can be found in, for instance, Gary Shteyngart's *Super Sad True Love Story* (2010).

Works Cited

Primary Sources

Barry, Kevin. 2011. *City of Bohane*. London: Jonathan Cape.
Berger, John. 1992. *Lilac and Flag: An Old Wives' Tale of a City*. London: Bloomsbury.
Ebstorfer Weltkarte. Facsimilie [original destroyed in Hannover, 1945]. Handschriftenabteilung, Staatsbibliothek: Berlin, 1284.
Miéville, China. 2000. *Perdido Street Station*. New York: Del Rey.
Miéville, China. 2011. *The City & The City*. London: Pan Books.
Schedel, Hartmann: *Weltkarte*. In: *Liber Chronicarum*. Nürnberg, 1492. Woodcut.
Thomson, Rupert. 2006. *Divided Kingdom*. London: Bloomsbury.

Secondary Sources

Adami, Esterino. 2013. "Beyond the Border and the Word: Wandering Subjects in Three Anglophone Texts". *Communication and Culture Online*: 1–14.
Alber, Jan. 2013. "Pre-Modernist Manifestations of the Unnatural: Instances of Expanded Consciousness in 'Omniscient' Narration and Reflector-Mode Narratives". *Zeitschrift für Anglistik und Amerikanistik* 61.2: 137–153.
Allen, Claire. 2008. "Young Protagonists in the Contemporary London Novel: Hanif Kureishi and Rupert Thomson". *Literary London: Interdisciplinary Studies in the Representation of London* 6.2. <http://www.literarylondon.org/london-journal/september2008/allen.html> [accessed 18 June 2014].
Altnöder, Sonja. 2009. "Die Stadt als Körper: Materialität und Diskursivität in zwei London-Romanen". In: Wolfgang Hallet and Birgit Neumann Birgit (eds.). *Raum und Bewegung in der Literatur. Die Literaturwissenschaften und der Spatial Turn*. Bielefeld: transcript: 299–318.
Arikha, Noga. 2007. *Passions and Tempers*. New York: Harper Perennial.
Bachmann-Medick, Doris. 2014 [2006]. *Cultural Turns. Neuorientierungen in den Kulturwissenschaften*. Reinbek bei Hamburg: Rowohlt.
Barker, Chris. 2000. *Cultural Studies: Theory and Practice*. London: Sage.
Barthes, Roland. 2000 [orig. 1970; transl. 1982 Richard Howard]. *Empire of Signs*. New York: Hill and Wang.
Beck-Bornholdt, Hans-Peter and Hans-Hermann Dubben. 2001. *Der Hund, der Eier legt. Erkennen von Fehlinformation durch Querdenken*. Rowohlt.
Berger, John. 1979. "Historical Afterword". In: Berger, John (ed.). *Pig Earth*. London: Writers and Readers Publishing Cooperative: 195–213.
Bonnett, Alastair. 2014. *Unruly Places. Lost Paces, Secret Cities, and Other Inscrutable Geographies*. Boston/New York: Houghton Mifflin Harcourt.
Botting, Fred. 1996. *Gothic*. London: Routledge.
Brotton, Jerry. 2012. *A History of the World in Twelve Maps*. London: Allen Lane.
Bulson, Eric. 2007. *Novels, Maps, Modernity: The Spatial Imagination, 1850–2000*. New York: Routledge.

Certeau, Michel de. 1984 [orig. 1980; transl. Steven Rendall]. *The Practice of Everyday Life.* Berkeley: University of California Press.

Deleuze, Gilles, and Félix Guattari. 2009 [orig. 1987, transl. 1988]. *A Thousand Plateaus: Capitalism and Schizophrenia.* London: Continuum.

Di Liddo, Annalisa. 2009. *Alan Moore. Comics as Performance, Fiction as Scalpel.* Jackson: University of Mississippi.

Doležel, Lubomir. 1998. *Heterocosmica: Fiction and Possible Worlds.* Baltimore: Johns Hopkins University Press.

Döring, Jörg. 2009. "Zur Geschichte der Literaturkarte (1907–2008)". In: Döring, Jörg and Tristan Thielmann (eds.). *Mediengeographie. Theorie – Analyse – Diskussion.* Bielefeld: transcript: 247–289.

Dünne, Jörg. 2013. "Die Unheimlichkeit des Mapping". In: Picker, Marion (ed.). *Die Zukunft der Kartographie: neue und nicht so neue epistemologische Krisen.* Bielefeld: transcript: 221–240.

Ehlers, Monika. 2007. *Grenzwahrnehmungen: Poetiken des Übergangs in der Literatur des 19. Jahrhunderts; Kleist – Stifter – Poe.* Bielefeld: transcript.

Engelke, Jan. 2009. *Kulturpoetiken des Raumes. Die Verschränkung von Raum-, Text- und Kulturtheorie.* Würzburg: Königshausen & Neumann.

Esposito, Elena. 2007. *Die Fiktion der wahrscheinlichen Realität.* Frankfurt/Main: Suhrkamp.

Eßbach, Wolfgang. 1999. "Anthropologische Überlegungen zum Begriff der Grenze in der Soziologie". In: Fludernik, Monika and Hans-Joachim Gehrke (eds.). *Grenzgänger zwischen Kulturen.* Würzburg: Ergon. 85–98.

Fludernik, Monika. 1999. "Grenze und Grenzgänger: Topologische Etuden". In: Fludernik, Monika and Hans-Joachim Gehrke (eds.). *Grenzgänger zwischen Kulturen.* Würzburg: Ergon. 99–108.

Frank, Michael C. (2006). *Kulturelle Einflussangst. Inszenierungen der Grenze in der Reiseliteratur des 19. Jahrhunderts.* Bielefeld: transcript.

Frank, Michael C. 2009. "Die Literaturwissenschaften und der *spatial turn:* Ansätze bei Jurij Lotman und Michail Bakhtin". In: Hallet, Wolfgang and Birgit Neumann. *Raum und Bewegung in der Literatur. Die Literaturwissenschaften und der Spatial Turn.* Bielefeld: transcript. 53–80.

Freedman, Carl. 2015. *Art and Idea in the Novels of China Miéville.* Canterbury: Gylphi.

Gabaude, Florent & Veronique Maleval. 2013. "Mapping als Bildrhetorik: Das karto- und abstrakt-graphische Denken der frühneuzeitlichen Publizistik". In: Picker, Marion (ed.). *Die Zukunft der Kartographie: neue und nicht so neue epistemologische Krisen.* Bielefeld: transcript. 135–157.

Gehrke, Hans-Joachim. 1999. "Einleitung: Grenzgänger im Spannungsfeld von Identität und Alterität". In: Fludernik, Monika and Hans-Joachim Gehrke (eds.). *Grenzgänger zwischen Kulturen.* Würzburg: Ergon. 15–24.

Gehrke, Hans-Joachim. 1999b. "Artifizielle und natürliche Grenzen in der Geschichtswissenschaft". In: Fludernik, Monika and Hans-Joachim Gehrke (eds.). *Grenzgänger zwischen Kulturen.* Würzburg: Ergon. 27–33.

Genette, Gérard. 1993. *Palimpseste. Die Literatur auf zweiter Stufe.* Frankfurt/Main: Suhrkamp.

Goetsch, Paul. 1999. "Grenzen und Grenzüberschreitungen in der Literatur aus der Perspektive des Lesers". In: Fludernik, Monika and Hans-Joachim Gehrke (eds.). *Grenzgänger zwischen Kulturen.* Würzburg: Ergon. 63–74.

Gordon, Joan. 2003a. "Hybridity, Heterotopia, and Mateship in China Miéville's *Perdido Street Station*". *Science Fiction Studies* 30.3: 456–476.
Gordon, Joan. 2003b. "Reveling in Genre: An Interview with China Miéville". *Science Fiction Studies* 30.3: 355–373.
Hallet, Wolfgang. 2009. *"Fictions of Space:* Zeitgenössische Romane als fiktionale Modelle semiotischer Raumkonstitution". In: Hallet, Wolfgang and Brigit Neumann (eds.). *Raum und Bewegung in der Literatur. Die Literaturwissenschaften und der Spatial Turn.* Bielefeld: transcript. 81–113.
Harley, J.B. 1989. "Deconstructing the Map". *Cartographica* 26.2: 1–20.
Harley, J.B. 2001. *The New Nature of Maps. Essays in the History of Cartography.* Baltimore, MD: Johns Hopkins University Press.
Hertel, Ralf. 2005. "John Berger". Malcolm, Cheryl Alexander (ed.). *Dictionary of Literary Biography: British and Irish Short Fiction 1945–2000.* Columbia: Bruccoli Clark Layman. 25–33.
Huck, Christian. 2010. *Fashioning Society, or, The Mode of Modernity. Observing Fashion in Eighteenth-Century Britain.* Würzburg: Königshausen & Neumann.
Kaplan, Amy. 1988. *The Social Construction of American Realism.* Chicago: University of Chicago Press.
Langer, Jessica. 2010. "The Shapes of Dystopia: Boundaries, Hybridity and the Politics of Power". In: Hoagland, Ericka, and Reema Sarwal (eds.). *Science Fiction, Imperialism and the Third World. Essays on Postcolonial Literature and Film.* Jefferson, C: McFarland & Co. 171–187.
Lefebvre, Henri. 1991 [orig. 1970; transl. Donald Nicholson-Smith]. *The Production of Space.* Oxford: Blackwell.
Lefebvre, Henri. 2003 [orig. 1970; transl. Robert Bononno]. *The Urban Revolution.* Minneapolis: University of Minnesota Press.
Lehan, Richard. 1998, *The City in Literature. An Intellectual and Cultural History.* London: University of California Press.
Löbbermann, Dorothea. 2005. "Weg(be)schreibungen: *Transients* in New York City". In: Stockhammer, Robert (ed.). *TopoGraphien der Moderne. Medien zur Repräsentation und Konstruktion von Räumen.* München: Fink. 263–285.
Löw, Martina. 2008a. *Soziologie der Städte.* Frankfurt/Main: Suhrkamp.
Löw, Martina. 2008b. *Einführung in die Stadt- und Raumsoziologie.* Opladen: Budrich.
Löwy, Michael. 2010. "The Current of Critical Irrealism: 'A moonlit enchanted night'". In: Beaumont, Matthew. *A Concise Companion to Realism.* Oxford: Wiley-Blackwell. 211–224.
Lotman, Yuri M. 1990 [transl. Ann Shukman]. "The Semiosphere". *Universe of the Mind: A Semiotic Theory of Culture.* London/New York: I.B. Tauris & Co. Ltd. 123–214.
Luckhurst, Roger. 1994. "The Many Deaths of Science Fiction: A Polemic". *Science Fiction Studies* 21.1 [#62]. <http://www.depauw.edu/sfs/backissues/62/luckhurst62art.htm> [accessed 07 August 2014].
Luhmann, Niklas. 1997. *Die Gesellschaft der Gesellschaft.* Frankfurt/Main: Suhrkamp.
Luhmann, Niklas. 2008. *Schriften zu Kunst und Literatur.* Niels Werber (ed.). Frankfurt/Main: Suhrkamp.
Luhmann, Niklas. 2000. *Die Religion der Gesellschaft.* Frankfurt/Main.
Luhmann, Niklas. 1982. *Liebe als Passion. Zur Codierung von Intimität.* Frankfurt/Main.
Luhmann, Niklas. 1984. *Soziale Systeme: Grundriß einer allgemeinen Theorie.* Frankfurt/Main: Suhrkamp.

McDonagh, Josephine. 2010. "Space, Mobility, and the Novel: 'The spirit of place is a great reality'". In: Beaumont, Matthew (ed.). *A Concise Companion to Realism*. Oxford: Wiley-Blackwell. 50–67.
McLuhan, Marshall. 1962. *The Gutenberg Galaxy*. Toronto: University of Toronto Press.
Merrifield, Andy. 2006. *Henri Lefebvre. A Critical Introduction*. New York: Routledge.
Meyer, Kuno. 1910. *Fianaigecht. Being a Collection of Hitherto Inedited Irish Poems and Tales Relating to Finn and his Fiana, With an English Translation*. Dublin: Hodges.
Meyer, Stephan. 2001. *Die anti-utopische Tradition: eine ideen- und problemgeschichtliche Darstellung*. Frankfurt/Main: Lang.
Middeke, Martin. 2012. "The Victorian Age". In: Middeke, Martin, Timo Müller, Wald, Christina and Hubert Zapf (eds.). *English and American Studies. Theory and Practice*. Stuttgart: Metzler. 56–77.
Miéville, China. 2009. "Weird Fiction". In: Bould, Mark (ed.). *The Routledge Companion to Science Fiction*. London: Routledge. 510–515.
Mokre, Jan. 2000. "Kartographie des Imaginären. Von Ländern, die es nie gab". In: Petschar, Hans (ed.). *Alpha & Omega. Geschichten vom Ende und Anfang der Welt*. Wien. 21–42.
Molesworth, Jesse. 2010. *Chance and the Eighteenth-Century Novel: Realism, Probabilism, Magic*. Cambridge: Cambridge University Press.
Moylan, Tom. 2000. *Scraps of the Untainted Sky. Science Fiction, Utopia, Dystopia*. Boulder, Colorado: Westview Press.
Nassehi, Armin. 2015. *Die letzte Stunde der Wahrheit. Warum rechts und links keine Alternativen mehr sind und Gesellschaft ganz anders beschrieben werden muss*. Hamburg: Murmann.
Neumann, Birgit. 2009. "Imaginative Geographien in kolonialer und postkolonialer Literatur: Raumkonzepte der (Post-)Kolonialismusforschung". In: Hallet, Wolfgang and Birgit Neumann (eds.). *Raum und Bewegung in der Literatur. Die Literaturwissenschaften und der Spatial Turn*. Bielefeld: transcript. 115–138.
Murphy, Graham J. 2009. "Dystopia". In: Bould, Mark (ed.). *The Routledge Companion to Science Fiction*. London: Routledge. 473–477.
Nurmi-Schomers, Susan. 2007. "Trojan T(r)opoi: The Spectre of the Cosmopolis in John Berger's *Into Their Labours*". In: Stilz, Gerhard (ed.). *Territorial Terrors. Contested Spaces in Colonial and Postcolonial Writing*. Würzburg: Königshausen & Neumann. 263–279.
O'Flinn, Paul. 2001. *How to Study Romantic Poetry*. Houndmills/New York: Palgrave Macmillan.
Ortag, Felix. 1995. *ICA Mission*. 1995. International Cartographic Association. <http://icaci.org/mission> [accessed 03 March 2014].
Parker, Mike. 2009. *Map Addict. A Tale of Obsession, Fudge, & the Ordnance Survey*. London: Harper Collins.
Pavlik, Anthony. 2010. "'A Special Kind of Reading Game': Maps in Children's Literature". *International Research in Children's Literature* 3: 28–43.
Piatti, Barbara. 2009. *Die Geographie der Literatur. Schauplätze, Handlungsräume, Raumphantasien*. Göttingen: Wallstein.
Poovey, Mary. 1998. *A History of the Modern Fact: Problems of Knowledge in the Sciences of Wealth and Society*. Chicago/London: University of Chicago Press.
Pratt, Marie Louise. 1992. "Introduction. Criticism in the Contact Zone". *Imperial Eyes. Travel Writing and Transculturation*. London/New York: Routledge. 1–11.

Reinfandt, Christoph. 1997. *Der Sinn der fiktionalen Wirklichkeiten. Ein systemtheoretischer Entwurf zur Ausdifferenzierung des englischen Romans vom 18. Jahrhundert bis zur Gegenwart*. Heidelberg: Winter.
Reinfandt, Christoph. 2000. "Markierungen der Transzendenz in Hoch- und Populärkultur: T.S. Eliots *Four Quartets* und Van Morrisons *Hymns to the Silence*". In: Jahraus, Oliver and Nina Ort (eds.). *Beobachtungen des Unbeobachtbaren: Konzepte radikaler Theoriebildung in den Geisteswissenschaften*. Weilerswist: Velbrück. 101–124.
Reinfandt, Christoph. 2012. "Systems Theory". In: Middekke, Martin, Timo Müller, Christina Wald and Hubert Zapf (eds.). *English and American Studies. Theory and Practice*. Stuttgart: Metzler, 2012, p. 231–237.
Rupp, Jan. 2009. "Erinnerungsräume in der Erzählliteratur". In: Hallet, Wolfgang and Birgit Neumann (eds.). *Raum und Bewegung in der Literatur. Die Literaturwissenschaften und der Spatial Turn*. Bielefeld: transcript. 181–194.
Sarkowsky, Katja. 2014. "The Spatial Politics of Urban Modernity: Henry James's *Washington Square*". *Amerikastudien* 59.1: 7–25.
Sennett, Richard. 1996. *Flesh and Stone. The Body and the City in Western Civilization*. New York: Norton.
Schlögel, Karl. 2003. *Im Raume lesen wir die Zeit. Über Zivilisationsgeschichte und Geopolitik*. München: Carl Hanser.
Schmid, Christian. 2008. "Henri Lefebvre's Theory of the Production of Space: Towards a Three-dimensional Dialectic". In: Goonewardena, Kanishka (ed.). *Space, Difference, Everyday Life: Reading Henri Lefebvre*. New York: Routledge, 2008, p. 27–45.
Schneider, Ute. 2006. *Die Macht der Karten. Eine Geschichte der Kartographie vom Mittelalter bis heute*. Darmstadt: Wissenschaftliche Buchgesellschaft..
Sieverts, Thomas. 2000. "Mythos der alten Stadt." In: Wentz, Martin (ed.): *Die kompakte Stadt*. Frankfurt/New York: 2000, p. 170–176.
Schroer, Markus. 2006. *Räume, Orte, Grenzen: auf dem Weg zu einer Soziologie des Raums*. Frankfurt/Main: Suhrkamp.
Schweitzer, Beate and Tobias L. Kienlin. 2001/2002. "Das Troia-Symposium in Tübingen. Eine Diskussion um Geschichte und Archäologie." *Hephaistos* 19/20: 7–38.
Schwengel, Hermann. 1999. "An den Grenzen der Gesellschaft". In: Fludernik, Monika and Hans-Joachim Gehrke (eds.). *Grenzgänger zwischen Kulturen*. Würzburg: Ergon. 35–39.
Staggs, Matt. 2011. "A Brief Interview with China Mieville [sic], Author, Embassytown." Del Rey and Spectra Science Fiction and Fantasy. New York: Penguin Random House. <http://sf-fantasy.suvudu.com/2011/05/a-brief-interview-with-china-mieville-author-embassytown.html> [accessed 24 February 2016].
Stallybrass, Peter and Allon White. 1986. *The Politics and Poetics of Transgression*. London: Cornell University Press.
Stichweh, Rudolf. 2000. *Die Weltgesellschaft. Soziologische Analysen*. Frankfurt/Main: Suhrkamp.
Stilz, Gerhard. 2013. "Coming to Terms: Voice and Perception in the Transcultural Contact Zone". *ZAA* 61.1: 7–16.
Stockhammer, Robert. 2005. "Verortung. Die Macht der Karten und die Literatur". *TopoGraphien der Moderne. Medien zur Repräsentation und Konstruktion von Räumen*. München: Fink. 319–340.
Stockhammer, Robert. 2007. *Kartierung der Erde: Macht und Lust in Karten und Literatur*. München: Fink.

Stockwell, Peter. 2000. *The Poetics of Science Fiction*. Longman: Pearson Education.
Stross, Brian. 1999. "The Hybrid Metaphor: From Biology to Culture". *Journal of American Folklore* 112: 254–267.
Surkamp, Carola. 2002. "Narratologie und *possible-worlds theory*: Narrative Texte als alternative Welten". In: Nünning, Ansgar and Vera Nünning. *Neue Ansätze in der Erzähltheorie*. Trier: WVT. 153–183.
Waldenfels, Bernhard. 1999. "Schwellenerfahrung und Grenzziehung". In: Fludernik, Monika and Hans-Joachim Gehrke (eds.). *Grenzgänger zwischen Kulturen*. Würzburg: Ergon. 137–154.
Walsh, Chad. 1962. *From Utopia to Nightmare*. London: Bles.
Warnke, Martin. 2011. *Ebskart. Die Ebstorfer Weltkarte*. Lüneburg University. <http://weblab.uni-lueneburg.de/kulturinformatik/projekte/ebskart/content/start.html> [accessed 18 June 2014].
Watt, Ian. 1995. *The Rise of the Novel: Studies in Defoe, Richardson and Fielding*. London: Hogarth.
Weigel, Sigrid. 2002. "Zum 'topographical turn'. Kartographie, Topographie und Raumkonzepte in den Kulturwissenschaften". *KulturPoetik* 2.2: 151–165.
Welz, Stefan. 1996. *Ways of Seeing – Limits of Telling. Sehen und Erzählen in den Romanen John Bergers*. Eggingen: Edition Isele.
Williams, Raymond. 1973. *The Country and the City*. London: Chatto & Windus.
Wirth, Louis. 1974 [orig. 1938]. "Urbanität als Lebensform". In: Herlyn, Ulfert (ed.): *Stadt- und Sozialstruktur. Arbeiten zur sozialen Segregation, Ghettobildung und Stadtplanung*. München: Nymphenburger. 42–66.
Wokart, Norbert. 1995. "Differenzierungen im Begriff 'Grenze'. Zur Vielfalt eines scheinbar einfachen Begriffs". In: Faber, Richard and Barbara Naumann (eds.). *Literatur der Grenze – Theorie der Grenze*. Würzburg: Königshausen & Neumann. 275–289.
Wood, Denis and John Fels. 1986. "Designs of Signs: Myth and Meaning in Maps". *Cartographica* 23.3: 54–103.
Wyatt, John. 2013. *The Use of Imaginary, Historical, and Actual Maps in Literature: How British and Irish Authors Created Imaginary Worlds to Tell Their Stories (Defoe, Swift, Wordsworth, Kipling, Joyce, Tolkien, etc.)*. Lewiston: Edwin Mellen Press.
Zähringer, Raphael. 2015. "'Strange Tricks of Cartography': The Map(s) of *Perdido Street Station*." In: Edwards, Caroline and Tony Venezia (eds.). *China Miéville: Critical Essays*. Canterbury: Gylphi. 61–87.
Zähringer, Raphael. [forthcoming 2017]. "China Miéville, *Embassytown* (2011)". In: Reinfandt, Christoph (ed.). *Handbook of the English Novel of the Twentieth- and Twenty-First Centuries: Text and Theory*. Berlin/New York: De Gruyter.

Dictionaries

CCAD = *Collins Cobuild Advanced Dictionary*. 2009. Ed. Joe Dougherty et al. Boston: Heinle Cengage Learning.
CDCM = *A Concise Dictionary of Classical Mythology*. 1990. Ed. Pierre Grimal. Oxford: Blackwell.

Name Index

Adami   215, 218, 220 f.
Alber   227
Allen   168
Altnöder   79, 84, 96, 104, 121
Arikha   152 f., 155, 160, 163 f.
Austen   226

Barker   161
Barry   6, 22 f., 49, 72, 76 f., 129, 132, 264
Barthes   40, 57 f.
Beck-Bornholdt and Dubben   230
Bentham   16
Berger   6, 26, 28, 133 f., 138 f., 142, 144, 146, 148–150, 254 f.
Bonnett   194, 245
Botting   33
Bradbury   150
Brotton   35, 38, 42, 67
Bulson   50–52
Burgess   18, 72, 77
Butler   85, 191

Christopher   22, 208

de Certeau   18, 37, 39–41, 47–49, 53, 56 f., 61, 65, 69, 74 f., 85, 103 f., 115, 121, 123, 218, 242
Deleuze   61
Di Liddo   33
Dickens   39, 45, 51, 143
Doležel   44, 232
Doyle   39, 226
Dünne   42, 52

Ehlers   170, 173
Eliot   143
Engelke   79, 82
Enquist   42, 44, 55
Epicurus   167
Eßbach   170, 172, 182, 184, 194 f., 198
Esposito   222, 228–231, 232 f., 238, 240, 242 f., 246, 248–250, 259

Fest   12
Fludernik   5, 169, 171–174, 176
Frank   46, 169, 172–174, 176
Freedman   237, 247
Fukuyama   12

Gehrke   169 f., 176
Genette   43, 67
Glauser   73
Goethe   50
Goetsch   176, 203, 212
Gordon   50, 55, 100 f., 177 f., 181, 184, 187, 190, 192

Habermas   11
Harley   54, 58
Harris   68
Haussmann   97
Hertel   139, 148
Hippocrates   29, 151 f., 160, 213
Hoban   18
Homer   138, 254
Huck   37, 41
Huxley   3, 9

Jameson   176
Jesse   12
Joyce   72

Kaplan   265
Keller   73
Korzybski   38

Langer   175–180, 182, 185, 187, 191 f., 221, 236
Lefebvre   5, 28, 62, 79–85, 88–90, 92 f., 96, 110, 117, 151, 155, 191
Lehan   143
Leibniz   11
Löbbermann   53 f., 56, 74 f., 77, 123, 206
Lotman   5, 54, 69, 71, 173–176, 182–184, 188, 192, 208
Löw   64, 79, 84, 88, 94, 102, 106, 113, 115, 199

Löwy   222 f., 226–228
Luckhurst   14
Luhmann   81, 112, 175 f., 222–224, 230 f.
Lukács   227

McDonagh   226 f.
McLuhan   63
Melville   50
Merrifield   83
Meyer   7–9, 11, 18 f., 22, 31–33, 89, 124, 151, 157, 165 f., 192, 207, 236
Miéville   5, 7, 15, 19, 49 f., 52–55, 57, 63–65, 89, 97–101, 110, 113, 116, 178 f., 181, 184, 192, 195, 206, 224, 227, 237, 243, 248, 263
Mokre   43
Moore   18
More   2, 7 f., 70
Moylan   2, 7–9, 11, 13 f., 17, 109, 223, 225, 228, 234, 243, 256, 266
Murphy   8

Nassehi   222, 232–234, 236, 244, 246, 249, 254, 258
Neumann   172
Nurmi-Schomers   26, 134

O'Flinn   2
Ortag   38
Orwell   1–3, 13, 150, 153, 190, 207
Ossian   124

Parker   43, 71
Pavlik   55
Piatti   39, 42, 44–48, 55, 67 f., 70–73, 75, 260
Plato   2, 8
Poovey   229
Pratt   171, 175, 195, 199

Reinfandt   81, 112, 130, 222–225, 231, 234, 242
Rupp   122
Russell   190

Sargent   7, 13
Sarkowsky   13, 265
Schedel   36 f., 41, 59
Schlögel   39 f., 43, 87 f.
Schnabel   50
Schneider   35, 37 f., 42, 51 f., 55, 59, 63
Schroer   21, 114 f., 191
Schwengel   172
Sennett   86, 96–99, 101, 109, 120, 135
Sieverts   114
Soja   26
Staggs   179
Stallybrass and White   171
Stevenson   46
Stichweh   174
Stifter   50
Stilz   171, 174, 195, 210
Stockhammer   35, 38 f., 42–44, 47 f., 50 f., 54 f., 65, 68 f.
Stockwell   190
Strawson   190
Stross   178, 180, 187, 189, 193
Suvin   9, 223, 235, 243
Swift   50

Thomson   6, 29, 68, 71, 153, 160 f., 257
Tolkien   39, 73

Virgil   143

Waldenfels   170
Walsh   8, 11
Warnke   36
Wells   3
Welz   28, 135, 139 f.
Williams   133, 142–144, 148 f., 151
Wirth   84
Wokart   170, 172
Wood and Fels   42
Wordsworth   143
Wyatt   39

Zähringer   49, 179
Zamyatin   3, 193
Zipfel   46

Subject Index

actual world   2–4, 9, 11f., 14, 17, 28, 38, 42–46, 49, 67f., 71, 77, 138, 222f., 225–231, 234, 236, 243, 252, 255, 258f.
alterity   63, 85, 104, 169, 173, 181, 195, 221
anti-utopia   2, 4, 7–9, 11–13, 142, 150f., 167, 192, 224, 235, 245, 252, 262, 264
appropriation   41, 85, 88, 95, 109, 121, 129, 135, 192, 215
archaeology   138
ascription   159, 161, 168f., 210, 212

border   5, 19, 29f., 33, 67, 69, 71, 81, 113, 115, 157f., 160, 162, 168–178, 180–182, 185–187, 191, 194–206, 209–212, 214, 216–221, 244, 246f., 256, 266
Brave New World   9f., 22, 78, 155, 166, 208, 236

cartography   35, 37, 44, 49, 58f., 74, 95, 101, 210
collectivism   3, 10, 22, 33, 252
conceived space   79–81, 83, 86, 88, 90f., 104, 109f., 117, 151, 155, 159, 164, 167, 247, 257
constructedness   79, 150f., 154, 170, 209, 247
contact zone   171f., 174f., 178, 181, 183, 188–190, 192, 195, 199, 202, 208, 210, 240, 244f., 248
contingency   223, 228, 232, 236, 238, 242f., 246
cultural studies   4

deictics   172–175, 177, 181
differentiation   4, 81, 84, 112, 114, 195, 228, 231, 247
discourse   37, 41, 82, 96, 118, 167, 174, 251, 262, 265f.
discursivity   5, 63, 79–81, 84f., 100, 102, 104, 107f., 110, 116, 118, 121, 124, 132, 135, 137, 144f., 196, 198, 200, 203–205, 215, 251, 257

dominated space   88, 90
dystopia   2, 4, 7–9, 12f., 18f., 28, 77, 109, 157, 224, 245, 263f.

effect of realisation   44, 48, 234, 260
etymology   136, 138, 166
exclusion   172–175, 177, 182, 186, 213

fantasy   5, 39, 43, 49, 224f., 243
fiction   1, 3f., 6f., 11, 14, 32, 35, 39f., 42f., 45f., 49, 56, 118, 132, 138, 158, 193, 222, 224–228, 231, 234–236, 238, 240, 266
fictional world   1–3, 14f., 39, 42–46, 51, 67f., 79, 82f., 179, 223, 226–229, 232, 234
fictionality   3f., 7, 35, 42–44, 48, 223f., 238, 266
focalisation   17f., 24, 31, 51, 94f., 116, 130f., 133, 139, 141, 182

geography   35, 40, 44, 49, 68, 73, 105, 201, 260

habitus   85, 102, 111, 113, 117, 201, 205, 247
historicity   38, 48, 120, 124, 135
humourism   29, 153, 155, 163, 168, 211, 213, 218f., 257, 259, 264
hybridity   100, 178–187, 190f., 193, 243

identity   6, 31, 63, 84f., 104f., 107, 118, 157–159, 160f., 161–163, 165, 167, 169, 172f., 177, 181–183, 195, 213f., 214, 217f., 220, 225, 235, 245, 251, 260, 263
ideology   33, 83, 117, 152, 154, 157, 162, 164, 167, 207, 221, 257
integration   220, 225, 261–265
irrealism   4, 222f., 226–228, 232, 234f., 240, 243f., 247, 253, 260, 265

literary history   2, 5, 235
literary studies   4, 7, 79, 174, 222, 224

lived space   40, 79f., 82f., 86, 88f., 91, 110, 117f., 132, 151, 155, 157, 159, 167, 247, 249
lust   39, 43, 53, 55, 57, 60, 65, 69, 77, 210f., 213, 221

map   5, 16, 23, 29, 35–39, 41–44, 46–59, 61–77, 100, 123, 170, 197, 209, 233f., 242f., 253, 260
mappamundi   35
marginalisation   59, 195
materiality   5, 63, 79–81, 83–85, 100, 102–104, 106–108, 110, 113, 115, 118–120, 122, 132–135, 137, 141, 144, 145f., 147, 149, 198, 204f., 215, 255, 257, 266
mediation   14, 82, 119, 229
mimesis   227
modernisation   2, 139, 265
modernity   12f., 242, 258
mythology   26f., 77, 123f., 129, 132, 138, 142, 262

narration   7, 17, 27, 31, 82f., 94, 116, 118, 138f., 141, 151, 227
narrator   18, 23f., 27, 31, 76, 81f., 82, 94, 116, 118, 123, 126, 130–133, 139–142, 144, 149f., 182f., 216, 227f., 243, 247, 249, 252
Nineteen Eighty-Four   1, 10, 33, 150, 153, 190, 207f., 236
nostalgia   23, 28, 76, 126, 158

observation   6, 30, 37, 64, 81, 112, 114, 131, 220, 225, 228f., 232f., 258
observer   37, 40f., 47, 61, 69, 75, 205, 250
omission   6, 29, 38, 49, 67, 69–71
ontology   188
outsider   5, 10, 31, 56, 105, 168, 178, 191–193, 206, 220, 261

paratext   43
perceived space   79–82, 86, 88f., 110, 112, 151, 155, 247
performance   6, 19, 84f., 102, 106, 110, 113, 115, 123, 162, 168, 176, 178, 182, 191, 194f., 198f., 201–203, 205, 210, 213–220, 223, 225, 244f., 248

philosophy   100, 151, 154, 167, 229
power   9, 11, 15f., 18f., 23, 25, 39, 43, 48f., 57f., 61f., 65, 70, 81, 83, 89, 92, 96, 104, 109, 123, 125, 131, 142, 145, 171, 188, 192, 198, 204, 209–211, 213, 221, 227, 239f., 248, 250f.
projection   38, 41, 48, 63, 85, 104, 143

racism   16, 21, 33, 156, 161, 166, 184, 187, 210, 236, 259
realism   9, 12, 52, 222f., 225–228, 231, 266
reality   3f., 7, 35, 38–40, 43–46, 48, 52, 60, 65, 68, 80, 113, 116, 125, 176, 207, 211f., 219, 222–224, 226–229, 231f., 234f., 240f., 265f.
referentiality   39, 42, 44–46, 48, 56, 64, 68
reflexivity   223, 225
reintegration   48, 221, 243, 251f.
representation   3f., 11, 35, 37, 43, 46, 48, 52, 55, 63, 65, 67, 79, 82f., 92, 226f., 235f., 249, 260, 266
rhizome   61
Romantic period   2, 243, 266

Science Fiction   4, 7f., 11, 13f., 17, 61, 190, 223–225, 236f., 266
selection   6, 29, 38, 40, 51, 67, 71, 74, 76, 104, 114f., 172, 195, 230, 233
social space   79, 85, 104, 109
sociology   84, 88, 161, 188
space   3–5, 8, 15f., 23, 38, 40f., 44–46, 51, 53–56, 58, 60, 63f., 68, 73, 82–84, 89f., 92–96, 100f., 108–110, 115, 118, 121–123, 127, 129, 132, 150, 157, 159, 163f., 170–174, 177, 191f., 196, 199, 201–203, 218, 225f., 240, 244, 247, 251, 264
spatial turn   4, 14, 48
story world   14, 17f., 20, 24, 28f., 49f., 63f., 67f., 71, 76, 82, 116, 118f., 131, 133, 139f., 142, 173, 176, 226f., 250, 254, 261, 263
systems theory   4, 222–224, 230

The Production of Space   5, 79, 83f., 88
topography   6, 20, 22, 24–26, 39, 45, 49, 52, 58, 64, 67–69, 73, 75f., 94f., 105,

115, 135, 137f., 149, 164, 245, 249, 253f., 257, 262
totalitarianism   3, 10, 16, 157
tour   39, 41, 48, 53, 69, 74–76, 123, 242
tourist   53f., 74–77, 107, 160, 206
transgression   5, 168f., 173, 176–178, 180–182, 185–188, 190–194, 196–201, 203f., 206, 211, 215, 218f., 221, 246, 261
treading   173, 176f., 182, 194, 196, 200, 206, 211, 221

unmarked space   81, 112, 114–116, 173, 175f., 232

unseeing   6, 19–22, 110–116, 177, 194–200, 202f., 205, 207, 244f., 247f., 261, 263
urbanity   13f., 120, 235f., 244, 249, 251, 263
utopia   1, 4, 7–9, 11–13, 25, 28, 70, 142, 145, 149–151, 167, 192, 207f., 223f., 235, 245, 252, 254, 261–264
Utopia   2, 7, 10, 12, 70, 264

voyeur   39–41, 52f., 57, 61f., 123

walker   18, 39f., 53, 56, 61f., 121f.
Weird Fiction   100, 179, 224, 243

www.ingramcontent.com/pod-product-compliance
Lightning Source LLC
Chambersburg PA
CBHW082103250426
43661CB00079B/2620